STUDIES IN IMPERIALISM

general editor John M. MacKenzie

Established in the belief that imperialism as a cultural phenomenon has as significant an effect on the dominant as on the subordinate societies, Studies in Imperialism seeks to develop the new sociocultural approach which has emerged through cross-disciplinary work on popular culture, media studies, art history, the study of education and religion, sports history and children's literature. The cultural emphasis embraces studies of migration and race, while the older political and constitutional, economic and military concerns are never far away. It incorporates comparative work on European and American empire-building, with the chronological focus primarily, though not exclusively, on the nineteenth and twentieth centuries, when these cultural exchanges were most powerfully at work.

New frontiers

MANCHESTER
UNIVERSITY PRESS

AVAILABLE IN THE SERIES

Britain in China
Community, culture and colonialism, 1900–1949   Robert Bickers

Western medicine as contested knowledge
ed. Andrew Cunningham and Bridie Andrews

Imperial cities
Landscape, display and identity   ed. Felix Driver and David Gilbert

Unfit for heroes
Reconstruction and soldier settlement in the Empire between the wars
Kent Fedorowich

Emigration from Scotland between the wars
Opportunity or exile?   Marjory Harper

Empire and sexuality
The British experience   Ronald Hyam

'An Irish Empire?'
Aspects of Ireland and the British Empire   ed. Keith Jeffery

The South African War reappraised
Donal Lowry

The empire of nature
Hunting, conservation and British imperialism   John M. MacKenzie

Propaganda and empire
The manipulation of British public opinion, 1880–1960   John M. MacKenzie

Imperialism and popular culture
ed. John M. MacKenzie

Gender and imperialism
ed. Clare Midgley

Guardians of empire
The armed forces of the colonial powers, c. 1700–1964
ed. David Omissi and David Killingray

Colonial masculinity
The 'manly Englishman' and the 'effeminate Bengali'   Mrinalini Sinha

The imperial game
Cricket, culture and society   ed. Brian Stoddart and Keith A. P. Sandiford

Jute and empire
The Calcutta jute wallahs and the landscapes of empire   Gordon T. Stewart

The French empire at war, 1940–45
Martin Thomas

Travellers in Africa
British travelogues, 1850–1900   Tim Youngs

Forthcoming
Science and society in South Africa
Saul Dubow

France and Algeria 1830–1962
From colonialism to independence   Martin Evans

Aviation and empire
Gordon Pirie

Imperialism and music
Jeffrey Richards

The space in between: Frontiers and boundaries in settler colonies
Lynette Russell

New frontiers

IMPERIALISM'S NEW COMMUNITIES IN EAST ASIA, 1842–1953

edited by Robert Bickers and Christian Henriot

MANCHESTER UNIVERSITY PRESS
Manchester and New York

distributed exclusively in the USA by St. Martin's Press

The publication of this book has been assisted through
the financial support of Jean Moulin-Lyon 3 University

Copyright © Manchester University Press 2000

While copyright in the volume as a whole is vested in Manchester University Press, copyright in individual chapters belongs to their respective authors, and no chapter may be reproduced in whole or in part without the express permission in writing of both author and publisher.

Published by Manchester University Press
Oxford Road, Manchester M13 9NR, UK
and Room 400, 175 Fifth Avenue, New York, NY 10010, USA
www.manchesteruniversitypress.co.uk

Distributed exclusively in the USA by
Palgrave, 175 Fifth Avenue, New York NY 10010, USA

Distributed exclusively in Canada by
UBC Press, University of British Columbia, 2029 West Mall,
Vancouver, BC, Canada V6T 1Z2

British Library Cataloguing-in-Publication Data
A catalogue record for this book is available from the British Library

Library of Congress Cataloging-in-Publication Data
A catalog record for this book is available from the Library of Congress

ISBN 978 0 7190 5604 8 *hardback*
ISBN 978 0 7190 8932 9 *paperback*

First published by Manchester University Press 2000

First digital paperback edition published 2012

Printed by Lightning Source

CONTENTS

List of tables — *page* vii
List of figures — viii
General editor's introduction — ix
Preface — xi
The contributors — xii
Abbreviations — xiv

1 Introduction   *Robert Bickers and Christian Henriot*   page 1

2 Colonialism 'in a Chinese atmosphere': the Caldwell affair and the perils of collaboration in early colonial Hong Kong   *Christopher Munn*   12

3 Marginal Westerners in Shanghai: the Baghdadi Jewish community, 1845–1931   *Chiara Betta*   38

4 Indian communities in China, c. 1842–1949   *Claude Markovits*   55

5 Foreigners or outsiders? Westerners and Chinese Christians in Chongqing, 1870s–1900   *Judith Wyman*   75

6 The Japanese and the Jews: a comparative analysis of their communities in Harbin, 1898–1930   *Joshua A. Fogel*   88

7 Japanese colonial citizenship in treaty port China: the location of Koreans and Taiwanese in the imperial order   *Barbara J. Brooks*   109

8 Denied and besieged: the Japanese community of Korea, 1876–1945   *Alain Delissen*   125

9 'Little Japan' in Shanghai: an insulated community, 1875–1945   *Christian Henriot*   146

CONTENTS

10 Who were the Shanghai Municipal Police, and why were they there? The British recruits of 1919
    Robert Bickers — 170

11 The Russian diaspora community in Shanghai
    Marcia R. Ristaino — 192

12 In search of identity: the German community in Shanghai, 1933–1945 *Françoise Kreissler* — 211

13 The Shanghai American community, 1937–1949
    Mark F. Wilkinson — 231

14 Afterword: a colonial world *John Darwin* — 250

Bibliography — 261
Index — 280

LIST OF TABLES

4.1	India's China trade and opium exports, 1828–1911	page 57
4.2	The Indian population of Hong Kong, 1845–1941	58
4.3	The Indian population of Shanghai, 1851–1935	60
4.4	Indians registered at British consulates, by community, in 1915	62
8.1	The changing hierarchy of Japanese urban settlements in Korea	139
9.1	The Japanese population in Shanghai, 1870–1949	148
9.2	The family structure of the Japanese community, 1944	151
9.3	Distribution of Japanese firms in Shanghai by district	156
9.4	Business sectors of Japanese firms before 1937	157
11.1	Russian refugee arrivals in Shanghai, 1922–36	195
12.1	German firms and nationals in China, 1875–1928	214
13.1	Americans registered in Shanghai, 1936–49	233

LIST OF FIGURES

1.1	East Asia	*page* 3
1.2	Shanghai, 1937	8
8.1	Patterns of Japanese residence in the Korean peninsula, 1876–1945	133
8.2	The distribution of Japanese settlement in Korea, c. 1940. Source After Hermann Lautensach, *Korea: a Geography based on the Author's Travels and Literature*, trans. K. and E. Dege, Leipzig, Koehler, 1945; reprinted Berlin, Springer, 1988	138
8.3	Reappearing Koreans in the 'open port' of Mokp'o. Source Lautensach, *Korea*, fig. 79, p. 372	140
8.4	A new town in northern Korea: Nanam. Source Lautensach, *Korea*, fig. 41, p. 209	141
8.5	Split settlement in Wônsan. Source Lautensach, *Korea*, fig. 65, p. 307	142
9.1	Geographical origin of Shanghai's Japanese residents, 1943. Source *Kai-in meibo* (List of Members [of the Japanese Club]), Shanghai, Shanhai nippon kurabu, 1944	150
9.2	'Little Tokyo': Japanese neighbourhood associations, 1938. Source *Shanhai nihonjin kakuro rengokai no enkaku to jiseji* (Events and Evolution of the Japanese Street Unions in Shanghai), Shanghai, Shanhai nihonjin kakuro rengokai, 1939, pp. 19–55	153
9.3	Year of foundation of Japanese firms, 1941	155

GENERAL EDITOR'S INTRODUCTION

As this volume demonstrates, imperial approaches to East Asia were multi-faceted, multi-ethnic and both international and local. These complex social and economic, cultural and political histories of the penetration and inter-penetration of East Asian societies in the nineteenth and twentieth centuries are exciting increasing attention. They offer considerable insights into imperialism in general, not least in the manner in which different ethnicities are employed and manipulated in the economic, social and controlling mechanisms of the relationship between imperial power and East Asian cultures and polities. They also provide significant routes into the history of the host territories of the period. This has been recognised in Japan, where the history of the treaty ports and other forms of Western settlement is carefully analysed and presented in museums and galleries. The most important Western treaty port figures, like Thomas Blake Glover, are a source of considerable fascination.

Japan, which was able to overthrow the treaties in 1899, can view such individuals and communities as a necessary part of its own economic response to the West. For China, itself the victim of Japanese as well as Western imperialism, the situation is more complex and ideologically fraught. Foreign communities tend to be treated only in a uni-dimensional way. Yet it is only through international comparative approaches that the role of such communities can be fully appreciated. This volume builds on earlier work in the 'Studies in Imperialism' series and on new work appearing in the United States.

Through their tight focus on East Asia these essays allow an examination of different Euro-American and Asian imperialisms at work in one region. At the same time they aim to break down traditional national labels such as 'British' and 'Japanese' in this context by highlighting the multifaceted and transnational character of these establishments. Parsis were part of British imperialism, Koreans agents of Japanese expansion into China, and Chinese Christians added a further twist to the problem of identity and agency. The essays here also help highlight 'through contrast and comparison' the differing roles played on the one hand by metropolitan/domestic factors and on the other by the specific character of transnational treaty port colonialism in the shaping of these new communities. All these essays are themselves rooted in a three-year international collaboration project, and methodologically draw on East Asian and colonial history historiographies. They deal with port, coastal province and interior, with the relationships among several religions, and among others with Indians, Russian, Baghdadis, Japanese, Americans, and Koreans in Chinese contexts.

GENERAL EDITOR'S INTRODUCTION

Although this volume represents a considerable advance in the historiography, there is still more to be done. For example, French East Asian colonialism is much understudied. But this volume constitute an excellent starting point which should help to stimulate further research.

John M. MacKenzie

PREFACE

This volume has grown out of several years of collaboration between the editors, which had as its principal manifestations a one-day symposium at Nuffield College, Oxford, on 'Settlers and Sojourners: Foreign Communities on the China Coast' on 28 November 1995, and an international conference on 'Foreign Communities in East Asia, 19th–20th centuries', held at the Institut d'Asie Orientale, Lyon, on 20–1 March 1997. We would like to thank all those who participated at those events or who helped us organise them; in particular we would like to thank Chang Ning (Academia Sinica, Taiwan), Christine Cornet (Lumière–Lyon 2 University), Marjorie Dryburgh (University of Sheffield), Feng Yi (IAO), Martine Raibaud (La Rochelle University), Eileen P. Scully (Princeton University), Mariya Sevela (Japan Centre, EHESS), Rudolf Wagner (Institute of Chinese Studies, Heidelberg University), Catherine Yeh (Institute of Chinese Studies, Heidelberg University), Yuki Honjo (St Antony's College, Oxford), and Zheng Zu'an (Institute of History, Shanghai Academy of Social Sciences). Subsequent to the Lyon conference a panel of participants presented papers at the International Convention of Asian Scholars, held under the joint auspices of the American Association of Asian Studies and the International Institute of Asian Studies, Leiden, on 25–8 June 1998. The editors would like to acknowledge the generosity of the Warden and Fellows of Nuffield College for making the 1995 workshop possible, and the British Academy's overseas conference grants scheme, which took some participants from Britain to Lyon. We would also like especially to acknowledge the support of the French Ministry of Foreign Affairs and the Programme Francobritannique of the Centre National de la Recherche Scientifique. For assistance in the preparation of the text we would also like to thank Paula Warburton. The volume is a direct testimony to the pertinence of collaborating in co-ordinated and long-term research on topics that by their very nature call for cross-country studies.

THE CONTRIBUTORS

Chiara Betta teaches Chinese language and culture at the University of Indianapolis in Athens (Greece). She received a Ph.D. from the School of Oriental and African Studies, London, in 1997 with a dissertation on 'Silas Aaron Hardoon, 1851–1931: Marginality and Adaptation in Shanghai', which is being revised for publication.

Robert Bickers is Lecturer in East Asian and Colonial History at the University of Bristol. He has published various papers on the history of Sino-British relations and is the author of *Britain in China: Community, Culture and Colonialism, 1900–49* (1999).

Barbara J. Brooks teaches history at the City College of the City University of New York. Having completed *Japan's Imperial Diplomacy: Consuls, Treaty Ports and War in China, 1895–1945* (forthcoming), she is writing a book about the culture of Japanese settlement in Korea and treaty port China.

John Darwin is a fellow of Nuffield College, Oxford, and the author of *Britain and Decolonisation: the Retreat from Empire in the Post-war World* (1988) and *The End of the British Empire: the Historical Debate* (1991).

Alain Delissen is Associate Professor of Korean History at the Ecole des hautes études en sciences sociales, working on Korean urban history, and in particular the twentieth-century history of Seoul. He is preparing for publication *Seoul Urban Landscapes and Korean National Identity*.

Joshua A. Fogel is Professor of History at the University of California, Santa Barbara. His most recent publications include *The Literature of Travel in the Japanese Rediscovery of China, 1862–1945* (1996) and an edited volume, *The Nanjing Massacre in History and Historiography* (forthcoming).

Christian Henriot is Professor of East Asian history at Lumière–Lyon 2 University and a fellow of the Institut Universitaire de France. He serves as director of the Institut d'Asie Orientale (France) and is the author of various books on the history of Shanghai: *Shanghai, 1927–1937: Municipal Power, Locality, and Modernization* (1993), (with A. Roux) *Le Shanghai des années 30* (1998) and *Belles de Shanghai: prostitution et sexualité en Chine aux XIXe–XXe siècles* (1997: forthcoming in English translation).

Françoise Kreissler is an associate professor at the Université Paris 3 (Sorbonne Nouvelle) and the author of *L'Action culturelle allemande en Chine de la fin du XIXe siècle à la Seconde Guerre mondiale* (1989). She is preparing her thèse d'Etat on the German community in Shanghai.

Claude Markovits, Directeur de Recherche at the Centre National de la Recherche Scientifique, Paris, is the author of *Indian Business and National-*

THE CONTRIBUTORS

ist Politics, 1931–1939 (1985) and of *The Global World of Indian Merchants 1750–1947: Traders of Sind from Bukhara to Panama* (forthcoming). He also edited *Histoire de L'Inde moderne, 1480–1950* (1994).

Christopher Munn completed his doctorate at the University of Toronto in 1998. His book *Anglo-China: Chinese People and British Rule in Nineteenth-Century Hong Kong* will be published in 2000.

Marcia R. Ristaino is a China specialist at the US Library of Congress and author of numerous works on modern and contemporary China. She formerly served on the faculties of the University of Maryland and of Trinity College, Washington DC.

Mark F. Wilkinson received his doctorate from the University of Michigan in Ann Arbor in 1982. He is Professor of History at Virginia Military Institute, where he teaches American foreign relations and modern East Asian history. His essays on the Shanghai American community have appeared in *The Southeast Review of Asian Studies* (1995) and in Larry Bland, ed., *George C. Marshall's Mediation Mission to China* (1998). He is preparing a book on the internment of foreigners in Shanghai during the Second World War and continuing his research into the Shanghai Americans during the years of the Chinese civil war.

Judith Wyman works as Senior Program Manager for the Hubert H. Humphrey Fellowship Program at the Institute of International Education in Washington DC.

ABBREVIATIONS

FSU	Federation of Street Unions (Shanhai nihonjin kakuro rengôkai)
JRA	Japanese Residents' Association (Shanhai kyoryû mindan)
NCDN	*North China Daily News*
NCH	*North China Herald*
NSDAP	Nationalsozialistische Deutsche Arbeiter-Partei (Nazi party)
SMC	Shanghai Municipal Council
SMP	Shanghai Municipal Police
SORO	Council of United Russian Public Organisations at Shanghai
SVC	Shanghai Volunteer Corps

CHAPTER ONE

Introduction
Robert Bickers and Christian Henriot

Despite its grossly tangible historical presence, imperialism is a spectre which haunts the historiography of East Asia by its absence. Despite the redrawing of the maps, the renaming of cities, the creation of new borders, cities, countries, languages and identities, historians of China, Japan and Korea mostly content themselves with placing imperialism within nationalist narratives of subjugation, humiliation, resistance, and liberation. Historians of British or Japanese imperialism have also pared their analyses down fine to manageable national narratives (although these are only now being intertwined with domestic narratives), excluding the confusions of imperial process and multiple colonial presences. The high politics of imperialism, rather than the low pragmatism of colonialism, have also provided manageable frameworks for analysis. The social history of colonialism in East Asia has received little attention; and even then the social and political history of colonialism and imperialism has obscured what is mostly obviously a part of the international history of migration. This volume restores to the historiography agents and opportunists at present excluded by virtue of their nationality, their status, their silence, or through sheer neglect: destitute White Russian refugees, wealthy Baghdadi Jewish merchants, working-class British men, Japanese petty bourgeois traders, German anti-imperialists, French and American citizens, and the indigenous subjects (and agents) of empire – Chinese, Korean and Taiwanese. Imperialism made a wild frontier zone of East Asia, and the story of decolonisation in the region is the story of the reassertion of state control over the new communities that developed there, and the suppression of the power and autonomy they carved out for themselves.

More than merely adding colourfully to the narrative of imperialism, the examination of these communities and groups serves to force us to grapple with fundamental questions about empire in East Asia.

This volume explores two themes at the heart of the colonial process: agency and identity. The agents of British empire in China included the usual suspects – Britons from the official and military castes – but also the less usual: Iraqi Jewish merchants, Parsis and Indian Jews, Eurasians, South East Asian Chinese. The agents of Japanese penetration and its consolidation included Japanese migrants, Korean and Taiwanese colonial subjects, as well as Chinese nationals who voluntarily took colonial citizenship and Sindhi merchants from India. Not surprisingly, the relationship between the imperial state and its multiple agents was never unproblematic. In 1914, as Alain Delissen argues in Chapter Eight, the Japanese state effectively abolished its Japanese settler agents in Korea by making Koreans and Japanese alike citizens of Chôsen; in China it worked hard to use proxy subjects to bolster its claims to action in defence of its nationals' interests there; Korean independence activists, meanwhile, took advantage of the looseness of jurisdiction in China to launch attacks on Japanese officials. British diplomats never formulated a coherent policy towards the non-Britons who so strikingly made up the British presence, except to try and prevent too great abuse of the British flag; but at the same time the British state found itself in charge of a Shanghailander community of overseas Britons who demonstrated little but contingent loyalty to British aims in China. The German community in Shanghai increasingly found itself at loggerheads with Nazi foreign policy towards China after 1933, despite being effectively brought to heel in other ways by Nazi policies to co-ordinate overseas German communities. Many of these communities were strongly linked with their metropolitan centre then (although British subjects in China had two centres, British India and Great Britain), but their aims and those of the centre for them often conflicted.

Clearly, at the root of this picture is the question of the uses and abuses of extraterritoriality. It is also clear that far from the simple dichotomy of imperial states/subjects and colonised states/subjects we must re-envisage the East Asian experience for what it was: a network of multiple overlapping imperialisms, in the interstices of which opportunistic groups carved out new livelihoods and new roles.

The 1842 Treaty of Nanjing, which ended the first Anglo-Chinese Opium War, set out the framework for a new order on the China coast that British and Indian merchants and their Chinese collaborators had been agitating for throughout the 1830s. The most significant outcomes were the establishment of a right of residence for foreign merchants in Chinese cities outside Canton (Shanghai, Fuzhou, Ningbo,

INTRODUCTION

Figure 1.1 East Asia

Xiamen (Amoy)), the cession of Hong Kong and the creation of a system of consular jurisdiction over British subjects in China. Qing sovereignty was undermined by these concessions, but British control over British subjects in China did not wholly succeed to the sway of its Manchu predecessor and collaborator in the new system. Far from sharply demarcating a new frontier between Qing and foreign, the treaty system in fact led to the creation of new grey areas of contested sovereignty and control, pushing that frontier into new geographical regions, but also into less tangible areas: who was to exercise ultimate jurisdiction over Chinese subjects in Hong Kong, for example. Under most favoured nation clauses in subsequent treaties, British advantages were extended to all other treaty-signing nations and nationals; the treaty system was also exported to Japan (1858–99), and then to Korea (1876). Local agreements, notably at Shanghai, mapped out a new *modus vivendi* between foreign residents and Chinese power. At the time of the embassy of Lord Macartney to China in 1792–94, Qing officials had worried that the British would alienate Chinese subjects from their loyalty to the dynasty.[1] They were right to do so: the treaty system had precisely that effect, because entrepreneurial Chinese, as much as British colonial subjects, saw how advantageous the new system could be to those who were well placed to make use of it, and the new identities created out of the treaties led inexorably to new loyalties. In practice, as well as the legal framework, the system was founded on collaboration, and on agency. Those with the skills (languages), and resources (networks, contacts, finances, violence), were at a premium. Those who were there already were at an advantage. Parsi and Baghdadi Jewish merchants clearly benefited swiftly as a result, as Chiara Betta and Claude Markovits demonstrate in Chapters Three and Four, and so did Chinese-speaking men like Daniel Caldwell, as Christopher Munn shows in Chapter Two.[2]

Existing historiographies largely see the treaty system as serving the interests of states, and of those groups (country traders, finance imperialists, China lobbies, diplomatic lobbies, military lobbies) informing the policy making of such states.[3] The aim broadly might be described as the proper integration of East Asia into the developing Euro-American-dominated world order, and the supersession of existing orders in East and South Asia which did not serve Euro-American interests. For nationalist historians this translates as the effective exploitation of markets and resources by imperialist power. However, that tidy model is undermined first by the role of Japan, imperialist victim and latterly imperialist aggressor. More important, the model is at fault because a clear distinction between aggressor and exploited can hardly be effectively identified, because of the wholesale interpenetration of interests, because of the multiplicity of actors operating under the shadow of any one state, and because of the way in which the treaty system actually worked in practice. Principally, the treaty system allowed groups of metropolitan nationals to develop new identities, as Shanghailanders, as Shanghai Russians, as the Japanese of Chôsen, or as 'Amoy *sekimin*', Fujianese who had never lived in Taiwan but who registered as Taiwan residents in 1898 to take advantage of the extraterritoriality they could enjoy as Japanese colonial subjects. These identities were no less important or problematic because of the size of the communities. Shanghailanders exercised a tenacious hold on British

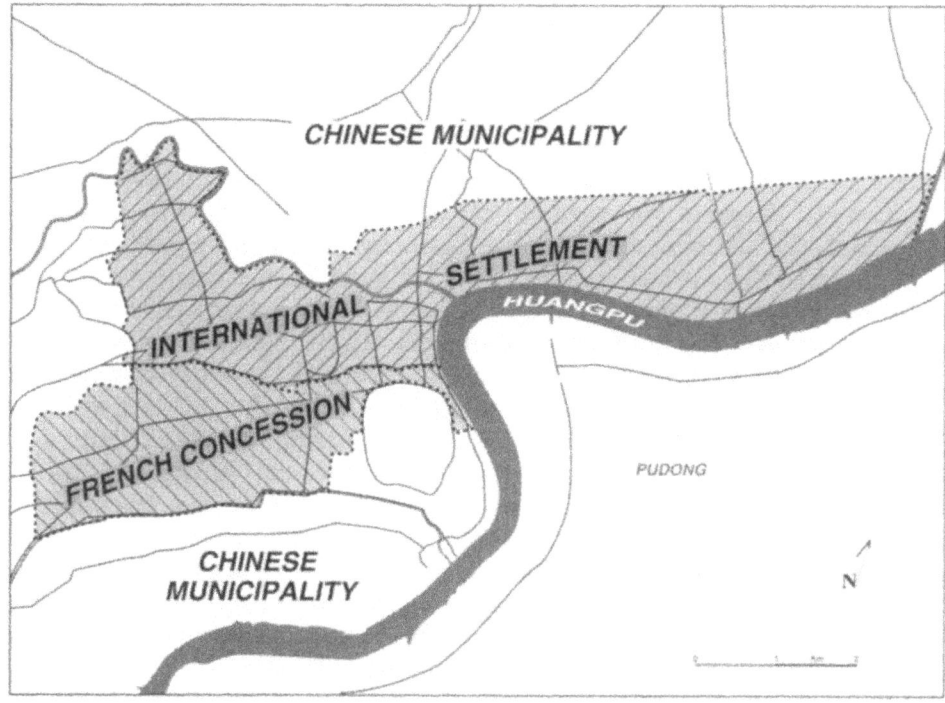

Figure 1.2 Shanghai, 1937

or more cynically to move along with imperial expansion and its economic benefits.

For Japan the treaty system worked, and was worked, in a number of ways. In China Japanese officials used as agents, or attempted to use, Japanese migrants who themselves, especially in Shanghai, were not averse to attempting to draw metropolitan power into China to further their own aims. They also used Japanese colonial subjects, Chinese abusers of Japanese extraterritoriality, White Russians and British colonial subjects. Japanese designs were sometimes resisted, as Marcia Ristaino shows in Chapter Eleven, on the Russian community, but Japanese power could not be successfully thwarted in late 1930s Shanghai. Russian refugees presented a useful target for an expansive colonial apparatus to adopt. Just as the French state found it useful to demand and acquire the role of protector of Chinese Catholic converts, so in a similar manner the Japanese repertoire sought to protect the Russians. For all these groups, the Russians apart, the benefits were transparently mutual: extraterritoriality conveyed full citizenship in the treaty system. The dangers were also apparent in an era of devel-

demonstrate a reconceptualisation which integrates foreign groups and individuals into their histories. But the process has only just begun, and unevenly so to date. As Joshua Fogel shows, for all the attempts of historians in China to locate a date for the creation of the city of Harbin in the late eleventh century, it was in fact a city built by Russian Jews and Japanese migrants after 1898. The history of Shanghai has mostly been written by settlers, who largely ignored the Chinese, by Chinese historians, who have ignored or caricatured the foreign presence, or by Western historians, whose questions about Shanghai's social, political or economic history have largely evaded the need to confront the issue. Where the issue of the foreign is dealt with, as Claude Markovits perhaps suggests, analysis relies on hostile caricatures of violent, colonialist Britons more suited to the pages of Tintin's Shanghai adventure. More than a tale of the upper-class British of the International Settlement, the foreign communities of Shanghai also included Russians, Baghdadi Jews, Germans, French citizens and colonial subjects, US citizens, British Indians, Japanese, lower-class Britons (all analysed here), as well as Portuguese, South Americans, Eurasians and other communities not dealt with in this volume. The most consistently effective source of authority in the city of Shanghai from the 1850s until the 1940s was the Shanghai Municipal Council of the International Settlement, which was dominated by these communities, or by their interests. Through presenting the histories of these communities for the first time, and by demonstrating the tensions within them, and between communities, and in their relations with metropolitan power, the book also offers opportunities for creating for the first time the history of Shanghai as an internationalised Chinese city in what ought to be its proper context of such fellow international cities as New York or Alexandria.

For Korea the treaty system was a prelude to full-scale colonial occupation by Japan. Despite a formal discourse on Chôsen as an integral part of Japan and an official policy of erasing ethnic and national differences, the Koreans were subjected to a particularly harsh regime of assimilation and negation of their own identity. But if the tale is of the conflicting relationship between Japanese migrants and Japanese colonial agencies, and Japanese migrants and Koreans, it is also the tale of Koreans taking advantage of extraterritoriality in China, of the Korean subjects of Chôsen as being colonised and at the same time living the role of 'colonialist'. The Japanese occupation, as in Taiwan, eventually produced a whole array of elite and middle-class groups who saw fit to use to their advantage their capacity to act as bridges, to penetrate societies that were hostile to Japan,

For China the system meant that Qing subjects became the colonial subjects of Japan in Taiwan, and subject to British colonial authority in Hong Kong and Weihaiwei, German authority in Jiaozhouwan and French in Guangzhouwan, and to the farmed-out authority of the foreign oligarchies and their Chinese bankers or clients in treaty ports such as Shanghai and Tianjin. Judith Wyman describes how Chinese Christians found themselves (mostly unwittingly) denationalised in the eyes of their neighbours as a result of conversion and of their concomitant withdrawal from local social and cultural practices. It is also clear that conversion was sometimes a strategic move to enable groups or individuals to take advantage of the perceived advantages of what might be termed a 'vulgar' extraterritoriality that was offered through the protection of converts' interests in local affairs by missionaries. As Barbara Brooks shows, Chinese in Fujian, aware of the advantages offered by extraterritorial status, willingly sought the protection offered by Japanese officials as a tool for expanding and consolidating Japan's penetration of China. Chinese actors also sought private collaborators from among treaty nationals newly empowered by extraterritoriality. Christopher Munn shows how a pirate like Ma-chow Wong sought and found effective collaborators among influential British colonial officials in the 1840s and 1850s. Chinese merchants became compradores, and a multiplicity of groups in time sought the protection offered by the missionaries of foreign religion. New frontiers were created within China. Imperialism changed Chinese identities in the treaty ports, and, as Judith Wyman demonstrates, new tensions were created and old ones metamorphosed deep in China's 'interior'.

The book also points to the fact that the national history of China is also the history of its immigrant communities, as is the provincial history of China: outsiders were not simply foreigners. Moreover, the paradigmatic concern with imperialism has obscured the history of these foreign communities as immigrants, by tarring all such groups with the same colonialist brush, and also because the communities were broken up and dispersed overseas by the upheavals of war and revolution. Although, as the present volume shows, some of these communities have generated a substantial memoir literature, and sometimes histories too, such scattered works are often insularly restricted to their immediate communities and concerns. As a result these literatures have been devalued and ignored. But no historian of the United States, or of the United Kingdom or France, could exclude immigrant histories without comment, or without prompting comment. We should apply the same criterion to China, especially as there are small signs that local historians in China are starting to

INTRODUCTION

China policy until the 1930s, *sekimin* usefully served Japanese interests.

Instead of clearly identifiable colonialist communities serving their own states, this book shows a vast array of nationals (and the stateless) engaged in the pursuit of their livelihoods and interests in the interstices of empire, adroitly operating on the margins of treaty legality, using extraterritoriality, and the grey areas offered by colonial citizenship and settler autonomy, to further their own ends. They took the world as they saw it, and as they found it, when applying for jobs, when planning to escape persecution in Tsarist or Bolshevik Russia, or later in Nazi-occupied central Europe, or when drifting in search of opportunity. We can also see that the treaty system was an integral part of the national histories of China, Korea, and Japan. Nationalist historiography places imperialism effectively outside the normal narrative of national history, which imperialism is shown to have perverted. Western historiography, especially of China, has compounded this by evading engagement with non-native elements in the national narratives, largely out of concern to avoid framing all questions in terms of relations with the West. The underlying assumption is based on an idea of a 'national' identity derived from the state (and from the state as constituted at the end of the twentieth century). But the treaty system, broadly defined, effectively replaced the state as the defining organisational framework for East Asia's international relations, and the treaty system and its citizens were international.

The Chinese treaty ports in particular demonstrated the denationalised nature of the new order that developed after 1842. Each city developed in its own way as a result of the local agreements between Chinese and British officials that mapped out the new spheres of semi-autonomous foreign activity on Chinese soil. In Shanghai, where the system developed most brazenly beyond the control of any single colonial power, the Shanghai Municipal Council of the International Settlement developed a powerful repertoire of institutions and practices that demonstrated settler might, and facilitated settler expansion and consolidation. In the space created by the interplay of local and colonial power, the Shanghai settlement unleashed entrepreneurial energy, and drew in to itself individuals and groups – gangsters, refugees, traders, police recruits – who sought to maximise their own ability to take advantage of the system. The cohabitation of the interests of institutional authority and Chinese social organisation that characterised the main treaty port settlements served to draw Chinese interests further into the treaty system as much as to demonstrate the limits of settler power over Chinese society.

INTRODUCTION

oping nationalist tensions. Chinese who were Japanese colonial subjects were attacked by Nationalist troops, the National government's occupation of Taiwan after the Japanese surrender at the close of the Pacific War was fraught with tensions for Taiwanese Chinese, which exploded in the brutal slaughter of the island's elite by Guomindang forces after 28 February 1947.[4]

These dramatic instances of violence apart, there is also a sense in which the existence of Chinese within the country who voluntarily took the proxy citizenship of Japan, or demonstrated a primary loyalty to the treaty system, served to facilitate a new conception of Chinese citizenship. Some degree of caution must be exercised here, as becoming a servant of Japan (a country at war with China, and thereafter a defeated nation) or more benign forms of collaboration with foreign and basically Western-dominated institutions in the former settlements, was not perceived in the same way by those who acted or those around them. Such nationalist reconstructions notwithstanding, the Chinese involved in the treaty port system embodied a form of interaction with things foreign, with the world and, ultimately, with Chinese modernity. As scholars have argued about the institution of slavery – and 'slave' was an epithet regularly used of Chinese entwined in the treaty system – the existence of another type of Chinese meant much more for Chinese identity. It certainly helped build up a political identity which had previously been based mostly on shared cultural values rather than on a sense of the nation. In turn, however, the political challenge raised by the treaty system and the foreign presence on Chinese soil reshaped what it meant to be Chinese, a process that acquired a new character under the post-1949 regime in attacks on those with foreign connections, especially during the Cultural Revolution. These issues have come back with even more force and relevance in contemporary China.

New frontiers and new tensions were also created by the commingling of bodies, languages, ideas and roles in the East Asian new world. Communities imagined themselves in various and at times conflicting ways: as pioneers, as progressives, as cosmopolitans, as educators, as liberators, as agents of empire. Economically and practically they were yoked together by the treaty system. But at the same time they ring-fenced themselves against their particular others ('natives', 'races', different nationalities) through social, sexual, marriage and other taboos, although individuals often treated such barriers as contingent, or convenient, fictions. Within communities, then, tensions and fissures were evident, while communal practices towards other groups effectively denied the essential polygamous reality of the treaty world. They were also sometimes evident in the activities of individuals: Chiara Betta's exploration here and elsewhere of the worlds of the businessman Silas Aaron Hardoon, a Baghdadi Jew who married a Eurasian, dramatically highlights the difficulties and opportunities facing treaty port actors. The political and social history of colonialism has only recently turned to examine the cultures of the coloniser; this book offers reports on colonialism's multiplicity.[5] Such tensions served to heighten the importance of nationality-derived identities, at the same time as the treaty system and the high policy of imperial expansion undermined them by seeking collaborators, auxiliaries and proxies.

This volume challenges existing orthodoxies concerning the treaty port world, and presents the new work that has largely stemmed from the opportunities offered by the steady opening up of archives in China to historical researchers. Most of the topics could have been written on a decade ago, but the richness of the archival materials now available would have necessitated their rewriting. More tellingly, however, there has been what may be termed a change of perspective in the 'political economy' of research, which has stemmed from the patent failure of communism in East Asia and the fading away of nationalist liberation narratives which had previously made it difficult to assess accurately the role of the foreign. The call for China-centred history, for example, made with such urgent clarity in 1984 by Paul Cohen, needs fresh nuance when official backing is given in contemporary China to the internationalised treaty port capitalism of the pre-1937 era.[6] The chapters that follow stem largely from broader research projects undertaken by their authors, all of whom are making use of the new materials we now have access to in their narratives. The volume is still far from comprehensive. Missing groups include the Portuguese and Eurasians, for example, and the chronological scope could be extended to include Soviet experts in post-1949 China, for example, or US citizens in Taiwan. Much more work needs to be done on Chinese Christian converts, on overseas Chinese in the treaty system and even in this context on the role, for example, of Cantonese migrants in the development of the system elsewhere in China after 1842, and of Chinese merchants in Japan after 1858.

As editors we have sought to bridge the divide between the historiography of colonialism and that of East Asia. By mapping out the main contours of the communities which grew in and because of the treaty system the book is designed to facilitate the repositioning of future research into the treaty port world. We still need national narratives, and we still need narratives of nationals, but we can understand the treaty port system, in practice, only if we internationalise and denationalise it at the same time.

INTRODUCTION

Notes

1 James L. Hevia, *Cherishing Men from Afar: Qing Guest Ritual and the Macartney Embassy of 1793* (Durham NC, Duke University Press, 1995), 190–1, 196–7.
2 On the evolution of the treaty system see John K. Fairbank, 'The Creation of the Treaty System', in *The Cambridge History of China* (Cambridge, Cambridge University Press, 1978), X, *Late Ch'ing, 1800–1911*, Part 1, 213–63.
3 Rhoads Murphey, *The Outsiders: The Western Experience in India and China* (Ann Arbor MI, University of Michigan Press, 1977).
4 Lai Tse-han, Ramon H. Myers and Wei Wou, *A Tragic Beginning: the Taiwan Uprising of February 28, 1947* (Stanford CA, Stanford University Press, 1991).
5 Examples of such work can be found in Ann Laura Stoler and Frederick Cooper, eds, *Tensions of Empire: Colonial Cultures in a Bourgeois World* (Berkeley CA, University of California, 1997). The editors' introduction provides a comprehensive survey of the literature: Ann Laura Stoler and Frederick Cooper, 'Between Metropole and Colony: Rethinking a Research Agenda', in *Tensions of Empire*, 1–56.
6 Paul A. Cohen, *Discovering History in China: American Historical Writing on the recent Chinese Past* (New York, Columbia University Press, 1984); Tim Wright, '"The Spiritual Heritage of Chinese Capitalism": Recent Trends in the Historiography of Chinese Enterprise Management', in Jonathan Unger, ed., *Using the Past to serve the Present: Historiography and Politics in Contemporary China* (Armonk NY: M. E. Sharpe, 1993); Arif Dirlik, 'Reversals, Ironies, Hegemonies: Notes on Contemporary Historiography of Modern China', *Modern China*, 22:3 (1996), 243–84.

CHAPTER TWO

Colonialism 'in a Chinese atmosphere': the Caldwell affair and the perils of collaboration in early colonial Hong Kong
Christopher Munn

In July 1857, during his trial before the Hong Kong Supreme Court, the American pirate Eli Boggs made the allegation that one of the most powerful officials in the colony was in league with pirates. Daniel Caldwell, Registrar General and Protector of Chinese Inhabitants, had, Boggs claimed, fallen under the influence of his chief informant, the notorious gangster Ma-chow Wong, and had been assisting Wong in his piratical enterprises up and down the China Coast. The Attorney General, Thomas Anstey, demanded an inquiry into the activities of Wong, whom he described as 'the tyrant of our Chinese population': 'the Chinese tremble at his name so long as he seems to enjoy the influence over Mr Caldwell which he, most untruly, no doubt, but most effectually parades on all occasions.' Wong, Anstey alleged, had held people to ransom with threats of prosecution before the Hong Kong courts. He had even used his influence over Caldwell to dupe the Royal Navy into undertaking expeditions to exterminate alleged pirates who had refused to purchase his protection.[1]

The arrest of Ma-chow Wong later that month set off a series of investigations that were to implicate Caldwell in a scandalous web of corruption. In July 1858 these investigations culminated in a lengthy and controversial commission of inquiry into Caldwell's activities: the commission failed to confirm the main charges against Caldwell and, instead, they rebounded on Caldwell's principal accuser, Anstey, who was dismissed from the service. A second inquiry two years later, however, concluded that Caldwell's long association with Ma-chow Wong rendered him unfit to remain in the public service. Yet, even after his fall from grace, Caldwell continued to act as an essential intermediary between colonial government and Chinese community. His 'intimate knowledge of the Chinese, their language, their habits, and their haunts'[2] made him indispensable in a deeply troubled colonial relationship that lacked effective channels of communication between government and people and depended heavily on a series of narrow, personal and highly unstable connections formed between certain well placed European officials and their Chinese collaborators.

The reliance of colonial regimes on local middlemen has, since Ronald Robinson sketched out his model of indigenous collaboration in 1972, become an essential part of any explanation of colonialism, though it is only very recently that the model has been systematically applied to Hong Kong.[3] The more respectable Chinese middlemen of early colonial Hong Kong have nevertheless been the focus of much productive research, which has traced their eventual transformation into an organised and powerful elite.[4] The less respectable among them, like Ma-chow Wong, deserve greater prominence, not least because the manner in which they bolstered colonial power while simultaneously undermining the principles that it purported to embody raises interesting questions about the intricate relationship between collaboration and resistance. The collaborative roles of their European counterparts have also perhaps received less attention than they merit. These European intermediaries included well-known missionaries whose principal loyalties were not necessarily with the colonial state: among them were the deeply incompetent Karl Gutzlaff, whose mistranslations of proclamations provoked fatal clashes between government and people, and the more productive James Legge, whose various interventions saved many innocent men from the gallows. Far more important, however, were the less celebrated policemen, interpreters and other functionaries who operated in the wide margins between official colonial power and the informal, and often illicit, networks that organised the Chinese communities in the colony. These men were usually of obscure origin and occupied precarious positions in the colonial hierarchy: they were prone to corruption and the abuse of power; some were racially indeterminate; and, in the eyes of bourgeois colonial society, they mixed far too freely with the Chinese criminals they were supposed to be suppressing. Yet they were vital to the running of this troubled frontier colony.

Daniel Caldwell, the archetypal European middleman in a frontier colony, was Hong Kong's most successful example of this class of men. The powers he accumulated through a mixture of official authority and native connections made him the most influential official in the colony. His position as pirate catcher and Triad society suppressor bore some resemblance to that of the somewhat more respectable Indian official W. H. Sleeman, whose measures to put down *thag* robberies in northern India were founded on what Sandria Freitag has described as a conflation of overt and covert legal structures of crime control.[5] Contemporaries in Hong Kong were aware of the similarities, but the more critical among them were increasingly concerned that the various collaborations between Caldwell and his criminal informants were getting seriously out of hand. During the controversies that erupted in Hong Kong in the late 1850s, the tangle of formal and informal controls that Caldwell and his collaborator Ma-chow Wong had woven began to unravel. Caldwell's methods came into direct confrontation with an alternative, purist view of colonial rule, voiced by the Attorney General, Thomas Anstey, which held that, under Caldwell's management, the institutions of British rule, from the Royal Navy to the judicial system, had been usurped and sabotaged by Chinese gangsters and undermined by the very officials on whom they most depended.[6]

The controversies also point to deeper fears about the contamination of colonial government and European life by what many Europeans saw as a polluting Asiatic backwash. Racial and social anxieties in the tiny and isolated colonial community surfaced in the discussions about Caldwell's own uncertain origins and in what many of his opponents saw as the key to the whole scandal: 'his alliance, by means of his wife, a Chinese girl from a brothel, with some of the worst of the Chinese in this colony'.[7] This chapter explores these problems and focuses on two themes: the freedom and power that the unstable early system of government gave to certain middlemen, both European and Chinese; and the notion that government institutions, European life, and the prestige of British rule were being corrupted by 'Asiatic' entanglements, or by what Hong Kong's radical early newspaper, the *Friend of China*, described as an 'Anglo-Chino conspiracy in crime.'[8]

Hong Kong in the 1850s

The Caldwell affair could hardly have broken out at a more difficult time for the young and problematic British colony at Hong Kong.[9] Founded in 1841, the colony had passed through a depressed 1840s. In the 1850s it rose quickly to prosperity as a centre for the coolie and opium trades and as a place of refuge for Chinese merchants fleeing civil war in southern China. At the same time, a sudden rise in the colony's Chinese population, coupled with a surge in piracy and other crime in the region, increased the sense of endangerment felt by the colonial community. A mere thousand or so, constantly measuring themselves against a Chinese population of around 75,000, the Europeans in Hong Kong depicted themselves as a beleaguered group threatened and disturbed by the crime, disease and noise of a large, unassimilated, yet all too close native populace. Beyond Hong Kong, and especially in the centre of anti-foreign activities in Canton, hostility against the British frequently erupted into violence. In the autumn of 1856 an alleged insult against the British flag in Canton, during the *Arrow* incident, triggered the Second Opium War between Britain and China and prompted attacks on the colony at Hong Kong by Chinese agents. Supplies were interrupted, Chinese official proclamations ordered all Chinese in the colony to return to their native places, some Europeans were murdered, and a campaign of terrorist attacks culminated in the attempt in January 1857 to murder the entire European community by lacing their morning bread with arsenic. The poisoning attempt narrowly failed, and the arrival later in the year of military reinforcements delayed by the Indian Mutiny provided greater security, but Chinese actions against the colony continued throughout the following year: the most disruptive was the mass boycott of the colony by about 25,000 of its Chinese inhabitants during the summer of 1858.

Though it survived the disruption of war, and did well out of the trade boom connected with the British expedition, the Hong Kong government was barely able to cope with the difficulties facing it. Its fourth Governor, the elderly radical parliamentarian, Sir John Bowring (1854–59), had sought to turn the colony into a model of British good government and of equal treatment for all races. Conservative interests within the government, however, and a pattern of misgovernment and miscarriages of justice obstructed his plans. The outbreak of war in 1856 (which Bowring had done much to engineer) prompted some of the most racist and repressive legislation that Hong Kong has ever seen. The powers under this legislation were concentrated in the hands of Daniel Caldwell. As the only European official with any great knowledge of the Chinese language or the Chinese community, Caldwell rose to prominence as Bowring's own prestige collapsed under the weight of bickering and scandal that now plagued the government. Much of this scandal was exposed by Bowring's highly strung and cantankerous new Attorney General, the former radical MP, Thomas Anstey, who saw it as his task to root out corruption and abuse of power. Since his arrival in 1856, Anstey had accused the outgoing Chief Magistrate of incompetence, the new acting Chief Magistrate of receiving bribes, the acting Superintendent of Police of gross breach of duty, the Chief Justice's clerk of embezzlement, and the Chief Justice himself of drunkenness. Within barely a year Anstey had turned the colony into a hotbed of controversy and had set off a chain of libel prosecutions that were to earn Hong Kong the nickname of 'libel land' in the London press. In 1858, in collaboration with journalists who had long-standing grievances against the government, he set his sights on some of the most powerful, and allegedly most corrupt, men in the government.

The Caldwell inquiry of 1858 was immediately preceded by a similar inquiry into allegations of corruption by Anstey against the barrister and acting Colonial Secretary, W. T. Bridges, in his handling of the revived retail opium monopoly. Another of the colony's most prominent officials, Lieutenant Governor William Caine, had since the early 1840s been the target of a succession of accusations, ranging from running protection rackets to accepting rake-offs in the award of government contracts. The man behind many of these accusations, William Tarrant, had lost his position as a civil servant in 1848 for drawing attention to corruption in Caine's office and had in 1850 purchased the radical newspaper, the *Friend of China*, largely for the purposes of prosecuting a campaign against Caine. Other journalists, such as Yorrick Jones Murrow of the *Hongkong Daily Press*, were pursuing their own campaigns against corruption, which increasingly targeted Bridges, Caine and Caldwell in a crusade against what Tarrant described as the ascendancy of 'the bloated bully over a craven-hearted, helpless section of the Chinese people'.[10] These campaigns reached their climax in the Caldwell inquiry of the summer of 1858. The inquiry took up seven weeks of some of the hottest months of the year and was held in an atmosphere of severe sickness: in addition to the usual catalogue of ill health among colonists, a cholera outbreak, barely noted in the colonial reports, had claimed hundreds of victims in the Chinese community.[11] The commission began shortly after the conclusion of the opium monopoly inquiry and ended just before the mass boycott of the colony by Chinese tradesmen and servants. The inquiry, reported Bowring (who took no part in its proceedings), 'more or less paralysed the action of every department of government' for a period of three months and involved nearly every senior official as participant or witness.[12]

Daniel Richard Caldwell

The man at the centre of the inquiry, Daniel Richard Caldwell, was born in 1816 on the East India Company's island of St Helena and was raised in Singapore. While he was still a boy, his father, 'a common soldier in a local militia corps', brought the family first to Penang and then to Singapore. In 1834 the younger Caldwell moved to the South China coast and took up a series of jobs on opium-smuggling ships, some of them Chinese-owned, mixing freely with 'river pirates of the most desperate character'.[13] Through his 'penchant for the fair celestials' he was able 'to learn and speak their language equal to a native' and could 'disguise himself so well, that the Chinese themselves are not able to detect that he is not one of their long-tailed tribe'.[14] Caldwell served as an interpreter to the British during the First Opium War. In 1842 he settled in Hong Kong and served the colonial government as court interpreter, head of detectives and guide to the Royal Navy in its expeditions against pirates. His fluency in various local dialects and his knowledge of the region made him indispensable to a colony chronically short of reliable intermediaries and deeply concerned about crime in and around the colony. A disproportionately low official salary left him in constant debt and caused him twice to resign from the government service: once in 1847, when he escaped creditors by fleeing to the neighbouring Portuguese colony of Macao; and again in 1855, when a rejected application for a salary increase prompted him to leave the government and enter into a business partnership with Ma-Chow Wong. Caldwell's obscure origins and his marriage to a Chinese wife were, one newspaper noted, 'incompatible with what is due to Government notions of society' and prevented him from receiving the rewards and recognition that many believed he deserved.[15] The crisis brought on by the Second Opium War was to change all that.

In late 1856, following the outbreak of war, the government re-engaged Caldwell on far more generous terms. Described by Bowring as 'the only government functionary through whom we have ever had satisfactory intercourse with the native population', Caldwell was appointed Registrar General and Protector of Chinese Inhabitants, and made a justice of the peace.[16] Emergency legislation in 1857 and 1858 concentrated authority in his hands and gave him extensive powers over the lives and businesses of Hong Kong's Chinese inhabitants. He was proclaimed to the Chinese population as the main intermediary between them and the government. He became Licenser of Brothels under the new 'Venereal Diseases Ordinance', which regulated prostitution with the aim of preserving the health of British troops. His power and influence, boosted by extensive connections in Chinese society, expanded accordingly. The Royal Navy called on him to guide its expeditions against pirates and the Chinese enemy. The colonial government relied on him to track down wanted criminals, communicate with the Kowloon authorities, advise on Chinese sentiment, make recommendations on pardons for convicted criminals, and cultivate support from the Chinese community.[17] Caldwell's usefulness was repeatedly demonstrated by his ability to apprehend spies, uncover plots and forestall some of the more pernicious attacks organised by the anti-British militia on the mainland: these included, in April 1857, the uncovering of a plot to assassinate both himself and Lieutenant Governor Caine.[18]

The bracketing together here of Caine and Caldwell, the Hong Kong government's two most 'orientalised' servants, is significant. Both had been recruited on the spot soon after the foundation of the colony for their special ability in handling the Chinese population, as military disciplinarian in the case of Caine, and as talented detective in the case of Caldwell. Both flourished in the liminal world between the colonial and Chinese communities. The Indian-trained Caine was, in Bowring's observation, 'altogether military and oriental' and had 'scarcely ever touched European soil'.[19] Caldwell himself had probably never even set foot in Europe and was of uncertain ancestry, possibly of mixed race. Much more than Caine, Caldwell, or Sam Kwei (Sangui), as he called himself, was a cultural hybrid, given to dressing up in Chinese costume and so fluent in the local dialects 'that natives take him for a brother'. Yet, despite these affinities, early descriptions also stressed his 'Englishness': he had 'blue eyes' and a 'truly English countenance'; he was 'a weak, slim, but well made man with peculiar largish dark blue eyes, which the natives cannot at all understand when they are set upon them'.[20] Uniquely among Europeans in Hong Kong at the time, Caldwell had 'gone native' by formally marrying a Chinese woman. In 1845 Caldwell married Chan-ayow, according to Chinese custom: in 1851 the Anglican Church sanctified the marriage, and Chan-ayow became Mary Ayow Caldwell. The evidence suggests that Mary Caldwell, an impressive and devoutly religious woman, exercised a stabilising influence on Caldwell's life: they raised a large and happy family and maintained a household that was remarked on by many for its warmth and generosity.[21] To Caldwell's accusers, however, the marriage was to become the key to his improper connections with the Chinese underworld and the gangster empire of Ma-chow Wong.

Ma-chow Wong

The career of Caldwell's Chinese counterpart, the notorious Ma-chow Wong, suggested to colonists not only that the Chinese community was being held in a grip of terror but that the government itself was coming increasingly under the control of gangsters. Ma-chow Wong symbolised the criminality that was thought to pervade Chinese life and to exert a powerful influence over some of the government's own senior servants. Colonists doubtless exaggerated the extent of Wong's 'reign of terror', but evidence from the Caldwell inquiry and independent reports suggest that Wong exerted an influence over the affairs of the colony that has been underestimated by many historians. By all accounts Ma-chow Wong was a prolific and accomplished criminal. As blackmailer, extortionist, burglar, expropriator, racketeer, arms dealer, trafficker in slaves, dealer in malicious prosecutions, receiver of stolen property, organiser of murderous piratical expeditions, and minor warlord, he appears to have tried his hand at nearly all the offences then current in Hong Kong.

Wong was a native of Nantou, the county town of Xin'an (the county of which Hong Kong was traditionally a part), where he began his career as contractor to supply hay for the horses belonging to the local magistrate.[22] In the early 1840s he fell in with pirates and was denounced to the magistrate, who offered a reward for his arrest. He then fled to Hong Kong with his family. In Hong Kong he became an organiser of 'a band of thieves, Triad street coolies, &c.', and made a living supplying pirates and disposing of pirated property. By the early 1850s Wong had consolidated a position of influence in and around the colony, and had learned enough English to be able to perform 'comprador pigeon' for various senior government officials. He bought the lucrative lease of the fish stalls at the Central Market, which, since they were supplied by fishermen from Xin'an, put him at the head of the large and notoriously unruly Xin'an faction in the colony and provided him with information on the movements of pirates.[23] His 'rowdies' from Xin'an were also reported to collect fees from gambling houses and other businesses on his behalf.[24] He acquired property in the newly reclaimed Bonham Strand at the western end of town and shares in lorchas and pawnshops.[25] He obtained appointments as chief of municipal police of Aberdeen (a village on the south side of the island) and the Central Market, 'the one the haunt of *pirates* and *fences*, the other of *pickpockets*'.[26] He became involved in a 'slave trade' carried on in the Straits and in emigration to California.[27] In 1854, a year of generalised rebellion in southern China, he fitted out an expedition of mercenaries to take his native place, the city of Nantou, but was foiled by the Chinese authorities.[28]

Wong's greatest source of power lay in his extensive control over pirates, which he secured through skilfully manipulating two great assets: a knowledge of the movements of pirates achieved through his connections and commercial undertakings; and an influence over Daniel Caldwell cultivated through personal and business relations. By feeding Caldwell with a steady stream of information about piracies sufficient to satisfy the needs of the colony's criminal justice system, Wong was able to demonstrate his own powers of denunciation to those who might attempt to resist his control. Wong's position as Caldwell's principal informant was no secret. Caldwell admitted that it was owing to Wong 'that I have been enabled to render those services for which I have been over and over thanked by my official superiors'.[29] The relationship began in 1843, when Wong adopted as goddaughter (or *qinu*) a woman known as Awoon, who had been kept by Caldwell as a mistress. By extension this was understood in the Chinese community to make Caldwell his adopted son.[30] In the 1850s Caldwell entered into various business speculations with Wong, including a partnership, formed during his absence from government employ in 1855 and 1856, for convoying Chinese junks along the coast and protecting them against pirates: this enterprise was allegedly hard to distinguish from the various illicit piracy protection societies current in the region, and it continued under Caldwell's official stamp into 1857.[31]

Whatever the origins of the connection with Wong, Caldwell's usefulness to his employers depended on his ability to maintain Chinese informants. The effects on the workings of government of such dependence had earlier been made clear by the Chimmo Bay piracy case of 1847, in which Chinese pirates had launched a murderous attack on ships belonging to Hong Kong's two largest opium firms. In this notorious miscarriage of justice, several convicted men were granted pardons after the principal witness, Caldwell's chief informant, Too-apo, had been exposed as a trafficker in malicious prosecutions. This system of narrow collaboration was now made even more destructive by the merging of the powers concentrated in Caldwell during the emergency of 1856–57 and the extensive resources of his protégé, Ma-chow Wong. Wong made himself 'the arbiter of the fate of all pirates, by either giving them protection, and necessarily deriving profit from it, being their agent in Hong Kong, or launching against them the British naval power'.[32] Through the protection and other services he could offer them, he maintained partnerships with prominent pirate chiefs in the region. He was 'the orbit round which the satellites of plunder revolved, the recognised head of the turbulent class of Chinese people, and a man of might and power for evil'.[33]

Wong's 'power for evil' was increasingly turning him into an embarrassment for Caldwell.[34] On 4 July 1857 the American pirate Eli Boggs told the Supreme Court that he had been framed by Wong, and gave evidence of Wong's criminal connections with Caldwell.[35] A few days later Wong was connected with a particularly atrocious piracy, in which a pirate fleet attacked a merchant junk off Lintin Island, killing four people, including the merchant's wives and son. Having been liberated after the junk was plundered of its cargo of sugar and indigo, the merchant sailed to Hong Kong, where he traced some of the booty to Wong's shop in Bonham Strand. Wong attempted to arrange the matter by undertaking to retrieve and restore all the cargo in return for a commission of $100. This transaction took place (and was recorded in Wong's account book), but on 16 July, acting on information received, the police arrested Wong and seized his account books, which revealed that he had also fitted out the piracy.[36] Wong offered Charles Bartlett, one of the arresting policemen, $10 if he would allow him to speak to a Chinese policemen, $50 if he would allow him to see Caldwell, and $1,000 (and a safe house near Macao) if he would let him escape.[37] When Bartlett successively refused each of these offers, Wong secured bail by appealing to the Supreme Court through his lawyer, Stace (whom he paid £250, or about $1,250, for the purpose), and spent the next few days threatening those who had informed on him before being rearrested.[38] Wong and his co-defendant Wong-atung were finally convicted on 2 September of confederating with pirates and were sentenced each to transportation for fifteen years.

The Caldwell Commission

Caldwell's response to Wong's arrest was suspicious. He rushed immediately to Wong's aid, helped him obtain bail, marshalled defence witnesses, persecuted some of the witnesses against Wong, and then mounted a vigorous campaign for Wong's pardon.[39] His long-standing connections with Wong were well known. Yet the inquiry nearly a year later into Caldwell's relationship with Wong might never have taken place had it not been for minor allegations of a very different kind that were only peripherally connected with Wong himself. In the Legislative Council on 10 May 1858 the Colonial Treasurer, Frederick Forth, gave notice of a motion accusing Caldwell, who was the Licenser of Brothels, of owning a registered brothel.[40] Since no one wished to second the motion, it fell to the ground. A few days later, however, Anstey wrote to the acting Colonial Secretary, Bridges, complaining of Caldwell's continuing connection with Ma-chow Wong. Feeling unable to sit on the same magisterial bench with such a person, Anstey submitted his resignation as justice of the peace.[41] Bowring refused to accept the resignation and on 14 May informed the council that his enquiries had revealed the allegations about Caldwell's ownership of brothels to have been made in error. At this, Anstey launched into a scurrilous attack on Caldwell in a scene which, in Bowring's words, had 'seldom been paralleled in any assemblage of Englishmen met in official conclave'. Anstey referred to Caldwell as 'a brothel-keeper and pirate' and to his wife as a 'harlot'.[42] When

Anstey refused to put his accusations into writing, Bowring appointed a commission of Legislative Councillors and JPs to investigate the Caldwell affair.[43]

The accusations made by Anstey and others were pieced together into a list of nineteen articles. The articles fall into two broad overlapping categories. About half of them refer to Caldwell's relationship with Ma-chow Wong and other disreputable characters: these range from the very specific ('with having procured bail for Ma-chow Wong') to the general ('with having passed a portion of his life among Chinese outlaws and pirates'); they also include the charges of having acted against people and their property on Wong's unsupported evidence and of drawing profits from Wong's depredations. The second category deals with Caldwell's alleged ownership of brothels and his relations with various women intermediaries, including his own wife, Ma-chow Wong's wife and the brothel keeper Shap-lok (or 'No. 16'). The bridge between the two categories appears in article six, which states that the 'principal link' in the connection with Ma-chow Wong 'is the bond of affinity by adoption according to Chinese law', a reference to Caldwell's former mistress, Awoon: Awoon was frequently confused with Caldwell's current wife, Mary Ayow, who was also rumoured to be related to Ma-chow Wong's wife, and who was anyway singled out in another article as being connected with 'some of the worst Chinese in this Colony'.[44] The articles form a curious hotchpotch of grave allegations, prurient innuendo and vague hearsay assertions: the commission's report complained that their difficult wording and 'distasteful' nature did not help the inquiry.

The commission's own credibility and effectiveness were in doubt from the very beginning. Its chairman, the Surveyor General, Charles Cleverly, was, like Caldwell and Bridges, a Freemason. One of its four other members, the Legislative Councillor George Lyall, was a close friend of Bridges and Caldwell.[45] The commission's counsel, John Day, had defended Ma-chow Wong in his trial the previous year and had worked with Caldwell to seek a pardon for Wong.[46] Throughout the inquiry, Caldwell interfered with Chinese witnesses 'by sign and gesture, to show the witness where to stand, to dictate to the interpreter, and to intercept the recording of the answer by a personal appeal to the examiner'.[47] Crucial evidence, the account books of Ma-chow Wong, had been destroyed on the orders of Bridges, ostensibly to save office space: these books allegedly contained entries firmly implicating Caldwell in Wong's piratical activities.[48]

The commission's report complained of the reluctance of Chinese witnesses to come forward, and commentators blamed the cowardice or the code of silence that prevailed in the Chinese merchant community.[49] They were perhaps sensible to stay away: Wong was still in gaol awaiting transportation and his imminent pardon was a persistent rumour. Wong's hold over the Chinese community, even from his prison cell, was still sufficient to force the leading Chinese inhabitants to petition for his pardon.

The commission relied mainly on a succession of unreliable European and Chinese witnesses. The most serious of the charges were dealt with largely through second or third-hand evidence from Anstey and the police chief, Charles May, who had long resented the erosion of his authority by Caldwell's rise to power. May referred to Caldwell's suspicious behaviour after Wong's arrest, to the suppressed account books, which he was certain would have incriminated Caldwell, and to the intimacy between the two men: 'Ma-Chow Wong's manner and bearing when I have seen him with Mr Caldwell,' he informed the commission, 'were different from those usually exhibited by a Chinaman in an Englishman's house.'[50] Thus the important questions about the extent of Caldwell's involvement in piracy and gangsterism were reduced to deliberations about whether or not Caldwell had treated Wong like a 'Chinaman'.

In the absence of specific evidence about Caldwell's connections with Wong, the commission dwelt mainly on lesser accusations about corrupt relations with the Chinese community. Reports of complex transactions, indirect control of property and indebtedness to Chinese creditors for sums amounting to $12,000 raised questions about conflicts of interest.[51] May testified that Caldwell appeared to be indifferent to the question of bribery and had sometimes boasted about the large amounts offered to him: 'I expressed my very strong disapprobation of his indifference to the opinion of the Chinese upon such a matter affecting so nearly the character of the British Government, but he did not appear to regard it in that light.'[52] A variety of inconclusive allegations about bribes received by Caldwell and his wife were brought forward by a succession of Chinese witnesses.[53]

As the commission focused its enquiries on Caldwell's alleged speculations in brothels, numerous witnesses were brought forward to comment on his ownership of buildings used as brothels and his connections with brothel keepers, but neighbours, agents, brothel keepers and business partners were unable to provide conclusive evidence. Although present in the colony, the intermediary in many of Caldwell's alleged dealings, the brothel keeper Shap-lok, was not available for questioning.[54] The sworn sistership between Caldwell's mother-in-law and Shap-lok's mother (which Caldwell admitted) and Mary Caldwell's own alleged corrupt dealings made Caldwell's marriage a central part of the inquiry. Much of the questioning turned on the rumours, exploited by May and others, that Caldwell had taken his wife from a brothel, even if she was not herself a prostitute.[55] She was, admitted May (who had for years enjoyed hospitality at the Caldwells' house), a woman of strict propriety,

> but the inherent character of the Chinese, derived from education, manners, and custom, are not in my opinion in her, more than in any of her countrywomen, eradicated by her marriage with Mr Caldwell. By inherent character, I mean the making use of position and power to obtain return for services rendered.[56]

At certain points in the inquiry it seemed that an unstated twentieth charge, that of being married to a Chinese wife, was the dominant concern of the proceedings: in Anstey's later speaking tours around England, this was indeed to emerge as a principal accusation against Caldwell.[57]

The focus of the inquiry on Mary Ayow Caldwell and on the other women who linked him with the Chinese community is striking. Of the nineteen original charges against Caldwell, five relate to his involvement in brothels, and five apply to the corrupting influence of his wife or other women. These obsessions suggest anxieties among some colonists that went deeper than mere questions of bribery or misgovernment. The Caldwell scandal erupted at a time when colonists were anxious about the prevalence of venereal disease among British troops yet divided over what should be done to address the problem. Concern was also emerging about the growth of a 'large population' of 'children of native mothers by foreigners of *all* classes' which was 'beginning to ripen into a dangerous element out of the dunghill of neglect'.[58] Such concern was to arise periodically in nineteenth-century Hong Kong, where men greatly outnumbered women, and where the system of racial apartheid made the growth of this Eurasian population an administrative problem and a social embarrassment.

Caldwell stood at the centre of these anxieties. The vesting in Caldwell of powers under the legislation introduced to regulate prostitution, combined with the suspicion that he held a financial interest in several brothels, naturally added fuel to the controversy. His marriage to a Chinese wife, and his connections with various female brothel managers, complicated matters further. The 'dangerous element' of children of mixed race derived mainly from the many liaisons and semi-permanent relationships between European men and Chinese women. Yet, with few exceptions, Europeans sought to keep these relationships as secret, as limited and as subordinate as possible. In openly marrying a Chinese woman according to Christian form, Caldwell had transgressed the tacitly agreed boundaries and provoked complex responses in the colonial community. These ranged from approval by the bishop and his wife to scorn among his detractors; they probably also included ambivalence from a large number of men who wondered what the implications might be for their own less public relationships. It was these questions about racial barriers, as much as concern about bribe taking or piracy, that, like May's observation that Caldwell had failed to treat Ma-chow Wong like a 'Chinaman', were at the heart of the inquiry.[59] As the scandal unfolded, not only did accusations emerge that Mary Caldwell had spent her early life in a brothel: questions about Daniel Caldwell's own racial identity also began to surface. The man who only a few years earlier had been emphatically differentiated from the Chinese with whom he mixed 'by his blue eyes and truly English countenance' was now increasingly described as a 'man of mixed blood' and 'a Singapore half-caste'.[60]

Finding himself increasingly on the wrong side of the racial barrier, Caldwell sought to draw his own boundaries by insisting on his respectability and by distancing himself from Ma-chow Wong and other Chinese of his type. Having pointed out that there was hardly one among his accusers 'who can be considered independent or unbiased', Caldwell denied the charges of bribery and brothel ownership and attempted to present his relationship with Ma-chow Wong as productive, legitimate and limited to that between superior and subordinate. Wong had supplied him with valuable information over a period of several years: 'I always had the most thorough reliance in him,' Caldwell insisted, 'as far as one can have in any Chinaman.' His business relations with Wong had been confined mainly to lending him money and a joint venture entered into when Caldwell was out of government employ. He denied any affinity with Wong: 'Ma-chow Wong is an inferior man, not an equal, and I consider this attempt to connect me with Ma-chow Wong nothing better than a villainous attempt to injure my reputation.'[61]

Despite its positive findings on some of the more important charges, 'coupled with the circumstance of Mr Caldwell's connexion with so notorious a character as Ma-chow Wong', the majority of the commission concluded that 'although Mr Caldwell's original appointment as Justice of the Peace may have been injudicious', their findings did 'not necessitate so strong a measure as his removal from office'. A Colonial Office minute observed that the mere establishment of Caldwell's connection with Ma-chow Wong 'and other bad characters' ought to have been sufficient to justify his immediate dismissal but suggested 'that the difficulty of procuring an efficient substitute for Mr Caldwell must have led the Commission to their conclusion, aided also by a lax way of viewing parity in the conduct of a public officer in a Chinese atmosphere'.[62] This was an acute observation. Bowring's lengthy summary of the mass of documents on the affair so distorted the facts that it amounted to a whitewash. 'To say the truth,' commented Bowring on the day the commission completed its enquiries, 'Caldwell is one of the most valuable of our public servants, while Anstey is a chronic pest.'[63] Anstey was suspended from office at the beginning of August and was finally dismissed in March 1859. Although Caldwell had had every opportunity to receive bribes, it was, Bowring pointed out, difficult to believe that he could have done so, since he continued to be so poor, despite his temperate way of life. 'Mr Caldwell's testimonials are most numerous and honourable,' he reported a couple of weeks later.

> I have constant occasion (as have our naval and military authorities) to avail myself of his special services, and at the moment in which I write he is accompanying a Naval expedition against pirates, being really almost the only trustworthy and well informed person on such matters to whom we have access.[64]

This remark was unfortunate, for stronger evidence was soon to emerge of abuses in this highly dubious system of pirate suppression. In March 1859 an old friend of Caldwell's named Seeko, an elder at the coastal town of Jiazi, more than 100 miles to the east of Hong Kong, sent word to Caldwell that some pirates had captured a junk of his: coincidentally, Ma-chow Wong, now serving out his time at the penal settlement in Labuan, possessed a share in the junk. Caldwell procured naval assistance and sailed to Jiazi, where he was joined by Seeko. Their search took them to the town of Hudong, a few miles down the coast from Jiazi, where some of the stolen cargo had been disposed of. With Seeko's concurrence, Caldwell demanded an indemnity of $1,000 from the inhabitants of Hudong: when they refused to pay, the naval ships fired rockets at intervals at the town. By 10.00 p.m. the amount demanded had been handed over and, without looking further for the pirates, the expedition returned to Hong Kong, where Caldwell decided not to make any report of the event to his superiors.[65]

In April 1859 a translation of a declaration by Chun Yook-teen and others, the Chinese government salt monopolists at Pengchengbu in nearby Xin'an county, appeared in the *China Mail*. It complained that a salt-smuggling boat intercepted by them and released when its master promised not to repeat the offence had petitioned Caldwell, who had taken three naval steamers to the monopolists' native village near the county town of Nantou. The steamers had destroyed four houses with cannonfire and had sent men ashore demanding $4,000 in ransom money. In order to save the village, the elders paid $1,000 immediately and agreed to pay the rest within a week to Caldwell. 'We think your honourable nation must have laws as well as ours,' declared the monopolists, in a well aimed protest. 'If [our boats] took a smuggler, and discharging her, should suffer such calamity, smugglers will become more and more formidable, and consequently national interests will be injured.' Caldwell's willingness to proceed on what became known as the 'Namtow Raid' may have arisen from the fact that his own shroff was allegedly a part owner of the boat captured by the monopolists.[66]

The *China Mail*, which first exposed these activities, remarked that such an 'ill-regulated interference' was turning minor disputes into serious piracies,

> for it is evident that if one of the parties in the dispute procures the services of our gunboats to knock the junks and villages of his opponents into flinders, the matter is at once made serious, and the natural consequence is that the Chinese begin to think they may as well be in for a pound as for a penny.[67]

Reacting to the press uproar, Caldwell announced in early June that he would participate in no more expeditions against pirates. Regretting this, the *China Mail* noted that the duty of guiding the navy in such expeditions would in future be in the hands of 'police *lookongs* and unnamed interpreters', which would amount to 'placing an engine of destruction in the hands of Hongkong fishermen and market boatmen'. One thing that the Hong Kong system of justice had at least taught colonists, the *Mail* pointed out, was that even apparently *bona fide* accusations against pirates could be highly dubious. Many alleged cases of piracy before the Supreme Court had broken down for want of evidence or because of clear proof that they had been trumped up. For naval officers on the spot there was:

> no opportunity for a proper examination of the complainant; and, of course, the accused have no opportunity of offering a defence, for the first intimation they get of the charge made against them is a gunboat steaming up to their junks and firing, when of course they take to the water and try to escape.[68]

This kind of warfare had become the favoured method of dealing with piracy from at least the mid-1840s, and had resulted in thousands of deaths and hundreds of thousands of pounds in head money for naval personnel. The question was therefore perhaps not so much what abuses lukongs and interpreters might introduce into the system but how many of the expeditions in the previous ten years had been motivated by revenge or rivalry. Or had Caldwell simply interpreted the findings of the commission and the faith placed in him by Bowring as a licence to do whatever he liked?

Caldwell's activities within Hong Kong in the aftermath of the commission certainly suggest that Anstey's failure had filled him with a new confidence. Five petitions, signed by no fewer than 918 Chinese residents, praying that Caldwell be retained as Protector of Chinese, were submitted to Bowring in early 1859 following a rumour that Caldwell was about to be removed from office.[69] Caldwell appears to have continued to protect the rackets of Ma-chow Wong and his associates by influencing proceedings in the Magistrates' Court and using his powers to silence his enemies.[70] The most extreme of these cases was the alleged framing of Shum-ahing, Wong's former godown keeper, who knew a great deal about Caldwell's activities and was believed to be willing to give evidence about them. Shum was convicted in February 1860 of kidnapping and slave dealing on evidence collected by Caldwell about a case involving the forcible carrying off of coolies to Cuba. He was sentenced to four years' penal servitude, and died half way through his sentence, having been severely abused by his gaolers. If the considerable documentation assembled by William Tarrant, Shum's fellow prisoner, is correct, the whole case was concocted by Caldwell with the assistance of Wong's wife and of men hired from Jiazi.[71]

The inquiry into civil service abuses

The aim of the vicious persecution of Shum-ahing, Tarrant alleged, was to prevent him from giving evidence at a second inquiry, due to take place later in the year, into Caldwell's relationship with Ma-chow Wong. The Colonial Office had not shared Bowring's confidence in Caldwell's innocence, and had merely waited for Bowring's final abandonment of the government over which he had already relinquished control. Bowring's successor, Sir Hercules Robinson, arrived in Hong Kong in early 1860 with detailed instructions to get to the bottom of Caldwell's alleged misdoings but also with a caution 'against stirring up again all that mass of mud which appeared to have encumbered society in Hongkong'.[72] The Colonial Office's desire to clear up the problem arose not only from its distrust of Bowring's judgement but also from campaigns led by newspaper editors and by Anstey in England to reopen the question of abuses in Hong Kong: these campaigns targeted not just Caldwell, but other senior officials, including Bowring himself.

Tarrant, in his *Friend of China*, used the Caldwell commission as an opportunity both to attack Bridges and to publish more exposés about his old enemy, Colonel Caine.[73] This led, in September 1859, to Tarrant's conviction on a charge of criminal libel, for which he was sentenced to a year's imprisonment and a fine of £50 and ordered to pay substantial costs.[74] This further persecution of Tarrant gave Anstey more evidence to support his campaign for an inquiry in England into the 'extortion, bribe-taking, corrupt alliances, malversation, resetting of pirates, felons, and murderers, and other offences' committed by British officials in Hong Kong.[75] In a 30,000-word letter to *The Times* in April 1859, he narrated in dramatic detail the whole 'reign of terror' that had been built up in Hong Kong through the corruption of its most senior officials.[76] During a series of lecture tours he aroused the support of public meetings and foreign affairs committees, whose members sent their equally dramatic petitions to the Colonial Office calling for the recall and trial of Bowring, Bridges and Caldwell.[77] At a meeting in Newcastle billed as 'The British Crown disgraced in China' Anstey described how Hong Kong, 'this little miniature representative of Great Britain, its laws, its manners, its institutions', had degenerated into a den of corruption and crime: from its shores Chinese, European and 'half-caste' desperadoes committed piracy and murder with the protection and encouragement of the colonial authorities.[78] The scandals in Hong Kong were discussed in the press and in Parliament, where the vast printed correspondence on the subject revealed 'hatred, malice, and all uncharitableness in every possible variety of aspect'.[79] 'It is a case for a dictator,' *The Times* commented, and urged the government 'to send out some sensible man with power to mediate, and, failing mediation, with authority to judge'.[80]

The 'dictator' was the new governor, Sir Hercules Robinson, who somewhat slowly and reluctantly carried out his special instructions to clean up the Hong Kong government. The inquiry into civil service abuses of 1860–61 was conducted by the Governor-in-Council. The only member of the public to volunteer information was the journalist Y. J. Murrow, who dominated most of the proceedings and whose twenty-four charges against Caldwell formed the basis of the inquiry. Half way through the inquiry Caldwell attempted to resign his position and then, when permission was denied, refused to perform his duties. In a published 'vindication' of his conduct, he tried to implicate May in brothel ownership.[81] He also appealed to the Chinese community in a statement published in the Chinese version of the *Hongkong Daily Press*, which traced the accusations against him to his investigations in 1857 into Murrow's coolie trading.[82] The inquiry, Robinson reported, was severely hampered by the absence of important witnesses, the wholesale destruction of evidence (including masses of papers that should have been in Caldwell's office) and 'the notorious incredibility of Chinese witnesses.'[83] The inquiry found decisively against Caldwell on the main charges: that he had maintained a relationship with a notorious pirate (Ma-chow Wong), who had used him to pervert the course of justice; that there were strong grounds for suspicion that, in his business associations with Wong, he was cognisant of a piratical association; and that there was every reason to fear that Caldwell had used the Royal Navy to carry out the 'nefarious designs' and strengthen the influence of a 'notorious pirate'. Still, Robinson's report added, there was 'no reason to suppose that our forces have ever been induced to capture or destroy any vessels or men undeserving of such a fate'. The inquiry concluded that 'Mr Caldwell's long and intimate connexion with the pirate, Ma-chow Wong, was of such a character as to render him unfit to be continued in the public service, and the Council recommended his dismissal therefrom.'[84] Resisting demands from Murrow that it should cast its net wider, the inquiry neatly placed the blame on Caldwell, Ma-chow Wong and their Chinese victims.

This was not, however, the end of the road for Caldwell, or even for Ma-chow Wong. Recognising, perhaps, that his real usefulness and support lay with the Chinese community, Caldwell quickly established himself as a 'Chinese agent'.[85] Within a year of his dismissal he had built up a lucrative business as arbitrator in Chinese disputes: many of these were referred to him by the colony's courts, which he continued to frequent as observer and freelance interpreter.[86] He speculated profitably in land and became involved in coolie broking on behalf of ships destined for Surinam and Peru: 'from the confidence reposed in him by the Chinese, he was enabled to secure unusually well qualified emigrants' for the plantations and guano mines in those places.[87] In 1866, after members of the Legislative Council had proposed that the government should re-employ him in some useful capacity, Governor MacDonnell took him on as the head of a semi-official secret police to assist in his crusade against crime. 'Whatever were Mr Caldwell's relations with Ma-chow Wong, and whether he was his tool or his dupe,' MacDonnell explained to a sympathetic Colonial Office, 'the result was eminently advantageous to the Public, as proved by the numerous cases in which Mr Caldwell was enabled to direct successfully the operations of our men of war against Pirates.'[88] Two years later the Chinese concessionaries under MacDonnell's experimental legalised gambling scheme engaged Caldwell as their manager. So respectable a member of the community had he become, MacDonnell pointed out in response to queries from London, that many now doubted whether he had been judged rightly in the Ma-chow Wong affair.[89] Caldwell died in Hong Kong in 1875 and is buried in the Colonial Cemetery there with an elaborate monument erected by his Masonic comrades.

As for Ma-chow Wong, after having had his sentence increased in Labuan by five years for organising a conspiracy to murder every European in the settlement (Wong himself later referred to this simply as 'a disturbance and fighting'), he was granted a free pardon in 1869 by the Governor of that colony, John Pope Hennessy, himself no stranger to controversy when later Governor of Hong Kong. In early 1870 Wong returned to Hong Kong to recover property and various debts amounting to $20,000: he was immediately arrested as a convict returning from transportation and (under the old 'emergency' legislation) charged with 'being a person dangerous to the peace and good order of the Colony'. His pardon having been substantiated, he settled in Hong Kong, where, declining offers of employment by the Chinese government, he lived a quiet life with his family until his death in 1892.[90]

Conclusion

More clearly and more extensively than any other issue, the Caldwell scandal brings out the problems and anxieties of British rule in early colonial Hong Kong. At one level it illustrates the difficulties that faced a colonial government out of touch with the majority of the colony's population during a period of war and emergency and unable to control the activities of its senior officials. Bowring, the colony's well-meaning but inept governor, had mortgaged much of his power to the only man in the colony who could bridge the gap with the Chinese community. Caldwell, in turn, had been unable to control the gangster informants on whom he relied for intelligence, and his methods of controlling crime had led to serious abuses of power. When the controversy erupted, in the commission of 1858, Bowring effectively abdicated his powers as Governor, and left his senior officials to squabble among themselves in a prolonged and very public battle that effectively froze the workings of government at a time of war and civil unrest.

At another level, the most cynical interpretation of the Caldwell affair, and one frequently put forward at the time, was that the controversy simply arose out of professional rivalry between May and Caldwell, blown out of proportion by Anstey's intemperate behaviour, and drawing in the personal antagonisms and rivalries spawned by the claustrophobia of tropical colonial life. Anstey's own penchant for controversy and his belief that he had been sent to Hong Kong to clear up 'villainy and rascality in high places'[91] bring in a third level of interpretation: the demise of Hong Kong as a beacon of British good government to the Chinese people. For Anstey, Tarrant and Murrow it was 'preposterous' to treat this clash of civilisations as 'one of mere provincial brawling and discord'.[92] What was at issue, in their opinion, was no less than 'the fame of the British Crown' in Hong Kong 'amongst the half-civilised people who crowd its public places, for honour, probity, and distributive justice' and 'the cause of the oppressed 400,000,000 of people who inhabit the empire of China, and of that colony whose name and reputation has been so much disgraced by the acts of its British officials'. The state of affairs that had arisen under Bowring's governorship marked the 'lamentable end' of 'the model colony of Hong Kong, which was to exhibit so favourable a contrast of the workings of our institutions with the operations of the heathen institutions of decrepid China'.[93]

'In a trial of skill like that,' Anstey remarked on Ma-chow Wong's influence over Caldwell, 'the Asiatic genius must triumph over the European; at all events the risk is prodigious.'[94] Both sides in the Caldwell controversy pointed to the vulnerability of European officials working on the margins of a 'decadent' civilisation. Abuse of power, the assumption went, was confined to subordinate Chinese functionaries and intermediaries who used their positions to extort money from Chinese residents accustomed to such practices under their own government: it was inevitable that senior European officials, innocent of the elaborate rackets conducted in their names, should be occasionally implicated. The findings of the Caldwell inquiry, and the extensive evidence of corruption among other officials at the time, suggest that Europeans needed no lessons in corruption from 'the Asiatic genius'. Colonial rhetoric in Hong Kong, however, depended on a firm contrast between 'British good government' (of which there was little evidence in Hong Kong at the time) and Chinese corruption. Too much probing into alleged abuses among high colonial officials was anyway, as Bowring admitted in the only case of the kind that went to court, bad for the reputation of the government.[95] Underlying these interpretations, and surfacing quite often in the mass of documentation on the scandal, is a sense of struggle between English and 'Asiatic' methods of government and a clear consensus that, whatever the culpability of individual European officials, the corruption emanated ultimately from the Chinese population. That corruption was not just political or pecuniary: it was also seen to be cultural, racial and sexual, as the concerns about Caldwell's relations with his wife and other women focused larger concerns about miscegenation and disease.

The convulsions of the late 1850s, the coming together of war, terrorism, uncontrolled piracy, corruption, misgovernment and rampant scandal, were exceptional even in Hong Kong's troubled history. But they illustrate, in extreme form, the many difficulties produced by the colonial relationship in a place like Hong Kong: the great gulf between government and people, narrowly bridged by a few talented but untrustworthy intermediaries; the crime and political conflict in the region which made such intermediaries all the more necessary and the scope for abuse all the greater; and the contradictions between the extravagant claims made for British rule and the sordid realities of government in a frontier colony. The Caldwell affair, and the problems of government that surrounded it, had lasting implications. The emergency regulations and the schemes of control for the Chinese population, centred on the office of the Registrar General and Protector of Chinese, remained in place for most of the century and were augmented in the mid-1860s by tight controls on the movement of Chinese ships into and out of Hong Kong harbour aimed at ending Hong Kong's role as the regional headquarters of piracy. From the 1860s onwards the Hong Kong government sought to reduce its reliance on men on the spot, like Caldwell and Caine, by introducing a 'cadet' scheme, under which university-educated men were recruited from Britain and trained in the Chinese language in Hong Kong in preparation for senior official careers in the colony: their purely British background and formal education would, it was assumed, inoculate them against the dangerous connections and 'Chinese atmosphere' that had brought Caldwell down. For their part, the leaders of the Chinese community organised themselves into quasi-political associations, recognised by the colonial government, capable of resisting the kind of 'reign of terror' enforced by Ma-Chow Wong, and able to supply many of the inadequacies of the colonial government: the District Watch Committee in 1866, the Tung Wah Hospital in 1872 and the Po Leung Kuk in 1878. These changes should not be exaggerated: corruption, extortion and miscarriages of justice continued to plague Hong Kong; misunderstandings and suspicions between government and people persisted; and a place still remained for men such as Caldwell, who, even after his fall from grace, continued to be an indispensable agent both to the colonial government and to the Chinese community.

Notes

1 Great Britain Colonial Office, Original Correspondence: Hong Kong, 1841–1951, Series 129 (CO 129), Public Record Office, London, CO 129/68, 352–61, Anstey to Bridges, 8 July 1857.

2 *Friend of China* (*FOC*), 2 January 1847, 2.
3 Ronald Robinson, 'Non-European Foundations of European Imperialism: Sketch for a Theory of Collaboration', in Roger Owen and Bob Sutcliffe, eds, *Studies in the Theory of Imperialism* (London, Longman, 1972), 117–42; John M. Carroll, 'Colonialism and Collaboration: Chinese Subjects and the Making of British Hong Kong', *China Information*, 12:1–2 (1997), 12–35.
4 See especially Carl T. Smith, *Chinese Christians: Élites, Middlemen, and the Church in Hong Kong* (Hong Kong, Oxford University Press, 1985), Elizabeth Sinn, *Power and Charity: The Early History of the Tung Wah Hospital, Hong Kong* (Hong Kong: Oxford University Press, 1989) and Jung-fang Tsai, *Hong Kong in Chinese History: Community and Social Unrest in the British Colony, 1842–1913* (New York, Columbia University Press, 1986).
5 Sandria B. Freitag, 'Crime in the Social Order of Colonial North India', *Modern Asian Studies*, 25:2 (1991), 227–61.
6 CO 129/69, Anstey to Lytton, 16 August 1858, 182.
7 Anstey to Bridges, 13 May 1858, *British Parliamentary Papers: China 24: Correspondence, Dispatches, Reports, Ordinances and other Papers relating to the Affairs of Hong Kong, 1846–60* (Shannon, Irish University Press, 1971), 339.
8 *FOC*, 1 December 1860, 105.
9 This section, and much of the analysis elsewhere in this chapter, draws on material in my forthcoming book, *Anglo-China: Chinese People and British Rule in Nineteenth-Century Hong Kong* (London, Curzon Press).
10 William Tarrant, *Hongkong I, 1839 to 1844* (Canton, Friend of China, 1861), 29.
11 Colonial Surgeon's Report for 1858, *Hongkong Government Gazette* (*HKGG*), 19 March 1859, 190.
12 Bowring to Lytton, 9 August 1858, *British Parliamentary Papers: China 24*, 302.
13 Thomas Chisholm Anstey, *Crime and Government at Hongkong: A Letter to the Editor of the 'Times' Newspaper; offering Reasons for an Enquiry, into the Disgraces, brought on the British Name in China, by the Present Hong Kong Government* (London, Effingham Wilson, 1859), 49.
14 John Fortescue Evelyn Wright, Diary, 1849–1853 (typescript and photocopy deposited at the Public Record Office, Hong Kong, by Wright's descendant, Mrs Jocelyn Scrymgeour), 28 April 1851.
15 *FOC*, 14 July 1855, 226.
16 CO 129/63, Bowring to Labouchere, 21 May 1857, 154.
17 CO 129/59, Bowring to Labouchere, 9 and 10 December 1856, 218–20, 241; CO 129/62, 28 March 1857, 576–7; CO 129/63, 23 and 30 April 1857, 20, 57–8; Great Britain, Colonial Office, Executive and Legislative Council Minutes: Hong Kong (from 1844) Series 131 (CO 131), Public Record Office, London, CO 131/3, Executive Council minutes, 27 December 1856, 278, CO 131/4, 9 February 1857, 51–2; CO 129/62, notification by Mercer, 10 January 1857, 104.
18 CO 129/67, Wade's translation of a Chinese official letter on the planned assassination of Caine and Caldwell, 10 April 1857, 31–8; CO 129/63, Bowring to Labouchere, 23 April 1857, 20–5; *FOC*, 6 May 1857, 143; *China Mail* (*CM*), 7 and 14 May 1857, 75 and 78.
19 CO 129/49, Bowring to Grey, 14 February and 10 March 1855, 175–6, 203.
20 *FOC*, 14 July 1855, 226; Wright, Diary, 28 April 1851.
21 For a discussion of Mary Caldwell and her household see Smith, *Chinese Christians*, 199–200.
22 Hence the nickname 'Ma-chow' (*macao*, or 'horse-grass'). *CM*, 24 February 1853, 30; CO 129/68, Inglis to Bridges, 14 July 1857, 380–3.
23 CO 129/68, Caldwell to Bridges, 15 July 1857, 361–5; CO 129/68, May to Bridges, 20 July 1857, 366–79.
24 CO 129/68, 'Ascertained by Inquiry': background of Ma-chow Wong, 13 May 1858, 409–15.
25 CO 129/68, May to Bridges, 20 July 1857, 366–79; CO 129/68, 'Ascertained by Inquiry', 13 May 1858, 409–15.

26 *CM*, 24 February 1853, 30.
27 CO 129/68, May to Bridges, 20 July 1857, 366–79; *CM*, 17 September 1857, 150.
28 *CM*, 24 February 1853, 30; CO 129/68, May to Bridges, 20 July 1857, 366–79; CO 129/68, 'Ascertained by Inquiry', 13 May 1858, 409–15.
29 Caldwell Commission minutes: Caldwell's defence, 14 July 1858, 447.
30 CO 129/68, Inglis to Bridges, 14 July 1857, 380–3; CO 129/68, May to Bridges, 20 July 1857, 366–79; Anstey, *Crime and Government*, 52; Caldwell Commission minutes: Inglis's evidence, 30 June 1858, and Caldwell's defence, 14 July 1858, *British Parliamentary Papers: China 24*, 412 and 453.
31 *Ibid.*, 447; CO 129/69, John Roberts, Deputy Inspector of Markets, to May, 31 July 1858, 413; Caldwell to Bridges, 6 August 1858, *British Parliamentary Papers: China 24*, 320; Anstey, *Crime and Government*, 52, 57; *CM*, 10 September 1857 (Supplement).
32 CO 129/68, May to Bridges, 20 July 1857, 366–79; Caldwell Commission minutes: Dixson's evidence, 28 May 1858, *British Parliamentary Papers: China 24*, 359–60.
33 *CM*, 17 September 1857, 150.
34 *FOC*, 15 July 1857, 222; CO 129/68, May to Bridges, 20 July 1857, 366–79; Caldwell Commission minutes: Inglis's evidence, 30 June 1858, *British Parliamentary Papers: China 24*, 414.
35 CO 129/68, Anstey to Bridges, 8 July 1857, 352–61; George Wingrove Cooke, *China: Being the Times Special Correspondence from China in the Year 1857-58* (London, Routledge, 1858), 68–9.
36 *CM*, 17 September 1857, 150.
37 Bartlett's pay was $24 a month. *Ibid.*, 10 September 1857 (Supplement); *FOC*, 22 July 1857, 230.
38 *FOC*, 22 July 1857, 230; CO 129/66, Murrow to the Earl of Harrowby, 2 August 1857, 472.
39 *CM*, 17 September and 17 October 1857, 150; CO 131/4, Executive Council minutes, 21 and 28 September and 12 and 27 October 1857, 124–31, 135–8, 140–3; CO 129/68, the case of Wong Akee alias Ma-chow Wong, by Bridges, 8 March 1858, 332–7; Caldwell Commission minutes: May's evidence, 18 June 1858, *British Parliamentary Papers: China 24*, 392.
40 CO 131/4, Legislative Council minutes, 10 May 1858, 494–5.
41 CO 129/68, Anstey to Bridges, 13 May 1858, 393–409.
42 Bowring to Lytton, 9 August 1858, *British Parliamentary Papers: China 24*, 303.
43 Bowring to Lytton, 21 July and 9 August 1858, *British Parliamentary Papers: China 24*, 295, 304–5.
44 Annotation by Bridges, in Inglis to Bridges, 14 July 1857, *British Parliamentary Papers: China 24*, 333. The nineteen articles and the commission's report are reproduced in James William Norton-Kyshe, *The History of the Laws and Courts of Hong Kong* (London, Unwin, 1898), I, 506–8.
45 See Cleverly's remarks on divisions in the Caldwell commission and on Bridges's statement that he wished to help Caldwell as a fellow mason in R. v. Tarrant, November 1858, *British Parliamentary Papers: China 24*, 620–1.
46 Anstey to Bridges, 30 July 1858, *ibid.*, 462.
47 This was Anstey's allegation, and it was certainly consistent with Caldwell's practice in the Magistrates' Court. Such interference was explicitly denied in the commission's report: *ibid.*
48 *HKR*, 22 June 1858, 114; Caldwell Commission minutes: evidence by James Mongan, Assistant Chinese Secretary, 23 June 1858, *British Parliamentary Papers: China 24*, 394; *FOC*, 28 July 1858 (quoted in *ibid.*, 500); Bowring to Lytton, 9 August 1858, *ibid.*, 307–8; R. v. Tarrant, November 1858, *ibid.*, 613–17; Anstey, *Crime and Government*, 77–83; *HKGG*, 23 April 1859, 218–20.
49 Caldwell Commission report, 17 July 1858, *British Parliamentary Papers: China 24*, 297.
50 Caldwell Commission minutes: May's evidence, 18 June 1858, *ibid.*, 391.

51 Caldwell Commission minutes: evidence by Lum-ateen, Caldwell and others, 1–3 and 11 June 1858, *ibid.*, 361–5, 375–6.
52 Caldwell Commission minutes: May's evidence, 10 July 1858, *ibid.*, 442.
53 Caldwell Commission minutes: Wo Hang's and Tong Kwong-sin's evidence, 9–10 July 1858, *ibid.*, 393, 395, 437, 439.
54 CO 129/69, Roberts to May, 31 July 1858, 415.
55 Caldwell Commission minutes: evidence by May and Inglis, 8, 11 and 16 June 1858, *British Parliamentary Papers: China 24*, 369–70, 374, 380.
56 Caldwell Commission minutes: May's evidence, 8 June 1858, *ibid.*, 369.
57 CO 129/75, Supplement to the *Newcastle Chronicle*, 25 June 1859, 228. See also Anstey, *Crime and Government*, 65–7, and *The Times*, 15 March 1859.
58 CO 129/49, Bowring to Grey, 1 March 1855, 197.
59 Caldwell Commission minutes: Caldwell's evidence, 14 July 1858, *British Parliamentary Papers: China 24*, 445–7, 453.
60 CO 129/66, Murrow to the Earl of Harrowby, 2 August 1857, 472; Bowring to Lytton, 9 August 1858, *British Parliamentary Papers: China 24*, 302; Anstey, *Crime and Government*, 49.
61 Caldwell Commission minutes: Caldwell's evidence, 14 July 1858, *British Parliamentary Papers: China 24*, 445–7, 453.
62 CO 129/68, Colonial Office minute, 21 July 1858, 139–40.
63 CO 129/68, Bowring to Merivale, 19 July 1858, 129–30.
64 CO 129/69, Bowring to Lytton, 30 August 1858, 152–3.
65 CO 129/73, Bowring to Lytton, 14 February 1859, 212–13; *FOC*, 19 January and 30 March 1861, 191–2, 312–14; Robinson to Newcastle, 16 December 1861, *British Parliamentary Papers: China 25: Correspondence, Dispatches, Reports, Returns, Memorials and other Papers relating to the Affairs of Hong Kong 1862–81* (Shannon, Irish University Press, 1971), 26–7; William Tarrant, *Hongkong – Supplement to the Minutes of Inquiry into Civil Service Abuses before the Executive Council 1860–61* (Canton [n.p.], 1862), 2 (copy in CO 129/87, 310–29).
66 *CM*, 21 April 1859, 62; CO 129/76, Anstey to Lytton, 30 May 1859, 42–4.
67 *CM*, 21 April 1859, 62.
68 *Ibid.*, 2 June 1859, 86.
69 As Anstey pointed out, these petitions, which seem to have fooled Bowring, were co-ordinated by the tepos of various districts, who were now the direct salaried subordinates of Caldwell. CO 129/73, Bowring to Lytton, 22 February 1859, 214–15; CO 129/76, Anstey to Lytton, 30 May 1859, 42–4.
70 These actions included allegedly harassing and arresting various tradesmen for refusing to pay blackmail to Ma-chow Wong's successors. *FOC*, 18 December 1858, 402; CO 129/73, Anstey to Lytton, 21 January 1859, 72–8; *CM*, 27 January 1859, 14.
71 CO 129/77, Robinson to Newcastle, 23 March 1860, 158–64; *CM*, 30 March 1860 (Supplement); *FOC*, 11 May 1861, 385; Tarrant to Newcastle, 3 September 1862, CO 129/87, 306–7; Tarrant, *Hongkong – Supplement to the Minutes of Inquiry into Civil Service Abuses before the Executive Council, 1860–61*, CO 129/87, 310–29.
72 Newcastle's speech in Parliament, 28 June 1859, quoted in Norton-Kyshe, *History*, I, 642; CO 129/73, Minute by Carnarvon, 4 February 1859, 234–5; Carnarvon to Anstey, 30 May 1859, *British Parliamentary Papers: China 24*, 675; CO 129/73, Colonial Office to Robinson, 11 January 1860, 243–61; CO 129/77, Robinson to Newcastle, 10 April 1860, 365–7.
73 *FOC*, 8, 11, 25 and 29 September 1858, 286–7, 291, 306–7, 310.
74 *CM*, 29 September 1859, 154–5.
75 CO 129/76, Anstey to Lytton, 17 May 1859, 23–7; Anstey, *Crime and Government*, 4.
76 *The Times*, of course, declined to print the letter, and Anstey published it himself under the title *Crime and Government at Hongkong*.
77 CO 129/75, Foreign Affairs Association of Sheffield to Lytton, 15 February 1859, 257; CO 129/76, John Wright of Keighley to Derby, 28 February 1859, 387–8; CO

129/75, Holbeck Foreign Affairs Committee to Colonial Office, 10 March 1859, 264–5; memorial from the inhabitants of Sheffield, 2 April 1859, *ibid.*, 269; petition of the inhabitants of Newcastle upon Tyne, 20 June 1859, *ibid.*, 227.
78 CO 129/75, *Newcastle Chronicle*, 25 June 1859 (Supplement), 228.
79 Lytton, quoted in Norton-Kyshe, *History*, I, 582.
80 *The Times*, 15 March 1859, 9c.
81 The resignation attempt was partly prompted by the disappearance of $2,011 from the public chest kept in Caldwell's office, for which he was made liable through deductions from his salary. CO 129/80, Robinson to Newcastle, 14 February 1861, 139–45, CO 129/81, 21 June and 8 July 1861, 251–6, 454–7; CO 129/84, Bishop Smith to Newcastle, 6 April 1861, 343–5; *FOC*, 6 July 1861.
82 *Ibid.*, 2 March 1861, 265.
83 Robinson to Newcastle, 16 December 1861, *British Parliamentary Papers: China 25*, 12, 24.
84 *Ibid.*, 11–28.
85 D. R. Caldwell, or 'Sam Kwei' [*Sangui*], is also listed in the local directory for 1863 (and subsequent years) as 'Chinese Interpreter'. CO 129/93, Jury List for 1862, 24 February 1862, 32; *China Directory for 1863* (Hong Kong, Andrew Shortrede, 1863), 11.
86 CO 129/88, Mercer to Newcastle, 12 December 1862, 233–5; *CM*, 18 December 1862, 202.
87 CO 129/139, MacDonnell to Granville, 14 September 1869, 160–3.
88 *CM*, 16 August 1866, 156; CO 129/114, MacDonnell to Carnarvon, 27 August 1866, 475–82.
89 Buckingham to MacDonnell, 2 December 1868, MacDonnell to Buckingham, 6 March 1869, MacDonnell to Granville, 6 March, 24 April and 3 July 1869, *British Parliamentary Papers: China 25*, 207–9, 214–24, 238–9, 249–50.
90 Robinson to Newcastle, 16 December 1861, *ibid.*, 14–15; *CM*, 28 January, 5, 8 and 9 February 1870; Norton-Kyshe, *History*, I, 554.
91 Quoted in Norton-Kyshe, *History*, I, 404–5.
92 Anstey, *Crime and Government*, 5.
93 Anstey to Lytton, 16 August 1858, *British Parliamentary Papers: China 24*, 658; CO 129/75, Anstey's speech at Newcastle, *Newcastle Chronicle* (Supplement), 25 June 1859, 228.
94 CO 129/68, Anstey to Bridges, 8 July 1857, 353.
95 The case was a prosecution by Anstey against the acting Chief Magistrate and Sheriff, W. H. Mitchell, in 1856, for malversation of office involving the alleged taking of bribes from Chinese prisoners. Mitchell was acquitted. CO 129/56, Bowring to Labouchere (with enclosures), 7 June 1856, 240–70; *CM*, 3 July 1856, 106–7.

CHAPTER THREE

Marginal Westerners in Shanghai: the Baghdadi Jewish community, 1845–1931

Chiara Betta

This chapter is concerned with the presentation of the Shanghai Baghdadi Jewish community from a fresh perspective, that of its marginal position within the Shanghai Western community.[1] For this purpose Baghdadi Jews will be considered in the following pages as 'marginal Westerners'. The definition used here is meant to be broadly inclusive, and indeed incorporates five generations of Baghdadi Jews who differed substantially in the attitudes to the West and the Western presence in Shanghai. It should also be noted that on a social level the term lumps together the Anglicised merchant elite and the 'Oriental' poorer sections of the Baghdadi community in the city.

The first part of the chapter attempts to delineate the *modus operandi* of the Baghdadi Jewish merchants in the India–China trade in the second half of the nineteenth century. It compares the Baghdadis' commercial role with that of Parsi and Ismaili merchants, and is therefore closely tied to Claude Markovits's contribution in the next chapter. The latter part of the chapter traces the Baghdadis' relationship with the British, focusing on a number of interdependent aspects: nationality, Anglicisation, and social interaction. The main aim of this chapter is to define the ambiguous positioning of the Baghdadis vis-à-vis the British, and to show that their marginality did not represent, as a whole, a significant hindrance to their sojourn in the Shanghai foreign settlements.

The gates of the Middle Kingdom open

This exploration of the trade diaspora of Baghdadi Jews to India and China starts in Ottoman Baghdad around 1829, when David Sassoon (1792–1865), the scion of the leading local Jewish family, was forced to leave the city by the Governor, Daud Pasha. The young man moved first to Bushire in Persia and then to Bombay around 1832–33.

Baghdadi Jewish merchants, trading in precious stones, rose water and Arabian horses, had already extended their commerce as far as Surat, Bombay and Calcutta by the middle of the eighteenth century. At the beginning of the 1830s possibly twenty to thirty Baghdadi Jewish families lived in Bombay and coexisted with the more consistent native community of the Bene Israel. The forced conversion of the Jews of the Persian city of Meshed in 1839 prompted a number of families to flee to Bombay and join the local 'Arabian Jewish trading community'.[2] It is therefore important to specify immediately that the term Baghdadi, especially in Bombay, included 'Jews from Syria and other parts of the Ottoman Empire, Aden and Yemen, all of whom were Arabic speaking, and even Jews from Persia and Afghanistan, who were not'.[3]

Upon his arrival in Bombay David Sassoon set up a trading house, and in less than a decade he became the most respected member of the local Jewish community. Significantly, he 'gradually extended into Central Asia and southern China, trading in Bombay yarn, English piece-goods, and opium'.[4] Sassoon's competitors in Bombay, such as Parsi merchants, were also heavily involved in the import of opium into China. Opium commerce, in fact, represented a lucrative line of trade for foreign merchants, who were eager to trade with China, but whose commercial activities were restricted to Canton (Guangzhou), the only Chinese port open to foreign commerce after 1759. Following the official ban on opium imports promulgated by the Jiaqing emperor in 1796, the drug was smuggled to an island near Canton by clippers under the licence of the East India Company. Such a system left 'numerous intermediary roles available for non-Britishers',[5] such as the Parsis, who were among the major traders of Indian opium by the 1820s.[6] David Sassoon was a comparatively late arrival but nevertheless a keen competitor.

New commercial horizons for traders were provided by the Treaty of Nanjing in 1842 that marked the end of the Opium War (1840–42) and sanctioned the opening of Canton, Xiamen [Amoy], Fuzhou, Ningbo and Shanghai (the first so-called treaty ports) to commerce with Great Britain, and the cession of Hong Kong island to the British. David Sassoon's second son, Elias David (1820–80), an adventurous character who possessed remarkable business acumen, immediately anticipated the great potentiality of the Chinese market and sailed to Canton, which he reached after a long, perilous voyage some time between 1843 and 1844.[7]

Upon his arrival Elias David reorganised the family business. His task was enormous, since, in contrast to his father in Bombay, he could not rely on existing networks of Baghdadi Jewish merchants. By the mid-1840s Baghdadi Jewish traders were represented in China only by the Sassoons, whilst at least twenty-four Parsi firms operated in the city of Canton. Notwithstanding the evident difficulties, Elias David expanded Sassoon commercial activities to the thriving Jiangnan city of Shanghai. Here he opened an office in 1845, although he apparently remained based in Canton.[8]

That same year the first British consul, Captain George Balfour, and the Shanghai Circuit Intendant (*Daotai*) reached a local agreement, the so-called Land Regulations, which regularised arrangements for foreign settlement. This was made necessary by the fact that the Treaty of Nanjing did not contain any precise provision on this key issue. An area situated north of the Chinese walled city was assigned to British residents and a committee of merchants was also put in charge of such communal matters as the building of roads and the hiring of watchmen within the limits of the foreign settlement.[9] In 1849 the French consul also obtained a tract of land south of the English Settlement, and thus the Concession Française came into being.[10]

By the late 1840s private residences, stores, a hotel and a club had been built in the English Settlement to ease the harsh life of the first wave of foreign pioneers – pioneers who included a number of these 'marginal Westerners'.[11] From the opening of Shanghai as a treaty port, a handful of Baghdadi Jewish, Parsi and Ismaili merchants sojourned in the city and competed with each other to occupy similar commercial interstices in the trade between Bombay and Shanghai. In 1850, of the roughly 200 foreigners who lived in the city, three were Baghdadi Jews and seven were Parsis. The three Baghdadis were employees of David Sassoon Sons & Co. Of the Parsis, C. Bomajee (the first Parsi to move to Shanghai around 1847–48) and F. S. and N. M. Langrane (Lungrana) ran their own import-export companies. The others were employed by P. F. Cama & Co. and the Langrane concern. Significantly, a Parsi cemetery was also established as early as 1854. Ismaili traders probably arrived in Shanghai in the footsteps of the Parsis.[12]

A dramatic demographic change took place in the foreign settlements in the middle of the 1850s when about 50,000 Chinese refugees from the Small Sword and Taiping rebellions swarmed into the foreign areas. The new circumstances suited the British, French and American consuls (the Americans had in the meantime also set aside their tract of land), who aimed to increase foreign power in their concessions. They immediately took the opportunity to demand that the Circuit Intendant should revise the Land Regulations. Under the New Land Regulations signed in 1854 foreigners were permitted to raise money through taxation in order to carry out public services, and foreign municipal councils on Chinese territory thereby came into being without the consent of the imperial court. In 1863 the British and American areas merged together into the International Settlement (where British influence remained paramount) which was administered by the Shanghai Municipal Council (SMC). The Concession Française remained apart under the jurisdiction of the Conseil Municipal Français (CMF).[13]

In these first decades of foreign presence in Shanghai, when the system of the foreign settlements was taking shape, underpinned by dubious legal foundations, Indian opium and cotton represented the major commodities imported, whilst exports remained mainly confined to silk and tea for Europe and the United States. Opium was smuggled by British, American, Parsi and Baghdadi Jewish (D. Sassoon Sons & Co.) merchants into Shanghai via Wusong until 1858, when it was recognised as a legal commodity by the treaty settlement which ended the Second Opium War (1856–58).[14]

As a whole, throughout the 1850s, Parsis controlled a larger share of the India–China trade than Baghdadi Jews, who were represented in Shanghai only by D. Sassoon Sons & Co. Nor could Ismaili traders challenge the commercial hegemony of the Parsis. However, from the 1860s onwards Baghdadi Jews started gradually to replace Parsis as the main ancillaries of the British in the trade between India and China.[15]

In the footsteps of the Sassoon firms

New impetus to the Baghdadi presence in Shanghai was provided by a second Sassoon firm, E. D. Sassoon & Co., founded by Elias David in 1867, three years after the death of his father. By 1868 E. D. Sassoon & Co. already operated in Shanghai and Hong Kong. As for the more established D. Sassoon Sons & Co., it had branches in Shanghai, Hong Kong, Ningbo, Hankou, Zhifu, Tianjin, Niuzhuang and also in Yokohama. Nevertheless, the Baghdadi community in Shanghai remained tiny. In 1868 the Sassoon firms employed about ten Baghdadis; by 1874 the number had risen to about twenty. Most important, some Baghdadi individuals, usually ex-employees of the Sassoon firms, had started to set up their own companies in Shanghai by the middle of the 1880s. In 1887 the companies of Moses & Elias, A. E. J. Abraham, Isaac Ezra, R. J. Solomon, R. E. Toeg, B. D. Benjamin, D. H. Silas and Raphael Sidka Raphael were operating as general merchants and brokers.[16]

Significantly, most of these merchants, as well as a number of the Sassoons' employees, did not return to India or Baghdad and chose to settle with their families in the Shanghai foreign settlements. Their spouses were probably the first significant group of Baghdadi women who took up permanent residence in Shanghai.[17] They remained, however, an invisible presence, as they were confined in the domestic realm and were generally not involved in their husbands' businesses. In contrast to Baghdadi Jews, Parsi traders left their families in Bombay, and the Parsi community in Shanghai was formed almost exclusively by male sojourners – at least until the first decade of the century.[18]

Following the arrival of new clerks of the Sassoon firms and merchants in search of fortune, the Baghdadi Jewish community grew slowly but constantly. According to the estimate of Jakob b. Abraham d. Sudea, the roughly 175 Baghdadis who worked in China in 1895 were mostly engaged in the import of opium and cotton from India.[19] In the following decades the economic activities of Baghdadis in Shanghai closely followed the economic expansion of the city, which blossomed into China's major industrial centre towards the end of World War I. By the 1920s the Baghdadis had diversified their commercial interests. The Sassoon firms, for example, held extensive shipping interests and numerous agencies and rated among Shanghai's main landowners. In 1923 E. D. Sassoon & Co. dealt in cotton yarn, cotton, metals, textiles, wool products, glass and other general merchandise. As for the bulk of Baghdadi merchants, they remained general traders, commission agents and brokers, and monopolised the Shanghai Stock Exchange.[20]

Most significantly, until the turn of the century the Sassoon firms played a central role in the early Baghdadi community and represented a protective shell for Baghdadi Jews in their relations with both the local Western community and the Chinese environment. The firms provided a known cultural and religious framework for their employees, who were almost exclusively of Baghdadi origin. This practice helped to cement ethnic cohesion, strengthened kinship ties and may have helped to mitigate the 'culture shock' felt by the new arrivals.[21] Importantly, much of the early religious life of the Baghdadi community was sponsored by the Sassoons. The first Jewish cemetery was established in 1862 with the financial support of David Sassoon and in 1887 the Beth El synagogue received the patronage of the Sassoon firms. Sir Jacob Sassoon then financed the building of the Ohel Rachel synagogue, which replaced the Beth El in 1920.[22]

In the last decades of the nineteenth century young single men could find comfort not only within the Sassoon firms but also in the houses of some pious settlers, like S. J. Solomon, whose 'home was a temple in miniature... and was open to all the young men in the

Settlement on Sabbath and Festivals'.²³ Nevertheless, psychological strain was at times felt by Baghdadi sojourners. The solitude and displacement of Baghdadi Jews in Shanghai were eased by the frequent contacts they had with other communities of the Baghdadi trade diaspora. There was frequent visiting, especially among those who resided in Hong Kong, Singapore, Rangoon, Calcutta and Bombay. These cities represented 'individual nodes' of the same trade diaspora 'united only by the solidarity that could be built on the sentimental ties of a common religion, language, or distant kinship'.²⁴ The regular interaction of Baghdadis who lived in those cities not only favoured the maintenance of kinship ties but also served the purpose of making it possible for Baghdadi men and women scattered in India, South East and East Asia to find a suitable partner within their own community.²⁵ Baghdadis, in fact, married almost exclusively among themselves, though marriages with Ashkenazim had started to take place already at the end of the nineteenth century. The marriage of Reuben Hey Elias to a Russian Jewish girl, of the Haimovitch family – which seems to have taken place at the onset of the 1890s – must have been one of the first such weddings. Their grandchild George Hayim, however, recalls that they could barely understand each other, their first languages being Judaeo-Arabic and Russian.²⁶

British protection, opium and land

Besides playing a major role in the India–China trade, Baghdadi Jews were, as a whole, deeply committed Anglophiles who staunchly supported the Crown. As far as national status was concerned, a large number of Baghdadi Jews remained Ottoman subjects until 1918 and like other Ottomans were supposed to receive French protection. Baghdadis, especially the merchant elites, however, were not eager to associate with the French, as their loyalties lay firmly with the British empire. The issue was solved by a compromise reached by the British consular authorities with their French counterpart, probably as early as the 1860s. British protection was extended (with the prior consent of the French Consul General) to the employees of the Sassoon firms and of British firms, and sometimes also to people who had resided for a long period in India or in other British possessions. Not surprisingly, the practice was stretched to the limit and sometimes merchants who did not meet the requirements were granted British protection and, at times, even registered as British subjects. The Foreign Office discovered Shanghai's practice only by accident in 1906. It immediately admonished Shanghai to the effect that in particular those Baghdadi

Jews who were not employed by the Sassoons or by British firms were entitled only to French protection.[27]

The consequent refusal to renew British protection of a number of Baghdadis was greeted with vocal and stubborn protests from a number of traders who did not wish to receive French protection. In their letters these merchants, who were born in Ottoman Baghdad, still spoke Judaeo-Arabic as their first language and had probably never been to Great Britain, attempted to delineate their own identity as British. As one Silman Somekh explained, 'I have all along identified myself with British interests, and, to the best of my ability, have acted as a good citizen, and . . . my moral obligations . . . would have always prevented me from repudiating the country of my adoption.'[28] Consequently, an ambiguous approach continued to be pursued by the Shanghai consular authorities, at least until 1918, and a number of Baghdadis managed to retain their coveted British protection. In the following years, after the creation of the state of Iraq under British mandate, many Jews whose roots were in Baghdad continued to be registered as British-protected subjects. However, their status in Shanghai was subject to occasional review.[29]

From a practical point of view there were clear advantages for the Baghdadis in being British-protected subjects rather than French protégés. The benefits of receiving British protection were especially evident in relation to the opium trade. The Baghdadi commercial elites, in fact, together with the Parsis and Ismailis, lodged protests and memoranda with the British consular authorities whenever their commercial interests in the trade were at stake.[30] Not surprisingly, the decision in 1908 by the British government gradually to reduce the import of Indian opium to China with the aim of ending the trade by the end of 1917 was not welcomed by the Baghdadi merchant elite. The latter, especially the Sassoon firms, S. J. David & Co. and E. I. Ezra & Co., in fact, controlled the largest share of the opium trade between India and China at the turn of the century. To cite one example of the extent of the commerce, E. D. Sassoon & Co. imported 45,532 chests of the drug between 1899–1901 and 1904–08.[31]

The prospective demise of a particularly lucrative line of trade prompted Baghdadi Jews, Parsis, Ismaili and even Persian companies based in Bombay to exploit together their loyalty to the British Crown. Therefore as 'British merchants' they pledged that 'Though we claim no voice on the question of the extinction of the trade, we do claim to be heard as to the manner in which such extinction should be carried out.'[32] The relevant point to be drawn here is that Baghdadi Jews, Parsis and Ismailis – middleman minorities that were otherwise in competition to occupy similar economic niches – formed an alliance at a time when their economic interests were challenged by outside factors.

The solidarity among Baghdadis and Parsis became even more apparent when they established the Shanghai Opium Merchants' Combine in 1913. The combine basically acted as a monopoly for the import of Indian and Persian opium, which was then distributed by Chaozhou opium merchants, in a period during which the availability of the drug was limited. It was dominated by Baghdadi merchants and its head was E. I. Ezra, the first councillor of the SMC born in Shanghai.[33]

Baghdadis – like other Chinese and foreign merchants – routinely reinvested opium profits in property in the foreign settlements, where land values increased about thirteen times between 1900 and 1930.[34] The link between opium and land was readily acknowledged by Shanghainese. In 1931 the *Shenbao*, Shanghai's major Chinese newspaper, acutely observed that the staggering wealth of the Baghdadi Jewish tycoon Silas Aaron Hardoon was due to dealing in *tu*, a term with the double meaning of 'opium' and 'land'.[35] Besides Hardoon, the Sassoon firms and E. I. Ezra especially had invested their opium profits in land and rated among Shanghai's major landowners.[36]

Most important, the vast assets Baghdadi Jews held in the International Settlement helped them gain a prominent role in its administration. Neither the SMC nor the CMF was a democratic body: both were elected only by a minority of foreign residents on a restricted property franchise.[37] Under this system a number of residents held multiple votes, a practice that was favourable to Baghdadi Jews, who were among the main landowners in the International Settlement. Hence, in such a pragmatic organisation of municipal life, wealthy Baghdadi merchants represented a needed ally for the British oligarchy that dominated the SMC and which like the Baghdadi Jews held large interests in land in the Shanghai settlements. In the Shanghai International Settlement the relationship between Baghdadi Jews and the British was therefore not that of coloniser and colonised but one of interdependence based on shared commercial interests.

To foster this alliance a representative of the 'British' Sassoon firms usually occupied one of the six seats reserved for Britons on the SMC almost every year between 1869 and 1904. Furthermore E. I. Ezra, another British-protected subject, was an elected councillor between 1912 and 1918. The real estate developer Maurice Benjamin, whose family had settled in Shanghai as early as the 1870s, was elected in 1920. In contrast Baghdadis were only sporadically represented on the CMF, possibly because they had not enough ratepayers to elect a councillor. Parsis, who unlike the Baghdadis and the British did not become a community of settlers, never elected a councillor to the SMC, partly because their commercial influence had dwindled but also because they did not have enough landed properties in the International Settlement.[38]

Orientals or Europeans?

The majority of residents of the Shanghai foreign settlements were Chinese sojourners. Baghdadi Jews had therefore to devise their own cultural strategy to confront the surrounding Chinese socio-cultural milieu. Overall they maintained a detached attitude towards the Chinese environment which resembled the one adopted by the British. As aptly observed by Robert Bickers, 'The only Chinese met by Britons, or by most other foreigners in China, were rickshaw pullers, servants, compradores and staff, and sometimes interpreters. They were often invisible.'[39] The superficial relationship between Chinese and the foreign communities is then summarised by Jerome Ch'en, who writes:

> The pattern of acculturation was not the one where the majority was to change the minority but vice versa. As neither community was profoundly intellectual and few intimate friendships existed between them, the acculturation of the Shanghai Chinese depended more on the mass media than on the aloof Caucasians themselves.[40]

Among prominent Baghdadi merchants the only one who 'went native' and experienced a visible process of cross-cultural adaptation into the Chinese socio-cultural milieu was the above-mentioned Silas Aaron Hardoon (1851–1931), one of the few Baghdadis who married outside the Jewish faith. His life has captured the collective imagination of Shanghainese since the 1920s and he remains the only foreign merchant still widely remembered in Shanghai. Numerous fictional works have remodelled Hardoon according to the prevailing political, social and economic moods of Chinese society and as a result Hardoon's story has attracted the attention of the 'petty urbanites' (xiao shimin) of the 1930s, the Chinese masses of the Maoist period and the entrepreneurs of the 1990s. Recently his life has even been depicted in a soap opera.[41]

Hardoon married in 1886 the Eurasian Buddhist Luo Jialing (1864–1941), illegitimate daughter of a Chinese woman and a Frenchman who may have been of Jewish origin. Hardoon's union with Luo Jialing not only represented a most unusual challenge for the first generation of Baghdadi Jews, those more faithful to their traditions and values, but also broke away from the accepted codes of behaviour of the Shanghai foreign community. Marriage to a Eurasian of low extraction defied one of the strongest social taboos of treaty port society. Whatever her mixed origins, Luo Jialing identified herself as Chinese and contributed to Hardoon's solid and wide interaction with the Chinese milieu. As a result of his constant participation in Chinese affairs in the last decades of his life he attempted to build a new social identity in Chinese society according to the model of the traditional Chinese merchant-philanthropist.[42]

Nevertheless, Hardoon continued to maintain contacts with the Jewish community and even sponsored the building of the Beth Aharon synagogue. His Jewish funeral on 21 June 1931 and the Chinese memorial service held a month later ostensibly showed that at the end of his life Hardoon had found himself in a position fraught with ambiguities, at the border of different cultural experiences. Both occasions created uproar within the Shanghai Jewish community. According to one member of the community the 'funeral procession was more of a Chinese character than Jewish' and 'A Buddhist seance had, in the complete sense of the word, permeated the whole atmosphere.'[43] Even more shocking was the Chinese memorial service, a sort of belated funeral, during which Hardoon's ancestral tablet was dotted (as was customary in Chinese funeral rites) and Buddhist monks and Daoist priests performed auspicious rites to help Hardoon go through hell and then safely on to reach the Buddhist paradise. Hardoon without doubt remained the only Baghdadi merchant who attempted to form a new social identity in the Chinese milieu. However, whatever efforts he made to integrate in Chinese Shanghai, he could never overcome the sharp distinction Chinese draw between *wai* (outer, outside) and *nei* (inner, inside). The dichotomy remained and Hardoon continued to be a *waiguoren*, a foreigner.[44]

As for the majority of Baghdadi merchants, they emulated the tastes of the English gentleman. Maisie Meyer has amply shown in her work that Baghdadis, who kept strong ties with their cultural heritage, underwent a remarkable process of Anglicisation during their stay in Shanghai. Significantly, they readily adopted British habits and hobbies and attempted to integrate with Shanghai British society. Around the turn of the century, in order to stress their European links, and also to differentiate themselves from Russian Jews, they then started to define themselves as Sephardi.[45]

The Anglicisation of Baghdadis had started in India after David Sassoon moved to Bombay at the beginning of the 1830s. In the 1850s David Sassoon still posed in pictures and paintings dressed in the traditional Baghdadi Jewish robe with a princely bearing appropriate to the scion of the family that had served as the chief treasurer (*Nasi*) of the governor of Baghdad. He represented the last well known example of a prominent Baghdadi trader in India who displayed with opulence his Middle Eastern origins. His sons, however, readily felt the pressure to Anglicise and conform to Western customs and mannerism. They eagerly adopted Western dress, posed in pictures like English gentlemen, and the eldest son Abdullah became known by the more neutral appellation (Sir) Albert.[46]

Baghdadi businessmen who reached Shanghai from the 1870s onwards were also eager to stress their Western inclinations. Many adopted a Westernised name like the stockbroker Reuben Elias Toeg, who became known as Raymond. Toeg acquired from the British a passion for breeding horses and his ponies won numerous trophies from 1886 onwards. His culturally hybrid lifestyle could also be noticed by the Westernised style of his house that unmistakably imitated Shanghai British homes, with high-ceilinged drawing and dining rooms, dark wooden floors, Western-style furniture and occasional Chinese *objets d'art*.[47] The domestic space of other Baghdadi tycoons was also Westernised. The magnificent residence of E. I. Ezra 'had Louis XV furniture throughout, a ballroom for 150 dancers, a music room to seat an audience of 80 in comfort, and elegantly designed French windows giving out on to 25 acres of garden'.[48] Not surprisingly, only Hardoon lived in a pagoda-roofed house whose interior decoration reflected the homes of the local Chinese merchant gentry elite. The house was situated in a traditional Chinese landscape garden of Buddhist Chan (Zen) inspiration.[49]

Baghdadi Jews became more English as they gradually abandoned Judaeo-Arabic in favour of English.[50] Written Judaeo-Arabic disappeared swiftly. Nevertheless elderly Baghdadis such as Hardoon still used to jot down short notes in that language in the late 1920s.[51] As for the spoken language, it was still used by Baghdadi families, especially the elderly, throughout the 1930s. In 1920 the Zionist envoy Israel Cohen observed that Baghdadis in Hong Kong 'had preserved the Arabic speech of their fathers, which they often used in conversation with one another, though few born in China could either read or write the language'.[52] It is also of some relevance to note that Judaeo-Arabic was still used in certain business environments such as the Shanghai Stock Exchange. Here the Baghdadis 'shouted' to each other in their ancestors' language with the aim of confusing their competitors.[53]

The process of Anglicisation experienced by Baghdadi Jews did not, however, imply their full acceptance among Shanghai Westerners.[54] As in India, they occupied an ambiguous positioning on the fringe of the

British and 'were sometimes treated as non-Europeans or, at least, comparable to other "anomalous" people like the Eurasians and Anglo-Indians'.[55] The pain of social marginality in Shanghai's British society can be observed by the fact that as late as 1921 only the richest Baghdadi merchants were accepted by the leading British club, the Shanghai Club. In contrast, membership was easily obtained by junior British employees.[56] Full integration into the British community was obstructed first of all by the fact that the Baghdadis, like the Parsis, were considered 'Orientals', at least until the turn of the century.[57] Prejudice against the Baghdadis was then reinforced by latent anti-semitism, which was ingrained in certain sections of the Shanghai British community. The vulnerable position of the Baghdadis and, more generally, of Jews of all origins in Shanghai's Western society is epitomised by a letter, interspersed with violent antisemitic harangue, sent by a British resident, under the pseudonym 'An Everyday young man', to the *Celestial Empire* in 1882.[58] Antisemitic prejudices also intersperse the account of the rise and fall of Benjamin David Benjamin, the major landowner in the International Settlement by 1879, published by the *Celestial Empire* in 1888.[59]

Finally, it needs to be stressed that though this chapter has dealt mainly with the merchant elites, the Baghdadi community, like the British community, was not homogeneous and wealth was not ubiquitous. They had to face their own Other: paupers mainly from Jerusalem, Baghdad and Bombay who were looking for petty employment and sometimes survived by beseeching alms in the communities of the Baghdadi trade diaspora. Most important, they threatened the image the Baghdadi merchant community wanted to project to the Shanghai Westerners: that of a community which aspired to be considered European and especially British. Beggars and adventurers could, in effect, not speak English, were not familiar with English customs and in some cases even kept to the 'Oriental' practice of having more than one wife.[60]

Though sources on the poorest section of the Baghdadis in Shanghai are scarce, it seems plausible that a constant flow of poor Jews from the Ottoman empire and British India reached Shanghai from the 1880s onwards. They were mostly sojourners, who rarely settled in Shanghai, and found accommodation in the cheapest areas of the Northern District of the International Settlement.[61] There was an apparent sense of fraternity and solidarity among them, which was, however, broken at times by disputes. Such was the case in 1894 with a certain Israel Abraham from Jerusalem. He accused a Baghdadi co-religionist of having stolen 'seven Turkish golden coins' after the latter had offered him free accommodation upon his arrival in Shanghai.[62]

Many of the vagrants stayed in Shanghai only for short periods and like other undesirable foreigners were, whenever possible, deported from the International Settlement.[63] When in 1882 a woman beggar and her child were forced to leave the International Settlement the *Celestial Empire* explained that:

> it is well known that the Jewish fraternity in Shanghai never allow members of their persuasion to be in want, if they are worthy of relief, and the fact that they have neglected her is another reason for the belief that she is a professional vagrant, and there is only one proper resort for such characters, – the gaol, or the strict surveillance of the authorities.[64]

The above clearly suggests that Shanghai British residents considered the poorest sections of Jews from the Ottoman empire and British India a similar threat to that posed by the 'distressed British subjects' mentioned in Chapter Ten. They therefore represented an underclass, often invisible, which survived on the edge of the Baghdadi merchant community and was ready to move on to a new destination whenever better opportunities beckoned. The contrast with the wealthy Baghdadi merchants, the grandeur of their lifestyles, their Westernised tastes and habits, could not have been greater. Whilst these paupers considered Shanghai one of a number of possible destinations, for many of the merchants and their families Shanghai had become their permanent home. Were it not for the abrupt change prompted by the establishment of the People's Republic of China we might still find there the descendants of some of the earliest settlers. Nowadays only buildings such as Edward Ezra's mansion (used as headquarters by the Shanghai People's Armed Police), the Kadoorie's Marble Palace (now the Children's Palace) and the Cathay Hotel (Peace Hotel) bear silent testimony to the wealth accumulated by Baghdadi Jews throughout the century they remained in Shanghai.

Conclusion

This chapter has, first of all, attempted to link together the commercial presence of the Baghdadis and Parsis in China in the second half of the nineteenth century. In particular, it has stressed that Baghdadis, Parsis and Ismailis shared similar commercial interstices in the India–China trade under the aegis of the British empire. It has also suggested that these groups identified as 'British' to foster their commercial interests and, in moments of uncertainty, forged pragmatic alliances to foster their economic interests. This last issue would, however, require a broader comprehension of the relationship between competition and solidarity among middleman groups in the India–China trade.

Delineating the positioning of the Baghdadis with respect to Shanghai Britons and, more generally, to the Shanghai Western community shows that, notwithstanding the gradual process of Anglicisation experienced by Baghdadis, a constant and tangible tension between marginality and acceptance remained predominant in their relationship with the British. This can be seen especially in their ambiguous national status and the difficulty of being fully accepted by the upper echelons of Shanghai British society. That said, the fact that the International Settlement was not a colony allowed the Baghdadi merchant elite to participate together with the local British oligarchy in the running of the administration of the settlement. It is arguable that, as a whole, social boundaries between Baghdadis and the British were slightly more porous in Shanghai than in other environments such as British India. It was a nuanced difference which, however, highlights the uniqueness of the Shanghai International Settlement.

Finally, the degree of Anglicisation of individual Baghdadis depended largely upon their economic position. The most affluent more readily felt the need to Anglicise and adopt Western customs. The poorest, who represented a minority, remained more attached to their Baghdadi traditions and tended not to remain permanently in Shanghai. As for the Baghdadis' relationship with the Chinese environment, it was marked by a strong degree of detachment. The only individual response, at least among the prominent members of the Baghdadi community, that was notably influenced by the surrounding Chinese environment was that of Hardoon. He thus added to his Shanghai experience a dimension that remained unexplored among his most of his coreligionists, as well as among most foreigners in Shanghai.

Notes

1 The only comprehensive work on the Baghdadi community, which focuses on its Baghadi, Jewish and Sephardi identity, is Maisie Meyer, 'The Sephardi Jewish Community of Shanghai 1845–1939 and the Question of Identity' (London School of Economics, University of London, Ph.D. thesis, 1994).
2 Thomas A. Timberg, 'Baghdadi Jews in Indian Port Cities', in Thomas A. Timberg, ed., *Jews in India* (New Dehli, Vikas Publishing House, 1986), 273, 275; Joan Roland, *Jews in British India: Identity in a Colonial Era* (Hanover NH, University Press of New England, 1989), 16.
3 Roland, *Jews in British India*, 15.
4 *Ibid.*, 16.
5 Timberg, 'Baghdadi Jews', 273.

6 David Edward Owen, *British Opium Policy in China and India* (New Haven CT, Yale University Press, 1934. Reprinted Archon Books, 1968), 115.
7 Letter of Jakob b. Abraham d. Sudea (1895) reprinted in P. G. von Möllendorf, 'Die Juden in China', *Monatsschrift für die Geschichte und Wissenschaft des Judenthums*, 39 (1895), 330–1; *North China Herald (NCH)*, 11 May 1880, 416.
8 *The Hongkong Almanack and Directory for 1846, with an Appendix* (Hong Kong, China Mail, 1846); Shanghai shehui kexueyuan jingji yanjiusuo (Shanghai Academy of Social Sciences, Economic Research Institute), ed., *Shanghai dui wai maoyi, 1840–1949* (hereafter *SDWM*) (The Foreign Trade of Shanghai, 1840–1949) (Shanghai, Shanghai shehui kexueyuan chubanshe, 1989), I, 69.
9 Nicholas R. Clifford, *Spoilt Children of Empire: Westerners in Shanghai and the Chinese Revolution of the 1920s* (Hanover NH, University Press of New England, 1991), 18.
10 On the Concession Française see Jean Fredet and Charles Maybon, *Histoire de la Concession française de Shanghai* (Paris, Plon, 1929).
11 (Sir) Rutherford Alcock, quoted in Arnold Wright (ed.), *Twentieth Century Impressions of Hong Kong, Shanghai and other Treaty Ports in China: Their History, People, Commerce, Industries, and Resources* (London, Lloyd's Greater Britain, 1908), 62.
12 *Anglo-Chinese Calendar for the Year 1848* (Canton, Chinese Repository, 1848); *NCH*, 3 August 1850; SSK, *SDWM*, I, 68–75; E. S. Elliston, *Shantung Road Cemetery, 1846–1868* (Shanghai, Millington, 1946), 45.
13 Clifford, *Spoilt Children of Empire*, 18–19. The New Land Regulations were subsequently amended in 1869 and in 1898.
14 SSK, *SDWN*, 39–64; F. L. Hawks Pott, *A Short History of Shanghai: Being an Account of the Growth and Development of the International Settlement* (Shanghai, Kelly & Walsh, 1928), 46.
15 Rhoads Murphey, *The Outsiders: The Western Experience in India and China* (Ann Arbor MI, University of Michigan Press, 1977), 85.
16 *The Chronicle and Directory for China, Japan, and the Philippines, for the Year 1868* (Hong Kong, Daily Press Office, 1868), 155, 201, 223, 234, 236, 238; *The China Directory for 1874* (Reprinted Taipei, Ch'eng Wen Publishing Company, 1971), 28J-29J; *The China Directory, 1887* (1887), 432, 435, 442–4, 447–8.
17 The first Baghdadi woman to be buried in Shanghai was the wife of Raphael Sidka Raphael, Simha, in 1875. Mendel Brown, 'The Jews of modern China,' *Jewish Monthly*, 3:3 (1949), 161.
18 *NCH*, 10 August 1880, 135; 6 July 1906, 36.
19 Jakob b. Abraham d. Sudea, in von Mollendorf, 'Juden in China', 331.
20 For listings of Baghdadi firms and the Shanghai Stock Exchange see *The Directory and Chronicle for China, Japan, Corea, ...* (Hong Kong, Hong Kong Daily Press Office, 1926), under 'Shanghai', 697–805; on the commercial activities of E. D. Sassoon & Co. see Zhang Zhongli and Chen Zengnian, *Shaxun jituan zai jiu Zhongguo* (The Sassoon Group in old China) (Beijing, Renmin chubanshe, 1985).
21 Chiara Betta, 'Silas Aaron Hardoon (1851–1931): Marginality and Adaptation in Shanghai' (University of London, Ph.D. thesis, 1997), 26–8.
22 Revd C. E. Darwent, *Shanghai: A Handbook for Travellers and Residents to the Chief Objects of Interests in and around the Foreign Settlements and Native City* (Shanghai, Kelly & Walsh, 1920), 30; Simon Adler Stern, *Jottings of Travel in China and Japan* (Philadelphia PA, Porter & Coates, 1888), 155. Another synagogue, the Shearith Israel, was set up in 1898 and was succeeded by the Ohel Rachel in 1927. The religious life of the Baghdadi community has been analysed at length in Meyer, 'Sephardi Jewish Community', chapter three.
23 *Israel's Messenger (IM)*, 5 April 1929, 18.
24 Philip Curtin, *Cross-cultural Trade in History* (Cambridge, Cambridge University Press, 1984), 6–7.
25 See for example the marriage of Katie Moosa of Shanghai to J. S. Abraham of Bombay: *IM*, 3 April 1908, 9.

26 See George Hayim's highly colourful *Thou shalt not Uncover thy Mother's Nakedness* (London, Quartet Books, 1988), 5. On marriage among the Baghdadis see Meyer, 'Sephardi Jewish Community', 78–81.
27 Betta, 'Hardoon: Marginality and Adaptation', 38–43; see also Myer Samra, 'The Immigration of Iraqi Jews into "White Australia"', 1901–1973', paper presented at the Second International Congress of Babylonian Jewry, Babylonian Jewry Heritage Centre, Or Yehuda, Israel, 15–18 June 1998.
28 PRO, FO 372/5/8691, Sir Pelham Warren (Shanghai) to Foreign Office, 31 January 1906, Enclosure 1, D. Silman Somekh to Sir Pelham Warren, 29 January 1906.
29 Meyer, 'Sephardi Jewish Community', 231.
30 'Memorial from the opium merchants', sent to Sir John Walsham, HBM's Envoy Extraordinary and Minister Plenipotentiary, Shanghai, 25 May 1886, published in *NCH*, 11 June 1886, 612.
31 Brian G. Martin, *The Shanghai Green Gang: Politics and Organised Crime, 1919–1937* (Berkeley CA, University of California Press, 1996), 45–6; Zhang and Chen, *Shaxun jituan*, 22.
32 PRO, FO 228/2415/7, Sir Pelham Warren to Sir John Jordan (HM Minister), 10 January 1907, Enclosure 1, Letter of opium traders, 7 January 1907.
33 Martin, *Shanghai Green Gang*, 46–7; Meyer, 'Sephardi Jewish Community', 188–93.
34 'Shanghai land values – a comparison', *Realty Market*, 44 (July 1931), 1.
35 *Shenbao* (Shanghai news), 4 July 1931.
36 See especially Betta, 'Hardoon: Marginality and Adaptation', chapter three; Zhang and Chen, *Shaxun jituan*, chapter three; Meyer, 'Sephardi Jewish Community', 193–200.
37 Clifford, *Spoilt Children of Empire*, 21. The councils were structured in fundamentally different ways: the CMF acted mainly as an advisory body to the French consular authorities, and was fully incorporated into the French colonial system, but it was not clear to which authority the SMC was ultimately responsible. See *ibid.*, 35.
38 Tang Zhijun *et al.*, eds, *Jindai Shanghai dashiji* (Chronology of major events in Shanghai from 1840 to 1918) (Shanghai, Shanghai cishu chubanshe, 1989), 914–31, 939–41; G. Lanning and S. Couling, *The History of Shanghai*, I (Shanghai, Kelly & Walsh, 1921), 465; *IM*, 5 August 1921, 7; 2 October 1921, 25.
39 Social boundaries, however, eased in the 1920s: Robert A. Bickers, 'Changing British Attitudes to China and the Chinese, 1928–1931' (University of London, Ph.D. thesis, 1992), 101.
40 Jerome Ch'en, *China and the West: Society and Culture, 1815–1937* (London, Hutchinson, 1979), 233.
41 Chiara Betta, 'Myth and Memory: Chinese Portrayal of Silas Aaron Hardoon, Luo Jialing and the Aili Garden between 1924 and 1995', in *Jews in China: From Kaifeng to Shanghai* (Sankt Augustin, Monumenta Serica, forthcoming).
42 Betta, 'Hardoon: Marginality and Adaptation', especially chapters four and five. On marriage to Eurasians see Bickers, 'Changing British Attitudes', 117, 119.
43 *IM*, 4 September 1931, 19.
44 Betta, 'Hardoon: Marginality and Adaptation', 227–38.
45 On Baghdadis' identification as Sephardim see Meyer, 'Sephardi Jewish Community', especially 54–60.
46 Roland, *Jews in British India*, 56–7 and figures 1 and 2; Wright, *Twentieth Century Impressions*, 224, 227.
47 *NCH*, 25 August 1893, 317; Wright, *Twentieth Century Impressions*, 501, 519; *NCH*, 9 June 1928, 430.
48 Austin Coates, *China Races* (Hong Kong, Oxford University Press, 1983), 235.
49 Betta, 'Hardoon: Marginality and Adaptation', 76–9.
50 Meyer, 'Sephardi Jewish Community', 84–5. Hindustani was also spoken by the section of the community that had resided in India: Jakob b. Abraham d. Sudea, in von Möllendorf, 'Juden in China', 331.

51 Shanghai House Property Administration Bureau Archives, Archives of the Hardoon Company, file *Yi* 2123. Judaeo-Arabic was used to keep business correspondence at least until the 1880s: *NCH*, 12 March 1884, 303.
52 Israel Cohen, *The Journal of a Jewish Traveller* (London, John Lane, 1925), 118.
53 Hayim, *Thou shalt not Uncover*, 3.
54 'The Sephardi Jewish community certainly identified itself as British but does not appear to have been regarded as such on a social level': Bickers, 'Changing British Attitudes', 81.
55 Walter Q. Zenner, 'The comparison of Jews of China and Jews of India', paper presented at the conference 'Jewish Diasporas in China: Comparative and Historical Perspectives', Harvard University, August 1992, 4.
56 *List of Members of the Shanghai Club* (Shanghai, Kelly & Walsh, 1921).
57 The oriental roots of Baghdadi Jews are highlighted in *Twentieth Century Impressions of Hong Kong, Shanghai and other Treaty Ports in China*. Here Baghdadi Jewish, Parsi and Ismaili firms in Hong Kong (with the exception of S. J. David) are listed under 'The Oriental Mercantile Community', together with Chinese, and not under 'The European Business Community'. Wright, *Twentieth Century Impressions*, 'European Business Community', 224–8.
58 *Celestial Empire* [*CE*], 22 April 1882, 304.
59 George Thirkell, *Some Queer Stories of Benjamin David Benjamin and Messrs E. D. Sassoon & Co.: Wealth, Fraud and Poverty. Les Juifs entre eux* (Shanghai, Celestial Empire, 1888), 2, 7.
60 In 1904 one Rachel Reuben claimed maintenance from her husband after he had taken a second wife: *NCH*, 10 June 1904, 1232.
61 Meyer, 'Sephardi Jewish Community', 129–32.
62 *CE*, 30 March 1894, 387; *NCH*, 30 March 1894, 494.
63 *NCH*, 6 November 1894, 536.
64 *CE*, 4 October 1882, 278.

CHAPTER FOUR

Indian communities in China, c. 1842–1949

Claude Markovits

All readers of Hergé's 1936 Tintin adventure *Le Lotus bleu* are familiar with the Sikh policemen of the International Settlement in Shanghai. The Indian presence in nineteenth and twentieth-century China was not, however, limited to these tall, turbaned and bearded custodians of an imperialist order. In the Chinese treaty ports as well as in the British colony of Hong Kong, different groups of Indian subjects of the British Crown were employed in various capacities, primarily as policemen and watchmen but also as merchants, traders, commercial employees and clerks. They hailed from at least three different provinces of the Indian Empire, and belonged to four religious communities, the Hindu, Muslim, Sikh and Parsi. They were therefore, in spite of their small overall numbers (not more than a few thousand), a fairly diverse group, and to study them it is necessary to disaggregate the data as much as possible. Although towards the end of the period Indian nationalism had a growing impact on the political behaviour of these men, it would be misleading to view them as belonging to a closely knit 'national' group. An important point is that these were almost exclusively male communities. Very few Indian women came to China, and most Indians who resided there for long periods must have formed relations with Chinese women, an aspect on which unfortunately there is little evidence available. This chapter is in the nature of an exploratory exercise, aimed at presenting some very basic data about the various communities in the hope that further research can throw more light on other aspects. It deliberately leaves aside the Indian communities which traded with and resided in Xinjiang and Tibet, which deserve separate presentations. The first part deals with the general context, economic and political, in which Indians were led to settle in significant numbers in the colony of Hong Kong and in the Chinese treaty ports. The second part presents some basic data about the various communities, in particular the history of their settlement, some demographic data and their occupational structure. In the third part aspects of their economic, social and political life are looked at in a more detailed fashion.

Indians in China, c. 1842–1949: the economic and political context

The two giants of Asia have a long history of contact by land and by sea. In the first century AD, during the Han dynasty, Buddhist missionaries from India crossed the high mountain passes of the Himalayas to preach the message of the Enlightened One, and in turn Chinese pilgrims came to India to visit the holy places of Buddhism, leaving precious accounts of their travels which are still an important source for the historians of medieval India. At a later date Muslim traders from India were active in the trade of the China Sea, and Chinese junks regularly sailed to the ports of the Malabar coast. A colony of Hindu merchants resided in the port of Quanzhou, on the Fujian coast, in the thirteenth and fourteenth centuries.[1] Indian merchants were also involved in the caravan trade between China and Central Asia, mostly as financiers.

Modern intercourse between India and China, however, clearly derives its origins from the activities of the British East India Company. At the time when the company became master of Bengal (1765) it also started being involved in trade with China. A triangular pattern of trade developed between Britain, India and China in which Chinese sales of tea to Britain were increasingly paid for by the sale of Indian opium to China.[2] The story of the opium trade is well known, but it is sometimes forgotten that Indian merchants, particularly Parsi merchants, played a major role in it in close association, especially after the East India Company had withdrawn from the China trade in 1833, with British private traders. The opening of China after 1842 gave a new impetus to the export of Indian opium to China, which remained very significant till the 1880s and disappeared only after 1910. Table 4.1 shows the importance of China as a market for Indian exports during the nineteenth century, and particularly for exports of opium. It should be noted that, as practically all opium exported was directed towards China (except in 1839–40 when the Chinese interdiction of opium imports was actually implemented), column 3 is a rough equivalent of 'opium exports to China', allowing the derivation of a ratio of 'exports of opium to China' to 'total exports to China' which varied between a minimum of 65 per cent in 1890–91 and a maximum of 90 per cent in 1860–61. The most significant item, outside opium, in Indian exports to China was cotton yarn, which,

INDIAN COMMUNITIES IN CHINA

Table 4.1 India's China trade and opium exports, 1828–1911

Period	Exports to China as % of India's total exports	Imports from China as % of India's total imports	Opium exports as % of India's total exports
1828–29	25.4	13.8	17.0
1831–32	39.6	10.8	n.a.
1834–35	36.6	13.3	25.0
1839–40	10.1	3.6	10.0
1850–51	35.0	8.6	30.1
1860–61	34.5	4.8	30.9
1870–71	22.3	4.6	19.5
1880–81	20.0	3.7	18.2
1890–91	14.4	3.4	9.2
1900–01	11.0	3.2	8.8
1910–11	9.2	1.8	6.1

Source K. N. Chaudhuri, 'Foreign Trade and Balance of Payments, 1757–1947', in D. Kumar, ed., *The Cambridge Economic History of India, II, Circa 1757–c. 1970* (Cambridge, Cambridge University Press, 1983), tables 10.10, 842, 10.11, 844, 10.20, 861, and 10.21A, 864.

between 1870 and 1905, accounted for the bulk of non-opium exports. Indian imports from China consisted mostly of tea till about 1850, and then mostly of silk and silk goods.

What is of interest to us here, however, is the role of Indian merchants in the China trade. They have often been described as mere agents and auxiliaries of the East India Company and, later, of British private traders, but their role was actually more complex. Indian merchants entered the China trade as early as the 1740s through the export of cotton from western India to Canton and, at a later stage, were particularly involved in the export of 'Malwa' opium, which was the inferior but cheaper variety produced in central India, rather than in the export of 'Bengal' opium, of better quality, fetching a higher price, which was entirely controlled by the East India Company. Malwa opium, which was grown largely outside company territory, was, till 1825, exported mostly through the Portuguese ports of Damao and Diu, and therefore largely escaped company control. Parsi merchants based in Surat and Bombay were particularly active in this trade. One single Parsi merchant, Sir Jametsji Jejeebhoy, is said to have provided a third of the supply of Malwa opium to the Jardine warehouses in Canton.[3] When the trade in Malwa opium was progressively rerouted through Bombay, especially after the British annexation of Sind in 1843, their role did not diminish.[4] British private merchants trading with China all used the services of Parsi guarantee brokers, who advanced them funds. But most Parsi brokers traded also on their own account and many of the ships which carried the opium were built in Parsi-owned shipyards and belonged to Parsi merchants-cum-shipowners. Their active involvement in the opium trade led some Parsis to reside in Canton as early as in 1809, and in 1833 there were more Parsis than Britons in the Chinese port.[5]

Indian settlement in China therefore originated in the active involvement of Indian merchants in the cotton trade and then in the opium trade between India and China and it antedated the Opium War of 1839–42. It received a boost, however, from the 1842 Treaty of Nanjing and the opening of a growing number of Chinese ports to foreign settlement as well as from the formal annexation of Hong Kong. The new colony had close links with India and recruited personnel there. Apart from 2,700 Indian military personnel present at the landing of British forces on the island on 26 January 1841, there were also four Indian civilians, the beginning of a small stream which kept swelling rapidly. Table 4.2 shows the growth of the Indian population of Hong Kong between 1845 and 1941. Table 4.2 shows that, while growth in the nineteenth century was far from regular (the population reached a peak of 1,435 in 1870), in the twentieth century the curve was much more linear (although the inclusion of military

Table 4.2 The Indian population of Hong Kong, 1845–1941

Year	Total	Males	Females	Children
1845	362	346	12	4
1855	391	213	79	99
1863	1,268	1,014	139	115
1872	288	264	10	14
1881	754	705	7	12
1901	1,453	1,108	345	–
1911	2,012	1,548	464	–
1931	4,745	3,989	756	–
1941	7,379	n.a.	n.a.	n.a.

Source K. N. Vaid, *The Overseas Indian Community in Hong Kong* (Hong Kong, Centre of Asian Studies, University of Hong Kong, 1972), table II, 20.

personnel in 1931 and 1941 complicates matters). Since the volume of trade between India and China tended to decrease during the same period, we have an indication that Indian migration into Hong Kong was becoming less dependent on the vagaries of the trade cycle. Lack of sufficiently detailed data, however, prevents us from arriving at a firm conclusion regarding the relative importance of 'push' and 'pull' factors. Unfortunately, a detailed breakdown of the Hong Kong Indian population by occupations is available only in the 1931 census. It shows that half the Indians in employment worked for the government (two-thirds of them in the army); and that, of the other half, some 80 per cent were engaged in trade and commerce.[6]

This division between government-related occupations, on the one hand, and trading occupations, on the other, was more or less replicated in the treaty ports. The Indian population appears to have reached a peak in the mid-1930s, when it was estimated to be over 3,000 in Shanghai alone. The total Indian civilian population of Hong Kong and China must have been 7,000 or 8,000 strong by then, which made Indians probably the fourth largest foreign community, after the Japanese, the Russians and the British. In the treaty ports the main employer was not directly the British government but municipal authorities, particularly the municipalities of the International Settlements, and the police, not the army, was the major service. In the treaty ports Indians benefited from the extraterritorial status enjoyed by all the subjects of foreign powers in China, in particular the right to be tried by the consular courts and the mixed courts in civil and criminal cases.

Detailed estimates of the Indian population are available only for Shanghai, although official censuses probably understated the size of the Indian community. Table 4.3 charts the trend in the Indian population of the International Settlement between 1851 and 1935.

In Shanghai a sudden spurt in the growth of the Indian population from the 1880s onwards was clearly linked with the beginning of the recruitment of Sikhs to the Shanghai Municipal Police. The 1885–1915 period saw the Indian population, as recorded in the censuses, increase almost twentyfold. There was some stabilisation during the following decade, and again a doubling between 1925 and 1935, in spite of political instability and economic depression. What was significant in the early 1930s was the increase in the number of Indian women and children, which seems to indicate a growing shift from sojourning to settlement, which was, however, cut short by the Sino-Japanese War. There was a change over time in the economic role of the Indians, from a community, almost exclusively of traders to one more directly geared to performing services for the British, particularly in the field of secu-

Table 4.3 The Indian population of Shanghai, 1851–1935

Year	Total	Males	Females	Children
1851	21	20	1	
1876	16	n.a.	n.a.	n.a.
1880	17	14	2	1
1885	58	34	7	17
1895	119	108	7	4
1900	296	277	12	7
1905	568	n.a.	n.a.	n.a.
1910	804	680	61	63
1915	1,009	789	107	113
1920	954	811	80	63
1925	1,154	961	95	98
1930	1,842	1,517	174	151
1935	2,341	1,655	325	361

Sources North China Herald for 1851, *Annual Report of the Shanghai Municipal Council* for other years. I am grateful to Robert Bickers for providing me with these documents.

rity. This meant, of course, a decline in status and wealth, as service occupations did not carry the same prestige and did not bring the same kind of income as commercial pursuits.

As regards the trading section of the Indian population, the main question relates to the way it adapted to the decline in the opium trade which started around 1880 and led, by 1910, to the *de facto* end of the trade as a legitimate activity. It appears that Indian traders were able to survive by shifting gradually from opium to other sectors. Between 1870 and 1905 they played an important role in the export trade of Indian yarn into China. The new cotton mills which developed in Bombay after 1854 faced increasing competition from Lancashire on the domestic market for piece goods and they tended to specialise in yarn production, where there were greater economies of scale to be gained. From 1873 onwards, they found in China a growing market for their production.[7] Chinese hand-loom producers found Indian yarn cheaper and more suited to their needs than British yarn, and progressively the yarn produced in Bombay replaced the Manchester product on the Chinese market.[8] The fact that the rupee was a silver currency was an added attraction in an era of silver depreciation. The good times for Indian yarn came to an end around 1905 with the entry of the Japanese into the market in a big way, but Indian traders were able to shift to other lines. They found an alternative in general import trade and to a lesser extent in the export trade, mostly of silk goods. Basically they increasingly fulfilled a global middleman function which made them less dependent on Indo-Chinese trade. But many details of the story remain unknown.

The kind of general data presented here are certainly not going to detract from the widely held view of the Indians as forming an auxiliary community, whose development and growth were closely linked with the advances and retreats of British imperialism in China. While the overall validity of this view is not questioned here, a closer look at the particular stories of the different communities represented will introduce some nuance into the general picture.

The Indian communities of China: a pattern of diversity

Indians in China belonged to different communities which followed different occupations. There were basically two kinds of communities: the police-watchman communities, which hailed mostly from the north-west of the subcontinent (Punjab, North West Frontier Province), and the trading communities, which originated almost exclusively from the Bombay presidency. The latter in turn were divided along religious lines, with Parsis, Hindus and Muslims equally represented, and also linguistically between Gujarati-speakers and Sindhi-speakers. One should also mention the presence in Hong Kong and Shanghai of Baghdadi Jews from India, mostly belonging to the famous Sassoon family. They are dealt with in Chapter Three by Chiara Betta.

A fairly detailed, although incomplete, estimate of the strength and geographical spread of the various communities outside Beijing is contained in a document of 1915, reproduced as Table 4.4. This estimate is far from complete. In particular, it does not include Sikhs in the police force in Shanghai and some other towns. The Sikh and Punjabi Muslim communities of Shanghai were estimated to number 1,250 men in 1912.[9] It also leaves out the sizeable Hindu, Parsi and Muslim merchant communities of Canton and Macao. However, as an indication of the relative numerical strength of the various communities it is probably not far off the mark. It shows clearly that the police-watchmen communities of the Sikhs, Punjabi Muslims and 'Pathans' (a loose term applying to the inhabitants of the North West Frontier Province) accounted for the bulk of the Indian population of China outside Hong Kong. It also reveals that there were only four cities with

Table 4.4 Indians registered at British consulates, by community, in 1915

Consulate	Sikhs	Punjabi Muslims and Pathans	Hindus	Parsis	Bombay Muslims
Canton	28	6	n.a.	n.a.	n.a.
Shantou	3	3			
Fuzhou	1	8		5	1
Xiamen	29	16			
Macao		8	1		18
Hankou	152	23	3		13
Chongqing	5				
Zhenjiang	2				
Nanjing	44	1			
Niujiang	3			1	
Yizhang					1
Tianjin	93	7	n.a.	9	7
Kunming		1			
Harbin		6			
Changsha	4				
Tengyueh			3		
Shanghai	468	156	24	31	9
Total	832	235	31	46	49

Source Enclosed in Governor, Hong Kong, to British Minister, Peking, 22 December 1915, Public Record Office, Embassy and Consular Archives, China, FO 228/2299.

a sizeable Indian population: Shanghai, by far the major centre, Hankou, Tianjin and Canton. Xiamen and Nanjing, as well as Beijing, had smaller but not insignificant communities. Other towns had only small groups of Indians.

Sikhs were undoubtedly the largest single group. They were considered the best recruits for the police force, because of their military background and their reputation for loyalty (although by 1915 they were increasingly suspected of Indian nationalist sympathies), and were in great demand as watchmen, a position they often sought after a period of employment in the police force. The origins of Sikh employment in the police force in China went back to the late 1860s, when the Deputy Superintendent of Police in Hong Kong, C. V. Creagh, who had served in the Sind police, recommended that Sikhs should be engaged for the colony's police force. The first batch of recruits arrived in 1867, and until the 1940s Sikhs remained an important element in the Hong Kong police. Most of the early recruits came from the Amritsar, Jullundhar, Ludhiana and Ferozepore districts of central Punjab, and Creagh selected 'young and sturdy lads who were unmarried and had a clean-record chit from the police authorities of their native district'.[10] The Shanghai Municipal Police started recruiting Sikhs in 1884, and recruitment in Tianjin started in 1896. At the beginning, recruitment seems to have been done directly by the British authorities in India, but, as an increasing number of Sikh men with a military background made their way to the Far East to seek employment, local recruitment was sanctioned. This migration became part of a broader stream, which took Sikhs to various destinations in the Far East and across the Pacific to North America. Many of the Sikhs in China thus had previous experience in Burma, Singapore or Malaya, and, after a few years in Shanghai, Tianjin or Hankou, they attempted to move to America, often using the Philippines as a staging point.

Most of the Sikh migrants belonged to the Jat peasant caste, which accounted for approximately half the Sikh population of India. The motives of the Sikh emigrants are described thus by a recent author:

> Most of the families involved were neither very rich nor very poor; rather, they were commonly those of middling wealth, whose positions in their villages were threatened by fragmentation of land holdings and by inflation of land prices. Migration was thus a family strategy, an honourable alternative to reduction of status at home. Rather than cause the family's land holding to be further subdivided, younger sons who joined the army and/or went abroad could add to the family's fortunes and position in the village. The objective was enhanced status or prestige (*izzat*), to be acquired through purchase of additional land, construction of a *pukka* (brick) house, and arrangement of honourable marriages for women of the family. Those who were sent were almost all single men or young married men travelling without wives.[11]

There were many Sikh policemen in the British colonies of the Far East and they took early to the related profession of watchman, especially with European companies, who considered them trustworthy and reliable. Many Sikh watchmen also did some moneylending as a sideline, their fearsome reputation ensuring timely repayment of the loans. On the other hand, the estates of four Sikh policemen from Shanghai whose deaths straddle the period between 1895 and 1931 reach a total combined value of only approximately £200, an average of £50 per estate.[12] This reflects the fairly low scale of pay in the SMP but also seems to indicate that Sikh policemen remitted most of their gains to their families in the Punjab on a regular basis, which is exactly to be expected of that type of rural migrant.

Although these migrants were thus basically pursuing strategies centred on land, they nevertheless adapted easily to the urban environment in which they worked. Communal solidarity was of particular importance in facilitating this adaptation. It was maintained mainly through the central role the places of worship called *gurdwaras* played in the lives of the Sikh migrants. A *gurdwara* was not only a temple, where the sacred book, the *Adi Granth*, was enthroned, and where prayers and chants were offered; it was also a meeting place and a community centre, and the priest attached to it played the role of mediator in the community. Wherever they went Sikhs built *gurdwaras* and in that way maintained an active community life. A *gurdwara* was built in Shanghai in 1907, and two more at a later stage. Similar structures existed in Hong Kong, Hankou and Tianjin.[13] Sikh migration to China intensified in the 1920s largely owing to the closing of North America, which had been the Sikhs' preferred destination between 1907 and 1914.

Less is known about the Punjabi Muslims and Pathans, who performed basically the same function as the Sikhs and originated from the same region of the subcontinent. It seems that they were first recruited in Hong Kong as a deliberate counterweight to the predominance of Sikhs in the colony's police force. They hailed mostly from the Jhelum, Multan and Campbellpur districts of western Punjab, in present-day Pakistan. In India too many were in the army and the police but, once in China, they do not appear to have developed community institutions to the same degree as the Sikhs. In Hong Kong there were also Indians from other regions, engaged in a variety of occupations, but they do not appear to have formed permanent communities.

Of the trading communities, the Parsis were probably still in 1915 the most important in terms of economic clout, although they were already well past their prime. Why this community of Zoroastrians, who migrated to India around the eighth century AD and settled on the coast of Gujarat before moving *en masse* to Bombay in the eighteenth and nineteenth centuries, should have played such a prominent role in China's commercial life has to do with the close relationship they established with the East India Company, first in Surat and thereafter in Bombay. They were the main brokers of the company, supplying it with funds and information, and, when the company moved into the China trade it took the Parsis along. It seems, however, that the Parsi presence in China even antedated the development of company trade, since the first Parsi private trader, Hirji Jivanji Ready-money, appeared on the China coast as early as 1756.[14] In the next half-century Parsi participation in the China trade increased and in 1809 several Parsis were residing in Canton. In 1833 fifty-two resided there, as against thirty-five Britons. Although there was an exodus from Canton in 1839, when the Chinese authorities seized opium cargoes, Parsis quickly re-established themselves both in Hong Kong and in the treaty ports after 1842. In 1844 Parsis accounted for about one-fifth of the foreign trading community of the treaty ports, with nineteen firms (out of a total of ninety-four) and sixty-four resident members (out of a total of 300), and they were the second largest group after the British.[15] One firm, D. & M. Rustomjee, had fifteen partners in China.

Most Parsi fortunes in Bombay in the nineteenth century were actually made in the China trade, which meant mostly the opium trade. Among Parsi families which played a major role in the trade were the Readymoneys, Kamas, Wadias, Dadiseths, Banajis and Jejeebhoys, none of which settled in China. Parsi families which settled in the treaty ports always maintained close contact with their home base of Bombay. Although Parsi merchants often brought their wives to China, they did not put down deep roots there. They remained a community of sojourners and maintained a keen interest in the affairs of their community in India, playing an important role in the affairs of the Parsi *panchayat*. They started disengaging from the opium trade in the 1860s and invested heavily in real estate. Some then shifted to the yarn trade, in which they played a major role. They imported large quantities of yarn from Bombay, produced in mills which often belonged to co-religionists. Among the Indian trading communities the Parsis were exceptional in the attention they paid to education, and they made a lasting contribution to educational life in Hong Kong, as will be shown later.

They had three main areas of operation in China: Hong Kong, Shanghai and northern China. In Hong Kong, where they reached their maximum strength of 230 around 1916 before declining to around eighty in 1938, several Parsi firms played an important long-term role in the commercial life of the colony.[16] The firm of Cowasjee Pallanji & Co., set up in Canton in 1794 as a branch of the Bombay firm of Cursetjee Bomanjee & Co., and established in Hong Kong since 1842, after a successful stint in opium, spices and silk, became the pioneer of the yarn trade, in which it maintained a prominent position till the First World War. The firm of F. M. Talati & Co., which moved from Canton to Hong Kong in 1842, had diversified dealings in precious stones, jewels, silks, precious oils and quality goods, and remained a force in trade till very recently. The firm of Mody & Paul Chater pioneered the stock exchange and was involved in share brokerage and real estate on a large scale till the 1920s. A Parsi businessman called Dorabji Naorojee started the cross-harbour ferry services. The Ruttonjees had diversified interests in import-export, the liquor trade and real estate. In Shanghai pioneering firms were those of Pestonji Framjee Cama and F. S. & N. M. Lagrane. Among Shanghai-based Parsi firms the most famous was undoubtedly Tata, managed by a branch of the celebrated family of Bombay industrialists. Other prominent Shanghai Parsi firms were those owned by F. B. Petit and R. S. Kermani. In Beijing and Tianjin the firms of F. M. Talati and Painter were active in diverse fields in the 1920s and 1930s. The overall role of the Parsis in Chinese commerce and finance was considerable till the 1880s. It is significant that Parsi businessmen played an active role in the foundation of the Hongkong & Shanghai Bank in 1864.[17] Afterwards there was a decline, but they remained a significant group till the 1930s.

A look at six Parsi estates (extending over a quarter of a century between 1882 and 1907) from the archives of the Shanghai Consular Court shows both the wealth of these merchants and the shift in their investments in the late nineteenth century.[18] The estates had a combined value of almost £50,000, an average of over £8,000 per estate. Approximately 54 per cent of their value consisted in real estate, while shares, debentures and deposit receipts accounted for a further 25 per cent of the total. One can see a clear shift in the investments of Parsi merchants, from entrepreneurial activities to rent seeking. Most of the fortunes accumulated by the Parsis during the heyday of the opium trade between 1840 and 1870 were not reinvested in new trading ventures in China but divided between real estate and shares in 'safe' companies like the Hong Kong & Shanghai Bank. Of course the documents say nothing about entrepreneurial activities outside China, particularly in India. But they seem to indicate lack of confidence in the prospects of business in China.

The Gujarati Muslim communities, the Bohras and Khojas, both belonging to the Ismaili branch of Shia Islam, but separated by fine points of doctrine, followed a trajectory largely similar to that of the Parsis. They were active in the opium trade in Canton prior to 1839, then moved to Hong Kong.[19] They tended to replace the Parsis as intermediaries in the opium trade from the 1860s onwards but did not adapt very successfully to the decline in the opium trade. Members of those communities numbered some 240 in the colony around 1918, but the figure declined precipitously in the inter-war period to around sixty in 1938. Among prominent Ismaili families in Hong Kong were those of Currimbhoy Ebrahim, which set up the firm of E. Pabaney in 1857, one of the largest in the colony in the opium and yarn trades, and the Kayamallys and Tayebs. They rarely made substantial fortunes. Two Muslim estates from the archives of the Shanghai Consular Court are those of merchants of middling wealth: their combined value was some £2,500, and they consisted mostly of property.[20]

The most recently arrived of the Indian trading communities, in the long term the most successful, are the Sindhi Hindus of Hyderabad (Sind) in the Sind province of present-day Pakistan. These merchants, who were Hindus of a religious persuasion very close to Sikhism (Nanakpanthis), started travelling abroad in the 1860s and gradually set up a worldwide network of shops selling silk and curios which by the early twentieth century extended between Kobe and Panama.[21] At first they travelled mostly westwards towards Egypt and the Mediterranean, but one firm reached Singapore in 1873 and from there expanded into the whole Far East, laying the basis of a growing trade between China and Japan, where these merchants bought silk goods as well as curios, and other areas of the tropical and Mediterranean world, where they sold them mostly to a clientele of European and North American travellers. They seem to have reached China in the late 1870s or early 1880s, operating at first from Canton and Hong Kong. The 1889 *Hong Kong Directory and Hong List for the Far East* lists three Sindhi firms in Hong Kong among a total of thirty-one Indian firms, of which the majority were Parsi and Gujarati Muslim. The 1903 *North China Desk Hong List* lists two Sindhi firms in Shanghai. From 1917 onwards commercial directories reveal the increased importance of this group, which gained at the expense of the Parsis and the Gujarati Muslims alike. In the 1930s they became the dominant Indian trading community in Hong Kong: a list of Indian member firms of the Hong Kong General Chamber of Commerce for 1940 includes nine Sindhi firms out of a total of fourteen Indian firms (as against one Parsi firm, two Gujarati Muslim firms and two Jewish firms). Their rise was certainly in part due to their close links with the Japanese; in the 1930s Sindhi firms, hit by the depression in the luxury trades in which they had tended to specialise, often operated as agents of big Japanese trading firms, especially in British territories, where they benefited from their status as subjects of the Crown. Their network in China proper was extensive: they operated in Canton, Hankou, Tianjin, Beijing, Qingdao. Some firms also had branches in Japanese-occupied Manchukuo.

Documents from the archives of the Tianjin Consular Court throw some light on their activities between 1917 and the end of World War II.[22] There were at least four Sindhi firms in Tianjin engaged in the retail sale of silk goods in shops situated in the British concession on

Victoria Road. They were owned in partnership by Sindhi merchants from Hyderabad, some of whom had been in Tianjin for years. One was even married to a Chinese woman. These merchants and their employees formed a small, largely self-contained community of perhaps twenty persons, who sold goods purchased in Japan and in Shanghai from other Sindhi firms. Some of these Tianjin firms had branches in Manchuria, and one Sindhi merchant was killed in the Mukden incident of 18 September 1931 while he was carrying to Mukden a cargo worth $30,000. The Sindhi community of Tianjin was one of the northernmost outposts of a global trading network from which it drew its sustenance in terms of both goods and men. The profits earned in that kind of trade could be substantial: one merchant who died in 1931 left his wife an estate which was valued at almost £800, a very decent sum in Sind at the time.

The majority of Sindhis in China were employees of Hyderabad firms who spent a period of two and a half years in China before being generally sent to another destination. There were also, however, independent merchants who established themselves more permanently. This community expanded considerably in Hong Kong after 1947 as Sindhi Hindus massively left their province, which had become part of Pakistan, and many relocated outside India. Sindhis, as the dominant Indian business group in China from the 1930s onwards, were very different from the Parsis. In particular, their relationship with the British was much more distant. They were an international trading network whose dynamic lay much less in the exploitation of political connections. Their rise reflected in some way a weakening of the British position in Asia.

This survey of the main Indian communities in China is meant to emphasise the diversity of regional origins, religious affiliations and occupations among that population. The next section turns to look in more detail at some aspects of the lives and labours of Indians in China.

Aspects of Indian lives and labours in China

The lives of Indians in China, as far as we can judge in the quasi-absence of accounts written by themselves (one Hong Kong Sikh, however, wrote a personal memoir in Punjabi which was published in 1922), were very much centred on work.[23] Whether in the police or in trading firms, most Indians were salaried employees who worked long hours and had little time for leisure or cultural activities. The few rich merchants and the handful of professionals were also busy earning money, and, with the exception of some Parsis, of whom more will be said later, had neither the time nor the inclination to involve themselves heavily in non-economic activities. Lest this account of Indians be perceived as too functionalist, something has to be said on other aspects of their lives. Few Indians, outside Hong Kong and Shanghai, where there existed a more 'settled' community, had a proper family life in China. The majority, even in these two major centres, were young unmarried men who lived as bachelors, sharing quarters with colleagues in barrack lines or trading firm premises. Most of those who were married had left their wives in India and actually also lived the life of a bachelor. Obviously they had to find an outlet for their sexual and emotional needs: some probably found it with Chinese prostitutes, the only ones they could afford. (There is no mention of Indian prostitutes in China, though Anglo-Indian girls probably worked in the cabarets of Shanghai and Hong Kong.) But a minority appear to have formed more lasting liaisons with Chinese women, sometimes resulting in marriage. Sikhs, with their fine physique, had generally no problem in finding female company wherever they went. Children must have been born of these unions, but they remained very much in the background, as such relationships were strongly frowned upon by members of the two communities involved.

Whatever leisure time these men had, leaving aside that which was devoted to drinking, gambling and whoring, must have been largely occupied with participation in community life. This was particularly true of the Sikhs, who generally tended to form closely knit, though faction-ridden, communities. In the late nineteenth century Sikh communities in India went through a process of social and religious reform in which a major role was played by organisations called the *Singh Sabhas*. They tried to 'purify' Sikhism from what were perceived as 'Hindu' practices. *Singh Sabhas* were created in most Chinese cities where there were Sikhs and they were active in circulating religious literature from the Punjab, in organising tours by preachers from India and in ensuring regular observance of religious festivals.[24] The *gurdwaras* were the centre of Sikh religious and social life: one went there not only to pray but also to gossip about home and generally to unwind in a congenial atmosphere. Other communities did not have the same kind of communal institutions. Sindhis, although Hindus, tended also to frequent the *gurdwaras*, but Indian Muslims as a rule did not have their own mosques: they went to whatever Muslim shrines existed in the city where they were located. As for the Parsis, temples did not play a central role in their worship; the most important rituals for them were those of purification, but it appears that in China there were no Towers of Silence where the Parsi dead could be exposed to the vultures, thus sparing the living the defilement associated with death.[25] In Hong Kong however, there was a Zoroastrian house which served for community meetings, but not much is known about Parsi communal life.

The different Indian communities appear to have led very self-contained lives and to have had little contact with each other or with the wider society beyond the necessary economic transactions and the occasional sexual encounters. The fragmentation of the Indians had little to do with caste exclusiveness, but more to do with class and occupational differences. A Parsi business magnate and a Punjabi Muslim policeman had no particular reason to interact just because they happened to hail from India and to inhabit the same Chinese city. Nor did they have a common language. Even Punjabi Sikhs and Muslims, who shared a language, had little else in common and there was an undercurrent of hostility between the two groups. The only 'transcommunal' link was the one between Sikhs and Sindhis, due to the fact that they largely shared the same religious culture.

Indians' relationship with the wider society in the treaty ports was also limited. With the Chinese there was very little intercourse, barring brief or lasting sexual liaisons with women. Few Indians appear to have been fluent in Chinese, although shopkeepers must have had a minimal knowledge of the language to keep in touch with suppliers and customers. Some of the Indian business firms employed Chinese clerks specifically for the purpose of communicating with the Chinese economic environment. But, as a whole, Indian merchants tended to operate more in international trading or in certain kinds of specialised trade for a mostly European clientele, and they did not have very extended contacts with the Chinese trading communities. Relations with other foreign communities do not appear to have been intense either. With the British, barring a few rich traders, Indians were clearly in a relationship of servant to master: this was the case in particular between Sikh police constables and British officers, even between Sikh and British constables: they did not meet outside the barracks. With non-British foreigners, such as the Japanese or the Russians, relations were on a strictly economic basis. One should, however, mention two special cases: Jews from India, belonging to the Baghdadi community, did participate in the life of the Sephardic communities, and Indian Muslims worshipped in company with other Muslims; however, the fact that they were Ismaili limited their possibilities of intercourse with the mostly Sunni islamic world of China.

The political attitudes of Indians appear to have evolved over time. Prior to the First World War loyalty towards the British Crown seems to have been the dominant strand, although nationalist ideas from India did penetrate. After 1914 part of the Sikh community, under the influence of a revolutionary party based in San Francisco called the Ghadr (Revolution) Party, seems to have adopted a more militant nationalist attitude. British intelligence services became worried about 'subversive' activities among Sikhs and other Indians in China, and in 1916 a high Indian police official, Sir David Petrie, was sent to survey the political situation among the Indian communities in China and in the Far East.[26] From that time onwards, Indians in China were under close surveillance by British intelligence, and, in 1926–27, a special Indian section was created within the Special Branch of the Shanghai Municipal Police.[27] It is clear that the British were worried about a possible conjunction between Indian and Chinese nationalism, particularly since they used Indian troops in China on an important scale. It is, however, difficult to perceive, beyond the often alarmist reports sent by British officials, the reality of shifting political alignments among Indians in China. Some Sikhs developed communistic tendencies and may have helped the Chinese communists in Shanghai in 1926–27, but the vast majority of Indians seem to have just tried to pursue their usual occupations through the troubled times of the 1920s and 1930s. Only with the beginning of the Sino-Japanese War in 1937 did a fairly massive exodus of Indians from China take place: some 3,000 left then, a part of them relocating in Hong Kong. Some merchants remained, however, in Japanese-occupied China. Indians in Hong Kong in turn were trapped by the Japanese invasion of 1941. Their attitude to the Japanese occupation varied widely from overt resistance by a few to open collaboration by a small minority, the vast majority adopting a non-committed attitude meant to ensure survival. At the end of the Second World War the Indian presence had practically disappeared from China outside Hong Kong. Indian and Pakistani independence in 1947 led to the end of the Indian presence in the Hong Kong police, but a new migration of traders, mostly Sindhis, started. The history of Indians in Hong Kong since 1949 is an entirely new chapter, deserving of separate treatment.

After Hong Kong's return to China, which may well signal the end of the Indian saga in that country, while some of the Indians who remained in Hong Kong were *in extremis* awarded 'true' British passports, it is time to reflect on the history of a 200 year presence. Indians arrived in China as traders and it seems that they will leave China as traders. In the meantime some of them fulfilled other functions, mainly that of custodians of the law imposed in parts of China by British imperialism. British attempts at 'instrumentalising' the Indians were not, however, completely successful. A comparison with the case of the Japanese *sekimin*, dealt with in Chapter Seven by Barbara Brooks, reveals a greater capacity for operating outside the orbit of the colonial master. Politically, some of the Sikhs fought openly against British imperialism and supported the Chinese in their struggle. Note should also be taken of the specific contribution made by the Parsis to the early development of modern education in China, which did not directly serve British interests. Students of Hong Kong University still study in a building erected thanks to the generous donation of the Parsi merchant and benefactor Sir H. N. Mody. There are other traces of Parsi munificence dispersed around Hong Kong and some may also be surviving in Shanghai.

As regards the role of the Indians in the trading economy of China, there is no doubt that it tended to be auxiliary. The nature of the Indian commercial presence was strongly influenced by the political subjection of India to British rule. However, within this overall pattern, Indian merchants were not without agency. It could thus be argued that the Parsi network contributed to shaping the specific form that British economic penetration took in China. At a later stage the Sindhi traders acted as auxiliaries of Japanese economic penetration in China, although they had no direct political links with Japan. Seen from the point of view of the *longue durée*, the subordination of Indian merchants to European global interests can be seen as an interval in a longer history of inter-Asian trade of which Indian merchant networks were very much part. One should not forget that the gains realised in the China trade in the nineteenth century have been the foundation of Bombay's fortune and therefore contributed handsomely to the rise of modern capitalism in India. If India certainly gained more than China from two centuries of trade and war, the existence of a history of commercial contacts between the two largest countries of Asia could help in ushering a new phase of co-operation between them.

Notes

1 See Chen Dasheng and D. Lombard, 'Le rôle des étrangers dans le commerce maritime de Quanzhou ('Zaitun') aux XIIIe et XIVe siècles', in D. Lombard and J. Aubin, eds, *Marchands et hommes d'affaires asiatiques dans l'Océan indien et la Mer de Chine, XIIIe–XXe siècles* (Paris, Editions de l'EHESS, 1988), 21–9.
2 See M. Greenberg, *British Trade and the Opening of China* (Cambridge, Cambridge University Press, 1951), and D. E. Owen, *British Opium Policy in China and India* (New Haven CT, Yale University Press, 1934).
3 Asiya Siddiqi, 'The Business World of Jamsetjee Jejeebhoy', *Indian Economic and Social History Review*, 19:3–4 (1982), 310.

4 For a new interpretation of this event centred around the question of the opium trade see J. Y. Wong, 'British Annexation of Sind in 1843: An Economic Perspective', *Modern Asian Studies*, 31:2 (1997), 225–44.
5 C. Dobbin, *Asian Entrepreneurial Minorities: Conjoint Communities in the Making of the World Economy, 1570–1940* (London, Curzon Press, 1996), 84.
6 K. N. Vaid, *The Overseas Indian Community in Hong Kong* (Hong Kong, Centre of Asian Studies, University of Hong Kong, 1972), 23.
7 M. D. Morris, 'The Growth of Large-scale Industry to 1947', in D. Kumar, ed., *The Cambridge Economic History of India, II, Circa 1757–c. 1970* (Cambridge, Cambridge University Press, 1983), 577.
8 In 1905 Indian yarn accounted for approximately 70 per cent of total Chinese yarn imports: calculated from figures in H. B. Morse, *The Trade and Administration of the Chinese Empire* (London, Longman, 1908), 287.
9 A detailed estimate of 'Natives of India residing in and round Shanghai' figured in a letter from the Captain Superintendent's Office, Municipal Police, Shanghai, to the British Minister, Peking, dated 2 December 1912, Public Record Office (PRO), Foreign Office Records, Embassy and Consular Archives, China, FO 228/2299. It estimated that there were 1,000 Sikhs in Shanghai, of whom 449 were employed in the Shanghai Municipal Police, as well as 250 'Mohammedans', who were employed in the prison service and as watchmen.
10 Vaid, *The Overseas Indian Community*, 37–8.
11 V. A. Dusenbery, 'Introduction: A Century of Sikhs beyond Punjab', in G. N. Barrier and V. A. Dusenbery, eds, *The Sikh Diaspora: Migration and Experience beyond Punjab* (Delhi, Chanakya Publications, 1989), 5.
12 PRO, Foreign Office Records, Embassy and Consular Archives China, Shanghai Supreme Court Probate Records, Probates in the estates of Jhaba Singh, Nata Singh, Mayal Singh and Pritam Singh, FO 917/698, 810, 2699 and 3158.
13 See N. G. Barrier, 'Sikh Emigrants and their Homeland', in Barrier and Dusenbery, *The Sikh Diaspora*, 64–5.
14 Dobbin, *Asian Entrepreneurial Minorities*, 84.
15 John K. Fairbank, *Trade and Diplomacy on the China Coast: The Opening of the Treaty Ports, 1842–54* (Cambridge MA, Harvard University Press, 1964), 159, note b.
16 Vaid, *The Overseas Indian Community*, 53–6.
17 Three of the thirteen members of the provisional committee set up to establish the Hong Kong & Shanghai Banking Corporation were Parsis: Vaid, *The Overseas Indian Community*, 58.
18 PRO, Shanghai Supreme Court Probate Records, Probates in the estates of Dorabji Nussrewanjee Camajee, Pestonjee Cursetjee Mody, Hormusjee Dorabjee Camajee, Dharamsey Doorjeebhoy, Rustomjee Pestonjee Kapadia and Jwanbai Bomanji Karanjia, FO 917/278, 360, 370, 454, 956 and 1199.
19 Vaid, *The Overseas Indian Community*, 56–7.
20 PRO, Shanghai Supreme Court Probate Records, Probates in the estates of Rajab Abdool Curreem and Salemohamed Bhachoo, FO 917/ 2599 and 2981.
21 See C. Markovits, *The Global World of Indian Merchants 1750–1947: Traders of Sind from Bukhara to Panama* (Cambridge, Cambridge University Press, forthcoming).
22 PRO, Foreign Office Records, Embassy and Consular Archives: China Consulates, Personal estates, Correspondence, etc.', Agreement between Bulchand Nihchamall and L. Pinyamall, FO 678/1501, Agreement between R. S. Kathuria and L. Pinyamall, FO 678/1570, Agreement between Lalumal, Nomomal and L. Pinyamall, FO 678/1576, Probate in the estate of B. L. Pinyamall, FO 678/1733 B, Death of Master Lakhi D. Melvani, FO 678/1935, Will and estate of Tarachand Metharam Lalvani, FO 678/1938, Probate in the estate of Daloomall Phabiomall, FO 678/ 1979, Probate in the estate of Lalchand Pursumal, FO 678/1989.
23 Variam Singh, *Variam Sunehae* (Listen to Variam) (Hong Kong, n.p., 1922).
24 Barrier, 'Sikh Emigrants and their Homeland', in Barrier and Dusenbery, *The Sikh Diaspora*, 77.

25 See J. R. Hinnells, 'South Asian Diaspora Communities and their Religion: A Comparative Study of Parsi Experiences', *South Asia Research*, 14:1 (1994), 78.
26 Criminal Intelligence Office, Government of India, 'Note (by Sir David Petrie) on a recent tour to the Far East', dated 4 December 1916, enclosed in India Office to Foreign Office, 26 March 1917, PRO, Foreign Office Records, Foreign Office General Correspondence (Political), FO 371/3065.
27 Frederic Wakeman, Jr, *Policing Shanghai, 1927–1937* (Berkeley CA, University of California Press, 1995), 142–3.

CHAPTER FIVE

Foreigners or outsiders? Westerners and Chinese Christians in Chongqing 1870s–1900
Judith Wyman

This chapter differs from the others in this volume in two central ways: it deals with an inland rather than a coastal province, and it looks at the complexities of relations between the foreign and Chinese communities in a region of this province, rather than focusing on the structures and fabrics of the foreign communities themselves. In particular, it explores the ambiguities of the intense 'anti-foreignism' that led the south-western province of Sichuan to experience the highest incidence of attacks on Westerners and Chinese Christians in all of China.[1] Chongqing prefecture, the more specific focus of this study and the largest port of entry in the province, served as home to several of the most explosive and far-reaching of these movements. While historians have typically looked to theories of anti-imperialism and simple xenophobia as explanations for this hostility toward Westerners and Chinese Christians,[2] the situation in Chongqing reveals the shortcomings of such interpretations.

First, hostile responses to Western activity took place in the context of a frontier province peopled by Chinese migrants. In other words, while Western imperialism antagonised many in Sichuan, the 'anti-foreign' response it prompted was in fact part of a larger process, that of dealing with other outsiders, Chinese ones, who had been arriving for more than two centuries. Second, the inadequacies of xenophobia as an explanation also become apparent when looking at Chongqing. The term 'hatred of foreigners' by definition assumes clear distinctions between those who are Chinese and those who are foreign. This does not explain, then, why both types of outsiders, Chinese and foreign ones, were targets of these 'xenophobic' attacks, with Chinese Christians comprising by far the largest group of victims.[3] At the height of these campaigns in Chongqing, not one Westerner was killed or even seriously wounded. On the other hand, dozens of Chinese Christians died, many more were wounded and the number forced to flee from their homes reached the tens of thousands. To focus solely on anti-imperialist sentiment and xenophobia is to miss the complexities of the larger, domestic, picture. The significant distinctions were those made between insiders and outsiders, categories into which both Chinese and foreigners could be and were placed, with hostility against Westerners and Chinese Christians frequently motivated more by domestic competition for spheres of power than by staunch anti-imperialism or ardent xenophobia.

Chinese outsiders

Sichuan during the Qing was a province of Chinese outsiders. Devastation during the Ming–Qing transition of the mid-seventeenth century had reduced the population by nearly 75 per cent to an estimated 2 million people.[4] With an eye to repopulating the province, the Qing government had instituted generous land reclamation policies for Chinese living in other parts of the country. People came mostly from the neighbouring provinces of Hubei, Shaanxi, Gansu and Guizhou, but also from other Yangzi valley provinces, such as Hunan and Anhui, and the coastal provinces of Guangdong, Fujian and Jiangsu.[5] By the late nineteenth century, the population had mushroomed to approximately 40 million.[6]

As Sichuan's primary commercial port on the Yangzi river, Chongqing prefecture, an administrative unit of fourteen counties in the south-eastern region of the province, also experienced a population increase by migrants from different provinces. Over the course of the nineteenth century the population of Chongqing prefecture tripled, reaching 7 million in 1910, with groups tracing their ancestry back to Hubei, Hunan, Fujian, Guangdong, Jiangsu, Shaanxi and Tibet.[7] The importance of retaining close ties with one's ancestral province is reflected in the fact that, some 100 years later, many provinces were still represented by their own guilds.[8] Baxian, the county seat of Chongqing prefecture and home to the city of Chongqing, had reached approximately 1 million by the late nineteenth century,[9] including 3,000 Chinese Muslims[10] and approximately the same number of Chinese Christians.[11]

Such massive migration during the seventeenth and eighteenth centuries resulted in a Chinese population characterised by its diversity, with most of its people priding themselves on their non-Sichuanese origins. Qing officials working in Sichuan during the 1720s estimated that only 20–30 per cent of the population were native to the province.[12] In fact there were so many outsiders in Sichuan during this period that even the 'Hakka', a Chinese minority group whose name means 'guest people', were referred to not by that name but by the more specific appellation 'Guangdong people'.[13] A century and half later this legacy of migration still influenced local perceptions of Chinese insiders and outsiders, as reflected in a report filed in 1879 from Chongqing by British consul E. C. Baber: 'I have not yet found a Chinaman who would acknowledge himself to be a native of the province. To confess oneself a native is to admit that one is a savage, a national of the Lolo or Mantzu tribes who dwell on the Tibetan border and beyond.'[14]

The steady arrival of migrants throughout the eighteenth and nineteenth centuries led to a host of problems. Disappointment was inevitable on both sides as new people arrived with expectations of cheap land and easy living only to find that by the 1720s land was rarely available and earning one's livelihood no simple matter. New arrivals who did get land were resented by the locals because as migrants they were eligible for special tax exemptions. Weak administrative control and lack of accurate land surveys further complicated the picture. Land disputes became the most commonly litigated cases during the Yongzheng reign (1723-36).[15] The Yongzheng reign also marked a shift in the backgrounds of those who came to Sichuan. Whereas during the early Qing people were drawn to Sichuan in search of a better life, by the 1720s migrants were escaping desperate conditions at home. Many of the migrants left their own provinces poor and unemployed only to find a similar situation in Sichuan, where they became tenants, were sold undesirable land or fell into banditry. Qing efforts to control migration failed. By the late eighteenth century, Robert Entenmann has concluded, 'Sichuan itself was overpopulated and the province lacked a safety valve of its own.'[16]

By the late nineteenth century these problems had further intensified. As the region became a more important commercial centre,[17] Chinese migrated to Chongqing seeking employment, entertainment and illicit activity of any kind. Many became bandits or joined brotherhood societies, swelling the already substantial ranks of these groups, whose everyday movements were of concern to local officials.[18] For example, boats transporting cotton, silk and medicine to and from Chongqing city were routinely looted.[19] Crowds were robbed and plundered during regular celebrations and events such as the Dragon Boat Festival and prefectural examinations.[20] Local opera performances provided another opportunity for theft, in some cases resulting in the cancellation of performances.[21] Bandits also targeted the state-regulated salt industry and mobilised the poor to attack the rich during periods of famine.[22]

In addition to disrupting the economic and social order, bandits and brotherhood societies challenged the political structure.[23] This was an especially serious problem in Sichuan, where brotherhoods extended throughout the province and boasted a wide range of members, including many powerful local gentry. In numerous cases these organisations had so infiltrated the local village power structure that they acted as an alternative government, collecting taxes, controlling militia and making decisions in judicial matters.[24] Their power stretched horizontally as well, monopolising various trades. A case in 1900 in Chongqing, for example, indicates secret society control of labourers who worked the shipping docks.[25]

A particularly notable brotherhood society was the Gelaohui (Elder Brother Society), which by the mid-nineteenth century had emerged as one of the most powerful in the province. In addition to drawing members from a wide variety of occupations, including sailors, miners, labourers, salt smugglers, unemployed vagrants, actors, yamen runners, craftsmen, small shopkeepers, pawnbrokers, water carriers and sedan chair carriers,[26] members also came from the Hunan army organised by Zeng Guofan to fight the Taiping rebels.[27] Indeed, the dissolution in 1864 of Zeng's army of 100,000, many of them Sichuanese, contributed to the rapid growth of the Gelaohui in the province, especially in the eastern region which bordered on Hunan.[28]

Alone and together, the Gelaohui, other brotherhood societies and bandits laid siege to official institutions.[29] The Denghuahui (Lantern Society) was involved in salt bandit Ren Weituo's campaign against official salt offices in 1876, and other salt bandits were known to belong to the Guluhui.[30] In the 1880s, Governor-general Ding Baozhen indicated that 'secret society bandits in all quarters are in league with each other. They oppose officials and resist arrest, so the situation is gradually getting out of control.'[31] An anti-Qing uprising organised by sectarian leader Wang Jueyi in nearby Hubei province in 1883 also gave local officials in Chongqing cause for concern.[32] In a report to Governor-general Ding in April 1883, Baxian magistrate Guo Zhang wrote, 'Yu city [Chongqing] is on the river, making it convenient for our merchants to form companies with the merchants from Hankou. There is a lot of contact between the two places and, when the news [of this incident] arrived, everyone here paid close attention.'[33] Guo ordered neighbourhood committees to strengthen their local militia and to search for and arrest the 'bandits from the outside.'[34] Such was the situation when Westerners arrived in greater numbers during the second half of the nineteenth century – the Chinese community in Chongqing was already dealing with tensions between Chinese insiders and Chinese outsiders.

Foreign outsiders

Foreigners contributed to these tensions by threatening existing power structures. In religious spheres Christianity, already in existence in Sichuan since the seventeenth century, competed with other local religions. In economic spheres Western projects threatened to take jobs from the local workers. Politically, the foreign presence in the community was viewed as the first step toward foreign control of the province.

Compared with the treaty port cities of the coastal regions, as illustrated in the other chapters in this volume, foreigners came to Sichuan relatively late. With the exception of a few dozen French Catholic priests and a handful of British and American missionaries and trade representatives, Westerners did not come to the province in large numbers until Chongqing was forced open as a treaty port in 1891. Within a few years, consulates were set up by the British, French, Americans, Japanese and Germans, and missions established by Protestant missionaries. By 1906 there were approximately 100 foreigners in Chongqing and more than 700 living throughout the province.[35] Their numbers were small compared with places like Shanghai but large relative to the number of foreigners living in the province only several decades earlier.

Local Chinese resentment of foreign activity often led to violent results. French priest François Fleury saw such attacks not as an expression of hatred of foreigners but as a reflection of a fear that Christianity was taking over local religions. Describing the reasons for his six-month captivity during an incident in 1898, Fleury explained:

> I ... was not apprehended because I was European; what they saw in me, what they hated in me, was [my role as] the master of Religion, the propagator of the Christian faith. According to Yu's edicts ... Christian religion had been introduced in all the provinces in the Empire; the worshippers of Chinese Gods were fewer and fewer; the Empire of our Gods was threatening to disappear and to be supplanted by Catholicism. It was necessary to stop this trend; victory should reside in the Chinese Buddha, and to achieve this goal, the most reliable method was to exterminate all Christians in the Empire.[36]

The crowds cried out to him, according to Fleury, '[You] are the destroyer of our Gods; if [you] stay in the region, soon there will be no more followers of our great religion[s].'[37]

In addition, Western economic activity antagonised the local population. The most visible Western economic threat was the arrival of the first steam-powered boat to make the treacherous journey through the Yangzi gorges and reach Chongqing city in March 1898. Such a concrete example of mechanisation replacing tasks traditionally performed by manual labour (boats at the time were pulled manually by hundreds of trackers) gave credence to rumours circulating in nearby Dazu that Westerners were planning to mechanise the mines at the Western Hills and thereby threaten the livelihood of many of the workers.[38]

The Chinese were also no doubt aware that France and England were in fierce competition with one another to gain economic spheres of influence in this jewel in the crown of south-western China. France, in particular, was keen on strengthening its presence in the province. Such aspirations are illustrated in French and even in American diplomatic reports. A letter from the American consul Smithers in 1898 about the kidnapping of the French priest Fleury explains, 'I need hardly point out that France has had her designs on this part of China for some time past, and a case of this kind, involving the capture of one of her nationals and the destruction of property, offers her a good opportunity to make such demands on China as she thinks compatible with what other powers have lately obtained.'[39] The reports of French consul Haas confirm the speculations of his American counterpart. By 1899 Haas's wish list had grown to include the railroad concession from Chongqing to Chengdu, a consulate in Chengdu, a French concession area in Chongqing, mines for the Sino-French syndicat of Chongqing and a convention guaranteeing rights for French missionaries in Tibet similar to the rights enjoyed in the rest of China.[40] These demands were too much even for French minister Pichon, who advised that, in addition to demanding severe punishment for the guilty and indemnities for all damages, France should limit the other demands to mining concessions in Chongqing.[41]

On the political front, Western activity in Chongqing looked suspicious to the local Chinese, with stories circulating about possible European invasions of the province.[42] These suspicions prompted an attack on foreigners and Chinese Christians in Chongqing in 1886 when missionary attempts to build summer houses at Goose Neck Point, an area in the suburbs of Chongqing city, were misunderstood as Western attempts to build military forts for the purpose of invading the city.[43] In part, cultural differences about where to live prevented the Chinese from believing Western claims: 'As for the [other] benefits of these sites, the land is very poor, there are no markets in the vicinity, and there are no fields to cultivate. In terms of scenery, although these sites are high, there are neither trees nor bamboo groves. These are not places in which to pass serene and cultured leisure time.'[44] But international events, such as British activities in

India and French conquests in Indochina, certainly contributed to the Sichuanese notion that the Westerners were plotting to invade the province.[45] From the Sichuanese point of view, more was at risk than the defence of an inland city – the peace of the entire empire was at stake. One of the petitions explained, 'Sichuan is an important part of the Empire and Chongqing an especially important city in Sichuan. Throughout the dynasties we have seen that peace in the Empire depends upon peace in Sichuan, and peace in Sichuan depends upon peace in Chongqing'.[46] The patriotic responsibility was clear – if the people of Chongqing relaxed their vigilance, the entire empire would suffer.[47]

Chinese Christian outsiders

Chinese Christians, also perceived as a serious threat to the local economic, political and religious structures, comprised the bulk of the victims during the more than thirty attacks launched against Christians in the Chongqing region during the second half of the nineteenth century. Chinese Christians were killed or wounded, their property was destroyed and many were forced to leave their neighbourhoods and seek refuge elsewhere. An incident in Chongqing in 1886 disrupted over 150 Chinese Christian families.[48] The series of campaigns in nearby Dazu county from 1886 to 1900 displaced more than 10,000 people.[49]

The threat that Chinese Christians posed to the economic structure was most visible in Dazu and Chongqing. In Dazu, a county within Chongqing prefecture approximately sixty miles north-west of Chongqing city, Christians were accused of controlling prime retail space in the local coal market and engaging in dishonest trading practices.[50] In Chongqing, during an incident in 1886, the home of a wealthy Chinese Christian salt merchant was attacked and his store destroyed. Several days later the homes of his likewise wealthy Chinese Christians neighbours were also assaulted. In general, during times of famine, the homes of Chinese Christians were the first to be looted and plundered.[51]

Competition by Chinese Christians for local political power became a particularly serious problem in areas controlled by brotherhood societies. In 1876 the Gelaohui participated in attacks on Chinese Christians in Jiangbei county, just across the river from Chongqing city, and in Fuling, a county located down river but still within the Chongqing prefectural boundaries. In Dazu the Gelaohui was the main force organising campaigns against Chinese Catholics in 1886, 1888 and 1890, and finally, during what became known as the Yu Dongchen incident, in 1898.[52] Attacks on Chinese Christians in 1904 in southern Chongqing prefecture, along the border of Guizhou province, were led by the Gelaohui, the Gedihui and the local variant of the Boxer group, the Hongdengjiao (Red Lantern Society).[53]

Notably, many of these political disputes were turf battles among Chinese groups, not attacks on foreign power. In some cases there was little connection at all with foreigners.[54] Such was the case during repeated attacks in Youyang county (down river from Chongqing) in the late 1860s, where the church became the battleground for existing rivalries. After the Protestant missionaries arrived in the 1880s, these local feuds were also played out between the various Chinese Protestants and Catholics, with rival secret societies joining opposing sides.[55] Even some of the attacks directed specifically against the Catholic Church had more to do with local power struggles than with religious issues. In Dazu, the Catholic Church was attacked when it invaded a political sphere controlled by the Gelaohui. Although Catholics had been living in Dazu without incident since the 1780s,[56] violence broke out in 1886 when the Catholic mission built an imposing church in the middle of the main market town, Longshuizhen, which towered over the two main temples. Contemporary Chinese reports noted that the church was positioned in the centre of town and resembled an emperor's palace.[57] French missionaries were not unaware of these problems, with Père Fleury admitting, 'This church, erected in the market between two temples, offended the leaders of the secret society. From that day, its destruction was inevitable.'[58] Not surprisingly, the church was destroyed three times, in 1886, 1888 and 1890. The total damage in the latter incident included the deaths of at least twelve Chinese Christians, attacks on more than 200 Chinese Christian families and the destruction of three churches and one hospital.[59] The church was finally rebuilt in another market town in 1891 and the area enjoyed a respite from hostile campaigns until 1898.

The church, symbolically and literally, had usurped local Gelaohui power. It was no coincidence that the burning of the church took place on the birthday celebration of the Gelaohui's main deity, Lingguan, who was known as the God of War and the god who judged good and evil.[60] Gelaohui member and main leader of the incident of 1890, Jiang Zanchen, used Lingguan to legitimise his own authority. Before starting out, Jiang ordered his followers to check their divination in front of a Lingguan statue.[61] When the divination sticks showed that Lingguan supported their venture and would protect them, Jiang set off wearing Lingguan's cloak. After returning triumphant from one of the campaigns, he strutted around the market place proudly modelling the cloak.[62]

While Christianity was an important focus of the movement, the main point of contention was not its 'foreignness' but the power struggle between Christians and the competing religious group, the Buddhists inspired by Lingguan and led by the Gelaohui. Earlier we read the account by French priest François Fleury in 1898, attributing his captivity not to his foreign but to his Christian identity. In the description below, written eight years earlier by another French priest, Pons, we see a similar fear of Catholicism on the part of the local Chinese Buddhists:

> Yang and Zhen ... were seized and garrotted ... and taken to the market where they were promised their lives if they consented to renounce their faith; when taken to the Dongyoumiao Pagoda, these heroic Christians refused to prostrate themselves before the Lingguan idol. They were then chained with their hands tied behind their backs, and were exposed, completely nude, to a scorching sun near the door of the pagoda.... Then they were taken successively to the seven temples in the market place; in each one, they were again ordered to renounce their faith and worship the idols ...[63]

The perceived threat to Buddhism is clear: not only were these Chinese Christians tortured, but they were taken to all seven temples in the market place. With more at stake than revenge, it was crucial that they perform the Buddhist rituals and embrace the Lingguan God.

The hostility launched against Chinese Christians during the second half of the nineteenth century was not solely a product of anti-imperialism or xenophobia, but was a continuation of age-old domestic battles over competing economic, political and cultural resources. The evils of foreigners and foreign imperialist power may have appeared in the rhetoric, but they were barely apparent on the battlefields, where, during each of the campaigns in 1886, 1888, 1890 and 1898, the vast majority of the perpetrators and victims, on both sides, were Chinese.

Conclusion

When, how and why do people draw lines of inclusion and exclusion? The use of a term like xenophobia assumes exclusion based on race or national identity. Yet in Chongqing categories of insider and outsider and of domestic and foreign were shaped by many factors. Foreign identity played a role, but the domestic context into which this foreign identity was placed was as, if not more, important. Indeed, with the large influx of migrants to the province during the seventeenth and eighteenth centuries, the Chinese and Western Christians in Sichuan were considered merely a part of the diverse mix of communities peopling the province. It was not until the second half of the nineteenth century that they no longer lived in relative harmony with their non-Christian neighbours, but began to be seen as a group deserving of hostile treatment.

Any attempt to explain this change in perception cannot ignore the importance of the increase in Western power, both at the national and at the local levels, after the First Opium War of 1839–1842. The growth of imperialism, Western victories over China in a series of wars, and the ensuing harsh treaties, made the local Western and Christian presence much more threatening. These Westerners and Chinese Christians were also much more aggressive. Backed by the treaties, they pushed ahead in their quests to effect change or pursue selfish goals, paying little heed to whether or not the local communities were in agreement.

But Western and Chinese Christian challenges to local traditions became intolerable by this point mainly because they took place in a context of Chinese domestic unrest and uncertainty where local perceptions of Chinese insiders and outsiders were also in flux. The continued rise in population and increased commercialisation of the Chongqing region throughout the nineteenth century created new social fissures as different and unknown people moved in and out of the city daily. Some of these people, rootless and itinerant, single and unemployed, joined the organised networks of brotherhood societies that challenged the traditional cultural, economic and political structures. Such challenges would culminate ultimately in the overthrow of the Qing dynasty as the Manchu rulers themselves came to be viewed as foreign outsiders. But during the late nineteenth century they had the initial effect of reshaping local perceptions of Chinese insiders and outsiders.

Western imperialism in Sichuan, as manifest in the activities of Catholic and Protestant missions and their Western and Chinese congregants, the economic ventures of Western and Chinese merchants, and the political and military ambitions of Western governments, was interpreted and understood by the local Chinese in this context of domestic unrest and strife. In such an uncertain world, anti-foreignism was moulded by more than hatred of foreigners and foreign ideas. It was also formed by Chinese anxieties over Chinese problems which were then displaced, under the slogan of anti-foreignism, on to foreign and Chinese aggressors.

FOREIGNERS OR OUTSIDERS?

Notes

1 Of the more than 400 documented cases, 25 per cent took place in Sichuan: Mou Anshi, 'Zhongguo renmin fandui waiguo jiaohui qinluede douzheng he zhongguo jindaishide zhuyao xiansuo' (The Chinese People's Struggle against the Invasion of Foreign Missionaries and Important Strands in Chinese Modern History), in *Jindai zhongguo jiaoan yanjiu* (Studies of Anti-Christian Incidents in Modern China) (Chengdu, Sichuan Academy of Social Sciences Press, 1987), 1, 14 and n. 1.
2 See, for example, Paul A. Cohen, *China and Christianity: the Missionary Movement and the Growth of Chinese Antiforeignism, 1860–1870* (Cambridge MA, Harvard University Press, 1963); A. Sweeten, 'Community and Bureaucracy in Rural China: Evidence from "Sectarian Cases" (*jiaoan*) in Kiangsi, 1860–1895' (University of California, Davis, Ph.D. thesis, 1980); Joseph W. Esherick, *The Origins of the Boxer Uprising* (Berkeley CA, University of California Press, 1987); and E. Werhle, *Britain, China and the Anti-missionary Riots, 1891–1900* (Minneapolis MN, University of Minnesota Press, 1966).
3 Recent scholarship on Chinese outsiders and on the construction of race has influenced this conceptualisation: see Frank Dikötter, *The Discourse of Race in Modern China* (Stanford CA, Stanford University Press, 1992); Pamela Kyle Crossley, *Orphan Warriors: Three Manchu Generations and the End of the Qing World* (Princeton NJ, Princeton University Press, 1990) and 'Thinking about Ethnicity in Early Modern China', *Late Imperial China*, 11:1 (June 1990), 1–34; Barend J. ter Haar, 'Images of Outsiders: the Fear of Death by Mutilation' (work in progress, 1991) and *The White Lotus Teachings in Chinese Religious History* (Leiden, E. J. Brill, 1992); and Philip Kuhn, *Soulstealers: The Chinese Sorcery Scare of 1768* (Cambridge MA, Harvard University Press, 1990).
4 Robert Eric Entenmann, 'Migration and Settlement in Sichuan, 1644–1769' (Harvard University Ph.D. thesis, 1982), 59.
5 Entenmann, 'Migration', 157.
6 G. William Skinner, 'Sichuan's Population in the Nineteenth Century: Lessons from Disaggregated Data', *Late Imperial China*, 8 (June 1987), 1–79.
7 Inspectorate General of Customs (IGC), *Decennial Reports, 1892–1901*, Chungking, 157. Wang Di, *Kuachu fengbi de shijie: changjiang shangyou quyu shehui yanjiu* (Extending beyond the Closed World: A Social History of the Upper Yangzi Region, 1644–1911) (Beijing, Zhonghua shuju, 1993), 63.
8 IGC, *Decennial Reports, 1882–1891*, 119.
9 Wang Di, 'Qingdai Chongqing chengshi renkou yu shehui zuzhi' (Population and Social Organisation in Chongqing City during the Qing), in Wei Yingtao, ed., *Chongqing chengshi yanjiu* (A Study of Chongqing City) (Chengdu, Sichuan daxue chuban she, 1989), 316.
10 Wang Di, 'Qingdai Chongqing', 315, for population and household figures. Muslim figures in *Guangyi congbao*, 105, 1906.
11 Public Record Office, London (PRO), Foreign Office files, FO 228/829, Chungking, 7 July 1886, 284.
12 Entenmann, 'Migration', 119–20.
13 Entenmann, 'Migration', 177–8.
14 PRO, FO 228/627, Chungking, May 1879, 266.
15 Entenmann, 'Migration', 122, 133.
16 Entenmann, 'Migration', 156, 261–2.
17 Foreign and Chinese imports increased from 156,000 taels in 1875 to 17 million in 1899, and Chinese exports increased from 241,000 taels to 9 million. Y. T. Wei, *Jindai Chongqing chengshi shi* (A modern urban history of Chongqing) (Chengdu, Sichuan daxue chubanshe, 1991), 118–19 for the years 1875–91; and IGC, *1892–1901*, 148 for 1899.
18 Sichuan Provincial Archives (hereafter SPA), Baxian collection, (BX), neizheng (NZ) 1561, 28 September 1878; NZ 1584, 22 June 1881; NZ 1707, 13 August

1896; NZ 1708, 28 November 1896; junshi (JS) 3001, 26 January 1883; JS 2996, 23 May 1883.
19 SPA/BX, NZ 1729, 9 September 1900. Gentry and *juren* writing to Baxian magistrate Zhang.
20 SPA/BX, NZ 1695, 6 November 1895. SPA/BX, NZ, 1574, 14 May 1880.
21 SPA/BX, NZ 1758, 15 June 1906.
22 SPA/BX, NZ 1543, June 1886.
23 SPA/BX, NZ 1561, 28 September 1878; NZ 1584, 22 June 1881; JS, 3001, 26 January 1883.
24 R. H. Felsing, 'The Heritage of the Han: the Gelaohui and the 1911 Revolution in Sichuan' (University of Iowa Ph.D. thesis, 1979), 6, 64.
25 SPA/BX, NZ 1734, 22 November 1900.
26 Cai Shaoqing, 'On the Origin of the Gelaohui', *Modern China* 10 (October, 1984), 483. Cheng-yun Liu, 'The Ko-lao Hui in Late Imperial China' (University of Pittsburgh Ph.D thesis, 1983), 96.
27 Felsing, 'The Heritage', 34.
28 Felsing, 'The Heritage', 34. Cai, 'On the Origin', 498–9.
29 Wei Yingtao, *Sichuan jindai shigao* (A History of Modern Sichuan) (Chengdu, Sichuan renmin chubanshe, 1990), 1919–93. SPA/BX, JS 3029, 17 April 1876, 31 July 1877.
30 Wei Yingtao, *Sichuan jindai*, 192. Cai, 'On the Origin', 487.
31 Cai, 'On the Origin', 499.
32 SPA/BX, JS 2996, 23 April 1883.
33 SPA/BX, JS 2996, 23 April 1883.
34 SPA/BX, JS 2996, 23 April 1883.
35 PRO, FO 228/1628, Chungking intelligence report, 6 October 1906.
36 *Annales de la Société des Missions Étrangères et de l'Oeuvre des Partants*, 1900–01 (Paris) (hereafter *Annales*), 11, 15.
37 *Annales*, 1900–01, 10.
38 Hu Qiwei, *Dazu renmin fanyangjiao douzheng* (The Dazu People's Struggle against Foreign Religion) (Dazu, Dazu wenshi ziliao, No. 2 (no date)), 68.
39 Chungking, No. 40, 20 September 1898, US Consular Reports.
40 French Foreign Ministry Archives, Paris (FFMP), Nouvelle Série (NS) 322, 7 February 1899.
41 FFMP, NS 322, 7 February 1899.
42 Thomas W. Blakiston, *Five Months on the Yangtze* (London, John Murray, 1862), 222.
43 Société des Missions Étrangères Archives, Sichuan Oriental (SME), Vol. 536A, 8 September 1886. M. L. Wang, *Fanyangjiao shuwen tiezhan xuan* (A Collection of Letters and Placards against Foreign Religion) (Ji'nan, 1981), 259–60. *Jiaowu jiaoan dang'an* (Archives of Missionary Affairs and Missionary Cases) (Zhongyang yanjiuyuan jindaishi yanjiusuo: Taibei, series 1–6) (hereafter *JWJA*), Vol. 4 (1976), No. 648, 28 July 1886, 934.
44 Wang, *Fanyangjiao*, 260. Also in PRO, FO 228/829, Chungking, No. 8, 8 August 1886, 358–9.
45 *JWJA*, Vol. 4, No. 657, 15 July 1886, 14 August 1886, 951. Also quoted in PRO, FO 228/829, letter from Bourne to Walsham, Confidential Separate, 19 August 1886, 378. *Papers Relating to the Foreign Relations of the United States*, 1887, 159.
46 Wang, *Fanyangjiao*, 259–61. Also in PRO, FO 228/829, Chungking, No. 8, 8 August 1886, 358–9, and *JWJA*, Vol. 4, 657, 15 July, 14 August 1886, 952–3.
47 Bryna Goodman, *Native Place, City, and Nation: Regional Networks and Identities in Shanghai, 1853–1937* (Berkeley CA, University of California Press, 1995), 197–8.
48 FFMP, CP, 70, Constans, No. 13, 18 January 1887.
49 SME, Vol. 536B, Dangy, No. 428, 8 October 1898; Chouvellon, No. 430, 13 October 1898; Chouvellon, No. 437, 12 December 1898.
50 Hu, *Dazu renmin*, 68.

51 SME, Vol. 536A, Coupat, 9 August 1886; FFMP, CP, 70, Constans, No. 13, 18 January 1887.
52 Hu Hansheng, 'Sichuan Gelaohui Kao' (An examination of the Gelaohui in Sichuan) in *Sichuan jindai shishi sankao* (An Examination of three Aspects of Modern Sichuanese history) (Chongqing, Chongqing chubanshe, 1988), 146.
53 Judith Wyman, 'Social Change, Antiforeignism and Revolution in China: Chongqing prefecture, 1870s to 1911' (University of Michigan Ph.D. thesis, 1993), 104–10.
54 Hiroshi Tessan, 'Shinmatsu Shisen ni okeru hanshokuminchika to kyukyo undo' (The Semi-colonisation of Sichuan in the Late Qing and the Anti-Catholic Movement), *Rekishigaku Kenkyu* 6, No. 529 (1984), 220–2, as cited in Prasenjit Duara, *Rescuing History from the Nation: Questioning Narratives of Modern China* (Chicago, University of Chicago Press, 1995), 121.
55 PRO, FO 228/1550, Chungking, 30 September 1904.
56 *Annales* (1910), 265.
57 *JWJA*, series 5, Vol. 3 (1977), No. 1519, 1487. FFMN, Religious Protectorate – Sichuan, Box 36, missionary Blettery to French Minister in Peking, 15 June 1891. Chinese copy of Chinese notice.
58 *Annales* (1900–01), 4.
59 FFMN, Religious Protectorate – Sichuan, Box 36, missionary Blettery to French Minister in Peking, 15 June 1891. Chinese copy of Chinese notice.
60 *Shanghai Mercury*, 28 October 1890. View of Père Pierres, in *Société des Missions Étrangères (SME), Bulletin de l'oeuvre des partants* (1891), 337, and Fleury, *Annales* (1900–01), 15.
61 FFMN, Religious Protectorate – Sichuan, Box 36, missionary Blettery to French Minister in Peking, 15 June 1891. Chinese copy of Chinese notice.
62 SME, *Bulletin*, 1891, 462.
63 SME, *Bulletin*, 1891, 420.

CHAPTER SIX

The Japanese and the Jews: a comparative analysis of their communities in Harbin, 1898–1930

Joshua A. Fogel

One effective way to reach an understanding of the experiences of a given foreign community or colonial (or semi-colonial) situation in a given city is to compare it with another foreign community or colonial situation in the same city. This enables us to contrast degrees of assimilation, integration, interaction with the surrounding indigenous community and other foreign communities, and the like. Indeed, this volume, as a whole, will move us a large step forward in that direction. This chapter examines the experiences of the Jewish and the Japanese communities of Harbin in the three decades before the Manchurian Incident.

Harbin enjoys a unique place in East Asian history. Unlike the great majority of other cities in contemporary China, Harbin does not have a history stretching back hundreds, even thousands, of years.[1] It was constructed at the very end of the nineteenth century by Russian engineers and city planners, and it became something of a melting pot, a city of pioneers. It was a place where even the Chinese were newcomers. As a result of this newness, although there were not extraordinary levels of intermarriage and intercultural exchange, there was more in Harbin than in the other metropolises housing foreign communities in China.

For those leaving the Russian empire, Harbin offered Jews an opportunity unavailable elsewhere in the lands of the Tsars: a haven relatively free from the virulent strain of antisemitism so prominent in eastern Europe at the time. The elite of the late imperial regime supported this tolerant attitude toward the Jews in the hope that they would spur economic development and help extend Russian authority into Manchuria.[2] Thus Jews were used in Harbin by the authorities as an economic vanguard in Asia, at the same time that many Jews utilised this opportunity to escape the clutches of Tsarism and antisemitism. For Japanese, Harbin offered a second chance – and before

1931 it was not supported by Japanese military might. It was an opportunity to mix and do business in what was arguably the most international city in the world at the time – albeit a backwater from a world perspective – and it was a chance to escape back-breaking poverty for many at home.

Origins of Harbin and its Japanese and Jewish communities

The Japanese community in Harbin was the earliest settlement of Japanese in Manchuria. Earlier some Japanese had emigrated to Vladivostok in the Russian Maritime Province, which originally fell within Qing terrain and had been ceded to Russia in 1860 by the Manchu government. At the time Vladivostok was barely a sleepy fishing village; by 1877 there were approximately eighty Japanese living there, most working in the flesh trade servicing the large number of sailors whose ships called at port. Within a few years their numbers reached 140–50 – all from Nagasaki – and they had branched out into restaurants and several laundries as well. By 1890 there were nearly 400 Japanese in the city with a gender ratio of three women to two men; frontier cities usually have far more men than women and a thriving brothel world, but Vladivostok's experience was somewhat different. The Russians began construction of the Trans-Siberian Railway in 1891, and Vladivostok, being the eastern terminus, was overflowing with new businesses involved in the construction of the docks. There were some 500–600 Japanese recruited to the city from northern Kyûshû to work as labourers. By century's end, the number of Japanese topped 1,000, and communal institutions were beginning to emerge. However, the bulk of the population remained involved in prostitution.[3]

In the fall of 1896 the Ussuri line of the Trans-Siberian Railway – linking Vladivostok with Khabarovsk – neared completion, and China signed a secret treaty with Russia allowing the latter to construct rail lines throughout Manchuria. They were to become the Chinese Eastern Railway (CER), and a CER construction authority in Vladivostok was created in the spring of 1897. For the transportation of material, a base of operations was still needed near a river; a site was selected near the Sungari river (in Chinese Songhuajiang) that was sparsely populated. The materials were transported from Europe to Vladivostok by sea, loaded on to rail lines there and brought to Khabarovsk, and finally placed on riverine vessels and taken on the Sungari to this new site. The first group of men, led by A. I. Iugovich, chief construction engineer of the CER, with an armed Cossack guard, set out to establish this site in March 1898. It may be difficult to imagine now, with Harbin a teeming city of several million inhabitants, but what they found when they arrived the next month was a small settlement of local villagers in roughly twenty huts where low-grade alcohol was being distilled and opium grown along the banks of the river. The Russians bought it all, and soon the massive railway construction enterprise was under way; some 200,000 Chinese would eventually migrate north to find employment with it.

The Russian developers first set out to build a train station and narrow-gauge track from the Sungari wharf to the centre of the former settlement. This transport route was later to become the major thoroughfare of Harbin, known as Kitaiskaia Ulitsa (Chinese Street) in Russian and Zhongyang dajie (Central Boulevard) in Chinese. Within two decades, this avenue became the heart of non-Chinese Harbin, lined with an assortment of shops selling the latest fashions and foods from every corner of the European world.[4]

Russian city planners called this new site simply 'Posyolok Sungari' (the Sungari Settlement), but in a 1904 Japanese work introducing Manchuria it is already referred to as 'Harbin'.[5] The name must have come into popular currency within this period of six years. From that point forward, the Russian always called it 'Kharbin', and the Chinese used the three characters 'Ha-er-bin'. In Japanese writings of the pre-war era it was more often 'Harupin'. Even today both 'Harupin' and 'Harubin' are used as readings for this toponym.

The famed author Yokomitsu Riichi wrote an essay in 1932 entitled 'Rekishi (Harupin no ki)' (History: a Note on Harbin).[6] It recounts the story of Miyamoto Chiyo, a remarkable young woman who was one of the first Japanese to settle in Harbin. Born in 1879, she moved with her brother from her native Kumamoto to Vladivostok in 1888; there she earned her living as an assistant to the only Russian doctor in town. When, as part of the Russian development of Harbin, the doctor moved there in 1898, she accompanied him. Within a few years her close ties with the Russian community were sufficient grounds for all Japanese immigration matters to be put in her charge. The Boxer rising brought Sino-Russian border tensions to a high point, and in July of 1900 the Russian army routed or murdered the entire Chinese population of the city of Blagoveshchensk, altogether some 3,000–4,000 persons. Many Japanese fled Harbin for the relative security of Khabarovsk or elsewhere, as did many Chinese. Yokomitsu noted that only twenty-two of Harbin's Japanese residents remained during this massive withdrawal from the city; by the following year, however, the Japanese population returned to over 300.

The paperwork for such a group was now too demanding for

Miyamoto to handle by herself, and at this juncture a Japanese residents' association, the Sôkakai or Sungari Association, was founded. The name indicates that by that early date, 1901, the name 'Harbin' had as yet probably not become firmly established, at least among the Japanese population. By late 1902 the population of Harbin had reached about 30,000, of whom some 514 were Japanese, according to a report of the Sôkakai; Manchuria as a whole was now home to about 7,000 Japanese. In 1903–04, on the eve of the Russo-Japanese War, Harbin experienced a second mass withdrawal, though the city was otherwise unaffected by the fighting.[7] The Japanese population of Harbin finally surpassed its pre-war figure only in December 1907, when the number reached 627, at a time when the numbers of Japanese in the cities of China proper were much higher.[8] The gender imbalance continued to dog Japanese in Harbin for some time into the twentieth century. Even with a gender-skewed population and the bulk of it feeding the brothel business, Japanese in the city began quickly to branch out into other trades and to form a plethora of communal institutions.

Comparably precise data for the Jewish community of Harbin have as yet not been uncovered. The records of the Jewish community – minutes of communal meetings, taxation figures, and the like – have yet to be found. We do know, however, that there were Jews among the first settlers in Harbin, if not in the initial Tsarist construction team. Unlike the Japanese, who were leaving unemployment or poverty in their homeland, the Jews, many from Siberia and others from the Pale of Settlement in the Russian empire, were escaping waves of ferocious antisemitism and organised terror. However, the very first Jews to make Harbin their home were a breed apart. This intrepid group included a handful of former *Nikolaevskie soldati*, men who had been effectively kidnapped in their early to mid-teen years into twenty-five-year terms of military service for the Tsar's armed forces. If they survived this service, they were granted a privilege denied other Jews in Russia: to settle outside the Pale. A number of such men, hardy creatures that they were, chose to make the new city of Harbin their home.[9]

Other early settlers were equally intrepid souls. To help develop this new region of the empire, the Tsarist government allowed a handful of Jewish businessmen the opportunity to invest in various industries in the Harbin area and Manchuria more generally. The activities included furs and lumber, and some of the businessmen became fabulously wealthy. The principal early figure in the Manchurian export trade was Roman Moiseevich Kabalkin, who had made his fortune in the grain trade and served for fourteen years as a consultant on the

Riazan–Ural'sk railway. He was permitted to develop freight traffic from Siberia to Manchuria, to which end he established R. M. Kabalkin and Son around 1910. In the face of antisemitic pressures, he found support in the CER authorities. Another major Jewish player in the Harbin economy was Lev Shmulevich Skidel'skii, who was to become Harbin's only Jewish millionaire.[10]

Others were less wealthy men and women who simply gambled that they would do better on the more level playing field of Manchuria than in the pogrom-ridden cities and towns of the Pale. For example, the father of Eve Naftaly (née Greenwald) was a lumber and grain merchant who first visited Harbin in 1904 and brought his family there the next year. From the great Kishinyov pogrom in 1903 through the more widespread antisemitic acts associated with the Russian revolution of 1905, Jews began looking for opportunities outside the restrictions and abuses of the Pale. In Harbin, by contrast, a Jew could own land and there were no quotas on Jews in the schools: 'It was like Russia without the antisemitism of Russia.' Emile Katz's father brought his family to Harbin in 1906 for the same reason, as did the father of Abe Traig (né Treguboff) in 1907. As Mrs Traig put it in an interview in 1975, 'You see, the Jews in Siberia [by which she meant also Manchuria and the Maritime Province], once they got there, had much more rights than in Russia itself, because Siberia was a country that had to be developed.' Pearl Levin's father, responding to the horrors of 1905–06, moved his family to Harbin because he feared that his children would become revolutionaries as a result.[11] The Jewish community grew steadily in the early years of the twentieth century. By 1909 its population of approximately 5,000 amounted to 11·5 per cent of the overall total in Harbin, second only in Siberia to Irkutsk (6,100) where the numbers amounted to only 5·6 per cent of the overall population.[12]

What did they think of this strange young city on the other side of the world? Most were amazed by two facts. First, it was a perfect replica of a Russian city, although far removed from the centres of Russian culture and civilisation. Second, it was, as Eve Naftaly elegantly put it, 'a horrible place... You know, like in the westerns – a little town, a frontier town. There were no pavements. There were wooden sidewalks.' But, interestingly, she hastened to add, 'Harbin was a Russian town... on the Chinese soil.' 'It was a Russian city,' noted Pearl Levin bluntly; 'Harbin was absolutely Russian,' stated Sara Ossin most succinctly.[13] The city was a ramshackle frontier, much less sophisticated than anything with which they were familiar in the Pale, yet completely Russian, they all noted without any irony.

What made Harbin and a few other cities like it preferable to anything in western Russia or Poland or Ukraine at the time, it must be emphasised, was the almost complete absence of antisemitism, fuelled in Russia proper by the government itself, or restrictions, a topic to which we shall return. No memoirist remembers any serious incidents before the late 1920s, though there were certainly many minor incidents following the retreat of the White armies toward the end of the 1910s. This quality of life more than compensated for Harbin's lack of other amenities. As more Jews fleeing persecution in the 1910s made their way to Harbin, the early settlers took them in and together founded a full panoply of communal institutions.

Work in Harbin: occupations, businesses, shops

Unlike the Japanese community of Shanghai, which lived much like other foreign ethnic enclaves within its own small universe, in its early years Harbin remained under Russian control. Despite the concessions acquired by Japan after victory in 1905, Harbin was to all intents and purposes a CER fief unto itself, ruled by the general manager of the CER, Dmitri L. Khorvat. However, as prospects for a secure future looked better from 1907 and the immense untapped wealth of the region became known, a new infusion of Japanese capital from that time helped to revive Harbin's wayward economy; both Mitsubishi and Mitsui opened branches there that year. From this time, as well, there was a sustained return and growth in the number of Japanese in the city, following the withdrawal at the time of the Russo-Japanese War.

As early as 1905 there were five competing companies plying the sea lanes between Japanese ports and Vladivostok. Even before the war the Japanese had founded larger enterprises in Harbin, such as Tokunaga Shôkai, Suzuki Nichi-Man Shôkai and Moritomi Shôkai – these were not on a par with the great *zaibatsu*, but neither were they corner *bodegos*. A local survey of Japanese businesses in Vladivostok late in 1907, for example, revealed thirty-nine general stores, seventy-five laundries, thirty-six barbers, twenty-seven cobblers, thirty-six carpenters and sixty-two families in the *kashiseki* or 'rooms for rent' business, a euphemism for houses of prostitution. World War I brought prosperity to Harbin; trade exports rose dramatically and, by way of example, the number of oil refineries increased from seven to twenty. During the war years Japanese contacts throughout Siberia rose to make Japan second only to the United States for the volume of trade with the region.[14] Interestingly, even as the Japanese population grew and became more sophisticated and diverse through the 1910s, and even as fresh business opportunities enriched the local community, the number of Japanese linked with prostitution remained extremely high.[15]

The phenomenon of large-scale Japanese prostitution in Harbin was by no means unique in East Asia. Large numbers of young Japanese women, known colloquially as *karayukisan* (lit. those who go to China), were forced or deceived with offers of jobs to aid their impoverished families into travelling to many of the cities of mainland East and South East Asia, as well as Hawaii and even the west coast of the United States. If they survived the trip, they were faced with a future of indentured servitude as prostitutes, often for the rest of their lives. Morisaki Kazue has estimated that some 30,000 prostitutes were transported to Manchuria by unscrupulous Japanese.[16] One may see here the origins of what would later, also euphemistically, be called *ianfu* or comfort women, the young Asian women dragooned into sexual service for the expanding Japanese military, though others date this development to much later.

The Bolshevik revolution brought about a major shift in power relations within the city. There were struggles within the CER between Khorvat and the railway workers, exacerbated by demands from the local Chinese authorities for full sovereignty over both the railroad and the region. Russian culture continued to dominate non-Chinese (and even some Chinese) life in Harbin, but from this time forward Russian control of the city began a decline from which it was never to recover. The Russian presence in Harbin in fact only increased over time, with waves of White Russians and others escaping the Bolsheviks after 1917, but without Tsarist support many Russians were reduced to poverty, beggary and criminal behaviour. Harbin may have been the only city in East Asia in which Caucasian beggars outnumbered Asian beggars. Barely two decades old, Harbin remained a city of pioneers – Chinese, Japanese, Russians, Koreans and others – a city undergoing repeated political and social turmoil.

After the conclusion of the Great War, the joint powers invaded Siberia in an attempt to crush the young Soviet regime, but by the end of 1918 all the powers save Japan had withdrawn. Fearing the immediate consequences of Russian retaliation, Japanese forces remained in the region for over four years, despite worries voiced by the Japanese communities in Siberia and Manchuria of exacerbated tension with Russia and China. By this point there were thousands of Japanese expatriates (and far more Koreans, whose country had been annexed by Japan in 1910) living throughout the cities of North East Asia and along the Trans-Siberian Railway. When the decision was reached for the Japanese expeditionary force to withdraw in

1922, many local Japanese residents vociferously protested in the local press against such a move, fearing Russian reprisals because of the long intimacy of the Japanese military with the Whites and the Japanese support for such petty White Russian dictators as Grigorii Semenov.[17]

During the years of the Russian civil war the Russian *émigré* population of Harbin tripled to 124,000 by 1921, while the Japanese population rose by 75 per cent over the same period to 3,545 (excluding Koreans). The Chinese, far and away the largest portion of the local population, rose in number from 170,000 in 1917 to over 315,000 by early 1922. Thus, by 1922 the city had a total population of half a million, and nominal political control over the city was now in Chinese hands, but each of the constituent ethnic groups effectively managed their own affairs. To do so, each created its own array of communal institutions.

The Jewish community grew in response to waves of antisemitism in eastern and central Europe. While the great majority of Russian, Polish and Ukrainian Jews migrated to North America, a sizeable minority found their way along the Trans-Siberian Railway to cities in the east. Once the basis of a community had been laid, it began to grow. The population of Jewish Harbin reached its peak in the early 1920s at no more than 15,000 – small by international standards but important in other ways.

Continuing the direction set by the first generation of settlers, the majority of Jews in Harbin were in business. While the greatest wealth was probably to be made in lumber and furs, others dealt in grain, soap, textiles and similar products of daily use. Many were small businessmen who ran their own shops, such as Benjamin Alcone's father, who ran a jewellery store, and Pearl Levin's father, who, together with his brother, operated a music store.[18] Some Japanese visitors to the city claim that the brothels they visited were run by Jews and/or employed young Jewish women for their clientele, but they generally substantiate such claims by inane statements about someone 'looking Jewish' or having 'a long nose'.[19] There indeed may have been Jews in that trade, too, but the question requires further study. Harbin never became a noted centre of Jewish or secular learning; it spawned no great yeshivas or colleges for Europeans. Indeed, most young Jewish men and women went to Europe or the United States for a university education.[20]

Although no one has substantiated the role of Jews in Harbin prostitution, it seems clear that Jews were involved in the local entertainment industry to a considerable extent. Harbin was famous throughout East Asia as one of the liveliest and most freewheeling places on the world map, something that went well with its earlier frontier self-image. It was referred to generally as the 'Paris of the Orient' (as well as the 'City of Eros') by many travellers and settlers there, an appellation applied by others to Shanghai as well. It was renowned for its 'dance halls,' strip tease shows and bar-girls, and it was these institutions that were allegedly operated by Jewish residents.[21]

One of the enduring themes about Jewish life in Harbin was, with the exception of several notorious cases, the relative absence of organised antisemitism. Of course, the Whites brought their antisemitism with them to the city and taught it to the Japanese during the Siberian Expedition, to which time the first Japanese translation of the *Protocols of the Elders of Zion* can be dated,[22] but there were no Black Hundreds in Harbin, the setting being far removed from the traditional forces that stirred up antisemitic activities elsewhere. It was thus an extraordinary novelty: a Russian city without significant antisemitism, at least before the late 1920s. In the short history of the interface between Ashkenazi Jewry and China, Harbin was the only community which saw itself, more or less, as a terminus in the Exile (excluding, of course, the final ingathering of all exiles).

Communal and cultural institutions

By the 1910s, both the Japanese and the Jewish communities of Harbin had produced a wide array of local institutions supporting their respective constituencies. These institutions were, of course, by no means unique to Harbin; wherever either group settled away from home, they created comparable communal services. Neither the Japanese nor the Jews were content to rely on the local Chinese authorities to provide any but the most minimal political or policing service to the city; both assumed responsibility for the rest. This meant establishing social, educational, economic and religious institutions to provide for their people in Harbin. Harbin did have the additional circumstance of being such a young city that, unlike most other cities in continental Asia, it probably would have been in no position to offer such services even if its foreign constituents sought them.

As elsewhere outside Japan, it was the formal Japanese Residents' Association that took the lead in creating communal institutions. Although Harbin followed Vladivostok's lead in most civil matters, Japanese in Harbin formed a local residents' association, the Sôkakai, in 1901; Vladivostok did likewise in March 1902, where there were 2,875 Japanese residents (and a total of 4,334 throughout the Russian

Far East). The mass withdrawal of Japanese from the region over the following few years left few behind to run communal affairs. As Harbin's Japanese population returned to its pre-war level by the end of the first decade of the twentieth century, the first elementary school for Japanese pupils was opened – with a total of four students – in 1909 in a room of the local Nishi Honganji, a branch establishment of the Pure Land Buddhist sect. It acquired its own building only in June 1923, an impressive edifice built by the Sôkakai and the South Manchurian Railway Company (SMR) which from 1920 assumed half of all educational expenses for the local population.[23]

Despite these separate communal institutions, the Harbin community achieved a much higher degree of integration into the general Harbin population than did Japanese communities elsewhere in China. Whereas, for example, in Shanghai most Japanese lived in blissful ignorance of the surrounding Chinese population, in Harbin most Japanese learned Russian – they agreed with the assessment that it was, after all, a Russian city culturally – and many even made a stab at Chinese. Since those Japanese who settled in Harbin planned to remain there well into the future, it was only natural that they should attempt to learn the language of the predominant groups in the city, much as Japanese sought to learn English in the United States or Portuguese in Brazil. In September 1920 a Russo-Japanese School opened, the forerunner of the Harbin Academy which became famous as a training institute in the Russian language. The first principal, Inoda Kôhai, was a former student of Futabatei Shimei from the Tokyo Foreign Language School. A Sino-Japanese Evening School for language training opened in early April 1923 with similar aims of fostering Sino-Japanese understanding and friendship.

In addition, many Japanese who worked outside the home adopted Western styles of dress from the end of the Meiji period. In fact, Japanese in Vladivostok early on became tailors producing Western-style men's and women's clothing initially for the local Russian population. Fresh Japanese produce (mandarin oranges, apples, and other fruit and vegetables) was imported from numerous Japanese ports throughout the north-east as far as the Blagoveshchensk region with Chinese merchants serving as intermediaries. Japanese-language newspapers in Harbin abounded. In addition to journalists from all the major Japanese dailies and weeklies, Harbin produced a wide variety of its own, such as *Harubin nichinichi shinbun*, *Taihoku shinbun*, *Harubin tsûshin*, *Ro-A jihô*, *Hoku-Man denpô* and *Teikoku tsûshin*.[24]

In the aftermath of World War I and the Bolshevik revolution, Harbin became congested with countless new immigrants. The year

1919 was particularly difficult, with the Japanese military confiscating freight cars for their own use. That same year, though, the Japanese community founded the Harbin Commercial Exhibition Hall (*Harubin shôhin chinretsukan*) dedicated to stimulating Russo-Japanese trade and incidentally to calming Russo-Japanese tensions. It was headed by Mori Gyoin, who was to become a central figure in the local Japanese community for the next two decades. The Exhibition Hall began that year to publish a monthly magazine, each issue well over 100 pages, featuring all manner of local news, commercial statistics and a variety of human interest stories mostly from Harbin but with occasional reports from Vladivostok and elsewhere in the region. By October 1921 the Japanese Chamber of Commerce of Harbin had 113 members.[25]

These efforts at smoothing over the ethnic frictions in the city may be unique in the Japanese experience on the mainland, despite the fact that visitors to the city noted that Chinese, Japanese and Russians each had their own interests to protect and their own self-defence mechanisms. When the Japanese army withdrew in 1922, many Japanese residents of Vladivostok decided it was no longer safe to live there, and they resettled in Harbin, presumably because it seemed far more secure to them; others moved to the Korean city of Ch'ongjin to the south, but Harbiners did not move in any significant numbers. The decade from the evacuation in 1922 through the Manchurian Incident marked Harbin's Republican Chinese phase. The central government in Beijing and later in Nanjing was never strong enough to exercise control over Harbin, though, and the city thus fell under the sway of the massive Manchurian satrapy of warlord Zhang Zuolin, who turned affairs over to his underling, Zhang Huanxiang. The latter Zhang began a course of action aimed at Sinifying Harbin which met with considerable friction from the leaders of the other ethnic communities.[26]

History has sadly provided far more opportunities for Jews to find themselves forced to leave the country of their birth and migrate to a new setting in which they would carve out communal institutions. Jewish Harbin was a Russian Jewish enclave outside central Russian control. Russian Jews just longed to be left alone; in Harbin they were beyond the reach of the Russian government, and they prospered. Russian Gentiles had come to expect support from the regime; in Harbin they got none and did poorly.

The first generation of Jewish settlers were generally bilingual in Russian and Yiddish, though, as was the case elsewhere, Yiddish soon gave way to Russian monolingualism in civil affairs, though it is not entirely clear when the transition occurred. Most of those interviewed have denied any knowledge of Yiddish – for an assortment of complex reasons usually associated with a sense that Russian was a cosmopolitan, 'European' language while Yiddish was backward and old-fashioned. However, when Israel Cohen travelled through Harbin in 1920 or 1921, carrying the message of the Balfour Declaration around the world, he was asked by the beadle of the Great Synagogue to speak after the morning prayers one Shabbat: 'Reb Yisroel, vet ir efsher a bisl zogn?' (Israel, perhaps you could say a few words?) The ever-present Chinese military guards, fearful of the spread of Bolshevism, forbade the use of Yiddish, insisting on Russian, which they more or less understood and which Cohen did not know.[27] This story also indicates, as many interviewees have noted, that the Chinese, too, learned Russian far more often than Russian-speakers learned any Chinese. In addition, we have a survey dated 1913 on native language which gives 62 per cent Russian and 32 per cent Yiddish for Jewish Harbin; the 1897 Russian census produced a figure of 97 per cent Yiddish for Jews throughout Russia.[28]

A Jewish Nationality Committee was established in Harbin on 16 February 1903, and it elected a 'Spiritual Directorate'. They immediately set to work trying to establish a synagogue; at first, a place was rented while funds were sought among European brethren. In August 1904, W. Levin, Harbin's first rabbi, arrived; earlier that year, in January, a five-kopek communal tax per chicken for kosher slaughtering was levied by the Jewish leaders of the city. While Rabbi Levin departed in 1906, a new synagogue (known as the Main Synagogue) and Jewish primary school were completed in 1907. They soon created a *khevra kadisha* or burial society (like the hundreds of similar associations that exist to this day in Jewish communities through the world), a cemetery, a *mikvah* (ritual bathhouse), an old age home, a Jewish Women's Charity Committee in 1907, a library in 1912 and a Talmud-Torah in 1914. Many of the communal institutions established or expanded by Jews were in response to the wave of *émigrés* that came to the city later during the years of World War I and the Bolshevik revolution. These included a free kitchen, a Jewish hospital, a low-interest credit union, secular and religious schools, and a second synagogue. There were as well Russian secular schools that were not specifically Jewish and which Jewish students attended, such as the Harbin Commercial School.[29]

The foremost figure of Jewish Harbin, like Mori Gyoin for Japanese Harbin, was Abraham Kaufman. Born in Perm, Russia, Kaufman earned his medical degree in Switzerland before coming to Harbin in 1908. There he opened his practice and thereafter was involved in every aspect of communal life until the Soviet army invaded and occupied the city in 1945. Kaufman was promptly deported to the Gulag for the next eleven years. It was he who organised the Jewish hospital and numerous other communal organisations in the city. Not a single memoir about pre-war Harbin is complete without a paean to Dr Kaufman, the community *shtatlan* or intercessor. 'When [a] new group started,' remembered Eve Naftaly, 'he was the president.' He was famed as well as an orator; his moving speech on Kol Nidre night in 1912 about the trial of Mendel Beilis played an important role in his rise to prominence within the community.[30]

Unlike the other ethnic communities of Harbin, Jews did not share a single nationality, and citizenship became a serious issue for many who hoped to leave Harbin some day. Most had been Russian or Polish, but after the Russian Revolution, Soviet citizenship became a touchy issue. Some chose Soviet citizenship as a convenience, not necessarily as a sign of friendship for the new regime. Others retained the citizenship of Poland or Latvia or a host of other eastern European countries. Others opted for citizenship in the short-lived Far Eastern Republic (1919–24), and then found themselves without a country when that state collapsed. Many were simply stateless.

One thing that united the great majority of Jewish Harbiners was Zionism, the new movement that allowed them to take great pride in themselves as Jews, which they had not been allowed to do in Russia proper. Abraham Kaufman had been active in the young movement for a Jewish homeland from the beginning and even attended the 1897 Zionist Congress in Basel. In the long history of the Jewish Exile, Harbin was home to the only sustained Zionist press in the Russian language. The quintessential Zionist cultural and social organisation, Hashomer Hatsair (mostly left-wing), had a branch in Harbin. From within it was also formed Betar, the decidedly right-wing Zionist cultural and sports group.[31] In contemporary Jewish life, it would be unthinkable for these two groups to be so close; in Harbin early in this century, these political distinctions were less well understood and less important than the fact that both were Zionist. The Jewish Bund, a non-communist left-wing labour organisation later decimated by Stalin, also had representatives in Harbin, though its numbers tended to be small.

The quasi-military Betar helped the Jews of Harbin to learn the art (and hence the psychology) of self-defence in the face of antisemitic attack. Most Jews fleeing eastern Europe did not have this experience of relative freedom until they came to North America or Israel. Most of them discovered their capacity for self-defensive organisation only at this point, when the organised antisemitic groups in Harbin could not call on the support of the Russian government. Thus, the Jews of

Harbin effectively acquired this experience earlier in China. Whatever other failings it may have had, Betar did instil pride and the courage to fight back, enabling this group of Jews (unlike many others of their background and generation) to overcome the psychologically (and probably physically) scarring experience of antisemitism.

Thus a full Jewish cultural life was to be found in Harbin, as well as non-Jewish Russian cultural events in which Jews participated: clubs, artistic societies, dance companies, oratory groups, orchestras, and a wild night life of cabarets and revues. Harbin became a regular stop for touring companies, including the Bolshoi Ballet. All the principal Jewish holidays were celebrated in Harbin. Matzah was available every year at Passover, and kosher meat was available all year round. William Zimmerman remembers that, when his family lived in Vladivostok, they travelled regularly to Harbin to purchase kosher meat 'because Harbin is a good Jewish city'. Benjamin Alcone remembers that the Chinese even prepared gefilte fish for the Jewish families in whose homes they worked.[32]

The Jewish press of Harbin covered the full gamut from far right to far left. The great majority of its output was published in Russian. Evsey Domar remembered there being six daily newspapers in Russian in the 1920s. Some of these newspapers and newsletters (twenty, in all, for the years 1920–40), such as *Yevreyskaya zhizn'* (Jewish Life), lasted several decades; others, such as *Diaspora i Palestina* (Diaspora and Palestine), existed for only a few issues. The one Yiddish-language newspaper, *Der vayter mizrekh* (The Far East), represented the voice of social democracy and was sympathetic to what is now the oldest Yiddish newspaper in the world, the *Forverts* (Forward) of New York City. *Der vayter-mizrekh* appeared thrice-weekly for about fourteen months, 1921–22, and is a fascinating newspaper.[33] For a community not noted for the high level of education it offered, Harbin Jewry produced an impressive array of newspapers, periodicals and other publications, and supported a wide range of cultural events.

Conclusion: ethnic integration and assimilation in Harbin

On the whole Japanese memoirists who grew up in Harbin have gone to great lengths to describe how extraordinarily international, cosmopolitan and multicultural Harbin was. They frequently depict family interactions with Chinese and Koreans and even Russians. Sugiyama Kimiko, who has left an extremely valuable memoir of her nearly twenty years in the city, describes the disorientation in 1945 when her family was warned that it was time to go 'home'. She beautifully describes the eerie feeling of having to withdraw to a 'mother' country of which she knew next to nothing. Harbin *was* her home; it was where her parents had met and married and given birth to her.[34] In retrospect, though, especially after the experiences of the 1930s and 1940s, this portrayal is hard to accept in full. Perhaps, given the virtual absence of 'international', 'cosmopolitan' experience in Japanese history, cultural life in Harbin seemed to be the epitome of ethnic interaction to many Japanese.

Japanese did, though, before the 1930s bend to the Russian ways of the city. Many learned Russian, some – such as the famed diplomat, Sugihara Chiune – exceedingly well. There is no reason to believe that they all harboured evil intentions toward the Chinese or welcomed the arrival of the Guandong army *en masse* in the 1930s, despite the orchestrated parade in 1932 along the streets of Harbin. Nonetheless, Japanese born or raised in Harbin and elsewhere in Manchuria – Abe Kôbô, Ozawa Seiji, Etô Shinkichi and Sugihara to name but four – have made an unusually international contribution to wartime and post-war Japanese society and culture, a contribution still not well understood or studied.

Jewish Harbin was much less well integrated into local society. Reading the issues of *Der vayter mizrekh* from 1920–21, one senses the almost complete absence of China. There were countless stories about the numerous Jewish war orphans in eastern Europe that needed homes and news from other East Asian cities about the Jewish communities there. This characteristic resonates with other expatriate presses, such as Shanghai's British *North China Daily News*, which frequently tended to be consumed with stories from 'home'. For local news, it would have been assumed, there were other sources, but in the continual shaping of communal identity the news from the home front played a critical role that could never be ignored.

Russian and eastern European Jews, even more than their co-religionists in western Europe, had lived apart from Gentiles – in part because they were compelled to and in part because they chose to do so. Life in Harbin, largely free of virulent antisemitism until the late 1920s, was more conducive to integration. However, integration never seems to have included the Chinese population that outnumbered all others. As Eve Naftaly put it bluntly, 'every nationality . . . to the great shame of them, treated the Chinese like dirt'.[35] This statement has been repeated in less blunt but equally sharp ways by many others. Few learned more than a handful of Chinese words; few even recognised the everpresence of the Chinese around them, except in business transactions or as their servants. Evsey Domar, a retired professor of economics from the Massachusetts Institute of Technology and an eminent figure in his field, made a fascinating observation during an interview when he admitted that he had never noticed in his twenty years in Harbin and Dairen how attractive young Chinese women were; only on a trip back to China many years later did that awareness dawn on him.[36]

As noted above, Harbin offered pre-World War II Jewish *émigrés* something denied most other Jews not living in North America or Palestine: a safe haven. Beyond the reach of government-sponsored antisemitic attacks, they learned to defend themselves in Harbin. Shanghai would later provide a similar escape for Jews, but it was never as secure, nor was Shanghai ever seen as more than an avenue of escape to somewhere else. In fact, the experience of Jews in Harbin encapsulated in roughly a generation much of the history of the Diaspora. Through the rapidly evolving circumstances of the time, the rise, brief efflorescence and decline of Jewish Harbin was telescoped into a few decades. Thus we find many of the institutions and organisations in Harbin that we find in almost all well articulated Diaspora communities, with the caveat that events unfolded so quickly that the same people often found themselves simultaneously members of two or more organisations, which their counterparts elsewhere would never have dreamed of.

Harbin underwent a complete transformation beginning in the late 1920s and culminating in the Manchurian Incident and the Japanese military seizure of the city in 1931. From that time forward, the Japanese population skyrocketed, increasing by a factor of ten over the first half of the 1930s from a figure of 3,600 in early 1932. From the late 1920s the city experienced a spate of kidnappings – usually supported by extremist elements in the Guandong army working together with extreme right-wing, antisemitic, and fascist elements from the Russian community – of wealthy Chinese and of Jews for huge ransoms. The 1932 case of Semyon Kaspé, the talented young musician, is only the most notorious and grisly of many similar incidents.[37] Following the Kaspé funeral, at which Abraham Kaufman gave the eulogy and denounced the perpetrators of the gruesome crime in no uncertain terms, 'Dr Kaufman ... a most cultured scholar, beloved by Gentiles and Hebrews alike,' reported Amleto Vespa, then allegedly being compelled to work for the Japanese secret police, 'was attacked daily for two months in two Japanese-owned papers. He was attacked on the street by Russians in Japanese employ. My new Chief assigned two Russian thugs to go at night and smash all the windows of the two synagogues.'[38]

The new mood in the city forced the great majority of Jews to flee for cities in China proper to the south, principally to Shanghai, and Tianjin to a lesser extent. When the young American reporter Edgar Snow visited Harbin in 1934, he had the following to say about the changes in the city's atmosphere:

> Harbin, once delightful, today notorious as a place of living death, the worst-governed city in Manchukuo.
> Probably in no other city of the world is life so precarious. Harbin residents, including the 100,000 White and Red Russians, who here bend to the law of the yellow man, risk their lives if they go unarmed anywhere, even in daylight. Holdups, robberies, murders, kidnappings are common occurrences...
> Some of the worst criminals are White Russians. Destitute, broken in spirit, unwilling to return to Russia under the Bolsheviks, unable to earn a living in China *under the Japanese*, they turn to crime, nourished on a diet of drugs, which are sold openly in shops infesting the city... In Harbin alone there are more than 2000 licensed shops for the sale of opium, heroin and morphine.[39]

In the new Harbin, the highly feared Tokumu kikan (Special Services Agency) of the Guandong army used the ethnic enclaves of the city to control it. Thus, according to sources that still need to be corroborated, they hired, for example, impoverished Cossacks to watch over the local Russian community. With the fox now guarding the chicken coop, this policy was virtually guaranteed to make everyone unhappy, except a handful of venal malcontents. As Edgar Snow noted, the Japanese police then sold off contracts to operate brothels and drug houses to local thugs and other unsavoury elements in the various sectors of the city, siphoning off a percentage of the take for themselves. That Japanese military take-over of prostitution in the city probably worked fist-in-glove with the rise of sexual slavery now being documented after a long hiatus. Many Japanese visitors to Harbin in the 1930s were horrified by what they found and lamented the fact that there were whole illicit industries thriving in Harbin which would have been completely illegal in Japan.[40]

Notes

1 Chinese scholars have in the past few decades devised some highly dubious theories for the origins of Harbin which place it in the late eleventh century. This theory empowers the Chinese to claim a long history in Harbin prior to the first Russian settlement of the turn of the century. See Søren Clausen and Stig Thøgerson (trans. and eds), *The Making of a Chinese City: History and Historiography in Harbin* (Armonk NY, M. E. Sharpe, 1995), 3–4, 12–16.
2 David Wolff, 'To the Harbin Station: The Liberal Alternative in Russian Manchuria, 1898–1914,' unpublished MS, introduction.
3 Sugiyama Kimiko, *Harubin monogatari* (Harbin Story) (Tokyo, Hara shobô, 1985),

JAPANESE AND JEWS IN HARBIN

14–15, 18–24, 27–8. She cites a source that claims there were over 200 young women working as prostitutes in Vladivostok already in the mid-1880s.

4 R. K. I. Quested, *'Matey' Imperialists? The Tsarist Russians in Manchuria, 1895–1917* (Hong Kong, University of Hong Kong Press, 1982), 32, 100–1, 129–31; Koshizawa Akira, *Harupin no toshi keikaku* (The City Planning of Harbin) (Tokyo, Sôwasha, 1989), 13–24; Matani Haruji, *Harubin no machi* (The City of Harbin) (Tokyo, published by the author, 1981), 1. There are numerous theories about the origins of the toponym 'Harbin' and none of them is especially persuasive. Five of them are summarised in Sugiyama Kimiko, *Harubin monogatari*, 52–4; a Japanese guidebook of 1924 mentions three but fails to support one over the others: *Harubin no gainen* (The Concept of Harbin) (Harbin, Harubin Nihon shôgyô kaigijo, 1924), 1. The most recent theory, not cited in Sugiyama, comes from Guan Chenghe in his *Haerbin kao* (Study of Harbin). There he argues for a Jurchen origin for 'Harbin' meaning 'honoured'; he also maintains that the city dates from 1097, thus supporting the aforementioned Chinese claim on the city and casting his linguistic theory in an equally dubious light. See Li Shuxia, *Haerbin lishi biannian, 1896–1926* (Historical Chronicle of Harbin, 1896–1926) (Harbin, Difang shi yanjiusuo, 1980), 3.

5 Wolff ('To the Harbin Station', chapter 1) has found a Russian map dated 1898 in which 'Kharbin' is pencilled in at this site.

6 Yokomitsu Riichi, 'Rekishi (Harupin no ki)' (History: A Note on Harbin), *Kaizô* (Construction), 14 (October 1932), 2–17.

7 Sugiyama Kimiko, *Harubin monogatari*, 30–2, 49–50, 56–60. On the impact of the Russo-Japanese War on Harbin see Yanagida Momotarô, *Harubin no zanshô* (Harbin's Afterglow) (Tokyo, Hara shobô, 1986), 97–130. In September 1900, Chiyo's sister Fuino gave birth to a daughter, the first Japanese born in Harbin; the first Jew was born in 1904.

8 For example, there were already nearly 6,000 Japanese in Shanghai at this point in time. In addition to Chapter Nine in this volume see Zhu Yong, 'Shanhai kyoryû Nihonjin shakai to Yokohama Kakyô shakai no hikaku kenkyû' (The Resident Japanese Population of Shanghai and the Chinese Resident Population of Yokohama: a Comparative Study), in *Yokohama to Shanhai, kindai toshi keisei shi hikaku kenkyû* (Yokohama and Shanghai: a Comparative Study of Modern Urban Formation) (Yokohama, Yokohama kaikô shiryô fukyû kyôkai, 1995), 401; Takatsuna Hakubun, 'Seiyôjin no Shanhai, Nihonjin no Shanhai' (Westerners' Shanghai, Japanese Shanghai), in Takahashi Kôsuke and Furumaya Tadao, eds, *Shanhai shi, kyodai toshi no keisei to hitobito no itonami* (History of Shanghai: the Formation of a Great City and the Occupations of its People) (Tokyo, Tôhô shoten, 1995), 120–1.

9 See the interviews with Boris Katz, whose father was a *Nikolaevsky soldat*, and Benjamin Alcone (*né* Alconovitch), whose grandfather was one, in *Bay Area Jews from Harbin, Manchuria*, transcripts and tapes from unpublished interviews held in the Judah Magnes Museum, Berkeley CA, in Russian and English. These interviews are on cassette tapes.

10 Shmuel Rabinovits, 'Hayishuv hayihudi be-Sin, sigsugo vekhurbano' (The Jewish Community in China: its Growth and its Demise), *Gesher*, 2:11 (July 1957), 108–21; David Wolff, 'To the Harbin Station', chapter 3.

11 *Bay Area Jews from Harbin, Manchuria*, interview with Eve Naftaly, 1, 2–4, 19; with Emile Katz, 7–8; with Abe Traig, 1, 3; with Mrs Traig, 5; with Pearl Levin on cassette. The same was true for the family of Leon Lerman, who came to Vladivostok in 1905, later moving to Harbin in 1913 or 1914.

12 David Wolff, 'To the Harbin Station', chapter 2.

13 *Bay Area Jews from Harbin, Manchuria*, interview with Eve Naftaly, 11, 17–18; interviews with Pearl Levin and Sara Ossin on cassette.

14 Higashi Kochiku, 'Urajio yori Harubin e' (From Vladivostok to Harbin), *Taiyô*, 24:9 (July 1918), 184–6; *Manshû nippô*, 18 December 1907, 1; Sugiyama Kimiko, *Harubin monogatari*, 64–8, 75–8, 90–2.

15 *Harubin tsûshin*, 1 February 1923, 3. This report contains a survey of the local population, broken down by neighbourhoods and suburbs of Harbin, and a detailed occupational breakdown. By this time, the gender ratio of men to women had levelled to five-to-four. See Song Shisheng, 'The Brothels of Harbin in the Old Society', in Søren Clausen and Stig Thøgersen, *The Making of a Chinese City*, 104–7. There is a fascinating listing of the businesses owned and operated by Russians in Harbin in *Urajio nippô*, 10 August 1922, 3. With the exception of the brothel business, Russians were engaged in many of the same businesses in that city as the Japanese, albeit in larger numbers.

16 Morisaki Kazue, *Karayukisan* (Karayukisan) (Tokyo, Asahi shinbunsha, 1976), 156–7; Mikiso Hane, *Peasants, Rebels, and Outcastes: The Underside of Modern Japan* (New York, Pantheon Books, 1982), 217–21; Kim Il-myon, *Nihon josei aishi* (The Sad History of Japanese Women) (Tokyo, San'ichi shobô, 1981), 182–267. See also D. C. D. Sissons, 'Karayuki-san: Japanese prostitutes in Australia, 1887-1916', *Historical Studies*, 17:68 (April 1977), 323–41; 17:69 (October 1977), 474–88; Ronald Hyam, *Empire and Sexuality: The British Experience* (Manchester, Manchester University Press, 1990), 142–3.

17 See the appeal to the Japanese government (dated 1 May 1918), signed by the heads of the Japanese Residents' Associations of Vladivostok, Harbin, Iman, Nikolsk and Spassk-Dal'nyi; it cautions the authorities on the use of military force in the region. Reprinted in Shinobu Seizaburô, *Taishô seiji shi* (A Political History of the Taishô Period) (Tokyo, Kawade shobô, 1951), II, 483–4; *Harubin shôhin chinretsukan shûhô*, 2:17 (23 July 1924); *Manshû tokuhon* (Manchurian Reader) (Tokyo, Tô-A keizai chôsakyoku, 1935), 356–8; Kazama Seitarô, 'Kokkyô no machi Harubin tayori' (News from Harbin, City at the Frontier), *Bungei shunjû*, 16:9 (June 1938), 254–5; *Harubin tsûshin*, 6 March 1923, 3. In the 15 March 1923 issue of this last newspaper there is a report from the Japanese Chamber of Commerce of Harbin in the form of a letter (written in *sôrôbun*) to the Diet: 'Taishô jûichinen Nihongun Shiberia teppei ni yoru hisongaisha ni tsugu' (Report on those Injured by the Withdrawal from Siberia by the Japanese Army in 1922), 2.

18 *Bay Area Jews from Harbin, Manchuria*, interviews with Benjamin Alcone and Pearl Levin on cassette tapes; see also interviews with Eve Naftaly, 1, with Abe Traig, 4, with Emile Katz, 9, and with Leon Lerman, on cassette. Interview with Evsey Domar, 5 October 1987.

19 See, for example, a chapter entitled 'Hana' (Noses) in Yamamoto Sanehiko, *Shina* (China) (Tokyo, Kaizôsha, 1936), 163–78.

20 Evsey Domar left Harbin in 1934, spent two years in Dairen, and then proceeded to UCLA to study economics. Interview with Evsey Domar.

21 Yamamoto Sanehiko, 'Harupin' (Harbin), *Kaizô*, 14 (October 1932), 337–40; Kiyozawa Retsu, 'Sekai no jiyû shi, yoru no Harupin' (Free City of the World: Harbin by Night), *Taiyô*, 32:7 (June 1926), 58–62; Higashi Fumio, *Chôsen Manshû Shina*, 39–48; Yamaura Kan'ichi, 'Kokusai ero toshi Harupin: Manshû ero no fukeizai' (International City of Eros, Harbin: The Wastefulness of Manchurian Eros), *Keizai ôrai* (Economic changes), 6 (October 1931), 175, 177.

22 Kobayashi Masayuki, *Yudayajin: sono rekishizô o motomete* (The Jews: in Search of their Historical Image) (Tokyo, Seikô shobô, 1977), 238–41, 250–9; Miyazawa Masanori, *Zôho Yudayajin ronkô: Nihon ni okeru rongi no tsuiseki* (Studies of the Jews, Expanded: In Pursuit of Japanese Debates) (Tokyo, Shinsensha, 1982), 36–8, 41–59, 71, 81; Sugita Rokuichi, *Isuraeru shi zakkô* (Studies in the History of Israel) (Tokyo, Kyôbunkan, 1964), 370.

23 Sugiyama Kimiko, *Harubin monogatari*, 66–7, 78, 116–17; Gotô Shinkichi, 'Harubin Nihon shôgakkô' (The Japanese Elementary School of Harbin), in Gotô Shinkichi, ed., *Harubin no omoide* (Memories of Harbin) (Kyoto, Kyôto Harubin kai, 1973), 68–82; Sugiyama Kimiko, 'Harubin no ki: watakushi ga doko de mita koto, kangaeta koto' (Notes on Harbin: Where I saw Things and thought Things), *Manshû to Nihonjin*, 7 (November 1979), 8.

JAPANESE AND JEWS IN HARBIN

24 Yanagida Momotarô, *Harubin no zanshô*, 234.
25 Sugiyama Kimiko, *Harubin monogatari*, 93–5, 97, 106, 111, 113–14; *Harubin tsûshin*, 17 March 1923, 3, 18 March 1923, 2; Yamamoto Sanehiko, 'Harupin', 357. A June 1922 document marked 'secret' in the Gaimushô (Japanese Foreign Ministry) Archives (JFMA) complained that Japanese in Manchuria had changed their clothing in accordance with the conditions of life and work in the region, which the author regarded as potentially deleterious to long-term planning, and the Japanese 'treat locals like slaves'. See Miyahara Tamihei, 'Man-Mô bunka senden kôenkai ni kansuru ken' (On the Symposium for Manchurian and Mongolian Culture), No. 4 in the series 'Hôjin no zai-Man seikatsu' (Life in Manchuria for the Japanese), JFMA, 2631 (June 1922).
26 Higashi Kochiku, 'Urajio yori Harubin e', 189; Sugiyama Kimiko, *Harubin monogatari*, 114–15. Higashi Fumio (*Chôsen Manshû Shina*, 46) reported that relations between young Japanese and young Russians were excellent, with some intermarriage, but this strikes me as somewhat exaggerated or propagandistic. His book was published in 1940. More typical was Yamamoto Sanehiko's comment ('Harupin', 346): 'Who must bear responsibility for the crime of turning Harbin into a street of flirtatiousness?' The White Russians, of course. 'All their great pride in the glories of the Tsarist era they now discard in the gutters of Harbin. They keep hordes of degenerate women, and they have transformed it [Harbin] into a prominent boil on the face of the earth.' Stunning comment, considering that it was the Japanese who pioneered prostitution in Harbin.
27 Israel Cohen, *The Journey of a Jewish Traveller* (London, Bodley Head, 1925), 171. Cohen offered to speak in Hebrew, but none of the Harbiners (Chinese or Jewish) could understand the language; he settled on English, which was then translated into Russian. (Yiddish romanisation corrected to conform with the standard transcription system.)
28 See David Wolff, 'To the Harbin Station', chapter 3.
29 Evsey Domar, interview; Tsvia Shickman-Bowman, 'The History of Harbin Jewish Community, 1898–1931,' MS; Herman Dicker, *Wanderers and Settlers in the Far East: A Century of Jewish Life in China and Japan* (New York, Twayne Publishers, 1962), 21–33; David Wolff, 'To the Harbin Station', chapter 3.
30 Eve Naftaly, interview, 68, 84; Pearl Levin, interview on cassette; Evsey Domar, interview; Herman Dicker, *Wanderers and Settlers in the Far East*, 24, 26–7; David Wolff, 'To the Harbin Station', chapter 3.
31 William Zimmerman remembered his mother collecting money for Palestine in the 1910s: interview, 26; Leon Lerman also remembered the importance of Zionist activities in Harbin: interview on cassette; Sara Ossin also recalled how important Betar was in Harbin: interview on cassette.
32 Herman Dicker, *Wanderers and Settlers in the Far East*, 24–9; William Zimmerman, interview, 15; Eve Naftaly, interview, 25, 33–5; Benjamin Alcone, interview on cassette.
33 Evsey Domar, interview; Rudolph Lowenthal, *The Religious Periodical Press in China* (Beijing, Synodal Commission in China, 1940). *Der vayter-mizrekh* ran a large congratulatory notice for the *Forverts* on the latter's twenty-fifth anniversary in 1922.
34 Sugiyama Kimiko, *Harubin monogatari*, 3–6, 9, 12–13, 15–16, 18–19; see also Kaetsu Mikio, *Nanasen mei no Harupin dasshutsu* (Seven Thousand who Escaped from Harbin) (Tokyo, published by the author, 1971). More recently similar works of Japanese caught at the end of the war or later seeking their 'roots' in Harbin have been published; see, for example, Watanabe Ichie, *Harubin kaikikô* (Return Voyage to Harbin) (Tokyo, Asahi shinbunsha, 1996); Kôno Fumie, *Harubin no sora: Nit-Chû no sokoku o motsu shô Nihonjin no kunan* (The Harbin Sky: Sufferings of a Little Japanese who had both China and Japan as Homelands) (Tokyo, On Times, 1996).
35 Eve Naftaly, interview, 20.

36 Evsey Domar, interview. Professor Domar died on 1 April 1997: see Boris Bresler and Gregory Grossman, 'Evsey Domar: In Memoriam', *Bulleten' Igud Yotsei Sin* (English Supplement), 350 (June–July 1997), 30–1.
37 John Stephan, *The Russian Fascists: Tragedy and Farce in Exile, 1925–1945* (New York, Harper & Row, 1978); Amleto Vespa, *Secret Agent of Japan* (Garden City NY, Garden City Publishing, 1941), 78–80, 89, 196, 198–203, 205–18, 238–9, 253, 272.
38 Vespa, *Secret Agent*, 241. Amleto Vespa was an Italian sympathiser of Mussolini, married to a Chinese woman, and working for Zhang Zuolin; he was compelled by threats to his family to work for the Japanese. See also *Bay Area Jews from Harbin, Manchuria*, interviews with Eve Naftaly (76, 78–9), Emile Katz (9, 14), and Sara Ossin (unpaginated). Mrs Ossin: 'The Japanese were indescribably cruel.'
39 Edgar Snow, 'Japan Builds a New Colony', *Saturday Evening Post*, 206 (24 February 1934), 81, 84, emphasis added.
40 Sugiyama Kimiko, *Harubin monogatari*, 136–7; Vespa, *Secret Agent*, 33–5, 51, 86. Vespa claims that by 1936 there were 172 brothels, 56 opium dens, and 194 licensed narcotics shops in Harbin alone, and that in Heilongjiang and Jilin provinces there were 550 licensed houses of prostitution with 70,000 girls servicing customers (Vespa, *Secret Agent*, 102). The Harbin figures, although high, are considerably lower than those proffered by Snow.

CHAPTER SEVEN

Japanese colonial citizenship in treaty port China: the location of Koreans and Taiwanese in the imperial order
Barbara J. Brooks

Recent scholarship on the culture of colonialism has brought a new focus on understanding the dynamics of coloniser and colonised through examination of issues of citizenship. Ann Stoler's work, for example, has illustrated the porous boundary between European colonisers and colonised natives in several studies of citizenship debates for mixed-blood individuals in such places as Java and Indochina in the first half of the twentieth century.[1] The French empire, with its assimilationist mission and cultural notions of 'Frenchness', stood out for cultural qualifications of citizenship that were applied to judge such mixed-blood cases. For many modern empires historians have failed to note or account for the changes in individual status that accompanied movements of colonised subjects from colony to metropole. In short, colonial citizenship across differing imperial realms can be used as one index of the constructions of empires and nations that can facilitate understanding both of emerging identities – national, bourgeois, subaltern – and of imperial purposes. In the case of the Japanese empire, an understanding of the status of its colonial citizens under extraterritoriality in China illuminates many facets of imperialism in East Asia. This chapter focuses primarily on Japan's imperialist advantages that resulted from the anomalous position of its colonised subjects, who, by moving a short distance into treaty port China, also moved into the lower and contradictory ranks of the Great Power colonisers.

The categorisation and instrumental use of different types of colonial citizenship in the Japanese empire is quite striking. Recent scholarship has shattered the myth of pre-war Japan as a 'homogeneous' nation, pointing in particular to Japan's internal colonisations of the Ainu and the Okinawans, processes that preceded the acquisition of the formal colonies of Taiwan in 1895 and Korea in 1910.[2] While issues of citizenship for people moving between both 'internal' and external colonies and the Japanese metropole were also complex, after 1895 Japan's status as a Great Power with regard to China also opened up new vistas for countless of her colonial citizens who ventured to the north and south of China to seek their fortunes while benefiting from the exploitative system of extraterritoriality. Scholarship to date has begun to probe the Japanese colonial or treaty port community in China, but very little has illuminated the presence of the far greater number of Japan's colonial citizens (who were registered in the *gaichi koseki* or 'outer family registration system' and enjoyed extraterritorial protection in China) and their contribution as well as their resistance to Japanese imperialism.[3] From the perspective of China, the contributions of Koreans and *sekimin* ('registered people', not all of them from Taiwan: there were also southern Chinese families who elected Japanese citizenship on their own initiative) to Japanese imperialism far outweighed their resistance to it through most of the prewar period.

Sekimin in treaty port China

The 1895 Treaty of Shimonoseki not only established the people of Taiwan as subjects of the Japanese empire; the Japanese interpretation of it offered the option of citizenship to large numbers of Fujian and Chaozhou Chinese resident on the mainland itself. The treaty stipulated that Chinese residents of Taiwan would become Japanese citizens (obtain *gaichi kokuseki*) at the Japanese government's discretion if they had not sold their property and left the colony within two years of the signing of the treaty – by May 1897. About 4,500 people (0.2 per cent of Taiwan's population) did have the resources and will to leave, but the vast majority, of course, did not. In addition, the Japanese authorities, eager to enlist as many Han Chinese as citizens as possible, permitted many categories of people residing on the mainland far past the May 1897 deadline to apply for and receive citizenship (they became termed *Taiwan sekimin*). The official reasoning was that during the military disturbances of the pacification many Taiwanese had temporarily sought safety on the mainland or were simply abroad, perhaps visiting relatives on the mainland. In practice, as one Japanese consul in Amoy (Xiamen) wrote in 1926, 'viewed from a policy basis, we consciously facilitated Chinese in obtaining *Taiseki* status,' and this created a new class of 'Amoy *sekimin*', Fujianese individuals who had never sojourned in Taiwan.[4] He added that many wealthy citizens of Amoy had sought such status, given the advantages of imperial citizenship under extraterritoriality. Most commonly, Japanese authorities referred to both Taiwanese who left Taiwan for the treaty ports of China and other Chinese who had simply registered for Japanese citizenship as *sekimin* or 'people with Japanese citizenship (*kokuseki*)'. Consuls in south China, especially in the port cities of Amoy, Shantou and Fuzhou, found their time taken up with the care of this complex community.[5]

Official figures for the population of *sekimin* in China vastly underestimate their true presence, and mainly reflect the individuals who registered in the *Taiwan kôkai* (Taiwan civic associations) of southern Chinese cities or complied with the passport regulations implemented by the Taiwan Sôtokufu (colonial government) from 1907. Under these regulations, *sekimin* sailing from Taiwan had to obtain passports that would be deposited with the appropriate Japanese consul at their destination city in China, although if they entered China from a Japanese port, they, like *naichi* (homeland) Japanese, might enter China without papers. Official statistics for Amoy, by far the largest official community, show steadily increasing numbers: 1917, 2,883; 1920, 3,765; 1926, 6,832; 1933, 9,000; 1937, 10,217.[6] Wakabayashi Masahiro, a noted scholar of Taiwanese history, however, judges these as only partial statistics for a community that especially swelled after the Manchurian Incident. For 1935 to 1936, he estimates, a community of about 30,000 *sekimin* contributed to Amoy's reputation as the 'Shenyang of southern China', a term that became widespread in the Chinese press in the 1930s.[7]

If Amoy came to be seen as the 'Shenyang of south China' the term was also an indication of popular Chinese attitudes towards Chinese who held *sekimin* status. Such terms as *Taiwan daigou* ('Taiwan running dogs' [of Japanese imperialism]) became commonplace in southern China and only increased across the wartime period. The larger issue of Taiwanese collaboration with Japanese wartime regimes across China and South East Asia has troubled historians from Taiwan as they have ventured to understand a Taiwanese diaspora during the period of the Japanese empire.[8] While there were, in fact, many *sekimin* who were conscious agents of Japanese imperialism, far more either wanted the individual benefits of extraterritoriality or could not have changed their status in the eyes of the Japanese authorities if they had so chosen. Foreign Ministry archive files today attest to the watchfulness of the Japanese authorities over their colonial subjects in China and their insistence that colonial citizens not be permitted to naturalise in China or elsewhere.[9] Regardless of the intent of the individual *sekimin*, Japanese policy (often opposed by consuls, however) sought to use them and their numbers as important components of economic, cultural and social imperialism in China.

Many *sekimin* had no fixed jobs or were engaged in illicit activities under the umbrella of extraterritoriality. In 1926 Amoy consul Inoue reported that only half the city's *sekimin* residents had 'proper professions'; the other half were students or engaged in any number of illicit businesses, but especially the operation of brothels and opium dens (smoking establishments) or other aspects of the opium business. They were often running the businesses in name only; the real financing came from rich Chinese bosses who had no extraterritorial protection.[10] As Fujian was not far from the rich opium-producing sites of southern China, there was extensive involvement of *sekimin* opium traffickers with Chinese bosses and warlords.[11] This involvement fits the pattern of Japanese complicity in opium traffic throughout the pre-war period and is strikingly similar to the northern Chinese case of Korean involvement in opium. In oral interviews Wakabayashi even discovered that informants believed that pre-war Japanese authorities in Taiwan sent half the convicted criminals in the colony to penal servitude on an isolated island and the other half to freedom 'on the opposite bank' (*taian*) in China.[12] *Sekimin* engaged in many other types of shady or illicit activities. Aside from the *Taiwan kôkai*, Inoue also noted the importance of the 'Restaurant Union' (*ryôriya kumiai*), established in 1923, that served to represent some ninety entertainment establishments employing some 220 *sekimin* prostitutes under the extraterritorial umbrella. He added that *sekimin* prostitutes were not subject to the heavy taxes or fines levied by Chinese authorities and that this had contributed to the precipitous decline of Chinese and the rise of *sekimin* establishments now being protested by Amoy Chinese leaders. *Sekimin* 'restaurants' were more flourishing every day; the sex workers they employed were said to be sending several thousand yen per month back to their homes in Taiwan.[13]

But the perception that all *sekimin* were 'running dogs' or otherwise shiftless petty criminals was misleading. Many of Amoy's most powerful Chinese entrepreneurs themselves took advantage of 'flexible citizenship' to get themselves listed as *sekimin* to enjoy business and other advantages.[14] Some of their families had become powerful overseas Chinese families with members scattered throughout South East Asia and even San Francisco. Second generation members gained professional credentials in Taiwan and Japan and joined the growing professional community of doctors and lawyers in Fujian, in which *sekimin* stood out in their numbers. In 1930, Consul Terajima Kôbun reported that about twenty *sekimin* doctors, graduates of Taipei Medical School, were authorised to practise around Amoy, but there was a growing problem with falsification of credentials that also attested to the good reputation of *sekimin* doctors. Of 'Japanese' businesses registered at the consulate, twenty-nine households were *naichi* Japanese, 606 households were *sekimin* and one was Korean. He added that many of the *sekimin* businesses were really so-called 'joint (*goben*) ventures' using the *sekimin* partner as a legal front. Additionally, lawyers trained in Taiwan were greatly on the rise and had a reputation for representing *naichi* Japanese clients in consular and Chinese courts.[15]

In 1930, Consul Terajima, in response to a question about possible abolition of consular courts and extraterritoriality, wrote a lengthy report on the *sekimin* community of at least 7,000 in his jurisdiction. These households joined the Taiwan Association (*Taiwan kôkai*), an organisation devoted to aiding the community with some similarity to the *Nihonjinkai* or Japanese residents' associations of other treaty port settlements. Amoy *sekimin*, however, lived in mixed residence with Chinese; they displayed on their houses a plaque indicating their membership of the Taiwan Association (*kôkai kaiinshô*). The plaque asserted their rights of extraterritoriality and served, for example, to prohibit Chinese law enforcers from entering the premises. Terajima, however, asserted that recently more and more Chinese in Amoy fabricated this informal proof of national status to benefit from such extraterritorial immunities. He went on to list in detail many other legal complications that had arisen between the consulate and the Chinese authorities, including Chinese reluctance to remand *sekimin* when they did commit a crime and were arrested by Chinese authorities. Recently unusual cases involving traffic accidents where professional drivers revealed their *sekimin* status (they were actually Taiwanese who had learned to drive in Taiwan) and sought the jurisdiction of the consular court plagued his dockets. Even bicycles were a problem: they might be registered in a *sekimin* name but actually ridden by Chinese criminals armed with guns. Amoy civic authorities had also taken to demanding more and more Japanese financial contributions to the entire city's burgeoning modern infrastructure, with so many *sekimin* residents of great wealth and extensive settlement. While Terajima was clearly out of his depth in adjudicating such cases with his consular court and consular police staff, he nevertheless recommended only gradual abolition of extraterritoriality because of the enormous effect it would have on his diverse community.[16]

Despite Terajima's misgivings about the consular court burden, extraterritoriality was not given up in south China or elsewhere; rather, its uses for the knitting together of Taiwan and southern China under increasing Japanese influence continued. This is nowhere more evident than in the extensive records of consular meetings in south

China that also included many representatives of the Taiwan government-general. These meetings discussed greater facilitation of Taiwan-based investment and entrepreneurial expansion in south China, control over several Chinese-language newspapers and schools financed by the Taiwanese government-general and other details of economic, cultural and even political influence.[17] Influential *sekimin* in Amoy also collaborated in nefarious schemes proposed by such Japanese agents as members of the Manchurian-based Kantô army; in 1932 one *sekimin* provocateur murdered a local *naichi* Japanese schoolmaster in the attempt to provoke an incident that could justify the despatch of Japanese troops to Fujian. Arrested, he was sent to Taiwan for trial and sentencing, but wound up in a high position in the Foreign Ministry of the Manchukuo government.

As mentioned above, the Japanese authorities in principal refused to allow Taiwanese *sekimin* to claim Chinese citizenship. In 1928 Qingdao consul Kawai Tatsuo reported his grave concern that a Taiwanese who had attended Waseda was now employed in the Nationalist Chinese government (as a Chinese national) and had been appointed to head the Zhifu Customs Office.[18] Such surveillance of *sekimin*, who more often acted as Japanese sub-imperialists, was slight, however, compared with the vigilance of Japanese authorities in studying the empire's Korean subjects.

Koreans in treaty port China

The period of the Japanese occupation of Korea witnessed a diaspora of Koreans – to Manchuria, Japan proper, Sakhalin, the Siberian maritime provinces and the north of China – on a scale unprecedented in Asia.[19] By 1944 up to 11·6 per cent of Koreans resided outside Korea, with approximately 2 million in China's north-east. Unquestionably, changes brought on by the Japanese colonial regime in Korea spurred on the increasing outmigration from rural villages. In 1931 the eminent Japanese social scientist Amano Motonosuke, famous for his village studies in China, identified the primary cause of Korean migration as the impoverishment of farmers resulting from the introduction of capitalist practices, including laws enforcing ownership of land, registration of uncultivated or public terrain, and increasing concentration of ownership in the hands of large landlords and Japanese development companies such as the Oriental Development Company (Tôyô Takushoku Kaisha).[20] In the late 1920s, as Japan sought to close off the passage by ship from Pusan of poor Koreans seeking labour in the metropole, the Korean colonial government increasingly came to rely on northward migration to help solve socio-economic distress, and Koreans from the south became more numerous in Manchuria.[21]

During the nineteenth century Manchu restrictions on migration northward relaxed and Korean and Chinese migration into the Manchurian region increased. In the 1880s the Korean and Chinese governments both took measures to open up the border region on the Manchurian side to cultivation and settlement by Korean farmers forced to leave their villages because of increasing pressures on their land. Still, by 1904 the estimated Korean population in Manchuria was 78,000.[22] Conservative Gaimushô estimates of the Korean population indicate: for 1912, 238,403; for 1920, 488,656; for 1925, 513,973; for 1931, 629,000. The Foreign Ministry spokesman issuing these figures in 1932 added that they did not include large numbers of Koreans living in the interior; '1,000,000 at least' was his total figure for Koreans in Manchuria and Mongolia in 1931.[23]

Up to half the Korean population in Manchuria lived north of the Tumen river in the south-east corner of Jilin province, an area known as Jiandao (Kanto in Japanese, today known as Yanbian in Chinese). This borderland region on the edges of China, Korea and Russia was not considered part of the south Manchurian region, where after 1905 Japanese enjoyed a wider range of rights and privileges than in other areas of China proper. Nevertheless, as it was a place where up to 80 per cent of the population was Korean, Japan claimed the right to station consular police in scattered outposts (*hashutsujo*) in the area to 'protect' the community. These police numbered at least 400 on the eve of the Manchurian Incident.

The 'Jiandao problem' (*Kanto mondai*) was perhaps the most outstanding diplomatic issue between China and Japan down to 1931. A series of Sino-Japanese treaties regarding Jiandao indicate the continuing controversy between both governments regarding the Koreans who lived there. In 1909 the Japanese seemed to concede limited Chinese jurisdiction over Korean residents; in 1915 the Twenty-one Demands reversed this and insisted on their status as Japanese with the full range of new rights and privileges then enumerated; and in 1925 the Mitsuya Agreement laid out conditions under which both Japanese and Chinese authorities would pursue and apprehend Korean partisans.

While the 1920s witnessed an increasing discourse of fear and prejudice towards Koreans, there was no lessening in the competing Japanese discourse of inclusion.[24] Even before annexation, a specific strand of Pan-Asian thinking and scholarship asserted the common ancestry and many common features of Japanese and Koreans through examination of cultural attributes such as geographical place names, the structural similaries of the two languages, and shared historical experiences. This type of view, for example, saw the annexation of Korea in 1910 as the return of a 'branch family' to the 'main family'.[25] Such scholarly efforts in linguistics and classic textual study continued through the 1920s and contributed to a popular Japanese discourse of cultural similarity regarding Koreans that held particular meaning in the context of Manchuria.

In Manchuria, the outstanding and widely recognised affinity of Korean and Japanese culture was wet rice agriculture. Japanese officials reported that 90 per cent of Korean occupations in Manchuria were agricultural, and of those 30 per cent were in their field of special talent (tokui), wet rice farming: some 51,106 ha in all of Manchuria in 1923.[26] Other sources cite a nearly threefold increase in rice production in Manchuria between 1915 and 1930.[27] In 1921 a Fengtian consul-general wrote:

> Wet rice cultivation is a native-born skill for the Korean farmer. Their methods are natural and rudimentary either for large-scale or individual farming. They are satisfied to work every hectare, no matter how poor the land may seem. Moreover, in no time at all they transform even the vacant prairie lots on to which they move into rice paddies, reaping unimaginable harvests from such wild, abandoned, weed-infested land.[28]

Japanese officials stressed that in the 1860s Korean settlers had first brought this unrivalled skill, which claimed unused land, to the north of China, and documented the growth of rice paddies from that time.[29] While Japanese writers often hoped for more Japanese immigration to expand wet rice cultivation, it was recognised that almost all of this 'Japanese' contribution to life in Manchuria was in Korean hands. In 1922 Hori Isamu, the head of the Fengtian branch of the Oriental Development Company, emphasised the future importance of Manchurian wet rice cultivation to solve Japan's domestic shortage of rice production.[30] Indeed, by 1930 Japan imported about 50 per cent of the rice grown in Manchuria.[31]

Chinese farmers were said to have welcomed Korean settlers for their wet rice cultivating techniques until they, too, began to mimic this style of farming and sometimes demand the return of their land. In fact, Korean encroachment on these lands was often very complicated, especially the patterns of land leasing from Chinese landlords. Korean settlers also built irrigation networks that deprived neighbouring Chinese farmers of water, culminating in communal conflicts over land and water rights that grew worse after 1927.[32] The most notorious case was the Wanbaoshan Incident of the summer of 1931, which resulted in widespread rioting inside Korea against resident Chinese, causing injury, loss of life and property to that ethnic minority. Because only Chinese citizens could own land, a long-standing dispute between China and Japan over the rights of Korean settlers to naturalise simmered throughout the 1920s.

From at least the beginning of Japan's Korean protectorate the Japanese government began to make clear its position on Korean citizenship. In the wake of changes in Seoul, the Russian legation recalled one of their ethnic Korean officials who had served as official interpreter. This man owned land in the vicinity of the new government-general that was confiscated along with other Korean-held land by the Japanese army for its use. Russian officials protested at this action and demanded the return of the land. In 1907 the acting consul-general denied the request, insisting that 'a Korean subject naturalised in any foreign state without permission of the Korean government is not recognised by the latter as a foreigner'. The Russian consul-general persisted, insisting that the individual in question was born and grew up in Russia; his parents were naturalised. The Japanese response elaborated:

> [A] state has the perfect right of deciding whether or not its subjects shall lose their original nationality when they have acquired citizenship in a foreign country. It is true that no law or ordinance has yet been established in Korea regulating naturalisation of the Korean subjects in other states, but it may be observed that the inherent authority of a government can in no wise be affected by the non-existence of a law or ordinance governing such matters... As his parents' government's permission has neither been applied for nor given, it naturally follows that they still remain Korean subjects so far as the authority of the Korean government extends.[33]

After annexation officials extended the same logic to many cases that claimed ethnic Koreans as Japanese subjects, even if their parents or grandparents had left Korea during Yi dynasty times. In criminal cases on Chinese soil, records demonstrate Japanese refusal to recognise even the official papers of ethnic Koreans claiming Chinese or Russian citizenship. They also manipulated rules of extraterritorial jurisdiction to carry out swift retribution for some Korean political assassins. For example, An Changgun, the assassin of Itô Hirobumi in Harbin in 1910, was quickly tried and executed in the leased territory of the Kantôshû, bypassing Foreign Ministry jurisdiction that would have been more liberal. In another case in Shanghai in 1932, Legation Minister Shigemitsu Mamoru himself laid out the complicated case for the Japanese citizenship of an ethnic Korean criminal with a provenance far removed from Korean soil.[34] The individual in question was the radical, Yun Bong-gil, who carried out the infamous assassination attempt of 29 April 1932, when a bomb exploded on the dais at a military review in Hongkew Park. Shigemitsu lost a leg in this incident. Yun, who was born in Jiandao, was executed by the Japanese military on 19 December. Japanese consular officials, attempting to bring order to treaty port society, could thus apply this official position to prevent Korean and Taiwanese suspects from claiming alternative nationalities, a major 'weapon of resistance' to legal adjudication.[35]

In other instances, however, Japanese privileges of extraterritoriality worked to protect Koreans engaged in illicit activities from prosecution under Chinese law. Chinese fears of the large numbers of Korean immigrants and of their involvement in smuggling and opium production and trafficking led them early on to protest that Korean immigrants were simply the 'vanguard of Japanese penetration and absorption of Manchuria'.[36] In international meetings Chinese and Korean delegates protested that, because Korean immigrants were regarded as Japanese citizens, their widespread presence invited Japanese intervention in China's hinterlands: 'The charge is that, wherever Koreans go, Japanese consular police follow them.'[37] In a memoir of these years, one consul-general remarked that 'the opinion was that our economic development of Manchuria was to proceed with Koreans as the basis'.[38] Immigration from the metropole was insubstantial, but as Japanese subjects, often labelled 'compatriots' (*dôhô*) in the press, Koreans were touted for proving Japan's stake in settling Manchuria. In 1928, although the Japanese (*naichi*) residents in Manchuria did not exceed 200,000 and many were in government service, in a speech before the Diet, Prime Minister Tanaka Giichi stated that

> because we now have over one million Japanese subjects residing in Manchuria, we have important rights and interests in this region... We are resolute to prevent any event which would hurt our important rights and interests.[39]

Clearly the rhetoric of inclusion served the purposes of Japanese expansionists.

Significant Korean involvement in the illicit economic penetration of Manchuria and China continued through the pre-war period. Cultivation of opium poppies in Manchuria began as late as 1907, but the Chôsen Sôtokufu estimate for opium production in 1921 was 22,500 *jin*, and:

The special characteristics of Korean agriculture, wet rice farming and cultivation of poppies, are more and more evident, and it is not too much to say that the market produce of these two great crops accounts for almost all of the Korean commercial production.[40]

Through the late 1910s many Korean cultivators switched to raising poppies as a sole crop. During the harvest Korean labourers headed to the hills for seasonal wages, and in areas such as those near the Russian border or the railways, where the traffic in refined opium flourished, living standards rose and secondary businesses – tea houses, *reimenya* (noodle shops), inns, gambling and drinking establishments – sprang up. While on the Manchurian side Chinese bosses were involved in opium smuggling, across the Russian border 30,000 Koreans were thought to be engaged in the opium business.[41] In 1923 Yamazaki Masao, a traveller to Harbin in northern Manchuria, was struck by the wealth, education and Russian cultural attributes (even the offering of Russian tea with a lump of sugar) of Korean merchant families there who were engaged in the opium business. His shock at the loss of their Korean culture – some knew no Korean language and seemingly had no recollection of their homeland – echoed the concerns of Japanese proprietary claims as to the 'common culture' of Japan and Korea.[42]

In such statements diverse Japanese voices indicated an embracing, adjunct role in the project of imperialism for Korean immigrants to Manchuria, welcoming their numbers and their cultural and economic influences. Koreans leaving their homeland, where the colonial ordinances were very restrictive, found advantages derived from Japan's official policies of inclusion. In the metropole they had better access to higher education and jobs, and after 1925 they could even vote if they met residential and literacy requirements. In the 1930s some Koreans even achieved election to public office in Japan. In Manchuria before 1931 most of their advantages derived from extraterritoriality. The discourse of inclusion there was ambivalent and often instrumental. A South Manchurian Railway report of 1936 even admitted that, prior to the Manchurian Incident, claims to protection over Koreans had been a pretext for increasing Japan's police and military presence in Manchuria.[43] In fact, Japanese protection and state services for Koreans were far from adequate. When it suited Japanese powerholders to categorise Koreans as citizens, they did so, but the shifting boundary of that inclusiveness often placed Korean residents in Manchuria in grave danger. In the same way, the situation of the other *dôhô* (compatriots), the *sekimin* of southern China, grew just as dangerous.

Conclusion

This chapter has distorted the nature of these communities of colonial citizens in painting Koreans and *sekimin* primarily as witting and unwitting Japanese sub-imperialists. Both communities had substantial numbers of resisters to Japanese rule, although the Korean partisans are far better known. In 1926 Amoy consul Inoue recounted the 'common knowledge' that 'Koreans are characterised by their founding of a rebel government and their anti-Japanese actions, while *sekimin* merely plot to increase their individual profits from under the shadow of the Japanese imperial flag' but warned that while *sekimin* still came to the consulate to participate enthusiastically in imperial holiday rituals or the viewing of naval exercises, increasingly anti-colonial ideas had spread from Taiwan to the *sekimin* community in China, and *sekimin* students and others were also stirred by the new nationalism of the Guomindang.[44]

Consular reports from treaty port China tend to confirm the quotidian existence of both Korean and *sekimin* communities during times of relative peace and stability. The majority of members of both groups were pursuing their livelihoods as best they could; many had come to treaty port China seeking a better life than could be had in their Japanese-held homelands.

What is striking here is that Japanese policy across the time consistently sought to manipulate the citizenship of these individuals to effect far-reaching imperialist goals in China. The Treaty of Shimonoseki itself seems designed to aid the Japanese to build up the presence of colonial citizens in southern China, and Japanese officials pushed its interpretation to the limit. Refusing to permit colonials to naturalise as Chinese served many imperialist purposes: it increased 'Japanese' numbers at the same time as it assured Japanese consular or police authorities the right to apprehend and imprison dissidents. In Fujian, where the Taiwanese colonial government also gave financial aid to schools and cultural organisations, a new class of modern *sekimin* professionals, trained in Taiwan and Japan, contributed to a 'positive' Japanese influence of modernity. After the Manchurian Incident, increasing numbers of professional or bourgeois Koreans joined in this type of imperialism in Manchukuo.[45]

But these colonial citizens did not enjoy the protection that Japanese treaty port authorities extended to *naichi* Japanese. Their contradictory location in the Japanese order became more than apparent during violence and crisis points in China. During the Manchurian Incident, Chinese troops under Zhang Xueliang's command slaughtered some 7,000 settled agricultural Koreans outside the South Manchurian Railway corridor as they fled from arriving Japanese troops.⁴⁶ Koreans were the expendable and often despised subjects who imperialist schemers hoped would arouse tensions in the Chinese hinterland, giving rise to justification for Japanese military actions.

Sekimin fared no better after the beginning of the Sino-Japanese War in 1937. First, Amoy fell to Chinese troops. Despite the urging of Japanese consular authorities, many *sekimin* refused to evacuate. Nationalist troops entering the city rounded up and summarily shot many of these *Hanjian* (Han traitors); among them were a prominent *sekimin* businessman and his son, who was only home on a brief visit from engineering school in Tokyo. The Fujian provincial government confiscated other *sekimin* property and placed survivors in an internment camp under terrible conditions before Japanese re-entered the city the following year. Under Japanese wartime occupation *sekimin* numbers in Amoy increased again and with it the Chinese perception that they were all collaborators. After the war, most tellingly, such perceptions of Taiwanese and *sekimin* collaborators helped fuel the violence of the 1947 'February 28' incident, when Nationalist troops slaughtered thousands of well-placed Taiwanese on the island of Taiwan itself.⁴⁷

Both Japanese colonial citizen communities of Koreans and *sekimin* were a dynamic presence in Chinese treaty port communities. Overlooking their stories has contributed to gaps in our understanding of Japan's further expansion of the extraterritorial system for national benefit. While many individual Koreans or Taiwanese resembled the refugees who made up treaty port China's Jewish or other ethnic communities, their collective presence contributed to the extension of the Japanese imperial community into China, notably also into its hinterlands. During the wartime period Japan actually stepped up its embrace of these colonial citizens in *kōminka* (imperialisation) campaigns and eventually put them under conscription (a true hallmark of Japanese citizenship). Japan planned to extend *naichi* status to Korea and Taiwan, demonstrating this in 1942 when the two colonies were placed under Home Ministry supervision. Bureaucrats were moving to merge the *gaichi* and *naichi* registers as the war ended, to grant Koreans and Taiwanese rights and duties indistinguishable from *naichi* Japanese. As the war worsened for Japan, planners realised more than ever that the empire needed to further smooth out the contradictions of colonial citizenship, in order to obtain now desperately needed support from the colonised. What had proved to have worked well might be strengthened to avert the coming defeat. This final trend only underscores the importance of Japan's manipulation of colonial subjects for the purposes of empire; extraterritoriality in China provided a rich and complex site for such manipulation.

Notes

1. Ann Laura Stoler, 'Rethinking Colonial Categories: European Communities and the Boundaries of Rule', in Nicholas B. Dirks, ed., *Colonialism and Culture* (Ann Arbor MI, University of Michigan Press, 1992), 319–52, and 'Sexual Affronts and Racial Frontiers: European Identities and the Cultural Politics of Exclusion in Southeast Asia', in Ann Laura Stoler and Frederick Cooper, eds, *Tensions of Empire: Colonial Cultures in a Bourgeois World* (Berkeley CA, University of California Press, 1997), 198–237.
2. Alan Christy, 'The Making of Imperial Subjects in Okinawa', *positions*, 1:3 (1993), 607–39; Richard Siddle, *Race, Resistance and the Ainu of Japan* (London, Routledge, 1996).
3. Japanese treaty port life is best treated in Mark Peattie, 'Japanese Treaty Port Settlements in China, 1895–1937', in Peter Duus, Ramon Myers and Mark R. Peattie, eds, *The Japanese Informal Empire in China, 1895–1937* (Princeton NJ, Princeton University Press, 1989), 166–209; Kimura Kenji, 'Zai gaichi kyoryû no shakai katsudô' (Social Activities and Operations of Japanese Residents on the Empire's Periphery), in Ôe Shinobu et al., eds, *Iwanami kôza kindai Nihon to shokuminchi* (Iwanami Series on Colonialism and Modern Japan), V (Tokyo, Iwanami shoten, 1993), 166–209; Barbara Brooks, *Japan's Imperial Diplomacy: Treaty Ports, Consuls and War in China, 1895–1938* (Honolulu, University of Hawaii Press, 2000), chapter 3.
4. Inoue Torajirô, 'Kamon ni okeru Taiwan sekimin mondai' (The Taiwan *Sekimin* Problem in Amoy), a 1926 consular report reprinted in *Taiwan kindaishi kenkyû* (Modern Taiwan Studies) 1980, No. 3, 129–46.
5. The actions of British consular officials of the China service in Amoy contrast with those of their Japanese counterparts. Amoy was also a port of entry for many Straits Chinese who could lay claim to Chinese and British dual nationality, but consular officials, on the whole, extended recognition of British colonial citizenship to such Chinese only reluctantly, and in the nineteenth century only on the basis of their 'British' dress and overall presentation. Additionally, British consular officials were always admonishing British missionaries that under no circumstances would extraterritoriality or privileges of British citizenship be extended to Christian converts. See P. D. Coates, *The China Consuls* (New York, Oxford University Press, 1988), 206–9.
6. Dai Guohui, 'Nihon no shokuminchi shihai to Taiwan sekimin' (Japan's Colonial Rule and Taiwan *Sekimin*), *Taiwan kindaishi kenkyû*, 1980, no. 3, 114.
7. Wakabayashi Masahiro, *Kaikyo: Taiwan seiji e no shiza* (The Straits: The View towards Taiwan Politics) (Tokyo, Shimizu Insatsujo, 1985), 183–4.
8. Liang Huahuang, for example, condemns almost all *sekimin* individuals and activities in southern China while at the same time illuminating their tragic plight in 'Taiwan sôtokufu no taian seisaku to "Taiwan sekimin",' (The Taiwan Government General's Policies for China and 'Taiwan *sekimin*'), in Ôe Shinobu et al., eds, *Iwanami kôza kindai Nihon to shokuminchi*, V, 77–102; Dai Guohui, 'Nihon no shokuminchi shihai', 105–10, remains impartial while shocked by the popular memory of Taiwanese collaboration that he encountered in the 1980s when visiting Japanese-occupied cities like Singapore and Hong Kong.
9. See, for example, Japanese Foreign Ministry Archives (hereafter JFMA) A 5.3.0.8, 'ZaiShi Senjin oyobi Taiwan sekimin to kokumin seifu to no kankei Chôsa ikken' (Item relating to Investigations of the Relationship between the Nationalist Government and Koreans and Taiwan *Sekimin* in China), a catalogue of colonial

citizens in China seen to be collaborating with the Nationalist Chinese government.
10 Inoue Torajirô, 'Kamon ni okeru Taiwan sekimin', 133–5.
11 Dai Guohui, 'Nihon no shokuminchi shihai', 120.
12 Wakabayashi Masahiro, *Kaikyo*, 193.
13 Inoue Torajirô, 'Kamon', 139.
14 'Flexible citizenship' is a useful concept to explain diasporic or transnational behaviour both today and earlier in the century: see Aiwha Ong, 'On the Edge of Empires: Flexible Citizenship among Chinese in Diaspora', *positions*, 1:3 (1993), 745–78.
15 JFMA D 1.2.0.2, 'ZaiShi teikoku ryôji saiban kankei zakken' (Miscellaneous Items regarding Japanese Consular Courts in China).
16 *Ibid.*
17 JFMA S 13.2.3.0–3, 'ZaiMan teikoku ryôji kaigi gijiroku' (Records of the Meetings of Japanese Consuls in Manchuria).
18 JFMA A 5.3.0.8, 'ZaiShi Senjin oyobi Taiwan sekimin to kokumin seifu to no kankei Chôsa ikken' (Item relating to Investigations of the Relationship between the Nationalist Government and Koreans and Taiwan *Sekimin* in China).
19 Bruce Cumings, *The Origins of the Korean War* (Princeton NJ, Princeton University Press, 1981), 54.
20 Quoted in C. Walter Young, 'Korean Problems in Manchuria as Factors in the Sino-Japanese Dispute', *Supplementary Documents to the Report of the Commission of Inquiry*, Study No. 9 (Geneva, 1932), 59–60.
21 Usui Katsumi, 'Kindai Nihon to Chôsen, Chûgoku' (Modern Japan and Korea, China), '*Chôsen mondai*' *konwakai* (Discussions of the 'Korean Problem') No. 26 (Tokyo, Gakushû kenkyû shiriisu, 1984), 20.
22 Ki-hoon Kim, 'Japanese Policy for Korean Rural Immigration to Manchukuo, 1932–1945' (University of Hawaii Ph.D. dissertation, 1992), 37.
23 C. Walter Young, 'Korean Problems in Manchuria,' 253.
24 See Barbara Brooks, 'Peopling the Japanese Empire: Koreans in Manchuria and the Rhetoric of Inclusion', in Sharon Minichiello, ed., *Japan's Competing Modernities: Issues in Culture and Democracy, 1900–1930* (Honolulu, University of Hawaii Press, 1998), 25–44.
25 For example, Kita Sadakichi, *Kankoku no heigô to kokushi* (Japanese History and the Annexation of Korea) (Tokyo, Tôko shoin, 1929) and Kanazawa Shozaburô, *Nissen dôsoron* (Studies on the Common Ancestors of Japanese and Koreans) (Tokyo, Tôko shoin, 1929). See also Peter Duus, *The Abacus and the Sword: The Japanese Penetration of Korea, 1895–1910* (Berkeley CA, University of California Press, 1995), 413–23.
26 See Chôsen sôtokufu naimukyoku shakaika (Social Section, Bureau of Internal Affairs, Korea Government General), *Manshû oyobi Shiberia chihô ni okeru Chôsenjin jijô* (Situation of Koreans in the Manchurian and Siberian Regions) (Seoul, Keijô insatsusho, 1923), 123, 140, and also its 1927 report of the same title, reprinted in Kankoku shiryô kenkyûjo (Institute for Korean Documents), *Chôsen tôchi shiryô* (Documents on Japanese Rule over Korea), X (Tokyo, Sansei bijutsu insatsu, 1972), 486.
27 C. Walter Young, 'Korean Problems in Manchuria', 256.
28 Akatsuka Shôsuke, 'ZaiMan Senjin mondai' (Problems of Koreans in Manchuria), 1921 report reprinted in Kankoku shiryô kenkyûjo, *Chôsen tôchi shiryô*, X, 225–61.
29 See, for example, Chôsen sôtokufu naimukyoku shakaika, 'Manshû oyobi Shiberia chihô', 1927, 510–12.
30 'Manshû no suiden keiei ni tsuite' (On the Development of Manchuria's Rice Paddies) *Chôsen oyobi Manshû* (Korea and Manchuria) (May 1922), 22–4.
31 C. Walter Young, 'Korean Problems in Manchuria', 256.
32 Chôsen sôtokufu keimukyoku (Bureau of Prison Affairs, Korea Government General), *ZaiMan Senjin to Shina kansen* (The Chinese Authorities and Koreans in Manchuria), (Seoul, Gyôsei gakkai insatsujo, 1930. Reprinted Seoul, Seishin bunka sha, 1974), 157–227.

33 JFMA 8.3.8.7.19, 'Chôsenjin kika kankei zakken' (Miscellaneous Items regarding Naturalisation of Koreans).
34 JFMA Z 1.3.0.11, Chôsenjin no Shinakoku kika mondai ni kansuru senrei' (Precedents regarding the Naturalisation of Koreans as Chinese).
35 Eileen P. Scully, 'Taking the Low Road to Sino-American Relations: "Open Door" Expansionists and the Two China Markets', *Journal of American History*, 82:1 (1995), 77.
36 C. Walter Young, 'Korean Problems in Manchuria', 259.
37 J. B. Condliffe, ed., *Problems of the Pacific, 1929: Proceedings of the Third Conference of the Institute of Pacific Relations* (Chicago, University of Chicago Press, 1930), 195.
38 Hayashi Kyûjirô, *Manshû jihen to Hôten Sôryôji* (The Manchurian Incident and the Mukden Consul General) (Tokyo, Hara shobô, 1978), 82.
39 Translation from Ki-hoon Kim, 'Japanese Policy for Korean Rural Immigration', 80.
40 Chôsen sôtokufu naimukyoku shakaika, 'Manshû oyobi Shiberia chihô', 1923, 140, 165.
41 *Ibid.*, 166–72.
42 'Senjin o chûshin to seru Haerbin no kosatsu', (Reflections on Harbin, mainly on its Koreans), *Chôsen oyobi Manshû* (December 1923), 33–6.
43 Minami Manshû tetsudo kabushiki kaisha, chihôbu nômuka (Regional Agricultural Affairs Section, South Manchurian Railway (SMR) Corporation), 'ZaiMan Chôsenjin nôgyô mondai' (Agricultural Problems of Koreans in Manchuria), 1936 report, in Minami Manshû tetsudô kabushiki kaisha keizai chôsakai (Economic Survey Group, SMR), eds, *Manshû nôgyô imin hôsaku* (Policies for Agricultural Immigrants to Manchuria), No. 2, Vol. 1, No. 8, *Ritsuan chôsa shorui* (Survey Materials for Policy Design) 1937, 257.
44 Inoue Torajirô, 'Kamon ni okeru Taiwan sekimin mondai', 144–5.
45 For Koreans and Manchukuo see Carter J. Eckert, 'Total War, Industrialization and Social Change in Late Colonial Korea', in Peter Duus, Ramon Myers and Mark Peattie, eds, *The Japanese Wartime Empire, 1931–1945* (Princeton NJ, Princeton University Press, 1996), 3–39.
46 Usui Katsumi, 'Kindai Nihon to Chôsen, Chûgoku', 30–1.
47 Lai Tse-han, Ramon H. Myers and Wei Wou, *A Tragic Beginning: the Taiwan Uprising of February 28, 1947* (Stanford CA, Stanford University Press, 1991).

CHAPTER EIGHT

Denied and besieged: the Japanese community of Korea, 1876–1945
Alain Delissen

> In order to achieve the harmonious merging of the Japanese and Korean people, nothing was more necessary than the [1914] reform which placed both of them on an equal footing in the same administrative framework.[1]

Just when the Japanese migration to Korea was soaring – eventually bringing about one of the largest new communities in the colonial world – the colonial authorities in Seoul curiously set out to dissolve it within a unified political body, Chôsen, which was neither Korea nor Japan. And just as the peninsula was not formally labelled a 'colony', Japanese settlers were expected to forget about making their own community. Were the Japanese, then, doomed to disappear as such once they had taken a foothold in Korea?

Persistent denials of colonisation have characterised Japan's discourse regarding its sixty years' presence in Korea. From the founding – and legitimising – myths positing a common ancestry for the two people (dôso) to more brutal patterns of imperial assimilation (dôka, kôminka) in the 1930s, Japanese policy in Korea contrived colonial forms and norms that were certainly original in nineteenth and twentieth-century Asia. Political practice and the social realities of the period tell us a very different – but well documented – history of contempt, prejudice and violence in the peninsula, and unveil the foundations of this colonial ideology. As its flip side, the denied Japanese community of Korea itself aimed to conceal a more substantial denial. For what was doomed to disappear was in fact the age-old Korean nationhood. And since the Korean nation obstinately struggled to exist for its own sake, the Japanese community itself was forced back by reality into a besieged existence.

As well as providing an overall sketch of this – scantily researched – community, this chapter will focus on a paradox: how did a community whose existence was formally denied in both ideology and law manage to exist and maintain itself *vis-à-vis* the Korean people? Eschewing the interior analyses of Japanese communities adopted by Christian Henriot and Joshua Fogel, the emphasis here will be on the various outer borders of the Japanese in Korea. The physical, territorial, administrative, even imaginary frontiers of this community were as instrumental in shaping its identity as were its Shintô rites, neighbourhood associations, entertainment districts or vernacular newspapers. Moreover, while examining these forms in comparison with other colonial communities, we also hope to supplement a general morphology of imperialism that tends to become mute when tackling the Japanese empire.

Birth and development of a community, 1876–1945

The relative lack of knowledge about Japanese settlers in the peninsula appears to echo the general forgetfulness comparative studies of colonisation have fostered regarding the Japanese case. It is hardly surprising that Korean historiography chose to channel its efforts towards surveying the 20 million or so Korean people under Japanese administration, and this focus does not stem purely from a nationalist-inspired narrative. Structural change and colonial politics have clearly been more important to historical studies, leaving the scene almost free from real faces.[2] What comes as more of a surprise is the discovery that mainstream Japanese historiography of the empire has devoted so little energy to knowing colonists better, whether as individuals, as groups or as a community.[3] Western historiography, despite the recent vitality of this field in American academia, partly triggered by the three pioneering Princeton volumes on the Japanese empire, has left us still with no clear and substantial depiction of the Japanese of Korea.[4]

Peter Duus's 1995 volume, *The Abacus and the Sword*, should therefore be heralded as an important breakthrough, offering us a vivid portrait of a community (1876–1910) then only a few thousand strong.[5] These were the human spearhead which preceded by a generation the final military take-over of the peninsula. As Kimura Kenji recalled: 'According to *Imperial Annuals*, between 1876 and 1905 a yearly average of 2,686 Japanese migrants left their homeland for Korea. Before officially sponsored migration to Hawaii was initiated (1885), Chôsen was the magnet that captured the bulk of Nippon expatriates.'[6] If we now skip over decades towards the final years of the colonial period, German geographer Hermann Lautensach's following remarks sound amazing: 'The Japanese proportion of the total population ... always remains small. In view of [the] surprisingly slow development of the Japanese population element, despite the favourable nature of the environment, the question arises as to the reasons.'[7]

Indeed, by contrast with its slow but decisive beginnings, the subsequent massive character of this colonisation is probably one of its most striking features. Throughout the 1920s editorials in the *Tonga Ilbo*, one of the most influential Korean daily newspapers, were lamenting it as a genuine invasion. Viewed from the mid-1940s, when it reached its peak population (712,583 people in the 1944 census), the Japanese of Korea need to be examined in comparison not only with other settlements within the empire, but also with other communities of settlers in the colonial world. According to *Colonial Statistics from 1939*, 650,000 Japanese people were then living in Chôsen. Although almost on a par with the Japanese communities in China, it was by far the largest community of the formal empire (41 per cent), followed far behind by the Karafuto (346,000 – 22 per cent) and Taiwanese (323,000 – 20 per cent) communities.[8] At the very same time, in the multi-faceted French empire, *pieds-noirs* in Algeria were certainly the sole colonial community that exceeded the size of the Japanese figures in Korea, with over 1 million settlers. There were 200,000 settlers in Morocco but barely 34,000 colonists in Indochina.[9]

A final set of comparisons can still be made regarding the local populations of target countries. However large the Japanese community may have been, it was dwarfed by the Korean population (24·3 million in 1940). At best, the Japanese element accounted for 3 per cent of the Chôsen colony, other foreigners (mostly Chinese) accounting for less than 0·3 per cent of the total. To go no farther than in North East Asia, this stands in clear contrast with the Japanese element in Karafuto (97·5 per cent). And if we look at Western empires in South East Asia, the 3 per cent colonists-to-colonised ratio in Korea still compares favourably with the low ones to be found in French Indochina (0·2 per cent), British Malaya (0·7 per cent) or the Netherlands East Indies (0·4 per cent).[10] In short, the Japanese community of Korea happened to be a rather large community, quite uncommon in other colonial empires, but not so large *vis-à-vis* the Korean population. Natural factors (geographical closeness, territorial depth) partly explain the success of this populating process, which was not sustained by a long tradition of migrating to Korea. For centuries, down from Hideyoshi's invasions in the late sixteenth century, Japan had been for Korea a cumbersome and disquieting neighbour to be cautiously kept at bay. Only within the framework of 'managed trade' between kingdoms had a small community of Japanese sojourners been licensed to operate and take a sporadic foothold in the vicinity of Tongnae (Pusan).

With the extorted Treaty of Kanghwa (1876) as a critical turning point, the years following laid the institutional bases of Japanese settlements. Between 1876 and 1905 Korea experienced the fateful lot of a country exposed to the logic and harsh realities of 'unequal treaties'. In the name of free trade and the law of nations, it was compelled to open more and more of its territory to foreign powers and merchants. Such a situation – sovereignty and monarchy going adrift – was not new in the collapsing Chinese regional order. New, though, was the fact that, for the first time, those exorbitant political and economic privileges had been granted to a non-Western country: and Japan succeeded in opening up this 'hermit kingdom' that had kept itself hidden in the utmost seclusion since the early seventeenth century. This gave it a decisive advance on its rivals in the peninsula. Even though Western and other regional powers (including imperialised imperialist Qing China) struggled to catch up, insisting on the principles of an open-door policy, it took thirty years and two wars for Japan to wipe its challengers off the Korean landscape.

In this process, the quickly growing community of Japanese traders and adventurers, eager to make a living from the penetration of Korean markets, was not so simply the direct result of military and political thrusts. They were, conversely and co-extensively, one of the major causes prompting increasing Japanese meddling in Korean affairs. Between 1880 and the Sino-Japanese War (1894–95) the community of settlers had grown tenfold, reaching 8,000 people. Between that date and the Russo-Japanese War (1904–05) it doubled again. However, as examined below, even though Japanese rice traders penetrated farther and farther into the interior, the Japanese community of Korea was still dwelling in enclaves carved out of a foreign land.

The protectorate in 1905 and annexation in 1910 opened up an entirely different situation for Japanese migrants. The striking take-off in population, which went largely unabated throughout the colonial period, is well attested from more accurate census data provided from 1920 on. After a sharp rise at the turn of the century (1900: 16,000 settlers, 1910: 170,000 settlers), the community gained a yearly average of 13,000 people between 1910 and 1930 to reach the half-million level, only to give way to a still higher growth rate (18,000 people per annum) during the next decade to peak at well over 700,000 in the 1940s.[11]

Two main factors contributed to the constant growth and increasing complexity of the Japanese community under full colonial auspices: security and economic opportunities. The annexation of the peninsula granted settlers both open space to expand into and solid institutional safeguards. The Japanese began spreading over the whole country, feeling all the more at home as, year after year, more Japanese faces were appearing in towns and counties. This would not have been sufficient to sustain a massive pattern of settlement had not colonial policy aimed at the exploitation of the colony in directions that changed over time. Thanks to an efficient and quickly developed infrastructure, Korea became a place where, from agriculture to industry through trade and services, life and social mobility were seemingly easier for the Japanese than in the home islands. Having become an economic semi-periphery, Korea looked all the more secure as, with war on the continent in the 1930s, it was no longer the outer border of the empire. Slogans of fusion (*naisen ittai*, Japan-Korea, one single body) and assimilation policies could make the Japanese settlers who were living entrenched in their large neighbourhoods believe that, somehow, the Korean people had disappeared from view. The Japanese were not a foreign community in a foreign country. They were, beside the Japanese of Kantô or Kyûshû, the Japanese of Chôsen.

Migration to the peninsula was certainly a process that deserves more precise analysis. Unfortunately, whereas the topic has been covered in detail, from Kimura Kenji to Peter Duus, for the period before 1910, we are left with fewer references for the subsequent period, when it became much more massive. Some tentative conclusions may be drawn from Mark Peattie's remarks about immigration into mainland China in the early twentieth century and from my own research into the prosopography of a limited group of colonial technicians in the late 1930s.[12] First, it appears that the bulk of Japanese migrants originated from western Japan. At the turn of the century more than 70 per cent of them had their roots in the Kyûshû, Chûgoku and Kinki regions, five of their prefectures (Nagasaki, Oita, Fukuoka, Hiroshima and especially Yamaguchi) supplying the greatest number.[13] Afterwards, in accordance with the rise of the new capital city in Japanese geography, people from the Tokyo area (possibly rural to urban migrants in the first place) logically formed a larger share of the migrants. Chain migration, a phenomenon that shows early adventurers being followed by kinsfolk, neighbours and fellow villagers, adds a powerful social network dimension to the simple proximity factor.[14]

As in China, the sociological content of migration changed over time, and early, male, adventurist, petty business sojourners were replaced later by more stable, lower middle-class and middle-class families. Throughout the colonial period, female colonists were thus only slightly less numerous than male colonists. Second, even though state policies contributed to migration, once an institutional and psychological distinction was introduced between the status of migrant (*imin*) and of colonist (*shokumin*) – the former as second-rate Japanese leaving for the Americas, the latter as overseas pioneers of the Japanese nation – government-sponsored immigration was anything but a success. Between 1910 and 1929 the grand design of a widespread farming settlement conceived by the 1908 Oriental Development Company (Tôyô Takushoku Kaisha) 'was able to settle only 3,971 families' in Korea.[15] Third, such a setback clearly relates to the economic – and individual – reasons for emigration into Korea. If the drive to Chôsen is to be understood within the more general framwork of rural to urban industrialising migration in the home islands, and does not provide an indisputable push factor, conversely the pull factor is more solidly identified. Founded or not, the lure of work and quick money, hopes of better personal success and social advancement were more powerful than publications extolling the peninsula as 'the paradise next door'.[16] Hence the army of 'penny capitalists', to use Peter Duus's happy expression, that flocked into the once hermit kingdom to give it its peculiar occupational profile.

From migrants to colonists, 1876–1910

As a foreign settlement in an alien country, the Japanese community of Korea could (and should) be defined by the outer border of its territory, by contact with the 'host' state and 'host' society. However obvious it may sound, it should first be recalled that the Japanese community of Korea did not have the same legal meaning before and after the full colonial take-over of 1910. Before then there was still, although ailing, a sovereign Korean state that made Japanese migrants foreigners in the peninsula. With provision for new diplomatic principles, the opening of one port (Pusan) to Japanese free trade and residence (*kôryuji/kyoryûchi*), the Nippo-Korean treaty of Kanghwa (29 February 1876) was certainly a major breakthrough for the Japanese.

Still more important, however, were international treaties signed in the following two decades which opened up many more ports and cities – Wônsan (1881), Inch'ôn (1883), Mokp'o (1897), Kunsan (1899) – and were all modelled on the Sino-Korean treaty of 1882. Patterns borrowed from Chinese 'unequal treaties' were transferred to Korea to accommodate foreign communities and regulate their activities. As in China, they were defining settlement areas of extraterritorial jurisdiction to be held on a long-term lease. They also included clauses about tariffs and licensed zones of trading (*kanhaeng ijông*) around the open ports (within a radius of 400km in 1884[17]). In practice, though, each newly opened port conveyed its own formula and vocabulary. Commonly held international concessions (*kakkuk kongdong chogye*) were designed to accommodate the handful of Western settlers in neatly planned settlements that were managed by a municipal council (*sindong kongsa*), while two countries, China and Japan, benefited from more favourable conditions – and much larger areas of settlement – defining zones of exclusive residence (*chôn'gwan kôryuji/senkan kyoryûchi*).[18]

Even though Japan was not the only imperialist power to own concessions in Korea before 1910, once China had been defeated in 1895 it was clearly the dominant actor. The by then large group of Chinese merchants having been invited to leave the country, Japan's position was firmly strengthened *vis-à-vis* the remaining Western powers owing to its incommensurate community of migrants (95 per cent of the peninsular settlers[19]). As early as 1884 Japan had already been able to force its views on Western countries when it used the size of the community as a pretext for exacting from King Kojong a large area of its own, in the vicinity of Seoul, which would become the Yongsan military base.[20] Therefore, the formal distinction between concessions (*chogye*) and zones of residence (*kôryuji*) was less instrumental in shaping the Japanese community than was its incremental building up. Through the constant renegotiation and gradual acquisition of new land, Japanese *kôryuji* could take advantage of a flexible border. What is more, the idea of 'licensed settlement' should not distract from the fact that, little by little, 'illicit' Japanese settlers were steadily increasing their foothold elsewhere. Regardless of treaties, by forcing new markets open in the interior, the Japanese community was seeping in throughout the peninsula. Its ubiquitous presence triggered the anti-Japanese peasant uproar that was an integral part of the 1894–95 Tonghak rebellion.

In the aftermath of the treaty of Kanghwa, Japanese sojourners had flocked into the peninsula in search of quick tricks and easy money. Trade in all its forms was the main business of this hectic adventuring. In the subsequent period it still remained the main activity of Japanese colonists. In 1907, with only 6 per cent in the primary and 10 per cent in the secondary sectors, the occupational structure of Japanese residents was characterised by a 70 per cent presence in the tertiary sector. Close to 56 per cent of those jobs were in commerce, 18 per cent in public administration and 3 per cent in the professions.[21] To a greater or lesser degree, the peninsula became the kingdom of Japanese small business and petty capitalism. This is certainly most unusual for the formal colonial world. So much so that geographer Lautensach, imbued with patterns of colonisation implying farmer colonists, was unable to recognise the large Japanese community of Korea as a successful achievement. In short, Korea was neither a classical settlement colony (farmer colonists) nor a conventional command colony (bureaucrat colonists).

As in China, the colonisation of Korea was thus largely coterminous with the urbanisation of settlers. In contrast to China, however, newcomers did not only nestle in existing Korean cities and towns but also founded the modern cities of the peninsula. Yi dynasty Korea indeed had been reluctant to develop commercial activities and – apart from Seoul (Hanyang) – large urban settlements. Therefore, with the opening of Korea and Japanese immigration, its geography began to experience dramatic and sweeping change. Neither had old Chosôn been the place for the major port cities which Pusan, Inch'ôn or Wônsan rapidly became. Likewise, new cities began to mushroom in the interior, relating to transport nodes (Taejôn) crucial to the handling of Korean rice or mineral resources extracted from the north of the country.

Because they were mainly oriented towards small business activities and packed together in cities, Japanese settlers were not simply passive tools into the hands of consular authorities or Japanese politicians. They had interests of their own that needed proper recognition and organisation. It took some time, though, before they could obtain them from their reluctant and distrustful watchdogs. Owing to their often dishonest behaviour, unruly early sojourners pushing for stronger action against angered Korean citizens had at times constituted an embarrassment to plans for smooth and gradual control of the peninsula. Until the protectorate was firmly established in 1905, attempts to endow the Japanese community with some form of representation therefore came to naught.

So, once the original world of half-adventurist, half-lout penny capitalist sojourners had been replaced by a more stable and respectable one of clerks, innkeepers, teachers, soldiers, accountants, railwaymen, technicians, journalists, doctors and lawyers, a reform was carried out by the March 1905 imperial law that would apply to both China and Korea. From July 1906 onwards, residents' associations (koryûchi mindan) were created in twelve cities inhabited by a significant number of Japanese.[22] Although the heads of such local associations were to be nominated by the General Resident, elected assemblies (minkai) were established that could discuss local problems, issue local regulations, levy local taxes and allocate local resources. Community clinics, cemeteries and crematoriums, public

THE JAPANESE COMMUNITY OF KOREA

From migrants to colonists, Types of social and political dynamics, Penetration, Settlements

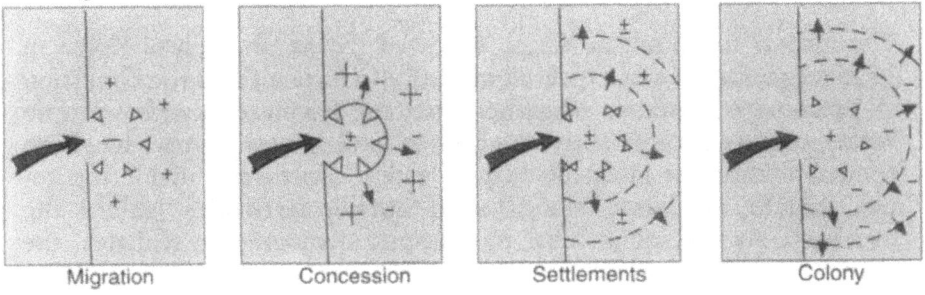

Settlement patterns in Korea

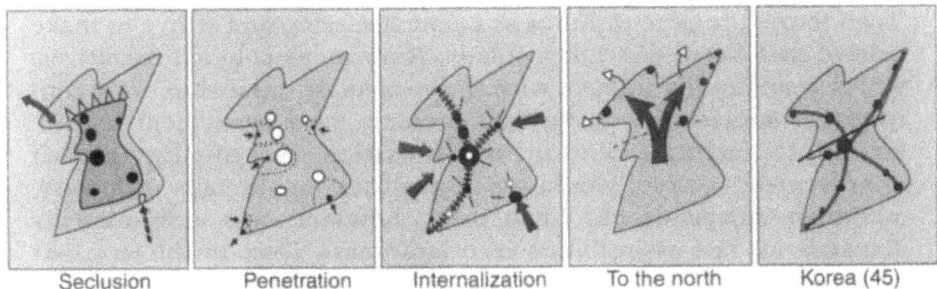

Colonial residential patterns, Types of contact

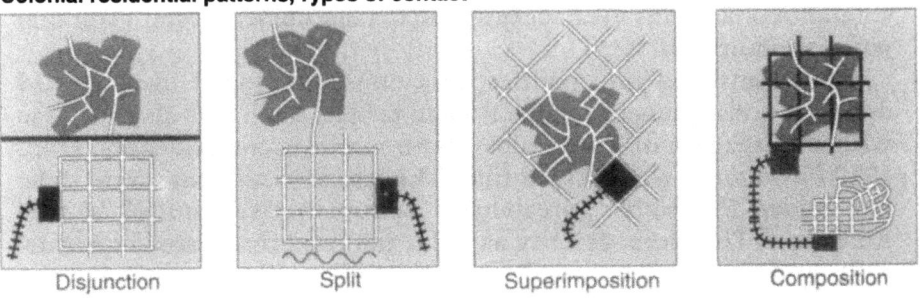

Figure 8.1 Patterns of Japanese residence in the Korean peninsula, 1876–1945

parks, schools, social aid organisations and real estate development were their main responsibilities.[23] At best, the *minkai* could stand for a consultative body whose pronouncements nevertheless remained engulfed in the almighty decisions of semi-colonial authorities. (See Fig. 8.1.)

[133]

NEW FRONTIERS

From colonists to gaichijin, 1910–45

The formal colonisation which followed the annexation of Korea in 1910 might have been expected radically to have altered the condition of Japanese settlement. Migrants from the Japanese islands were no longer a foreign community in a foreign land. A new frontier had been opened within the Japanese empire which contrasted 'inside territories' (*naichi*, the home islands) with 'outside territories' (*gaichi*, the overseas). At the social level too, despite demographic realities, the frontier with Koreans was reversed, with Japanese settlers being admittedly still a minority, but now a dominant minority.

The shift in terms from colonist (*shokumin*) to 'overseas Japanese' (*gaichijin*) was not neutral. As suggested at the start of this chapter, Japan refused to pose in Korea as colonial master, and strove to make believe that Korea was not a colony. Ambiguous colonial narratives, which were heavily imbued with the vocabulary of kinship, were contrived to suggest the provisional presence of a benevolent cousin, aiming to facilitate Korean modernisation. Supposedly, gradual improvement (*kairyô*) would put Korea back on the rails of history, and then independence. Gradualism, however, was subsumed by demands for fast assimilation into Japan-ness. Despite the fact that Japanese Governors General of Korea were endowed with a considerable degree of autonomy from the Japanese Cabinet, painstaking efforts were made to maintain the peninsula as a – fictitious – extension of Japan by transferring to it the Meiji constitution.[24] Even though only a handful of Koreans ever accepted such a discourse, Western colonial powers indulged it.

Once translated into politics, this unusual colonial ideology had dramatic consequences for the Korean people. Such was also the case with the Japanese of Korea, albeit with a milder consequences. From 1910 onwards, it was decided that 'The Japanese residents were to be put under the same bureaucratic administrative control as the Koreans.'[25] Therefore, as early as 1911, the recently created residents' associations were dissolved. From a political and legal standpoint the Japanese community of Korea had disappeared. What is more, the Japanese of Korea never were full-fledged Japanese citizens. If, in theory, they were protected by Japanese domestic law – which was never really applied to Koreans – they were also exposed to the hard-and-fast rule of Governors General. Although various types of associations could petition them in order to defend their vested interests, no overall organisation, either in Korea or in the imperial Diet, was ever devised to represent the hundreds of thousands of Japanese settlers.[26] The colonist of Korea was more a colonial subject than a colonial citizen: Taishô political experiences never crossed the Tsushima Straight. For all that, beyond the surface of laws and words, there was still a thriving community. How was it maintained?

In fact there was a huge gap between the theory and practice of Japanese colonisation that helped confirm the separate existence of the Japanese community. Between legal provisions and their implementation, and between amendments and their interpretation, a large span of space and time was opened surreptitiously to address the special needs of the Japanese. For instance, when the colonial authorities carried out their general land survey between 1910 and 1918 in order to record the properties of both the Japanese and Koreans, Japanese public servants were at liberty to call any place by the name they judged most convenient. As a result, ancient peninsular toponyms underwent massive alteration. The maps and trails of Korea took on a distinctly Japanese flavour.[27] More decisive, however, was another major characteristic of Japanese colonisation: over the forty years or so of its direct rule, it carried out a constant and curious administrative retooling. No sooner had a system of local administration been implemented than new reforms were already being prepared.

These adjustments were clearly meant to preserve the Japanese grip on Chôsen's administration by constantly changing the rules. For the Koreans had not only set out to protest, resist and fight the occupants. Some of them had even begun to take the Japanese colonial ideology at its word when it claimed a common, equal opportunity administrative policy. When the *pu* system was reformed in 1914 – it had been enforced in 1911 when foreign concessions were cancelled – the idea was not to take account of recent changes in population by producing a new list of cities. By law, *pu* were cities inhabited by 20,000 people or more. However, Kaesông, a former capital of Korea that was inhabited by nearly 40,000 people, received only the lesser designation of *myôn*, whereas Mokp'o with its 12,782 inhabitants gained an unexpected *pu* administrative category. Why the distortions? Suffice to say that only a handful of Japanese settlers were living in Koryô's former capital, Kaesông, while thousands of them were residing in the southern modern harbour of Mokp'o. Given the fact that the 1914 reform was also aimed at introducing *pu* local councils whose members were to be appointed according to density of population, it was certainly more convenient for geography and demography to be rearranged to meet Japanese needs. In the process, disturbed only by a tiny minority of Korean appointees, the former Japanese *mindan* had been surreptitiously recreated.

From the creation in 1917 of 'special *myôn*' (*chijông myôn*) to the reform in 1930 which gave birth to elected decision-making local councils (*gikai*), administrative retooling strove at once to apparently satisfy Korean claims while actually reinforcing safeguards for the Japanese community. For this reason the principle of electing members in the purely deliberative local councils (*hyôgikai*) (established in 1920) was associated with poll tax conditions that disqualified most Korean voters, by ensuring the eventual overrepresentation of the Japanese, who were much wealthier. On account of frequent shifts in underlying administrative regulations beneath the shining surface of fair and stable laws, the Japanese community of Korea under full colonial auspices was thus more concealed than denied. *Vis-à-vis* growing Korean pressure, it was sheltered by a fortress of paperwork which befitted its territorial and demographic expansion.

Territories within territories

During the 1910s Korea was intended by the colonial authorities to become the rice granary of Japan. As already suggested, in Korea this clear-cut colonial division of labour (agriculture overseas, industry at home) failed to make settlers farmers. All in all, despite dramatic internal shifts in property, Korean people largely remained the owners and farmers of their own land. If rice production was the major activity of the Koreans, rice processing was the activity that opened up Chôsen to Japanese settlers. As rice traders inventing new markets, not only could they go farther and deeper into the interior, but also, through contracting and transactions, they could provide the bulk of Korean people with evidence of their ubiquitous presence. Without settling on rural farm land but through having critical marketing control of rice, they gained command over a whole country and over a whole people. By so doing, they could settle in cities and townships which became centres of economic command.

In the 1920s, when the first campaigns for agricultural improvement were carried out and restrictions on creating industrial and other enterprises were being lifted, opportunities were seized by Japanese colonists to develop small industries connected with rice production (rice mills, distilleries, etc.) that reinforced this pattern. This turned many merchants into petty manufacturers more often than not associated with Korean 'junior' partners. At the same time, the upper crust of Japanese colonial capitalists started bigger and more modern enterprises in the textile, banking or general trading sectors. Cities were industrialised and towns grew quickly in size and population.

The 1930s were an important watershed in colonial development policies. With Korea secured as an 'old' colony and designed to become the rear base of new imperialist inroads into the continent, *zaibatsu* capital poured in to establish large factories in energy and resource-rich northern Korea. A once sleepy mountainous border was thus turned into a quickly growing zone of pioneer settlement, centred on chemical and war-related industries. New cities were designed to accommodate new migrants and new types of migrants: technicians, and industrial blue and white collar workers.

On the eve of defeat in the Pacific War, however, more than 70 per cent of the Japanese residents were still earning their livelihood in the service sector. New facts were the growing importance of industrial employment (28 per cent) and, in the tertiary sector, the marked rise of public servants and professionals (25 per cent) *vis-à-vis* commerce and transport (23 per cent).[28] If small business had somehow receded, it was nonetheless in the context of the enlargement and growth of the overall business sector. With such an occupational distribution, Korea might well stand somewhere between the home islands and the Japanese settlements of China, but a more meaningful comparison could also be made with another Asian colony the size of Korea, such as French Indochina, which was dominated by a handful of colonial administrators and large industrialists.

All in all, no part of Korea was left untouched by the dynamics of Japanese command and by the mobility of Japanese settlers. Through colonisation its geography underwent drastic change. Highly mobile in both time and space, the Japanese community of Korea offered the two major sub-forms of pioneering settlements and deepening settlements. The growing community of settlers entailed the existence of a less conquest-oriented sub-group, sheltered in cities and more and more differentiated in its occupational structure. In short, the territoriality of Japanese settlers in the peninsula featured an overall blanket of discrete settlement with heavy concentrations in urban centres.

The Japanese made up 3 per cent of Chôsen society, but Japanese settlers were nearly 70 per cent urban. At the same time, only 10 per cent of Koreans lived in cities and townships.[29] This does not mean, however, that, within cities, Japanese colonists formed the majority of the population. Situations varied too much in space and time for an average distribution by nationality to be meaningful. In 1915, for instance, Pusan was 49 per cent Japanese-populated, but P'yôngyang only 19 per cent. In 1944 Kaesông, which was never a beacon for Japanese settlers, still had only 2 per cent of them within its boundaries, whereas in Pusan the Japanese population had plummeted to 18 per cent of the total. Also, these percentages mask the absolute size of

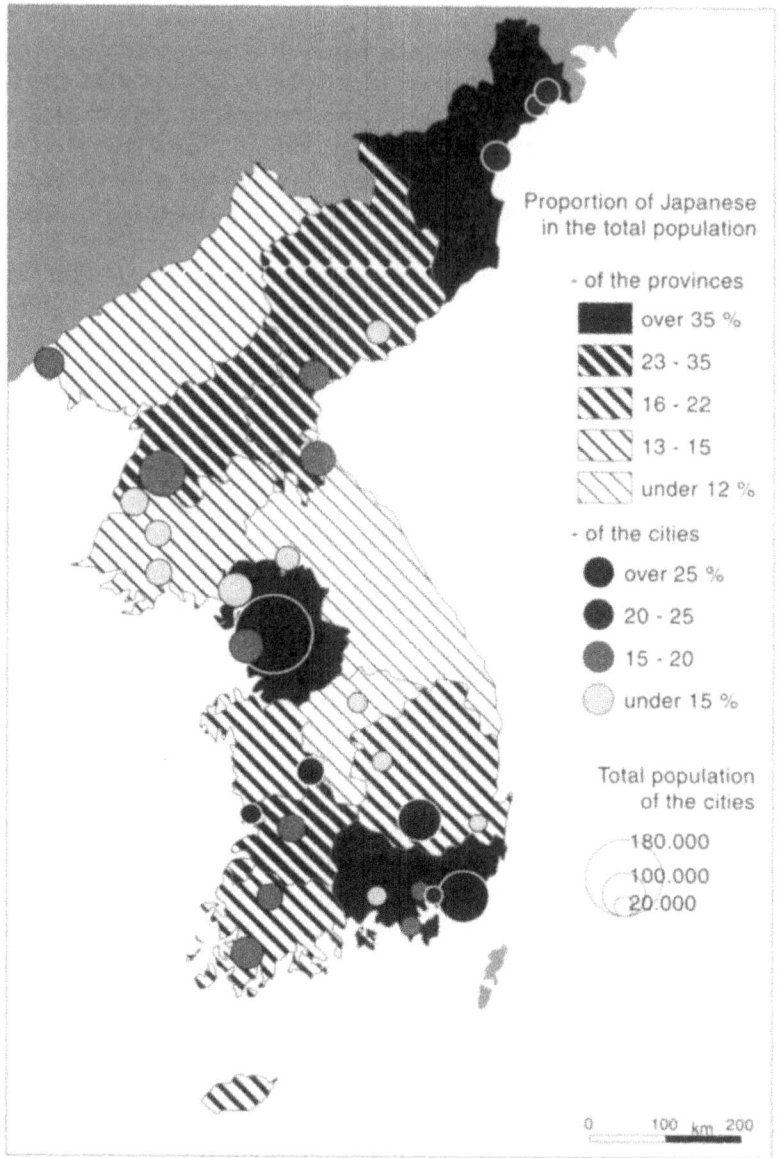

Figure 8.2 The distribution of Japanese settlement in Korea, c. 1940

Japanese urban communities. Table 8.1 provides the data for the six largest cities.

As Table 8.1 shows, the highly mobile territories of Japanese colonisation translate into the quickly changing scene of urban hierarchies.

THE JAPANESE COMMUNITY OF KOREA

Table 8.1 The changing hierarchy of Japanese urban settlements in Korea

Rank	1915	1930	1944
1	Seoul, 62,914	Seoul, 105,639	Seoul, 158,710
2	Pusan, 29,890	Pusan, 47,761	Pusan, 61,081
3	Inch'ôn, 11,898	P'yôngyang, 25,115	P'yôngyang, 31,804
4	Py'ôngyang, 8,670	Taegu, 19,426	Ch'ôngjin, 29,058
5	Taegu, 7,948	Inch'ôn, 11,758	Inch'ôn, 21,740
6	Wônsan, 7,082	Chôngjin, 12,411	Taegu, 20,649

Source Kwôn T'aehwan, 'Ilche sidae-ji tosihwa' (The Colonial Urbanisation of Korea), in Ilche singmin t'ongch'i-wa sahoe kujo-ûi pyônhwa (Colonial Policies and Change of Social Structures in Korea) (Sôngnam, Han'guk chôngsin munhwa yôn'gywôn, 1990), 289–92.

If Seoul and Pusan remained untouched by such changes, other large provincial cities experienced ups and downs. In a context of general urbanisation that saw the overall urban population jump from 13 per cent to 21 per cent (through natural growth, internal and external migration), these dynamics clearly relate to economic change spurred by Japanese penetration.[30] Formerly open ports thus became the bustling port cities that had never existed during the Yi dynasty (Pusan, Inch'ôn, Wônsan) whereas the older-established interior cities of the kingdom languished (Chônju, Hamhûng, Andong). Conversely, better situated interior cities developed, thanks to new administrative designations and railway development (Sinûju, Taejôn). Finally, new cities emerged from the northern 'desert' as a result of industrialisation in the 1930s (Chôngjin, Najin, Hûngnam). If the driving force prompting territorial change was to be found in the Japanese community, the bulk of urban population growth was supplied by Korean people through heavy and rapid internal migration. However clever administrative retooling might have been, cities were also to become the business of the Koreans.

A Japanese representation of Korean cities published by the general government of Korea in 1930 offers ample evidence of the way the existence of 'ethnic' boundaries was masked in official sources. If we take its map of Mokp'o, for instance, in a period when this open port was inhabited by some 35,000 people (75 per cent Korean) no specific types of settlements can be distinguished.[31] If we compare it with the same map as drawn by Lautensach in the same period after extensive field surveys, we discover that the whole Korean settlement, easily identifiable in the urban layout, had simply been erased from the former

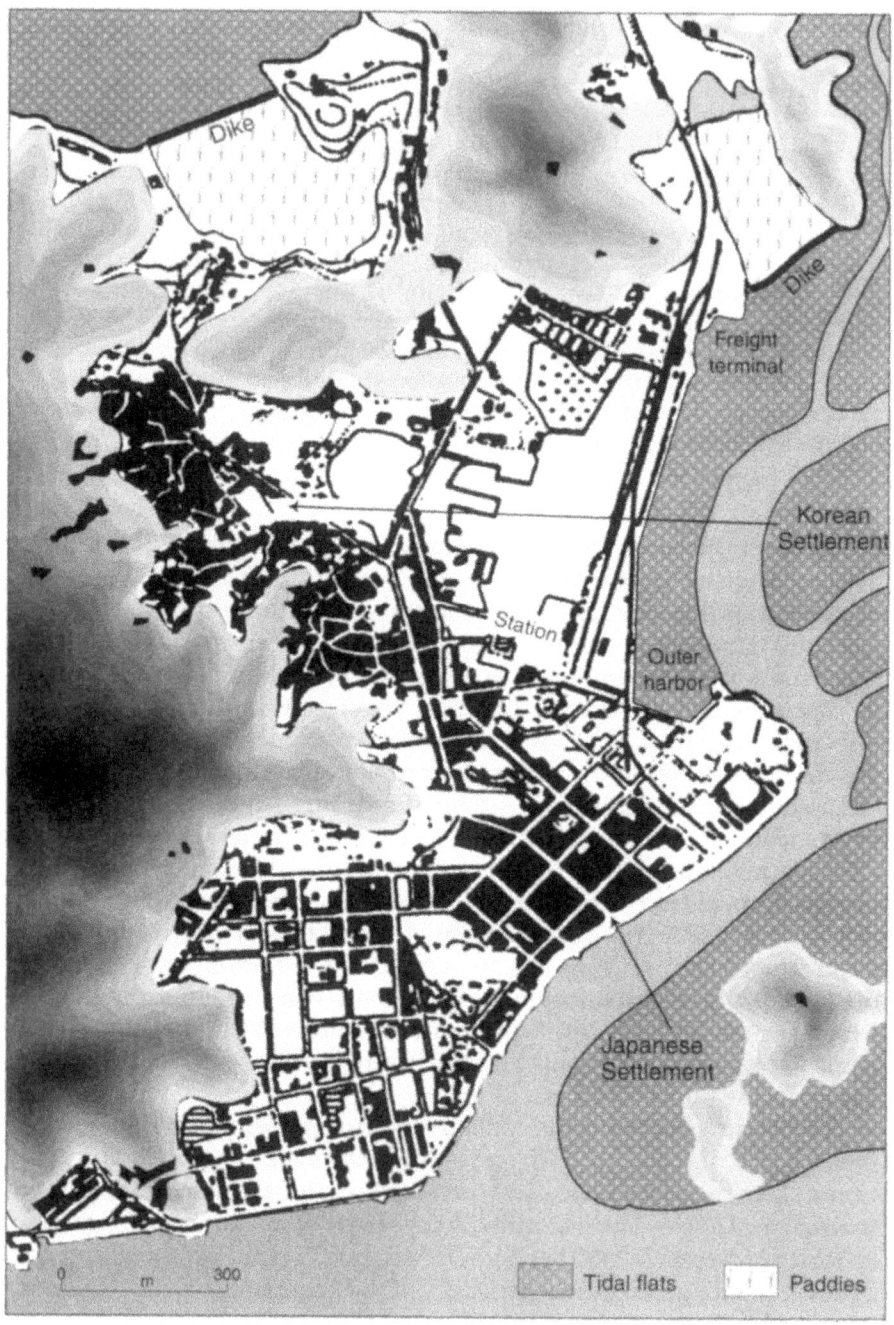

Figure 8.3 Reappearing Koreans in the 'open port' of Mokp'o

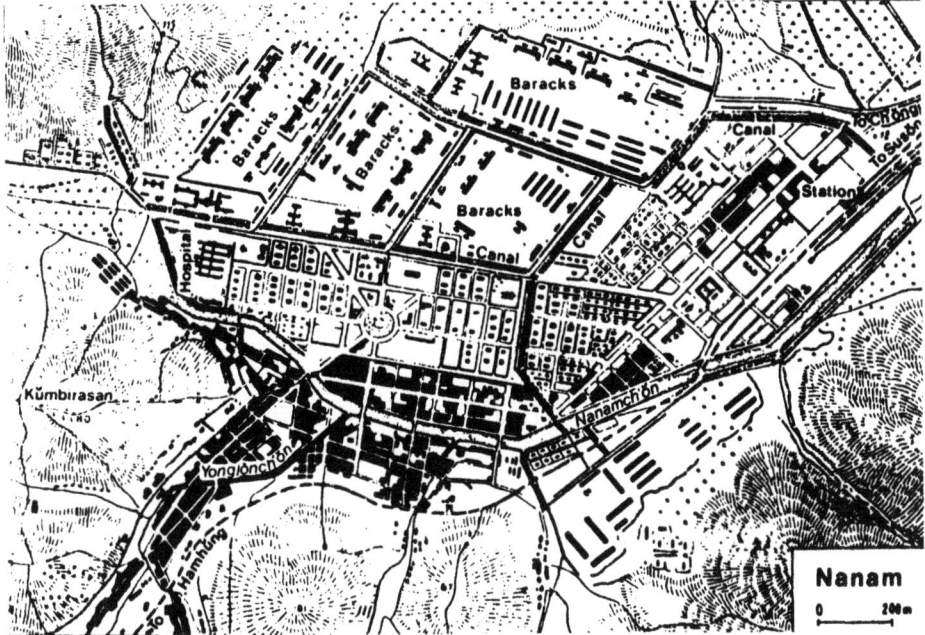

Figure 8.4 A new town in northern Korea: Nanam

publication; A German geographer of the old school happens to be a better source than most official Japanese documents for an assessment of this question.

In the many maps of his thick volume Japanese and Korean residential precincts do not simply show up as mere toponyms and distinct places, they also stand in sharp contrast in their gross urban forms. Japanese settlements are square, orderly, with a distinctly modern outlook, situated on flat land and connected to the sea or railways. By contrast, Korean settlements are disorderly, irregular, with a possibly archaic outlook, situated on slopes, unconnected with modern means of transport. Modern urbanism, generating modern urban forms, was a visible mark of Japanese territoriality.[32]

The first type of contact between the colonists and the colonised was actually a lack of contact. It corresponds to the few situations in which older Korean administrative centres were totally displaced for a new location. Sinûju and Nanam, in the north, and Taejôn in the south were cities in that category. The second type is certainly the more frequent. It consists in a simple separation of urban layouts such as the one recorded in Mokp'o. It can also be found in Wônsan. A third type could be characterised as a superimposition pattern, with Japa-

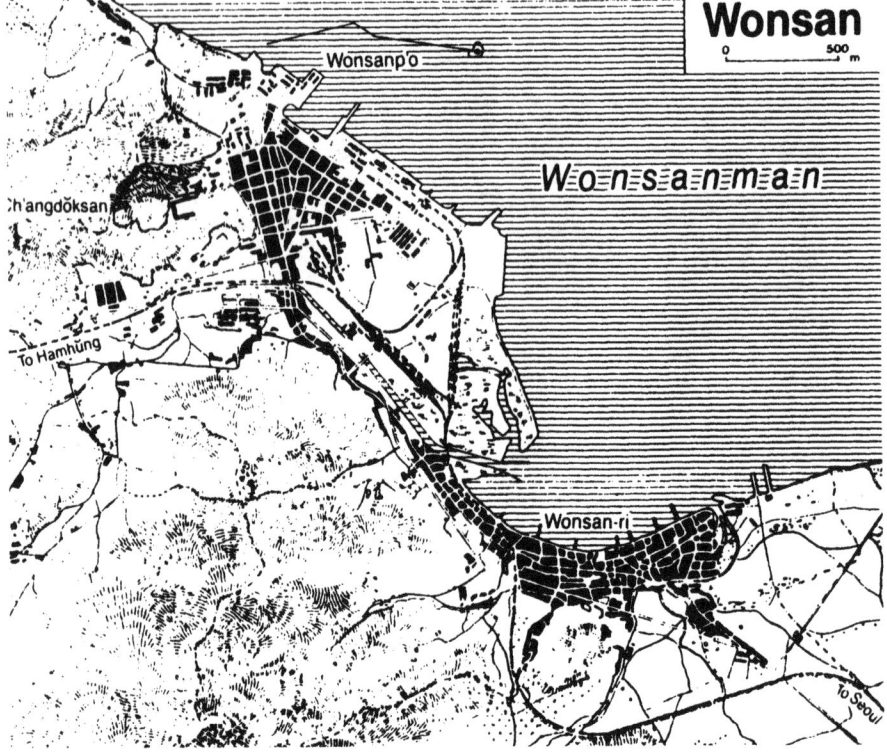

Figure 8.5 Split settlement in Wônsan

nese modern grid patterns cutting into or overlapping Korean traditional layouts. Such a pattern is to be found in Korea's oldest cities like P'yôngyang or Taegu. These types can generate complex compositions, as can been seen in the case of Seoul.

Neighbourhoods within cities could be just as revealing. In contrast to the cities of Indochina, where a thin layer of mixed settlement between the colonised and the colonists could be observed, supposedly Japanese and Korean settlements of Seoul inner city were so strictly separate from each other that it became a major topic of Korean newspapers in the 1920s. According to Son Chôngmok, a northern neighbourhood (*pukch'on*) inhabited by Koreans opposed a southern neighbourhood that was the kingdom of Japanese settlers (*namch'on*). It was there, on the slopes of Mount Namsan, that the Japanese had first established their consulate[33] and then developed a large Japanese-style city. If, in fact, the frontier between the two zones was neither clear-cut nor absolute – implying zones of mixed settlement whose meaning is still to be deciphered – the general pattern of estrangement tended to alter in the 1930s, opposing a Japanese-dominated inner city (the former citadel) to Korean-dominated slum suburbs.[34]

Locked tighter, more numerous and better aggregated in their city cores, Japanese settlers could forget that downtown areas (*shinai*), however good copies they were of their Japanese equivalents, were not the stuff of a real *naichi* (homeland). And since the constant drive to keep Koreans at bay through administrative sleight of hand, and their erasure from Japanese residential areas, proved insufficient, imaginary borders of the community also had to be rubbed out. Picturing Seoul in a thick book of the early 1930s, journalist Nagano Sueki provides a talking landscape of Japanese streets, shops and signs, Japanese factories and residences, Japanese modern buildings and shintô shrines, Japanese faces and dress.[35] This reassuring narrative served to deny the existence of the crowds of Korean people pressing in at the city gates. A fragile fortress of imaginings was thus the final (type of) border which gave a shape to the besieged Japanese of Korea.

Conclusion

A large new community such as the Japanese of Korea, about which extremely scant research is available, could hardly have been described over the long run of its history had not the concepts of shape and of border been called up to give undetailed but synthetic insights into its identity. Through social forms and occupational profiles, through territoriality and cities, through legal norms and administrative rules, and lastly through colonial ideology and representation, the Japanese community of Korea exhibited characteristics that were unusual in nineteenth and twentieth-century formal colonial Asia.

The apparent tension between the denied community and the besieged community was certainly alleviated by many kinds of devices, among which constant administrative retooling was probably the most efficient. However, neither those devices nor colonial ideology were powerful enough efficiently to provide the Japanese with a safe future in the peninsula. Facing the Japanese colonist was an existing Korean nation, not a would-be nation or non-aggregated ethnic groups. Moreover, the racial and cultural proximity of the colonists and the colonised may incline us to think of the Japanese of Korea as more comparable with British settlers in Ireland than, for instance, with Dutch settlers in Indonesia. And just as the Japanese colonial authorities managed to deny colonisation, Korean contemporary historiography conveys ideas of 'occupation' or 'invasion' when writing about this period.

A major contradiction arose from both colonial discourse and administrative practice: the Korean people were meant to be at once both similar to and different from the Japanese people. This had many consequences for the Japanese community of Korea itself, for, from the outset, it was a community whose identity *vis-à-vis* the Koreans and *vis-à-vis* the domestic Japanese was uneasy and troubled. Most communities in the formal colonial world were in a similarly uncomfortable position. However, whereas Western-style colonial policies of assimilation were founded on supposedly universal values to be applied to the colonised in a quite distant future, Japanese-style assimilation policies were founded on a far distant past, and on regional values to be applied to the colonised as rapidly as possible. Before this aim could be realised, the Japanese community of Korea was therefore exposed to a major ideological and practical tension: for how could a people who thought of themselves as exceptional in all respects (*kokutai*) have become a colonial power indulging in assimilationist policies?

Notes

1 *Shisei nijûgo nen shi* (Twenty-five Years of Administrative History) (Keijô, Chôsen Sôtokufu, 1935), quoted in Son Chôngmok, *Han'guk chibang chedo, chach'i sa yôn'gu* (A History of local Administration and Autonomy in Korea) (Seoul, Ilchisa, 1992), I, 129.
2 See for instance 'Singminji Chosôn sahoe-rul ottôkhe pol kôsinka' (Reconsidering Chosôn Colonial Society), *Yôksa-wa hyônsil* (History and Reality), 12 (1994), 11–113.
3 For a brief survey see Fumio Kaneko, 'Japanese Colonialism in Taiwan, Korea and Manchuria', *Historical Studies in Japan*, VIII, *1988–1992* (Tokyo, Yamakawa Shuppansha, 1995), 131–40, and *Kindai Nihon to shokuminchi* (Modern Japan and its Colonies) (Tokyo, Iwanami Kôza, 1992–93), 8 vols.
4 Mark R. Peattie, 'Japanese Treaty Port Settlements in China, 1895-1937', in Peter Duus, Ramon Myers and Mark R. Peattie, eds., *The Japanese Informal Empire in China, 1895–1937* (Princeton NJ, Princeton University Press, 1989), 166–209; Gregory Henderson, 'Japan's Chôsen: Immigrants, Ruthlessness and Development Shock', in A. Nahm, ed., *Korea under Japanese Colonial Rule* (Kalamazoo MI, Center for Korean Studies, Western Michigan University, 1973), 261–9.
5 Peter Duus, *The Abacus and the Sword: The Japanese Penetration of Korea, 1895–1910* (Berkeley CA, University of California Press, 1995).
6 Kimura Kenji, *Zai Chô Nihonjin no shakai shi* (A Social History of the Japanese of Korea) (Tokyo, Miraisha, 1989), 7.
7 H. Lautensach, *Korea: a Geography based on the Author's Travels and Literature* (Leipzig, 1945. Reprinted Berlin, Springer Verlag, 1988), 387–8.
8 *Takumu tôkei 1939* (Colonial Statistics from 1939) (Tokyo, Takumushô, 1941), as quoted in the 'Colonialism' entry of the *Kôdansha Encyclopeadia*. See also Chapter Nine of this volume.
9 P-Y. Trotignon, *La France au XXe siècle* (Paris, Bordas, 1976), 165 ff.; P. Brocheux and D. Hémery, *Indochine: la colonisation ambigué, 1858–1954* (Paris, La Découverte, 1994), 175.
10 D. McNamara, *Trade and Transformation in Korea, 1876–1945* (Boulder CO,

Westview, 1996), 37 and n. 49, quoting A. Booth, W. J. O'Malley and A. Weidemann, eds, *Indonesian Economic History in the Dutch Colonial Era* (New Haven CT, Yale Univertsity Press, 1990).
11 Note that growth in population was induced not only by migration but also by natural growth. Although data available do not allow us to assess a percentage, there were then different generations and types of settlers (including native Korean-Japanese).
12 M. Peattie, 'Japanese Treaty Ports', 170–2; Alain Delissen, 'Kim et Tanaka, techniciens dans la Corée des années 1930: modernisation et division coloniale du travail', *Le Mouvement Social*, 173 (1995), 97–111.
13 Duus, *The Abacus*, 315–16.
14 Kimura, *Zaichô nihonjin*, 30–7.
15 Lautensach, *Korea*, 389.
16 Duus, *The Abacus*, 322, quoting a 1911 *Kaigai risshin annai* (How to Succeed Overseas).
17 *Yongsan-gu chi* (Records of Yongsan-gu) (Seoul, Seoul t' ¡kpyôlsi, 1992), 80.
18 This development originates in Son Chôngmok, *Han'guk kaehanggi tosi pyônhwa kwajông yôn'gu – kaehangjang, kaesijang, chogye, kôryuji* (The Process of Urban Change in Korea, 1876–1905: Open Ports, Open Cities, Concessions, Settlements) (Seoul, Ilchisa, 1982), passim.
19 See Son Chôngmok, *Ilche kangjômgi tosihwa kwajông yôn'gu* (Colonial Urbanisation in Korea) (Seoul, Ilchisa, 1996), 356.
20 *Yongsan-gu*, 80–6.
21 Figures rearranged from Duus, *The Abacus*, 356–63.
22 Son Chôngmok, *Han'guk chibang, chedo, chach'i sa yôn'gu* (A History of Local Administration and Autonomy in Korea), I, Seoul, Ilchisa, 1992, 125–6.
23 For detailed accounts of the Inch'ôn *mindan*'s funds, *ibid.*, 146–8.
24 Kim Chang Rok, 'The Characteristics of the System of Japanese Imperialist Rule in Korea from 1905 to 1945', *Korea Journal*, 36:1 (1996), 20–49.
25 Duus, *The Abacus*, 363.
26 On chambers of commerce see McNamara, *Trade and Transformation in Korea*, 119–40.
27 Son Chôngmok, *Han'guk chibang*, 120–1.
28 Suh Sang-Chul, *Growth and Structural Change in the Korean Economy, 1910–1945* (Cambridge MA, Harvard University Press, 1978), 54.
29 Kwôn T'aehwan, 'Ilche sidae-ûi tosihwa' (The Colonial Urbanisation of Korea), in *Ilche singmin t'ongch'i-wa sahoe kujo-ûi pyônhwa* (Colonial Policies and Change of Social Structures in Korea) (Sôngnam, Han'guk chôngsin munhwa yôn'gywôn, 1990), 251–98.
30 *Ibid.*, 251.
31 *Chôsen no toyû* (Cities and Townships of Korea) (Keijô (Seoul), Government General of Korea, 1930), 22.
32 See my 'Kyôngsông chut'aek munje: crise de l'habitat ou crise du logement colonial?', *Revue de Corée*, No. 101, 29·2, 31 December 1997, 197–229.
33 Son Chôngmok, *Ilche kangjômgi tosihwa kwajông yôn'gu*, (Colonial Urbanisation in Korea) (Seoul, Ilchisa, 1996), 355–84.
34 See Lee Ki-Suk, *A Social Geography of Greater Seoul* (Seoul, Po Chin Chai, 1977), 97; Kang Man'gil, *Ilche sidae pinmin saenghwal sa yôn'gu* (Poor People's Lives under Japanese Colonialism) (Seoul, Ch'angjaksa, 1987), 237–86.
35 Nagano Sueki, *Keijô no omokage* (Scenes of Seoul) (Keijô (Seoul), Jijôsha, 1932).

CHAPTER NINE

'Little Japan' in Shanghai: an insulated community, 1875–1945
Christian Henriot

The image of Japan does not immediately evoke that of a colonial power. This may have to do with Japan's position as a latecomer into the club of predominantly European colonisers. Another explanation lies in the fact that its power and influence were not felt beyond Asia and did not seriously challenge the political and military supremacy of Western powers until the late 1930s. Yet Japan has a fairly long history of colonialism, which started within its own realm, and of population settlement abroad. Historians of imperialism have paid little attention to the Japanese experience. The outstanding exceptions are the ground-breaking studies on the Japanese empire edited by Peter Duus, Mark Peattie and Ramon Myers.[1] The present chapter will contribute to this reflection through the study of a unique Japanese settlement in China.

The Japanese community in Shanghai represents a special case in the Chinese context: 'While the city was the earliest and most important focus for the interplay of Japanese power, capital, and settlement in China, these elements did not operate within an exclusive Japanese concession.'[2] Both before and after the war, this situation created the conditions for conflict not only with the Chinese, but also with the foreign authorities, especially the Shanghai Municipal Council. Furthermore, although the Japanese community lived in a foreign enclave, it still established the self-governing institutions required by the Japanese Foreign Ministry, creating a proto-municipal organisation which increasingly challenged the legitimacy of Western power in Shanghai.[3]

The Japanese do not seem to have left an explicitly visible legacy. Foreign Shanghai was thought of as Western. The press did not devote much space to life in 'little Japan' at the time. The Japanese were a major topic for newspapers only when the imperial army fought in the city or when an anti-Japanese boycott campaign choked everyday life. But even then one would hardly find anything substantial about the civilian population and its activities. Nor have Western historians paid much attention to a Japanese community that appears only dimly in the background of their studies.[4] The present chapter will first outline the nature of the Japanese community in Shanghai and its major characteristics. Second, it will examine its major organisations and how they shaped community life. Finally, it turns to explore the major activities and challenges of the Japanese residents. The structure and self-contained nature of 'Little Japan' in Shanghai provide essential keys to our understanding not only of the behaviour of this major group of foreign residents, but also of its delicate interaction with the Chinese and the other foreign communities in the city.

The Japanese community: ecology and economy

The Japanese were latecomers to Shanghai, although they rapidly became the largest component of the foreign population. By 1915 they outnumbered the British by one and a half to one. In 1920 they overshadowed all the foreign communities taken together.[5] In sheer numbers, they ought to have been the most influential community, especially in the International Settlement. Nevertheless, the socio-economic profile of the Japanese population, and the peculiar electoral system which governed the election of the Shanghai Municipal Council, kept the Japanese in a subordinate role. Furthermore, the Japanese did not leave a strong symbolic image as a part of 'foreign Shanghai', either in contemporary literature or in journalism – their image as aggressors apart – or in Shanghai's collective memory.[6] The various and sometimes copious memoirs or city guides written by Japanese residents did not reach beyond their own community and they fell into oblivion after the war.

Table 9.1 gives a crude picture of the evolution of the Japanese population in Shanghai. It shows that, before the twentieth century, Shanghai was hardly a favourite destination for Japanese emigrants. During the 1904–06 period there was a real leap forward, with yearly increases close to 25 per cent. Thereafter, except for the years 1908–09 (10 per cent) and 1932 (10 per cent), there was a slow, though continuous, increase at 5 per cent a year.[7] In the mid-1930s there was even a relative falling off in the city's appeal, and Japanese community decreased in absolute terms. At times of acute tension, or fighting between Chinese and Japanese, the civilian population usually left for Japan. Regardless of individual preferences, the consulate would issue a repatriation order. Between 15 and 23 August 1937 eleven ships

Table 9.1 The Japanese population in Shanghai, 1870–1949

Year	Population	Year	Population	Year	Population
1870	3	1907	6,212	1935	27,299
1873	50+	1908	7,211	1936	26,135
1877	110+	1909	8,029	1937	26,070
1887	250	1914	11,138	1938	38,095
1890	644	1915	11,704	1939	54,308
1893	866	1920	15,551	1940	65,621
1894	1,000	1925	19,510	1941	87,277
1899	1,088	1930	24,207	1942	92,676
1900	1,172	1931	25,535	1943	103,968
1904	3,309	1932	28,438	1944	102,442
1905	4,414	1933	29,010	1945	72,654
1906	5,812	1934	28,801	1949	441

Sources Shanghai kyoryû mindan, 679, 805, 810, 822, 825, 843; Hiyoshi, Sonoda, *Sensô, jihen, Shanhai* (War, Incident, Shanghai) (Shanghai, Chûgoku tsûshimsha, 1944), 215–16; Kôsuke Takahashi, and Tadao Furumaya, *Shanhai shi, kyodai toshi no keisei to hitobito no itonami* (History of Shanghai: the Formation of a Great City and the Occupations of its People) (Tokyo, Tôhô shoten, 1995), 121; Xu Jie, 'Hongkou ribenren juzhuqu shulun', (A Presentation of the Japanese Quarter in Hongkou), *Shanghai yanjiu huncong* (Collected Essays of Research into Shanghai), 10 (1996), 297; *Zai chûshi hôjin*, 1944, 14.

evacuated women, children and the elderly, some 14,000 people. By 12 September – one month after the outbreak of the hostilities – fewer than 5,000 Japanese residents remained in the city.[8]

The end of the armed conflict in November 1937 and the occupation of Shanghai by imperial troops gave a new impetus to immigration into the city. Japanese residents were allowed to return to their homes after 14 November. Between September 1937 and March 1938, in addition to 17,912 returnees, 12,305 new immigrants disembarked at the Huangpu wharves.[9] The flow of Japanese grew at a brisk pace thereafter for four years (rising by 32 per cent in 1938, then by 30 per cent (1939), 17 per cent (1940) and 25 per cent (1941). Shanghai's reputation as a city of opportunities must have circulated broadly in Japan, and the city served as a magnet for a domestic population facing the scarcities of a rigorous war economy. Allied air raids may also have tempted many to chance their lot in an occupied city which in fact offered the conqueror a more secure and more promising environment than the homeland. Nevertheless, the rate of increase slowed down

'LITTLE JAPAN' IN SHANGHAI

substantially in 1942 (up by 6 per cent) and 1943 (11 per cent) and even led to a reversal in 1944 (down by 1·5 per cent).

The tremendous expansion of the Japanese community transformed it from a small enclave to a full-blown Japanese city in the heart of Shanghai. As we shall see, the strongly self-contained nature of the Japanese community and its pronounced insulation from the Chinese provides an explanation for this amazing boom. At the end of the war, all but a handful of Japanese residents were repatriated to their homeland. On the eve of the communist victory a few hundred Japanese still lived in Shanghai, but they were expelled, along with other foreign nationals, by the new authorities in the following months. Unlike the Western communities, the Japanese have left hardly any significant legacy. What remained in the popular mind was the opprobrium attached to the war and its tragedies.

The geographical origin of the Japanese who settled in Shanghai has been so far a matter of conjecture. The Japanese are not widely recognised as prone to emigration, even if small communities did develop abroad, in Brazil, Hawaii and the United States. Nevertheless, there was a tradition of emigration, even if it did not compare with those of China or India. This should not be surprising for a country usually described as an island (albeit in fact thousands of islands) and also, though erroneously, as a hostile environment owing to the lack of arable land. Parts of Japan nourished a sustained flow of emigrants to Korea and China, or toward the islands of the Pacific. Where did the Japanese living in Shanghai come from? The following analysis is based on the members of the Japanese Club – around 1,870 individuals in 1944 – a representative sample of the whole community.[10]

This analysis qualifies the accepted notion that the Japanese in China originated from 'the western prefectures of Kyushu – simply because they were closer to China than the rest of Japan – and from Tokyo, since its enormous population would inevitably make it a significant source of a 'urban-oriented' population.[11] Tokyo indeed ranked first as a source of emigrants, but provided only 12 per cent of the sample. It should be noted that all the prefectures of Japan are represented. Obviously, one group of prefectures outranked all the others. Figure 9.1 shows a distinct pattern with the dominant prefectures forming an arrow from Nakasaki to Osaka – through Fukuoka, Hiroshima, Okayama and Hyôgo – then to Tokyo. Aside from Nagano or Aichi, this distribution reflects the traditional pattern of Japanese emigration to Korea and China.[12] As Barbara Brooks indicates, the Japanese community also, of course, included Japanese subjects who were not ethnic Japanese, for example Koreans and Taiwanese. In 1944

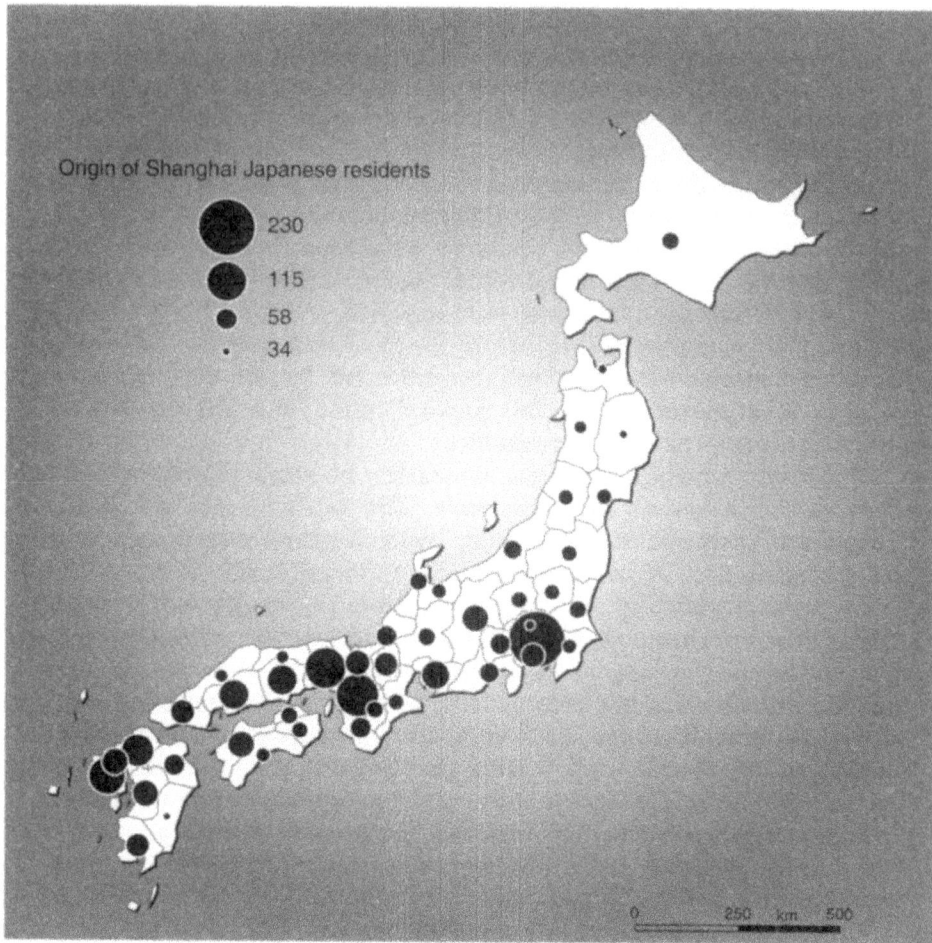

Figure 9.1 Geographical origin of Shanghai's Japanese residents, 1943

the two groups represented respectively 6 per cent and 4 per cent of the local Japanese community in Shanghai.

Male and female were fairly evenly balanced, men (52 per cent) slightly outnumbering women. This reflects the family situation of the large part of the population which was married (48 per cent). The war seems to have attracted an increasing number of unattached men and women: the average number of persons per family was fairly stable in the early 1930s at 4.6, but it started to decrease over the years, to 2.1 persons per family in 1941.[13] The large number of unmarried people can also be attributed to the age pattern of the Japanese community, which was rather young. Close to 62 per cent were under thirty in

Table 9.2 The family structure of the Japanese community, 1944

Category	Population (n)	Men (n)	Women (n)	Population (%)	Men (%)	Women (%)
Family heads	39,110	34,416	4,694	38.20	63.40	9.70
Family dependants	63,332	19,871	43,461	61.80	36.60	90.30
Total	102,442	54,287	48,155	100.00	100.00	100.00
Married	49,224	27,027	22,197	48.10	49.80	46.10
Unmarried	53,218	27,260	25,958	51.90	50.20	53.90
Total	102,442	54,287	48,155	100.00	100.00	100.00

Source Zai chûshi hôjin jittai chôsa hôkokusho. Shanhai no bu: shôwa 19-nen 2-gatsu 22-nichi (Survey Report on the Situation of Japanese Residents in Central China: Shanghai) ([Shanghai]: Zai Shanhai Nihon soryojikan, 1944).

1944 (children under fifteen making up 31 per cent). Those over sixty were a mere 1.5 per cent. A large segment of the work-age population was technically unemployed, mostly women who came as housewives (77 per cent). By contrast, the level of unemployment among men was very low (6 per cent).

The Japanese population was largely concentrated in just one part of the city, which set it apart from other non-Chinese communities. This general pattern of settlement 'north of Soochow Creek' – as it was then termed – seems to have arisen fairly early, although no specific factor can explain the preference for that area. The census data, for instance, show that the French Concession never attracted many Japanese – a few hundred at most – in spite of its reputation as a pleasant residential area. The International Settlement housed the bulk of the Japanese population, although a large segment settled in the Chinese districts adjacent to it. Within the settlement the favoured location was the Hongkou district, as shall be shown below. Then, from 1920 onward, Japanese residents started to extend their neighbourhoods into Zhabei and farther to the north of Hongkou. The latter became one of the contentious 'Extra-settlement roads' areas which the Japanese military later defended with the utmost vigour (hereafter called northern Hongkou).

In 1944 close to a quarter of the Japanese population lived in Hongkou, while a third had settled in northern Hongkou.[14] Another 15 per cent had their home in Yangshupu and 8 per cent in Zhabei. Taken together, these adjacent areas contained more than 80 per cent of the Japanese community. (See Fig. 9.2.) The war did not fundamentally alter the general pattern of distribution. The rate of concentration was even probably higher in the pre-war period. The Japanese army's occupation of the International Settlement in December 1941 and the abolition of the two settlements in July 1943 certainly offered the Japanese many opportunities to set up a firm and choose a home in the former Western-controlled areas south of Soochow Creek. By 1944 these areas harboured only 16·6 per cent of the Japanese community, while the rest of the Chinese municipality (Nanshi, Pudong and Wusong) had a mere 3 per cent.[15] In other words, there was a genuine Japanese city on the northern periphery of Shanghai. In this so-called 'Little Tokyo' whole rows of houses were Japanese, most of the shops were Japanese and the lingua franca was Japanese. A Japanese resident could live and work there as in Japan, without bothering to learn a foreign language, with limited interaction or even contact with the Chinese.

Another striking feature of the Japanese community in Shanghai was its insularity in terms of employment and job opportunities. Although the Japanese made use of the cheap Chinese labour force, they were more inclined than the other foreign communities to rely on their own strength. Japanese employees in 1940 amounted to 13,780 out of a total work force of 36,968.[16] The distribution of occupations according to size or business sector was very uneven. A majority of the Chinese (52 per cent) were to be found in the twenty-nine companies with industrial plants. Contrariwise, there were under a thousand Japanese employed in industrial plants.[17] Most of them worked in small companies, where they often outnumbered the Chinese staff. Another feature was the concentration of jobs in a few large enterprises: the sixteen largest firms (more than 300 employees) represented 54 per cent of the total work force. At the other end of the scale, the 306 smaller firms with fewer than twenty workers (59 per cent of the total number of firms) provided jobs for 8·2 per cent of the total work force.[18] In terms of qualifications, although the jobs of overseers were somehow distributed among Chinese and Japanese, most of the technicians (82 per cent) and senior executives (80 per cent) were Japanese. Either out of distrust of the Chinese, who were considered untrustworthy or because of Chinese nationalism, the result was the development of a wide range of job opportunities which included almost any type of craft, including menial jobs. A 1944 survey listed no fewer than 326 different professions in 272 business sectors.

By 1944 the Japanese labour force in the city as a whole amounted to 43,005 individuals. Two sectors – commerce and industry – dominated employment opportunities (60 per cent), followed by public ser-

'LITTLE JAPAN' IN SHANGHAI

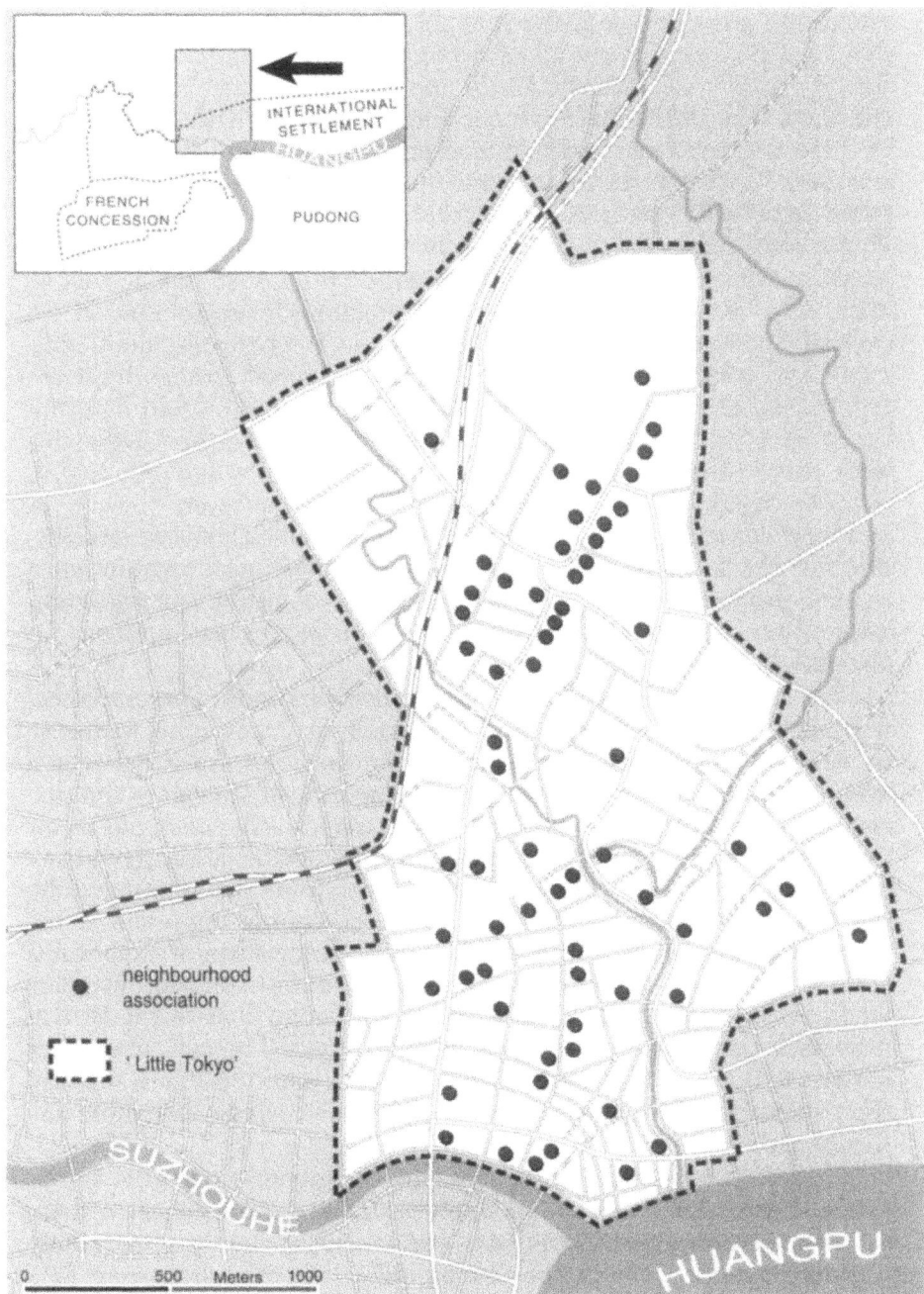

Figure 9.2 'Little Tokyo': Japanese neighbourhood associations, 1938

vices (20.5 per cent) and transport (14 per cent). Mark Peattie states that by 1931, 'nearly one quarter of the Japanese population ... was directly connected with the cotton industry, and a large proportion of the remainder did business of one kind or another with the mills'.[19] By 1944 the textile industry, including clothing, provided 2,898 jobs, less than 7 per cent of total employment.[20] Even if the trading companies involved in textiles are included, the figure does not even reach 10 per cent. Although there were changes in the composition of the Japanese labour force, the transformations were not so drastic that so many jobs were lost. The 1931 figure requires reassessment. If we exclude managers (10.2 per cent), technicians (5.9 per cent), public servants and professionals (8.6 per cent), the largest categories were employees (47.4 per cent) and workers (25.6 per cent). Their distribution among the various sectors shows an ordinary pattern: technicians were concentrated in industry, workers were evenly disseminated in industry, transport and commerce, and employees were present in industry, commerce, public services and transport. Characteristically, too, two-thirds of the 'entrepreneurs' category belonged to commerce and the rest to industry. These figures confirm that the Japanese community was composed mostly of shopkeepers and minor employees of Japanese firms.

This categorisation stems from Japanese administrative statistical work and can easily serve sociological analysis. From other writings, we know that there was a cleavage within the community between a minority of expatriates – the *kaisha-ha*, or company people – and the vast majority of lower and middle-class residents – the *dochaku-ha*, or 'natives'.[21] This division reflected itself in the organisation that structured the community: the Residents' Association was dominated by the former, while the Federation of Street Unions represented the interests of the latter. Although the small community of expatriates enjoyed privileged access to their consular authorities, one wonders whether they had an overall influence similar to that of the British expatriate community on the Shanghailanders.[22] The lack of sources has prevented us from examining what kind of conflicts, if any, divided the two parties and to what extent divisions existed regarding the 'China problem'.

In terms of economic presence, the development of Japanese enterprises in Shanghai was a late phenomenon, but it experienced a sharp increase after the First World War. As Douglas Reynolds noted, there was no Japanese firm in the city in 1871, whereas there were 221 British companies, forty German companies, and seventeen French firms. Two decades later, although forty-one Japanese firms had been established, only twenty-five of them had survived.[23] A 1940 Japanese

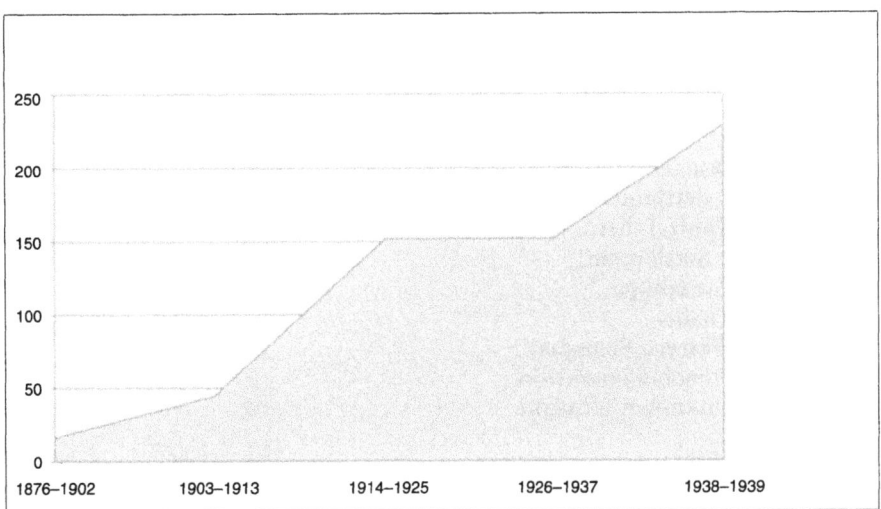

Figure 9.3 Year of foundation of Japanese firms, 1941

Chamber of Trade and Industry survey showed 596 firms, plants and shops in greater Shanghai.[24] This sample is large enough to give us an idea of the development of Japanese firms in Shanghai before and after 1937 (Figure 9.3). If we exclude five companies for which the date of foundation is not known, forty-six firms had been established earlier than 1913, and only fifteen of those before 1902. The 1914–25 period saw a sharp increase, with 151 new companies and shops in ten years. The following decade confirmed the Japanese interest in Shanghai with another 154 firms. Obviously the Sino-Japanese War provided new opportunities, as 228 new firms were established in the 1938–39 period, and this momentum continued. The movement never ceased. By mid-1941 there were 784 firms, and 909 three years later.[25]

Japanese firms were also concentrated in one district. Before 1937, 54 per cent were based in Hongkou and 34 per cent in the International Settlement's central district. Yangshupu came third, mostly for industrial plants, with 6 per cent. Zhabei and Huxi accounted for a mere 2 per cent each, although a substantial segment of the Japanese population lived in Zhabei. What is striking is the complete absence of the French Concession, save for three shops. After 1937 a slightly larger share of Japanese firms is to be found in the central district. After Pearl Harbor the distribution must have changed again, but this was the result of the take-over of the whole city by the Japanese army. As long as the settlements remained in foreign hands, Japanese entrepreneurs chose to remain where they felt secure and had their customers.

Table 9.3 Distribution of Japanese firms in Shanghai by district

District	No.	%
Hongkou (International Settlement/Chinese Municipality)	318	53.8
Central district (International Settlement)	198	33.5
Yangshupu	38	6.4
Zhabei	14	2.4
Western Shanghai	10	1.7
French Concession	3	0.5
Unknown location	10	1.7
Total	591	100.0

Source *Shanhai shôkô roku* (Yearbook of Japanese Commercial and Industrial Companies in Shanghai) (Shanghai: Shanhai shôkô kaigisho, 1941).

Firms located in the central district of the International Settlement were involved in trade, banking and transport; many banks were concentrated in Kiukiang Road, Shanghai's Wall Street. More than half the factories were located either in Yangshupu (49 per cent) or in Huxi, the westernmost part of the settlement.

In terms of business activity, the distribution of firms was biased toward trade. From the 1941 survey, close to 80 per cent of the companies were categorised as 'general traders' before 1937. Industrial enterprises formed the second largest group, although with only 7.2 per cent of the total.[26] In order of size, banks and insurance companies, construction and transport accounted for the rest. The inclusion of the companies established after 1937 reveals that the war and the increase in the number of firms did not alter this distribution pattern.

In summary, the Japanese who came to Shanghai were, above all, merchants and traders for whom the city and its vast hinterland represented a land of opportunities for the sale of Japanese goods and for the purchase of primary materials for export to Japan. Industry was not a major sector, except for textiles. Japanese immigrants settled in a specific part of the city, which, consciously or not, led to the emergence of a 'Japanese settlement'. Although they lived in an international metropolis, the Japanese formed a self-contained community with a strong tendency to preserve a large degree of autonomy *vis-à-vis* Westerners and the Chinese population. This created the condi-

Table 9.4 Business sectors of Japanese firms before 1937

Business sector	No.	%
General trading	300	79.2
Factories and manufacturing	30	7.9
Banking, finance and insurance	20	5.3
Construction	15	3.9
Transport	12	3.2
Miscellaneous	2	0.5
Total	379	100.0

Source Shanhai shôkô roku (Yearbook of Japanese Commercial and Industrial Companies in Shanghai) (Shanghai: Shanhai shôkô kaigisho, 1941).

tions for the development of a fully-fledged Japanese city that offered a myriad of jobs to people of almost any extraction. Other foreign communities were geographically evenly distributed in the various districts of the settlements and overwhelmed by the presence of Chinese residents.

A controlled community

Of all the foreign communities in Shanghai, and probably in China, the Japanese were beyond any doubt the most organised and regulated. Two major factors may explain this phenomenon: the strong involvement of the state in the control of its subjects, and the overreaction of Japanese residents to Chinese nationalism. Thus the development of associations, though spontaneous in the beginning, was reinforced and shaped by the forceful intervention of the Japanese state. Furthermore, a systematic pattern can be seen, whereby every Japanese association was formed in response to a specific event that was perceived to be an actual or imagined threat to their interests by the Chinese population.

It is not clear what kind of organisations existed among Japanese residents in the nineteenth century. Most likely the earliest form of organisation was the neighbourhood associations (Chônaikai). Given the untroubled nature of Sino-Japanese relations until 1915, the main purpose of these associations was to provide basic social services to their members, similar to those of the small guilds in Chinese society. The structuring of Japanese communities was given a new impetus in 1902 by the Japanese government with the promulgation of provisional regulations designed to govern its subjects in China, especially those who lived in exclusively Japanese settlements.[27] Three years later, on 7 March 1905, a more elaborate text, the Residents' Association Law (Kyoryû mindanpô), was enacted. It called for the formation of local residents' associations (kyoryû mindan) and the election of legislative and executive organs to serve as self-governing bodies. In fact, although various powers were delegated to these associations, residual power over all decisions rested with Japanese consuls.[28]

In Shanghai the consulate, the Japanese Club (Nihon kurabu) and the Japanese Industrial Club (Nihon jitsugyô kurabu) established an Association of Japanese (Nihonjin kyôkai) to take care of school management, a volunteer corps and other charitable activities.[29] The association had 226 members in 1905–06 and its thirty-member leadership was nominated by the consul. In August 1907 the Foreign Ministry issued a new decree that called for the organisation of a residents' association in Shanghai, in accord with the 1905 law.[30] The Shanghai association, founded in September 1907, was slightly different, as it operated within a settlement dominated by other powers. Nevertheless, although its structure and responsibilities were truncated, it worked indeed as a proto-municipal government for the Japanese community. The Residents' Association became the official representative of the community in its dealings with the Japanese consulate and with the Shanghai Municipal Council.[31]

From 1915 onwards, Japanese communities felt threatened by the rising tide of Chinese nationalism.[32] Occasional outbursts of violence against Japanese property or residents reinforced this sense of vulnerability, while the powerful anti-Japanese boycott campaigns hit Japanese economic interests hard.[33] In this context, the neighbourhood associations provided the basis for an organisation – the Federation of Street Unions (Shanhai Nihonjin kakuro rengôkai) – that came to play a very active role in the mobilisation of the Japanese population. It was formally established in 1915 as a federation (Shônaikai rengôkai), on the initiative of six neighbourhood associations, in order to cope with the strong anti-Japanese boycott movement generated by the Japanese government's 'Twenty-one Demands'.[34] Local Japanese leaders considered that they could not count on the Shanghai Municipal Police to protect them. In 1915 the federation already had forty member associations, and each outburst of Chinese nationalism brought renewed momentum.[35] In 1925 the May Thirtieth Movement again exposed the Japanese community to the effects of a boycott. The federation formed picket units to maintain public order, and the

Japanese consul ordered the establishment of neighbourhood associations in all districts where Japanese residents lived.[36]

Nevertheless, the federation did not include the entire Japanese population until well into the war period. There were some fifty-six associations with 25,000 members in 1937. In 1940 it had close to seventy neighbourhood associations with 30,000 members at a time when the whole population was well over 65,000 strong.[37] Control by the authorities of residents' associations, however, was reinforced by their reorganisation under a new system. The districts of the city where the Japanese lived were divided into nineteen sectors, each with its federation of neighbourhood associations and militia units. All the daily necessities of the Japanese community were monitored at this level, especially after the introduction of a rationing system or the launching of a campaign to collect metals.[38] On the eve of its dissolution in 1942, the federation included 200 member associations.[39] No individual could escape the thin net of surveillance that overshadowed the community.

Another body deserves special mention. In 1911 the sudden collapse of the Qing government took Japanese entrepreneurs by surprise and they feared that the new republican authorities might threaten their access to the Chinese market. These worries led to the establishment of the Shanghai Entrepreneurs' Association (Shanhai jitsugyô kyôkai) in December 1911, with twenty-nine companies and thirty-seven individual members.[40] Its official purpose was to study China's economic conditions and to defend Japanese interests. The association was the direct forerunner of the Japanese Chamber of Commerce (Shanhai Nihon shôgyô kaigisho), which was officially inaugurated in 1919, and which changed its name to the Japanese Chamber of Trade and Industry in 1928 (Shanhai Nihon shôkô kaigisho).[41] This was a less vocal body than the Residents' Association or the Federation of Street Unions, but it monitored the economic policies of the Chinese government very closely and prepared well documented surveys for the use of its home government in its negotiations with the Chinese authorities. By 1938 its membership included 148 individuals and 369 companies.[42] The latter increased tremendously after the war, from 664 in 1939 to 781 in 1941.[43]

The war was a real watershed for the Japanese organisations in Shanghai. Whereas they had previously served as the mouthpiece and representatives of the local community, and as the willing tool of Japanese policies in China, they became more clearly the docile instruments of the Japanese authorities in Shanghai.[44] At the end of 1941 the Japanese consul, on Foreign Ministry instructions, decided that the coexistence of two organisations ran against the necessity of keeping all residents in line, in view of the war developments. The Shanghai Youth Club (Shanhai Seinen Kurabu) had already been reorganised in February 1939, and again in August 1940, with a new name – the Shanghai Youth Corps (Shanhai Seinendan) – into a quasi-paramilitary group (14,000 strong) whose purpose was to prepare the local youth to fight for the homeland.[45] In January 1942 the consul ordered the Residents' Association and the Federation of Street Unions to merge, although in practice the Residents' Association took over the duties, powers and property of the federation.[46] Discussions were initiated in September but, although the dissolution was officially reported in June, the formal transfer of powers only took place in November, and the FSU grudgingly conceded its own dissolution.[47]

Although a volunteer corps was established as early as 1900, an organised militia did not come into being until 1925, when it was felt necessary to counter the anti-Japanese movement and the pressures and threats to Japanese residents of Chinese boycott organisations.[48] Furthermore, in 1927, when the Nationalist regime started to press for the recovery of foreign settlements, the chairman of the JRA and its secretary, both former army officers, decided to institute a local branch of the Imperial Military Reservist Association (Teikoku Zaigôgun-jinkai). These paramilitary organisations came to serve an important instrumental role in maintaining close links with the Japanese army.[49] In 1932 the militia assisted the army in its fight against Chinese troops by providing intelligence and guidance to military units in the city. It also fought fires which broke out during the battle, enforced a curfew, collected mail and distributed food and basic necessities to residents caught up in the conflict. But the militia also distinguished itself by brutal acts of reprisal against Chinese civilians living in Hongkou and Zhabei.[50] In 1937 the militia system was regularised. Each neighbourhood association was ordered to establish a militia unit and provide it with financial support. It assumed the same functions during fighting, taking care of wounded and sick soldiers and of the Japanese refugees from inland China. The militia increased rapidly in size with the growth of the Japanese population. It had seventy-eight units in March 1940 with 7,956 men and 179 units with 14,683 members in June 1942.[51]

With the outbreak of war all sectors of the Japanese community were mobilised. Women were assembled in a new organisation – the Women's Emergency Association (Shanhai jikyoku fujinkai) – created in February 1938, with thirteen departments covering every aspect of social welfare.[52] There were branches at the level of the neighbourhood associations, and one of their tasks was the running of rest centres established by the Residents' Association for Japanese soldiers. Some

200–300 soldiers were received daily in these centres, which also organised performances, raising funds for the benefit of local garrisons. One department mended uniforms.[53] The war inevitably brought economic difficulties for Japanese residents, but they did not feel the pinch of economic crisis until after 1941. The Japanese authorities were much concerned about the livelihood of their subjects, and between July 1941 and June 1942 carried out a detailed survey of Japanese residents' standard of living.[54] When severe shortages of rice and raw materials hit the city, a separate system of rationing was established for the sole benefit of the Japanese residents and their Chinese servants.[55] It was managed by the Residents' Association, under the supervision of the consulate and the Bureau of Liaison of the Asia Development Board.[56]

Activities and challenges

As a pressure group directed against their own government, the Japanese associations lobbied through three channels. The JRA was first of all a powerful lobbying group which asked for forceful action by the Chinese government to dampen each outburst of nationalism. Second, the establishment and maintenance of many schools and teaching staff represented a major financial burden, and the association lobbied for adequate funding from the Japanese government. Third, the JRA also pressured its government to grant relief funds in order to help the local community recover from war destruction in 1932 and 1937. After the first conflict, it received 1·4 million yen in the form of indemnities, but only after eighteen months of appeals was Tokyo convinced.[57] In 1937 it also obtained financial help from the metropolitan authorities, though in the form of a loan, which served partially to offset the damage caused by the bombing and fires that erased whole parts of Hongkou and Zhabei.[58] The drain on the resources of the Residents' Association caused by the influx of waves of residents forced it to negotiate a restructuring of its debts.[59]

The JRA was in charge of a variety of communal services: public health, welfare and above all schools. Its leaders were elected for a period of two years, but the consulate had a strong hand in the designation of the candidates. There was usually a single list of candidates (fifty-five) who were voted in by the annual assembly.[60] Participation in elections was fairly high, though not universal, even among eligible voters.[61] The association relied on its permanent departments (Secretariat, General Affairs, Education, Finance, Health and Social Affairs) and on a wide range of permanent or *ad hoc* committees (the Tax Investigation Committee [Kakin chôsa i-inkai], External Relations

Research Committee [Taigai kôshô kenkyû i-inkai], Welfare Promotion Committee [fukuri zôshin i-inkai], Land Value Assessment Committee [Tochi kakaku chôsa i-inkai]).[62] To assume its new responsibilities after the dissolution of the FSU, the Residents' Association created in November 1941 a new department – the Civil Affairs Department (*Shiminbu*) – which exerted overall control over the neighbourhood associations.[63] In 1942 another department was established to take charge of construction projects, mostly schools. By 1942 the JRA employed 330 persons.[64]

The erection of schools was a major concern for the Japanese community.[65] For decades in the nineteenth century the schooling of Japanese children had been arranged on an *ad hoc* basis, thanks to the initiative of a private tutor,[66] then with the support of a Buddhist temple (Higashi Honganji) after 1887.[67] In March 1906 a formal school opened on Wuchang Road. As the number of residents and children increased, new establishments were set up. From 1926 onward more primary schools were created, along with a junior high school and two vocational schools.[68] By 1937 there were nine schools. To relieve its burden, the JRA turned to the SMC for financial support and, after two years of difficult negotiations, succeeded. From 1931 onward the SMC contributed a regular sum to Japanese schools.[69] The massive immigration of the Japanese after the war required the founding of new schools. The JRA kept applying for subventions from the Japanese government.[70] By 1943 the association ran sixteen schools serving 13,359 children.

To finance these activities, the Residents' Association levied taxes on its members, although the latter were also subject to the taxes raised by the Shanghai Municipal Council in the International Settlement, or the Chinese Municipal Government in the Chinese municipality. This may explain why, in 1940, the Japanese opposed tax increases decreed by the SMC – a struggle which saw FSU chairman Hayashi Yûkichi attempt to assassinate SMC chairman W. J. Keswick on 23 January that year. They actually had to bear a heavier burden than the other foreign taxpayers.[71] As for other communities, the issue of taxes was a recurring headache for the JRA leadership, and a source of disputes and conflicts within the community. Several reforms were introduced over the years with the aim of increasing revenue and distributing the burden more equally. Twice, a tax expert was hired from Japan to head a reform committee.[72] Whatever the reforms, the largest share of taxes was borne by companies and shops, although individual income tax represented 18 per cent of the total revenue of the association.[73]

As a pressure group the Japanese associations started to claim a larger share of municipal power in Shanghai, especially in the International Settlement, where most of them lived. The Land Regulations that governed the structure of the SMC limited the number of seats available, and an informal agreement preserved an Anglo-American majority.[74] The Japanese were allotted one seat on the council in 1915, taken from the German community, and a second one in 1927.[75] Any change in favour of the Japanese would automatically call for a decrease of Western influence. The British were adamant about maintaining the *status quo*, particularly after 1937, when it was feared that pro-Japanese Chinese councillors would be installed in the five Chinese seats and that the Anglo-Saxon majority would be terminated. In 1936 the Japanese had demanded that a third Japanese councillor should be elected, were defeated at the polls, and accused the SMC of electoral fraud.[76] The same demand was expressed at each following election. The increasing number of Japanese residents, and hence of potential voters, eventually created a situation under which the Japanese could have their way, but in 1938 they failed for lack of eligible voters.[77] In the following years they definitely challenged the Western powers by presenting five candidates. The Japanese made careful preparations, mobilising both their own community and foreign communities they thought were subject to their influence (such as European Jewish refugees). A clever though clearly abusive use of the electoral system by the Anglo-Saxon bloc again kept Japanese ambitions in check.[78]

Although they failed to gain more power at the top of the SMC, from the 1930s onward the Japanese managed to make substantial inroads into the municipal administration. In 1916 a Japanese branch of the SMP had been established under the pressure of the FSU. It was manned by thirty men from the Tokyo Metropolitan Police,[79] and a Japanese assistant commissioner was also appointed in the 1920s.[80] New recruits were added, so that by 1937 the SMP had more than 180 Japanese constables, and 300 in 1940, while another thirty Japanese were employed in the SMC's various services.[81] The war provided the Japanese with a new opportunity to press for the recruitment of more Japanese in the SMC and in other bodies such as the Chinese Maritime Customs.[82] They pursued a systematic policy of lobbying until SMC leaders had to give in to their demands. In November 1941 it appointed two chief deputy commissioners and one officer attached to the politically sensitive Special Branch of the SMP.[83]

Conclusion

The Japanese community in Shanghai was a microcosm of Japan on Chinese territory. Its size was not unusual, at least until 1937, given the proximity of their home country, the fluidity of circulation between the two countries and their close cultural links. The war undoubtedly generated an anomalous expansion in a context which was perceived as favourable to Japanese interests. Commercial opportunities were the primary force that attracted tens of thousands of Japanese to Shanghai both before and after 1937. And the more it grew the more it offered all kinds of job opportunities to would-be emigrants. Eventually the Japanese community was made up of a large body of small shopkeepers, employees, and workers who left Japan in search of job opportunities and a better lifestyle than in their still poverty-ridden country. The privileges of extraterritoriality provided an additional incentive. This sociological profile and the context go a long way to explain the very conservative attitude of the Japanese community toward any challenge to the *status quo*.

The Japanese population evolved from an organised community into a militarised society. Even though the formation of associations can be traced to the initiative of private groups, the intervention of the state was a determining factor in the structuring of the Japanese community. From the 1902 regulations to the full mobilisation of the post-Pearl Harbor period, the consular authorities not only monitored their subjects very closely, they actually ruled over almost every aspect of the life of the Japanese population. The war obviously exacerbated this phenomenon, but at every stage the limited degree of autonomy of the Japanese community in Shanghai *vis-à-vis* their official institutions can be observed. This is not to say there was no contradiction or conflict between the residents and the authorities, but the latter clearly had the upper hand. The demands of the Japanese residents were either of a corporatist nature (funds for the schools, relief funds) or of a political nature. The fear of Chinese nationalism and the tendency to self-victimisation contributed to increased dependence on the diplomats and the military. On the 'China problem' there was a genuine united front.

The Japanese community had a strong sense of identity which, after 1915, expressed itself in an increasingly aggressive tone. The development of anti-Japanese movements generated a sense of vulnerability which in turn fed a defensive posture and sense of siege *vis-à-vis* the Chinese. The concentration of their living quarters, shops and firms in one district of the city created an insulated environment for Japanese residents. Although they lived in China they were hardly in touch with Chinese realities. They saw everything through their media, through their associations and through their consular authorities. The mountains of detailed and often accurate information Japanese agencies such as the chamber of commerce or the Shanghai Bureau of the South Manchuria Railway Company produced coexisted with an indifference to and ignorance of Chinese society. There was no understanding of what shaped Chinese public opinion, and the Japanese perceived themselves as the target of adverse forces manipulated by the Western powers in the midst of hostile Chinese masses.

Notes

1 Ramon H. Myers and Mark R. Peattie, eds, *The Japanese Colonial Empire, 1895-1945* (Princeton NJ, Princeton University Press, 1984); Peter Duus, Ramon H. Myers and Mark R. Peattie, eds, *The Japanese Informal Empire in China, 1895-1937* (Princeton NJ, Princeton University Press, 1989); *The Japanese Wartime Empire* (Princeton NJ, Princeton University Press, 1996); Peter Duus, *The Abacus and the Sword: The Japanese Penetration of Korea, 1895-1910* (Berkeley CA, University of California Press, 1995).
2 Mark R. Peattie, 'Japanese Treaty Port Settlements in China, 1895-1937', in Duus, Myers and Peattie, eds, *Japanese Informal Empire in China*, 181.
3 Although the Japanese had obtained the right to establish a settlement in Shanghai and other ports in China as early as 1896, the government does not seem to have pressed for the establishment of an exclusive settlement: Peattie, 'Japanese Treaty Port Settlements in China', 168, 172.
4 Silence about the Japanese is a feature of Albert Feuerwerker, 'The Foreign Presence in China', in *The Cambridge History of China* (New York, Cambridge University Press, 1983), XII, *Republican China, 1912-1949*, Part 1, 128-208; Nicholas R. Clifford, *Spoilt Children of Empire: Westerners in Shanghai and the Chinese Revolution of the 1920s* (Hanover NH and London, University Press of New England, 1991).
5 Zou Yiren, *Jiu Shanghai renkou bianqian de yanjiu* (A Study of the Evolution of the Population of Old Shanghai) (Shanghai, Renmin chubanshe, 1980), 145.
6 For a basic chronology of major events during the Meiji period (1868-1911) see Takatsuna Hirohumi and Chen Zu'en, 'Shanghai ribenren juliumin guanxi nianbiao' (A Chronology of the Japanese Residents in Shanghai), *Shilin* (The Forest of History), 1 (1995), 93-9.
7 We have no explanation for 1908 and 1909, but the crushing *Blitzkrieg* the Japanese army inflicted on Chinese troops in 1932 and the favourable terms of the settlement that followed worked as an incentive to would-be emigrants from Japan. On the 1931-32 conflict see Christian Henriot, *Shanghai, 1927-1937: Municipal Power, Locality, and Modernization* (Berkeley CA, University of California Press, 1993), chapter 4.
8 *Shanhai kyoryû mindan sanjûgo shunen kinenshi* (Commemorative Volume for the thirty-fifth Anniversary of the Shanghai Residents' Association) (Shanghai, Shanhai kyoryû mindan hen, 1942), 672-3.
9 *Shanhai kyoryû mindan*, 679.
10 *Kai-in meibo* (List of Members) (Shanghai, Shanhai nippon kurabu, 1944).
11 Peattie, 'Japanese Treaty Port Settlements', 171.
12 Philippe Pelletier, *La Japonésie: géopolitique et géographie historique de la surinsularité au Japon* (Paris, CNRS Editions, 1997), 345-6. I wish to thank Philippe Pelletier for his help in drawing Fig. 9.1.
13 Hiyoshi Sonoda, *Sensô, Jihen, Shanhai* (War, Incident, Shanghai) (Shanghai, Chûgoku tsûshinsha, 1944), 215-16.
14 For a general presentation see Xu Jie, 'Hongkou ribenren juzhuqu shulun' (A Presentation of the Japanese Quarter in Hongkou), *Shanghai yanjiu luncong* (Collected Essays of research on Shanghai), 10 (1996), 279-99.
15 This pattern of distribution was not the same among the other national groups

forming the Japanese community. The French Concession had long been a refuge for Korean nationalists fighting the occupation of their country by Japan (they were labelled 'foul' elements in Japanese official documents). They were also proportionately more numerous in the Chinese districts. As for the Taiwanese, it can be argued that, although they were Japanese subjects, they found it more congenial, culturally and for business purposes, to live among their kin: *Shanhai kyoryû mindan*, 999–1000.

16 This analysis is based on *Shanhai shôkô roku*. This source lists every Japanese firm in Shanghai (bar seventy-seven), with detailed data on their staff and a breakdown by sex, nationality and professional rank: *Shanhai shôkô roku* (Yearbook of Japanese Commercial and Industrial Companies in Shanghai) (Shanghai, Shanhai shôkô kaigisho, 1941).

17 In the 1941 yearbook only forty-three firms are listed as 'factory' with a total work force of 1,323 (six are unknown). In the *Shanhai shôkô roku*, however, firms originally listed as 'traders' in the 1941 yearbook appear to have industrial plant and workshops, with a total work force of 14,371, of whom 12,946 worked in plants. Altogether, therefore, the industrial work force in Japanese firms can be estimated at 15,206, including 2,831 Japanese (only 970 actually worked in plants).

18 When considering only the Japanese work force, there was a lower degree of concentration. The figures for the Japanese were 44·1 per cent and 12·3 per cent respectively.

19 Peattie, 'Japanese Treaty Port Settlements in China', 204.

20 *Zai chûshi hôjin jittai chôsa hôkokusho. Shanhai no bu: shôwa 19-nen 2-gatsu 22-nichi* (Survey Report on the Situation of Japanese Residents in Central China: Shanghai) ([Shanghai], Zai Shanhai nihon soryojikan, 1944).

21 The definition of the *kaisha-ha* is a difficult issue. From the 1944 survey, 10 per cent of the Japanese were categorised as 'managers', that is, 4,383 people, but that includes all the shop owners. The membership of the Japanese Club in the same year was 1,870. This smaller group gives a better indication of the nature of the local Japanese elite. Although it can be considered a 'small circle' (Peattie), it contained more than simply the representatives of 'the great commercial, shipping, banking, and industrial interests in Japan': Peattie, 'Japanese Treaty Port Settlements', 193.

22 Robert Bickers, 'Shanghailanders: The Formation and Identity of the British Settler Community in Shanghai, 1843–1937', *Past and Present*, 159 (1998), 161–211.

23 Douglas R. Reynolds, 'Training young China Hands: Tôa Dôbun Shoin and its Predecessors, 1886–1945', in Peter Duus, Ramon H. Myers and Mark R. Peattie, eds, *the Japanese Informal Empire in China, 1895–1937*, 213.

24 *Japanese Trade Directory of Shanghai* (Shanghai, Japanese Chamber of Commerce, 1940). It should be noted that, on later evidence, this figure is incomplete: *Shanhai shôkô roku* (Yearbook of Japanese Commercial and Industrial Companies in Shanghai) (Shanghai, Shanhai shôkô kaigisho, 1941).

25 *Shanhai shôkô roku*, 1941; *Shanhai shôkô roku* (Yearbook of Japanese Commercial and Industrial Companies in Shanghai) (Shanghai, Shanhai shôkô kaigisho, 1944).

26 As indicated in note 19, this classification did not reflect the actual field of activity of Japanese firms. If the firms which owned plant and workshops are included, the percentage of industry before 1937 amounts to 10·8 among Japanese companies (19 per cent in 1940).

27 The text was 'Provisional Regulations for Areas of Exclusive Japanese Settlement' (*Nihon senkan kyoryûchi karikisoku*): Peattie, 'Japanese Treaty Port Settlements in China', 189. Before that, the Japanese Foreign Ministry and the consulate in Shanghai had enacted various regulations to govern the lives of their subjects: 'Shinkoku zairyû nihonjin kokoroe kata kisoku' (Regulation on the Behaviour of Japanese Residents in the Qing Empire) (1873) and 'Shinkoku Shanhai kyoryû nihonjin torishimari kisoku' (Regulation on the Control of the Japanese Residents in Shanghai, Qing Empire) (1883): Hirohumi Takatsuna and Chen Zu'en, 'Shanghai

'LITTLE JAPAN' IN SHANGHAI

Ribenren juliumin guanxi nianbiao (A Chronology of the Japanese Residents in Shanghai), *Shilin* (The Forest of History), 1 (1995), 94, 95.
28 The system elaborated by the Japanese was not unlike the French system in which the Consul General had extensive veto powers over municipal organs when they existed and was the exclusive head of the police force: Peattie, 'Japanese Treaty Port settlements in China', 189.
29 *Shanhai kyoryû mindan*, 109.
30 *Shanhai kyoryû mindan*, 107.
31 For a brief sketch of the JRA see Cao Linhua and Ma Changlin, 'Shanghai Riben juliu mintuan gaishu' (A General Presentation of the Shanghai Japanese Residents' Association', *Dang'an yu lishi* (Archives and History), 3 (1990), 51–5.
32 On the impact of Chinese nationalism on both the Japanese and the British see Harumi Goto-Shibata, *Japan and Britain in Shanghai, 1925–1931* (New York, St Martin's Press, 1996).
33 Peter Duus, 'Zaikabô: Japanese cotton mills in China, 1895–1937', in Duus, Myers and Peattie, *Japanese Informal Empire in China*, 65, 79; Peattie, 'Japanese Treaty Port Settlements in China', 204.
34 The FSU explicitly claimed its foundation was related to the boycott movement that badly hit the Japanese community in 1915. Its statutes indicate that its purpose was to promote a spirit of unity among Japanese residents and to develop social services (*fukuri*). A quarter of that community is said to have left Shanghai during the campaign. In 1915 its immediate tasks were to form a self-defence organisation in collaboration with the consulate in order to protect Japanese property, assist residents in difficulty, and preserve the free movement of goods and the circulation of schoolchildren. The federation adopted its final name in 1925. *Shanhai Nihonjin kakuro rengokai no enkaku to jiseji* (Events and Evolution of the Japanese Street Unions in Shanghai) (Shanghai, Shanhai nihonjin kakuro rengokai, 1939), 61–2; *Shanhai kyoryû mindan*, 1181–4.
35 *Shanhai Nihonjin kakuro*, 1, 5, 77.
36 *Shanhai Nihonjin kakuro*, 65.
37 *Shanhai Nihonjin kakuro*, 8.
38 In 1942 a new regulation determined the duties of the associations and their structure. Neighbourhood associations were to consist of large groups of 50–300 families. The basis of the associations, however, were cells of ten neighbour families (*rinpohan*). Neighbourhood associations were directed by a small committee (president, vice-president, accountant and the heads of the various cells). *Shanhai kyoryû mindan*, 1049.
39 There were 179 associations in the traditional quarters of the Japanese, and another twenty in the former International Settlement, in the French Concession and in Nanshi. They were distributed as follows: Yangshupu: twenty-six; Hongkou: forty-one; North Hongkou: sixty-eight; Zhabei: seventeen; Central (IS): fourteen; Huxi: thirteen. *Shanhai kyoryû mindan*, 1056.
40 Its original name was the Shanghai Association of Japanese Industrialists (Shanhai Nihonjin jitsugyô kyôkai).
41 *Shanhai kyoryû mindan*, 1188.
42 *Showa jûyô nendo jimu hôkoku* (Annual Report [of the Chamber of Trade and Industry] for 1941), ([Shanghai], Shanhai Nihon shoko kaigisho, May 1942).
43 *Shanhai Nihon shôkô kaigisho nenpô* (Yearbook of the Shanghai Japanese Chamber of Trade and Industry) (Shanghai, Shanhai nihon shôkô kaigisho, 1938, 1939, 1941, 1943, 1944); *Shanhai kyoryû mindan*, 1188–91.
44 *Shanhai kyoryû mindan*, 855.
45 Sonoda, *Sensô, Jihen, Shanhai*, 194.
46 Sonoda, *Sensô, Jihen, Shanhai*, 194; *Shanhai kyoryû mindan*, 896. The Koreans had had their own association (*Shanhai Chôsenjin shin-yûkai*) since 1933; it merged with the JRA in April 1941: *Shanhai kyoryû mindan*, 999–1000, 1008, 1088.
47 *Shanhai kyoryû mindan*, 875, 1048.
48 A Volunteer Corps was founded in June 1900 and incorporated into the Shanghai

Volunteer Corps of the International Settlement a few months later. In 1907 the Japanese brigade of the SVC was dissolved and a separate Volunteer Corps was recreated by the Japanese. Takatsuna and Chen, 'Shanghai Ribenren juliumin guanxi nianbiao', 96, 98.

49 For a discussion of this association see Richard Smethurst, *A Social Basis for prewar Japanese Militarism* (Berkeley CA, University of California Press, 1974).
50 *Shanhai Nihonjin kakuro*, 71; on Japanese violence against civilians see *Month of Reign of Terror in Shanghai (A): What the foreigners see, say and think from January 28, to February 27, 1932* (Shanghai, China Weekly Herald, 1932).
51 *Shanhai Nihonjin kakuro*, 81; *Shanhai kyoryû mindan*, 1048 and 1056.
52 Sonoda, *Sensô, Jihen, Shanhai*, 194; *Shanhai kyoryû mindan*, 1231.
53 *Shanhai kyoryû mindan*, 1230–4.
54 *Shanhai kyoryû mindan*, 1193.
55 On the rationing system and its implementation see *Shanhai kyoryû mindan*, 1058–60. Chinese received two-thirds of the Japanese ration.
56 On the establishment and role of the Asia Development Board see Barbara Brooks, 'The Japanese Foreign Ministry and China Affairs: Loss of the Control, 1895–1938' (Princeton University Ph.D. dissertation, 1991), 335–54.
57 *Shanhai Nihonjin kakuro*, 88.
58 Even before fighting was over around Shanghai, the JRA formed a research committee for the settlement of the emergency situation (*jiyoku zengo shori kenkyû i-inkai*) on 6 September 1937. *Shanhai kyoryû mindan*, 776.
59 *Shanhai kyoryû mindan*, 814.
60 This number was reduced to twenty-five after the Foreign ministry modified the original law. *Shanhai kyoryû mindan*, 854–6.
61 In February 1937 there were only 4,579 eligible voters among a population of more than 26,000; there was an 85 per cent turn-out. In 1940 the number of voters rocketed to 9,887 (70 per cent) out of a total of 14,170 registered residents. The electorate numbered 4,664 in 1937, 5,167 in 1938, 9,931 in 1939 and 19,484 in 1941: *Shanhai kyoryû mindan*, 662, 858, 904–5.
62 *Shanhai kyoryû mindan*, 666.
63 *Shanhai kyoryû mindan*, 1047–8.
64 *Shanhai kyoryû mindan*, 1021, 898–9.
65 Wu Jianxi, 'Riben juliu mintuan he Shanghai Riqiao zidi xuexiao' (The Japanese Residents' Association and the Schools of the Shanghai Japanese Residents), *Shilin* (The Forest of History), 4 (1994), 51–9.
66 There were no more than a dozen children in the 1880s, fifty-four in 1900 and 185 in 1907, and 4,632 in 1937. *Shanhai kyoryû mindan*, 945; Wu Jianxi, 'Riben juliu mintuan he Shanghai Riqiao zidi xuexiao', 51, 54.
67 The Higashi Honganji Temple in Kyoto had branches all over Japan and overseas, forming an international network geared to religious and charitable work. *Shanhai kyoryû mindan*, 108.
68 *Shanhai kyoryû mindan*, 940.
69 *Shanhai Nihonjin kakuro*, 99.
70 *Shanhai kyoryû mindan*, 814.
71 *Bulletin mensuel de la police*, January 1941, Service politique, Archives diplomatiques de Nantes, 2–3.
72 There were reforms in 1920, 1926, 1930 and 1940: *Shanhai kyoryû mindan*, 906–10.
73 The 1942 budget shows that the company tax provided half the revenue. Shops and companies also contributed through the business tax (15 per cent), a leisure and food tax (12 per cent), an alcohol tax (3 per cent) and various excises. The whole budget amounted to 5,254,938 yen. The same source also mentions a land tax, but it does not appear in the 1942 budget. *Shanhai kyoryû mindan*, 902 and 906.
74 The Land Regulations could not be amended without the consent of the whole consular body and the Chinese authorities. Hence there was no hope of a change in favour of the Japanese.
75 *Shanhai Nihonjin kakuro*, 98.

'LITTLE JAPAN' IN SHANGHAI

76 *Shanhai Nihonjin kakuro*, 108–13.
77 From the beginning, the British Foreign Office was definitely opposed to Japanese demands for one more seat on the SMC, in peacetime as well as in wartime. It considered it preferable to let the Japanese press the issue at the level of the Land Regulations and involve all the powers concerned. The SMC systematically removed from its electoral register all Japanese residents who were in arrears with their taxes: PRO, FO 371/22083, 'Sino-Japanese war – situation in Shanghai', F924 (27 January 1938) and F1879 (14 February 1938).
78 As a result of the property-based franchise, British residents and companies could nominally divide their property and have the smaller parcels registered in the name of their employees. The British thus gained 3,000 more votes. The Japanese were deeply dismayed, since they thought they could win or at least increase the number of their councillors. The vote splitting mobilised the consul, the SMC and the British election committee (a private body). Although this gerrymandering was obviously hardly ethical (and 'un-British' according to one FO minute), it was perfectly legal. The consul-general, however, was aware that the procedure was tantamount to farce and undermined the Land Regulations. There was no other option, however, since the Japanese were using the same methods and since no one was eager to see them have a majority on the SMC. The Japanese press published several harsh articles and the Japanese organisations denounced British manipulation of the election. They decided to set up their own ratepayers' association. PRO, FO 371/24683, 'Situation in Shanghai' (March–October 1940), F3161; *Shanhai Nihonjin kakuro*, 124 ff. and 141.
79 *Shanhai Nihonjin kakuro*, 92.
80 Peattie, 'Japanese Treaty Port Settlements in China', 203.
81 *Shanhai Nihonjin kakuro*, 92, 95.
82 On Japanese pressure to have more Japanese agents in the Maritime Customs see File 693.002/442, 'Chinese customs administration', central decimal files (RG59), Department of State, National Archives and Records Administration, Washington DC.
83 PRO, FO 371/31677, 'Conditions in Shanghai', F2022.

CHAPTER TEN

Who were the Shanghai Municipal Police, and why where they there? The British recruits of 1919

Robert Bickers

Studies of colonial communities have tended to deal with elites, and to reflect the assumption that such communities were fairly homogeneous. The literature of colonial nostalgia has also perpetuated this assumption. The treaty port communities in China in particular have been characterised in both academic and popular literature as wealthy, well-born, even hedonistic, enjoying to the full their lives of privilege until their ship went down in Japanese waters in the late 1930s. There is no room in this picture for the workaday British servants of the world opened up to British empire. This chapter examines the lives, careers and mentalities of one such group in Shanghai: British men in the Shanghai Municipal Police (SMP). In particular it looks at seventy-four men recruited in 1919. Records of lower-class colonists have often failed to survive in the archives, except perhaps in court records. Fortunately, personnel and administrative files of the SMP, and files of the Secretariat of the Shanghai Municipal Council which oversaw it, survive in Shanghai.[1] When combined with the files of the Special Branch of the force, and surviving personnel correspondence and interviews, a detailed study can be undertaken of the men who sailed to Shanghai.

The chapter is in three parts. It begins with a survey of the British communities in the city, moves on to discuss briefly the functions of the SMP, and then looks at why those recruited in 1919 joined up, what police service in Shanghai offered them, and what it made them. In particular this chapter is concerned with the formation and maintenance of one type of British-derived identity in this society. Socialisation into the community, peer pressure, and formal and informal disciplinary regimes were very much concerned with policing the boundary between Briton and non-Briton. With the men of the SMP these issues are not only more starkly evidenced, they were also more sensitive. The person and behaviour of the low-ranking Briton in the

Shanghailanders and the International Settlement

Shanghai was not a colony, as Chiara Betta has shown in Chapter Three: the British state let a small once consular-controlled settlement of Britons develop a great deal of autonomy – ultimately too much so, and the independent-mindedness of the SMC and British residents became a significant problem in Sino-British relations in the 1920s.[2] The key event which changed everything occurred on 30 May 1925, when a patrol of Sikh policemen led by a British officer fired on a crowd of Chinese demonstrators, killing eleven. Two days of rioting followed in protest, together with a general strike leading to a nation-wide anti-British and anti-imperialist movement which almost toppled the whole British position in China.[3] May Thirtieth was the SMP's biggest test, and greatest failure, but it showed how far the force was at the centre of British informal empire in Shanghai, and in China.

The first question in the title of this chapter has two meanings. There are the issues of origins, and of identity; how many of these men came from Scotland, for example, but, more important, what was the nature of the identity they acquired and protected on arrival in Shanghai? The second question also has two parts, the personal and the institutional: what was in it for them, and what was in it for their employer? Both questions have been partly prompted by misapprehensions about the force current in the literature on Shanghai. 'The SMP and the French Concession Police were both part of global colonial networks of imperial control systems,' wrote Frederic Wakeman. 'Many of the officers had originally been recruited in England or Scotland to work for the East African or Hong Kong police before they moved on to Shanghai' because it was – and here he quotes Hong Kong historian H. J. Lethbridge – 'viewed as an arena more accommodating than Hong Kong to the adventurous and ambitious'.[4] 'A career' in the SMP, claimed another author, 'attracted thousands of Sikh, Anglo-Saxon, and Chinese men, whose familiarity with ammunition and killing might otherwise have led them into lives of crime'.[5] Such comments indicate pretty well how many people see the backgrounds and motivations of these men, and others like them in colonial police forces; but it is not how it actually was. Nicholas Thomas has noted the 'non-correspondence between idealised portrayals of colonists and their self-accounts' and argued for sceptical readings of 'colonial imaginings'.[6] This chapter argues that we should be more careful with our anti-colonial imaginings as well.[7]

British mores and structures dominated foreign life and the government of the International Settlement down to the Pacific War, but British society in the city was far from homogeneous. The British presence (about 7,000 in 1920)[8] was nominally multi-faceted, but in Shanghai parlance 'British' was also a term of exclusion. It did not include all those with British or British-protected status, notably Baghdadi Jews, Eurasians, Hong Kong and Straits Settlement Chinese, and British Indians. Dominions' subjects were included, but the term mostly meant fair-skinned Britons from England, Scotland, Wales and Ireland. Even this group was divided, however, the biggest chasm being between sojourners and settlers, a distinction correlating up to a point with the 'company' and 'native' divides in the Japanese community identified by Christian Henriot in Chapter Nine. British society in Shanghai consisted of an expatriate elite, made up of the managers and mercantile assistants of the big trading houses and the new multinationals, and a larger settler community – the people who called themselves Shanghailanders. Settlers were united economically in their common dependence on the existence of a foreign-controlled society in the Chinese treaty ports. Shanghailanders fell into three broad employment categories: the service industries of treaty port life and administration, property ownership and land speculation, and small business. So Shanghailanders were born, or made, as new recruits were quickly socialised into the community. There was an elite made up of the managers of the bigger trading houses, and property developers, leading staff of the council and the police. This was as unremarkably divided a British community as any other, and the fine gradations of domestic class divisions and perceptions were exported into this society.

Shanghailander identity was also grounded in social practices and injunctions, and assumptions which aimed to separate it from those outside the group (whether Chinese, White Russian or British Indian – this was no mere 'race' category). Taboos about interaction with groups outside this self-ascribed category were strong, especially regarding sex or marriage. Taboos also included social interaction, and, although language was obviously a crucial factor in Sino-British interaction, for settlers, in particular, learning Chinese was seen as a demeaning compromise with indigenous society. It is not surprising that these emigrants recreated the familiar in a foreign land, but in fact by doing so Britons in Shanghai aimed to protect their own identity in a city where they constituted a tiny minority of the population in 1919.[9]

WHO WERE THE SHANGHAI MUNICIPAL POLICE?

Police forces partly function to enforce social norms, especially, but not only, in the colonial context, where such norms can be new, and artificial. These norms were also imposed on the police; but men who joined the police were possibly the most likely of all groups to resist such impositions, especially in the Shanghai situation. Issues of class, of expectation, and opportunity, fuelled an ever present tension between the ideal and the reality of a Shanghai policeman's behaviour, and his role as exemplar of social norms. Shanghailanders looked down upon a floating population of the British poor, or the prospective poor. As it had in many British colonies, the fear of the growth of a white underclass in the city had taxed the energies of officials and oligarchs almost since foreign occupation of Shanghai began.[10] British seamen, discharged soldiers and discharged policemen represented one of the biggest threats because of the compromises with Shanghailander communal norms that they often made either because of poverty, or through the autonomy they enjoyed as men who had no managers, colleagues or peers to keep them in line. Those designated as 'Distressed British Subjects' could be shipped home by charity committees set up to deal with such issues if men requested assistance, criminals could be deported after serving their time, and dismissed policemen refused their superannuation (an end-of-service gratuity) unless they took it back to Britain, but ultimately the British state and Shanghailander society had few sanctions for those who kept out of trouble.

Why were they there?

An alliance of managers of the big British expatriate companies, notably Jardine's and Swire's, together with members of the settler elite (notably those with real estate interests), dominated the SMC, the administrative structures of which would hardly have looked out of place in a British city. For that reason, it was argued, British personnel were needed to staff the council, and a somewhat circular logic here kept the executive ranks of the council British until the 1930s. As well as governing, this administration served the additional function of forming a major route via which new recruits entered the Shanghailander community and its employees formed a large proportion of the British community in Shanghai in 1919. The police force, especially, inducted many Britons into the city: the men themselves, siblings, wives and children. The low pay and social status of the police had usually meant that the families of those who married were brought up in Shanghai, and children often married there.

In 1919 Commissioner K. J. McEuen, himself the son of a former chief of the force, commanded a mixed complement of 225 Europeans (nearly all Britons), 22 Japanese, 488 Sikhs and 1,354 Chinese constables and sergeants.[11] British constables and officers were the backbone of this force. On average, 11 per cent of the SMP at any one time in the twentieth century were European, and most of these were British. There was a small cadre of officers and officer cadets, groomed for the senior positions, or appointed with specific skills lacking in the SMP (often connected with the Sikhs), but the bulk of the Europeans entered at the level of constable. At the beginning of 1919 the foreign branch of the police had been severely depleted, and Maurice Tinkler (SMP 1919–30) and his cohort were recruited to bring the numbers back up to strength. Who were they and why were they there? These questions need answering in reverse order.

Obviously, the first answer to why were they there is: to police the International Settlement. The men who joined in 1919 were there, according to their contracts, to undertake 'routine police work of a modern business centre, modified as necessary to suit local requirements'.[12] They were policemen first and foremost; the priority was social order and the prevention or detection of crime. There was little scope for the adventurous, and not, as we shall see, a great deal of scope either for the ambitious, as dealing with ordinary crime in the settlement took up the greatest part by far of the SMP's time. But they *were* policing in Shanghai. The 'criminal classes', the service note continues, 'are chiefly Chinese'; given the relative proportions of the Chinese and foreign populations, this was quite true, but the note does have another reading: that the duties of the police were to protect foreign Shanghai as a whole from Chinese inside and outside the Settlement.

In the late nineteenth century the force had developed a specifically paramilitary character: the men were seen as a trained military reserve in case of an attack on the settlement. Partly this was out of necessity – after three decades of peace around Shanghai, British merchants lacked enthusiasm for their local militia, the Shanghai Volunteer Corps; partly it was a result of the nature of the force on which the SMP was remodelled in 1897, the Royal Irish Constabulary. This paramilitary function declined steadily after 1900, however, although the SMP certainly remained the first line of defence for the International Settlement in their role as custodians of public order. The second was the SVC, the third the warships and troops of the foreign powers. Many of these functions, however, especially in periods of emergency, were also undertaken by domestic police forces in Great Britain. The International Settlement's size and international status rendered more prominent the SMP's employment in these roles, but they were not necessarily unusual roles for a police force.

There are two further caveats to stressing the routine nature of the work. First, the force, especially its Special Branch, undertook activities which served to protect the communal identity of the Shanghailander. These involved implementing laws about cinema censorship, and efforts to suppress pornography featuring European women, and other areas that were the possible location of transgressions of the sexual norms which defined the Shanghailander. Special Branch also kept track of possible foreign delinquents,[13] while the uniform branch dealt with the foreign destitute in the settlement, a perceived danger to the 'prestige' of the 'race' rather than a mere nuisance.[14] The statues and memorials on the Bund, to Sir Robert Hart, Sir Harry Parkes, and the Taiping-era Ever Victorious Army, were key icons in Shanghailanders' imagined history. The police were enjoined to keep them free from beggars, hawkers and undesirables, and to prevent their defacement.[15]

Second, although British imperial planners did not see Shanghai as an imperial asset, and the SMP was not a colonial police force, close liaison was improvised as and when required in the face of the political emergencies of the early twentieth century. The SMP liaised with the government of India, initially in order to recruit Sikhs, latterly to police the British Indian community, and also with the British Secret Intelligence Service, and with colonial Special Branches, in efforts to identify, locate and suppress the activities of communists, nationalists, the Comintern and Soviet spies. Men such as Douglas B. Ross (SMP 1919–41) performed this latter task with enthusiasm, and some notable success, such as the smashing of the Noulens spy ring in 1931. In a similar fashion, however, the SMP also later co-operated, where interests converged, with the Guomindang's Public Security Bureau in the city.[16] The SMP collaborated with other organisations where interests converged, but remained protective not only over issues of sovereignty, but of its nominal international status, which remained the fiction through which it functioned.[17]

When Maurice Tinkler wrote home to his sister, however, there was little adventure or spying to report. Foreigners expect a detective to come out, he wrote, 'if they've lost a tool bag from the car or the canary won't sing'. 'It is a fact that one darned old lady wanted a foreign detective one day because her No. 1 House Boy wouldn't beat the carpets.' These comments and others like them reveal the hierarchical certainties of foreign Shanghai, for race and for class. A foreign policeman is peremptorily summoned to administer discipline to the Chinese servant of a socially superior foreigner.[18] There is also, again, insecurity here: the feeling that the police are needed to keep the Chinese obediently in order. A strong sense of class hostility is revealed in Tinkler's letters, and has been shown too in interviews with former policemen, although it is also quite clear that the police learnt to share the same attitudes. In 1923 one of the 1919 recruits was tried for complicity in the torture of a fellow officer's Chinese servant, who was suspected of having stolen some money. It was admitted that the man had been intensively interrogated but 'I thought it was face pidgin [a matter of face] for me; [the] money [was] lost in [the] Station. I thought other boys in [the] Station [were] concerned. I had him out and questioned him.'[19]

Tinkler did have the opportunity to take part in raids on opium 'dens' but 'All of this would be very interesting to any one just out from home, but you get used to it here and regard it as a matter of course.'[20] Bragging apart, this is actually close to the truth. The routine constabulary duties apart, the prime duty of the British men was to supervise the Asian personnel, who were little trusted to perform their duties, or to perform them well. The culture of distrust was predicated on views of the Chinese character, but poor pay and conditions hardly brought in good men, or kept good men from turning bad. It was also based on experience: in 1905 during the serious unrest in the settlement known as the Mixed Court Incident, significant numbers of Chinese constables had taken off their uniforms and gone home. In 1925, after the May Thirtieth incident, some 25 per cent of the Chinese Branch deserted the force, and the following two years of tension also saw high losses.[21]

Within the SMP there was a raced division of labour. This partly stemmed from, but also fed, the racism of Shanghai's foreign community, as European residents refused to accept the services of Chinese detectives, for example. In the uniform branch Chinese constables walked their beat or manned specific posts (bridges, park entrances). The force preferred to recruit Hebei and Shandong men, having imported into the China context a partiality for hierarchies of martial races that met existing Chinese prejudices. Shanghai men were also felt to be too prone to local loyalties.[22] Suborning of rank-and-file personnel twice became a serious problem in the 1920s, first over opium, latterly over organised illegal gambling. The SMP's reaction to such crises was to establish, or use, special units outside the formal uniform or detective structure and wholly staffed by Britons – another reason for the continued importance of the working class Briton to the force.[23] Sikh constables were set on point duty at road crossings, and became an iconic feature of the SMP's presence. The senior levels of the force remained purely British until 1919, when the first Chinese officers were appointed from the Beijing force. None of them gained substantive rank until the 1930s.

The CID employed more Chinese in more responsible positions.

WHO WERE THE SHANGHAI MUNICIPAL POLICE?

Trustworthy local men would be of more value than non-Chinese speaking Britons, but the trustworthiness of the Chinese detective always – rightly in many cases – remained a matter of suspicion. One prominent figure in the force in the 1930s, Detective Superintendent Lu Liankui, was also prominent in the Shanghai underworld.[24] Up to a point Britons in the SMP tolerated a flexibility that British colonial police forces might have balked at. Too much flexibility would have been too compromising, and would also have threatened the force's legitimacy; too little would have made policing almost impossible in this context. When it could, however, as the records of the Special Branch show, the SMP rooted out the corrupt.[25] There was no 'pact with the devil' in the International Settlement, and it is misleading to assume that the occasionally corrupt patterns and practices of the French concession were replicated in the settlement.[26] The supervisory capacity of British recruits must, however, have been limited, to say the least, by their lack of familiarity with Shanghai's languages, with the city itself, and with Chinese society, and modes of social interaction and social obligation. All the SMP could do was rely on rules which limited the arenas in which their Chinese personnel could exploit their positions.[27] If there was no identifiable institutionalised synarchy in Shanghai – that is, no cohabitation between British and Chinese structures – the SMP relied on Chinese to function, as PCs, detectives and as clerks (no British bobby typed his own reports). So although this was a British-structured force, there was what might clearly be termed a synarchy of practice. Such accommodations can be identified in the *modus vivendi* generally reached between the municipal authorities in the foreign concessions and their Chinese inhabitants, and between the foreign authorities and their Chinese employees at all levels. All foreign businesses and organisations in China relied absolutely on Chinese labour, goodwill, middlemen and, often, finance, to function; the British enterprise in China was ever, and at all levels, Sino-British.[28]

The foreign constables of the force formed the first level of interaction between the foreign oligarchs who administered the settlement and the Chinese population of the city. Comparisons have been made between the SMP and the former servicemen who joined the Royal Irish Constabulary Auxiliaries – the 'Black and Tans'[29] – whose violent personal ill-discipline and disciplined military violence against the populations they ostensibly policed made them infamous – an infamy handed on to the Palestine Police. But these two forces operated in different environments from Shanghai: there was no local consensus of civil support from the populace, which made ordinary policing difficult. Except during the brief periods of extreme political turbulence, the Chinese population of the International Settlement seems to have accepted the legitimacy of the SMP – as much as it accepted the legitimacy of any police force. Without such implicit consent the settlement would have been ungovernable.

The SMP needed Britons, then, it was argued, because it was simpler and made more sense to recruit Britons into what was already a British municipal structure, and into a force which used British policing practices. It also needed them because the British population of the settlement disdained being served or subdued by Asian policemen. Moreover Asian personnel were not trusted, nor were they expected to respect cheaper European alternatives, such as Russian refugees.[30] Against these practical needs, however, should be set traces of the self-importance and vulgar affectation of the Shanghailander elite. Constables were still under standing orders to salute members of the Municipal Council whenever they saw them in the late 1930s.[31] The oligarchs of Shanghai had their white servants of empire.

Why did they join?

Men like Maurice Tinkler, Harry Diprose (SMP 1919–41) and Bert Munson (SMP 1919–25) were recruited to police the International Settlement, and to serve as the first line of defence against internal and external threats. But what was in it for them? Why had these men chosen to leave their homes throughout the UK and journey thousands of miles to Shanghai, from which they would not officially return for at least three years? Most of them read of the SMP's openings through advertisements in British newspapers such as *The People* or *The Weekly Despatch* in March 1919. They applied for a variety of reasons. For some it was the only job they could get. Others wanted to get a job abroad. Some, in particular, wanted to escape the UK after the war. There were those who already had family links with the police – four members of the MacGillivray clan joined from Argyllshire, one of them in 1919, and five members of the Aiers family from Birmingham joined between 1889 and 1934 (another was a salesman for a British chemical company). Brothers Harry (SMP 1919–21) and Walter Hotchkiss (SMP 1919–36) left their labouring jobs in a Ludlow quarry to enlist and then joined the SMP together. Others were told about the force by serving policemen they met during the war. Some may have heard that opportunities for advancement were good, or that the pay and conditions were attractive – even the lowliest constable had access to a servant[32] – others may have heard that the opportunities for peculation and corruption were also rather good. Twenty-one-year-old

WHO WERE THE SHANGHAI MUNICIPAL POLICE?

Maurice Tinkler went for no good reason other than that he was unemployed after demobilisation, and largely estranged from his roots because of the war.

It has to be stressed, however, that our mental map has shrunk, or at least been redrawn. It is assumed that people would have actively sought employment in China only because they were attracted to its exoticism and wanted to see the world. But it certainly was not quite as exotic then as may now be thought. Britons in all walks of life would have some acquaintance with visitors to China or residents there; many local churches or other small groups, for example, supported particular missions; then there was the merchant navy. Moreover, aside from the hundreds of thousands of Britons who emigrated between 1911 and 1931, empire itself greatly broadened the range of employment opportunities available to British people of all classes.[33] In *The People* the 1919 advertisement for the SMP nestled next to those requiring recruits for the police in the Seychelles and in East Africa; Singapore's Harbour Board sought boilermakers and road foremen were wanted for Uganda.[34] Empire and its adjuncts beckoned the demobilised working-class male from the newspaper classifieds.

How did Shanghai strike them when they arrived there? For Maurice Tinkler it was love at first sight:

> Shanghai is the best city I have seen and will leave any English town 100 years behind – that's not exaggerated. It is the most cosmopolitan city of the world bar none and the finest city of the Far East. At night it is lit up like a carnival, and an orchestra plays in the Public Gardens along the river front. (Fountains beautiful trees etc.) . . . There is a splendid electric car service and everyone seems to own one of the latest type of American cars.

Like all recruits to Shanghai's communities he learnt quickly the habits and mores of his new world. He learnt to say 'tiffin' instead of lunch, to 'go about in rickshas mostly and throughout the East they get to be a habit with everyone', and he learnt that 'you have to know something to get the better of a Chinaman or a Jap'. Another recruit 'very soon got to know how to ring the bell if I wanted something done'. The accumulation of small names and habits helped perpetuate the way of life and thinking in the treaty ports. Of more immediate interest after the years of warfare, he noted that soap was expensive but cigars and silk were cheap. Food was inexpensive and plentiful, in contrast to England's blockade-occasioned shortages. After war service in France, and after Britain's post-war depression, Shanghai must have been intoxicating.[35]

Who were they?

On the face of it the first thirty-five men who shipped out from Glasgow with Tinkler in 1919 had very little in common except that they had all been on active military service during the war. Unlike the French Concession Police, which insisted on previous military service for its recruits, no 'familiarity with ammunition and killing' was actually necessary: the SMP advertisement specified only age, physique, that the men should be unmarried and that they should have good teeth. Harry Diprose had joined the army on 8 August 1914 from the farm in Kent on which he was born, and to which he had returned before signing up for Shanghai. James Young (SMP 1919–21) was a railway porter, Bert Munson a builder's assistant, Robert Hall (SMP 1919–42) a clerk. Two men had worked for the British Aluminium Company, one at Harrod's. Arthur Wadey (SMP 1919–20), a clergyman's son, had worked as an assistant to a county civil surveyor. There was a former policeman, a stoker, a clerk, a Post Office sorter, a railway dining car attendant, a labourer, a baker, a one-time professional footballer, an apprenticed engineer's fitter and a warehouseman, D. B. Ross.

These ordinary men had served, on average, roughly three and a half years on active service during the war. They had found it difficult to get work, or had failed to slip back comfortably into their old employment; former bank clerk John Crowley (SMP 1919–27) had 'been away from Banking too long to go back'. Alan Craig (SMP 1919–20) spent four and a half years as a private but reported, 'Having no trade am at a loose end,' after demobilisation. They were interviewed in London, given a health check, probably told next to nothing about Shanghai or China[36] and packed off second-class to Shanghai for six weeks' training. This was truncated by the SMP's desperate need to have men on the streets. They were then expected, within barely six months of demobilisation, to act as the guardians of law and order in Shanghai. 'As was only to be expected,' noted the Commissioner, 'a few erratically inclined individuals were found amongst the recruits.'[37]

They had no experience of the Far East and many had very little interest in it other than as source of employment and a potential standard of living unattainable at home. 'A white man can get a job out here ... He can't in England,' wrote Tinkler.[38] The SMC had no choice in the matter. It might have found local recruits, but experience showed that those who had already spent time in China had usually picked up too many of the less acceptable habits of Shanghailanders, especially their more violent attitudes towards Chinese.[39] The SMP had a long tradition of acquiring military men who while on postings in the East developed a taste for life there, but they often needed as much policing as they gave. Men recruited from police forces in Britain were not liked either. They were inclined to complain about conditions and facilities, which they considered inferior to those at home, and their attitude infected other recruits. In 1919 the thinking was that if the Shanghai police could acquire and mould men who already had experience of discipline as citizen soldiers, and who were a fairly representative section of British working-class and lower middle-class life, then it possibly stood a chance of creating an efficient cadre of good European policemen for the very first time.

Making Shanghailanders

So these men were recruited because they were British, and it was expected that they would become Shanghailanders and remain so. The processes employed are worth examining, because they show us what the British expected of new recruits to their society.

Socialisation into the Shanghailander world did not stop with learning about tiffin, rickshaws and Boys. Maurice Tinkler joined a club on arriving in China in 1919, then an Irish Masonic lodge (which had other police members) and through that the Shanghai Masonic Club. The club provided accommodation and recreational facilities, a library, a bar, meeting hall, and so on. Shanghai was 'the city in which a man is lost if he has not at least one club at his disposal'.[40] Tinkler got on well in the lodge and served as Secretary and Master. As an ex-soldier he joined the United Services Association. He was, like most of his compatriots, a keen shot, frequently hiring a boat with colleagues for the purpose and going on hunting trips into the Jiangsu countryside. (One of his 1919 companions was accidentally shot dead on one such trip.) Slightly more unusually for the average Shanghai policeman, Tinkler attended night classes in his earlier days, studying French.[41]

Tinkler's letters show how far these men were subject to the snobberies and prejudices of the community. They were mostly working-class, and they mostly remained working-class. Shanghailanders thought of themselves as meritocratic, and a man like Tinkler was certainly able to enjoy a life unthinkable in his native Ulverston, in England's damp north-west, but that was relative. Tinkler's fellow pupils at night school served to remind him of his class, and of his station in Shanghai. 'I wish [the Chinese] would have a real good riot, and murder a bunch of the petty, arrogant, local millionaires and profiteers. Then they might realise that the police force is here,' he wrote in 1921. The correspondence shows him mixing with his colleagues, with fellow Masons, soldiers and American journalists, but rarely with non-police Britons.[42]

The SMP's disciplinary regime served to remind them who they were in the new context in which they found themselves – a strictly subordinate part of the dominant Shanghailander minority – and it imposed local social norms on the men. Most important in this respect, it attempted to regulate their personal lives. 'Mixed marriages are not in the interest of the force,' declared the Commissioner of Police in 1927 to the SMC's Watch Committee, which broadly agreed with him.[43] Although the ban was formally lifted shortly thereafter, all constables were then forbidden to marry during their first contract in the hope that they would 'explore the marriage market at home' during their first long leave.[44] Taking a different approach, one senior officer's wife tried to engineer marriages for the men with governesses or probationer hospital nurses, the only other pool of working and lower middle-class Britons in the city: marriage registers show poor results for this strategy with the 1919 recruits. The economics of marriage, and the masculine culture of the force, and of treaty port life, meant that most of the men stayed single at this time.[45] Demographics also played a part: there were very few single British women around who were not nurses, and who were prepared to marry policemen. The police were also forbidden from keeping mistresses or frequenting brothels, houses of ill-fame, common and disreputable bars or cabarets, on pain of dismissal.[46] In response, Tinkler and his friends flaunted their Russian lovers. Marriages with Russians and Chinese still occurred. In 1927 Sergeant W. R. Parker (SMP 1922–42) was given permission to marry a Chinese woman of 'respectable parentage' as he was 'unlikely to rise to the more senior ranks of the Force'.[47] Maurice Tinkler saw keeping 'clear of the Asiatic ones' as a question of 'self-respect'.[48] While others in the force certainly agreed, evidence from the files shows men having close friendships with Japanese women. Sergeant Barnes (SMP 1930–31) grew very friendly with Matcha, a taxi-dancer at the Venus Cafe. E. W. Peters (SMP 1929–36) dedicated his published account of his service in the police to Sumiko, whom, he announced, he fully intended to marry when circumstances permitted. Four of the 1919 draft eventually married Russians, although none married Chinese.[49] The SMP was not unusual in making such interventions in the personal lives of its men. Soldiers, and colonial officials, in the British and other empires, were subject to differing injunctions depending on rank or status. The issue was usually tied to questions of institutional efficiency, and to the perceived integrity of colonial apparatuses.[50]

Drink was ever the greater problem. There was very little for many of these men to do off duty, except socialise in their station canteens, or Shanghai's bars and clubs. They mixed with their peers, and the men of the prison service, the Public Works Department or the Shanghai Fire Service, fellow servants of the foreign community. Sporting or recreational facilities were fairly inadequate, and the 1919 recruits were especially eager to relax after the years in uniform. Gone were the days when the whole force paraded weekly before the members of the council, whose chairman lectured them on drinking.[51] But in 1919, in an attempt to restrain the men, they were subject to a 1.00 a.m. curfew. The disciplinary files show that rooms were checked at that hour, and defaulters punished. Drunkenness on duty cost men their seniority; but even drunkenness off duty could cost them their jobs, as it did Maurice Tinkler in 1930. Excessive drinking led to men dying, being invalided out, sacked, bankrupted or corrupted; and alcohol was cheap.

Temptation went beyond drink. Patterns of conspicuous consumption in the foreign community were set by the Shanghailander and expatriate elite – Maurice Tinkler's first impressions of the city were dominated by his awe at the material goods available. Notions of 'White prestige' and 'self-respect', seemingly entangled with perceptions of what was expected of members of a colonial society, influenced the lifestyle and leisure of even the lowliest members of the Shanghailander community.[52] Keeping up with sports clubs, Freemasonry and shooting expeditions could cost more money than a policeman might earn. Moreover, the desire to be seen on Shanghai's public stage, at the night clubs, hotels and restaurants, and to be properly dressed for it, took a toll of wages and salaries. On his sudden death in 1926 James Douglas (SMP 1919–26) owed a third of his estate to three tailors, two garages, his shoemaker, four cafes, the SMP and Municipal Service Club bars, a watchmaker, as well as an unpaid newspaper bill. The total was equivalent to about five times his probable monthly salary.[53] The bulk of the estate of the majority of those who died in Shanghai usually consisted of their superannuation. In one way the system was self-defeating, as it encouraged men to consider all their net earnings as disposable income because there was always the superannuation safety net. The SMP were constantly reminded that they were at the bottom of the foreign pile, but foreign Shanghai was a community in which wealth, or conspicuous consumption, was tolerated and opened doors otherwise barred. Tinkler's letters show that he spent to impress, and to talk himself, at least, off the bottom.

The attempt to control the social lives of the men was also of course partly concerned with preventing them getting into debt. In a society in which most foreigners signed 'chits', that is, IOUs for goods and services, this was an easy path to tread. Debt made some men corrupt, such as the parson's son Arthur Wadey, who extorted cash at gunpoint from illegal private gambling parties but was dismissed shortly thereafter only for the theft of a watch. Bert Munson was suspected of stealing confiscated opium for resale, and was forced out. Debt also led men to borrow from moneylenders, often from or with the help of their Indian or Chinese subordinates. Both responses were felt to undermine the 'prestige', and therefore the efficiency, of the British element in the force in the eyes of their subordinates, and the Chinese population generally. Those men too far enmeshed in debt were not encouraged to stay. S. G. N. Bailey (SMP 1921–24) resigned when facing court writs for the payment of bills for 'clothes, liquor and motor cars'. Destitute and stranded in Shanghai in late 1925, he was given a third-class passage back to Britain, as 'he will invariably fall into the hands of the police unless something is done for him'.[54]

Low-level corruption appears to have been routine, especially tempting for new recruits with new debts to pay, who were happy to turn a blind eye. Opium placed 'extraordinary temptations in the way of everyone from Constable upwards', it was noted in 1926, and Britons were not exempt.[55] Acutely aware of its public image, the force preferred to refuse to extend men's contracts, or retard their promotion. There is, consequently, little evidence available of serious European corruption, but given the political prominence of the International Settlement after 1925 it seems more unlikely than otherwise that the wholesale suborning of senior personnel to ignore serious crime that occurred in the French Concession also took place in the SMP.[56] Assumptions about corruption in the SMP also need placing in the broader context of domestic police culture, which was far from ideally honest. Shanghai corruption ever gains in its alleged singularity from the context of race, and visions of the European brought down in Asia.

These prohibitions and injunctions served to protect the Shanghailander community as a whole from the possibly wayward activities of their working-class servants, the police. Regulation of personal lives was also intended to protect the race/nationality hierarchies on which the SMP was based and on which it operated. The final sanction available was to try men under King's Regulations for breaches of discipline. Such a strategy greatly risked antagonising the men, and broadcasting the inability of the force to police itself to the (foreign) electorate, the ratepayers, to the wider foreign community and to the Chinese. For their part, the men were not above complaining. Time and time again they rejected in their actions many of the restrictions placed on them, although they often paid a heavy price for disciplinary offences. In 1921 they held grievance meetings, and threatened to strike over issues of pay, promotion and barracks accommodation, earning, that way, an early pay rise and wholesale promotion to sergeant.[57]

What became of them?

On average the 1919 recruits served eight and a half years in the SMP, but the median length was four years, and thirty-three recruits, almost a whole draft, did not survive beyond their first three-year contract: five were transferred to the gaol service immediately, which was hardly an 'arena' for 'the adventurous and ambitious'; another ten left that first year. One was accidentally shot dead, three were dismissed for drink or theft-related reasons, and one was sent home still shell-shocked from the war. King's Regulations were invoked at least once: two men – one from each draft – were tried and jailed for a day in December 1919 for insubordination, to 'encourage' the others. 'Do you think you were playing the game,' asked the magistrate, 'setting a good example to the Asiatics in the Force?' 'No sir,' was the chastened reply.[58] At the end of the second three-year contract another nine left for various reasons. Thereafter the twenty survivors worked until family pressures, ill-health, death,[59] and then the Japanese, terminated their careers.

The 1919 recruits are broadly representative of the waves of domestic recruitment into the SMP. From 1928 onwards the force was under the reforming hand of F. W. Gerrard (SMP 1928–38), an officer recruited from the British police in India, initially to investigate the state of the force and suggest reform, but then to lead it. Many men were weeded out, and new drafts in 1929 – 128 recruits that year – represented an attempt to inject a new type of man into the SMP. Ex-army and ex-police seem to be roughly equal in numbers in the 1930s, but there was in general an attempt to get better-educated men into the service. Between 1919 and 1930 the size of the whole force more than doubled, and the SMP of the 1930s was a much more efficient force than it had been in the previous decade, until the years of attrition and terrorism after 1937 wore it down.[60] The attrition rate is high, however. Far from policing the Chinese, the SMP found itself spending a good deal of time and energy policing its own men: the human limitations on efficiently staffing and running an empire bear a great deal more consideration than they are given.

We can see, in this small but representative sample, what Shanghai offered such men, who ever formed the bulk of the British population.

Aside from the 'spoilt' life of servants and material comfort, they took paid annual leave – often in Japan; Tinkler also went to Indochina, visiting treaty ports on the way – and regular six-month sabbaticals. They dressed well and look dapper in the photographs they sent home – outwardly banished were the clerks, warehousemen and labourers. Although nearly all came from working- or lower middle-class backgrounds, there is certainly some upward social mobility to be seen in their career histories, despite the constraints put upon them as a group by Shanghai's foreign community. Eight of these men rose to chief inspector, six of those to superintendent, and two of those rose to deputy commissioner positions.[61] Few, however, were ever accepted into the wider British community; interviews and papers reveal an introverted sub-sector of the Shanghailander community. In that sense, the Shanghailander world was a real transplant, sophisticated enough for sections to ignore each other; there was none of the possibility of cross-class fraternisation which might accompany a very small community. And Shanghai also cut many of these men adrift from British society for good. The services it offered through the acquired privileges of race to those born into the British servant class led many to reject the option of any return home. For those who swaggered in Shanghai a return to the decent obscurity of Ulverston would have been shaming. Tinkler, demoted from inspector to sergeant for off-duty drunkenness during the new Gerrard regime, never returned, and never contacted his family again.[62]

And the SMP was not all swagger. The high attrition rate also reflected low opportunities for promotion in the early 1920s, primitive barracks accommodation, an intrusive disciplinary regime, homesickness, loneliness and disappointment. Although some men saved and prospered, others found Shanghai destroying their nerves, or health. The empire world was as much the scene of failure, and misery, as of success. At least six policemen committed suicide in Shanghai between 1926 and 1937, and the files of many others make sad reading. Still, at least seven of the 1919 recruits who left before 1942 decided to stay on in China. Charles Young (SMP 1919–27) joined the Harbour Police, George Matcham (SMP 1919–22) went to Hong Kong to work at the Race Club, William Slater (SMP 1919–29) resigned because of his debts and worked for Jardine's for three years before Great Depression cutbacks saw the end of his contract. G. E. Knight (SMP 1919–22) joined the council's Public Works Department. Maurice Tinkler resigned in 1930 after his demotion. His Shanghai fortunes reached rock-bottom when he worked as warden of a Salvation Army hostel for unemployed European men.[63] From 1935 he worked as security manager at a British cotton mill at Pudong, where he was killed by Japanese marines in 1939.[64]

Conclusion

How may we judge these men as representative of the SMP's front line of interaction with Chinese society? As half of them had left within three years, we could conclude that 50 per cent were definitely unacceptable – two, indeed, were dismissed for violence against Chinese. Of those that remained we know that one was tried for complicity in torture, that one other was disciplined for violence, and that Maurice Tinkler, who ill-treated an arrested student after May Thirtieth, became a loutish braggart described as late as the 1990s by one still living mild-mannered contemporary as a 'nasty piece of work' and by a former Chinese colleague as a 'lout'.[65] What comes through strikingly is the success with which British society in Shanghai reproduced its certainties and attitudes in these recruits to informal empire. In 1925 Tinkler visited Zhenjiang:

> (like Foochow) a glimpse of the 'good old China' of the earlier White men, when lavish . . . hospitality was the keynote of everything. In olden days in ports like this the foreigner did very little work . . . made money easily and spent it easily.[66]

This was a tantalising vision, but one which had little basis in reality, and certainly little basis in the reality of urban Shanghai for working-class British men.

What also comes though is the basic fact that these men thought in terms of work, and of police work in particular, and of the point of their presence as lying not in adventure, or in great professional success, but instead in the mundane benefits of their privileged position and, just as important, in doing their job properly. So internalised was this philosophy that the Japanese occupation of the International Settlement during the Pacific War posed few problems for them. 'We were still doing police work, we weren't doing anything for the Japanese.' And indeed, all those men still serving and in Shanghai on 8 December 1941 continued in their posts until sacked or interned by the Japanese – for about 120 of them that was in March 1943.[67]

The 1919 recruits of the SMP came from Britain's lower and lower middle classes; they were, not unusually for Britain-abroad, disproportionately Scottish.[68] They came to Shanghai for various personal reasons, but mostly in search of work. Even though life for most British men of their class in Shanghai had distinct advantages, half of them left, or were dispensed with, within three years. Most of those who left went back to Britain on the free passages supplied. They had gone in search of work, they went back in search of work. The remnants became members of the settler society that had developed in Shanghai. All the men were subjected to that society's distinctive rules, and to its attempts to make them Shanghailanders and share, or be forced to share, the social and sexual taboos which demarcated its identity and prevent it from dilution or disgrace. What comes through from a reading of the men's files is that, despite the injunctions, the discipline, Kings' Regulations and intense social pressures, men in the SMP made their own way through the treaty port world, and set their own limits as to what was acceptable or unacceptable behaviour. Some accepted Shanghailander norms calmly and in full, others rearranged Shanghailanders' frontiers to suit themselves. In one sense their lack of social discipline and their behaviour perfectly characterised the British-supported presence in Shanghai. At its worst it was violent, at its best brusque or incomprehensible in its relations with the Chinese: but by making their own accommodations these men created their own world within the world opened by British empire in early twentieth-century East Asia.

Notes

1 Unless otherwise noted below, details of the 1919 recruits have been taken from the personnel correspondence of 1919 recruit R. Maurice Tinkler (b. 1898–d. 1939) deposited at the Imperial War Museum London, and readings of forty-one of their individual personnel files in the U 1–9$_3$ [sic] series at the Shanghai Municipal Archives: no individual citations have been given to these files. This chapter also draws on a prosopographical database built using personal data taken from a number of sources, including newspapers (Shanghai's *North China Herald* in particular), marriage registers and Shanghai Supreme Court probate records in PRO, FO 971.
2 See my 'Death of a Young Shanghailander: The Thorburn Case and the Defence of the British Treaty Ports in China in 1931', *Modern Asian Studies*, 30:2 (1996), 271–300.
3 R. W. Rigby, *The May 30 Movement: Events and Themes* (Canberra, Dawson, 1980).
4 Frederic Wakeman, Jr, *Policing Shanghai, 1927–1937* (Berkeley CA, University of California Press, 1995), 142.
5 Tahirih V. Lee, 'Introduction', 'Coping with Shanghai: Means to Survival and Success in the Early Twentieth Century – A Symposium', *Journal of Asian Studies*, 54 (1995), 7.
6 Nicholas Thomas, *Colonialism's Culture: Anthropology, Travel and Government* (London, Polity Press, 1994), 167–8. For introductions to the literature on the history of colonial policing see David Anderson and David Killingray, eds, *Policing the Empire: Government, Authority and Control, 1830–1940* (Manchester, Manchester University Press, 1991), and the same editors' *Policing and Decolonisation: Politics, Nationalism and the Police, 1917–65* (Manchester, Manchester University Press, 1992).
7 For fuller development of this argument see my 'Shanghailanders: The Formation

WHO WERE THE SHANGHAI MUNICIPAL POLICE?

and Identity of the British Community in Shanghai, 1843–1937', *Past and Present*, 159 (1998), 161–211.
8 Zou Yiren, *Jiu Shanghai renkou bianqian de yanjiu* (A Study of Changes in the Evolution of the Population of old Shanghai) (Shanghai, Renmin chubanshe, 1980), 145–6.
9 See my *Britain in China: Community, Culture and Colonialism, 1900–49* (Manchester, Manchester University Press, 1999), chapters 2 and 3.
10 David Arnold, 'White Colonisation and Labour in Nineteenth-Century India', *Journal of Imperial and Commonwealth History*, 9:2 (1983), 133–58; P. J. Marshall, 'The Whites of British India, 1780–1830: A Failed Colonial Society?', *International History Review*, 12:1 (1990), 26–44.
11 SMC, *Annual Report, 1919*, 14a–17a.
12 SMA U 102-5-165, 'General Conditions of Service in Shanghai' (wording from 1930 edition).
13 The lists of 'Known and/or Suspected Criminals' for 1935–38 in National Archives and Records Administration, Washington DC, RG 263, Shanghai Municipal Police (SMP) D 1249 include S. H. Goodwin, swindler, A. C. Mack, swindler, G. R. Hulbert, thief, and F. A. Roche, fraud.
14 *North China Herald (NCH)*, 25 February 1928, 312. The police were instructed to note the names and particulars of 'destitute foreigners' found in Chinese lodging houses, and report the details to the pertinent station: W. H. Widdowson, comp., *Shanghai Municipal Police Guide and Regulations* (Shanghai, 1938), 285.
15 Bickers, 'Shanghailanders', 199; Widdowson, *Shanghai Municipal Police Guide and Regulations*, 308.
16 Frederick S. Litten, 'The Noulens Affair', *China Quarterly*, 138 (June 1994), 492–512; Wakeman, *Policing Shanghai*, 135–61.
17 Wakeman, *Policing Shanghai*, 60–77; Richard J. Popplewell, *Intelligence and Imperial Defence: British Intelligence and the Defence of the Indian Empire, 1904–1924* (London, Frank Cass, 1995) 268–76.
18 Imperial War Museum (IWM), R. M. Tinkler papers, R.M.T. to Edith, 9 January 1921, 27 November 1921.
19 PRO, FO 1092/356, Shanghai Supreme Court Notebook, J. F. Gabbutt, testimony, 20 April 1923, Rex v. J. F. Gabbutt and A. B. Balchin.
20 IWM, R. M. T. to Edith, 27 November 1921, 5 December 1920.
21 SMC, *Annual Reports*, 1925–27.
22 SMC, *Annual Reports, 1897*, 30; K. M. Bourne, 'The Shanghai Municipal Police: Chinese Uniform Branch', *Police Journal*, 2:1 (1929), 30.
23 SMA U 1-3-2660, Commussioner of Police to Secretary SMC, 29 January 1930.
24 Brian G. Martin, *The Shanghai Green Gang: Politics and Organised Crime, 1919–1937* (Berkeley CA, University of California Press, 1996), 32–3; Wakeman, *Policing Shanghai*, 287–8
25 See in particular the CS file series, e.g. SMP CS 143, 146, 178, 190.
26 Martin, *Shanghai Green Gang*, 32–4, 69, 216.
27 SMC, *Police Guide and Regulations* (Shanghai, Kelly & Walsh, 1926), 138; *Shanghai gonggong zujie Gongbuju jingchaju huapu zhiwu shunzhi* (Rules and Regulations for the Chinese Branch, Shanghai Municipal Police) (Shanghai, n.p., c. 1930, 94–6.
28 More generally on this point see Yen-p'ing Hao, *The Commercial Revolution in Nineteenth-Century China: The Rise of Sino-Western Capitalism* (Berkeley CA, University of California Press, 1986).
29 Nicholas R. Clifford, *Spoilt Children of Empire: Westerners in Shanghai and the Chinese Revolution of the 1920s* (Hanover NH and London, University Press of New England, 1991), 80–1.
30 SMA U 102-5-2/4, unsigned memorandum, 'Employment of White Russians', [1927].
31 Widdowson, *Shanghai Municipal Police Guide and Regulations*, 407.
32 One 'boy' to every three constables or two sergeants: Widdowson, *Shanghai Municipal Police Guide and Regulations*, 301.

33 The net population loss though migration of England, Wales and Scotland between 1911 and 1931 was 1,429,000: N. L. Tranter, *British Population in the Twentieth Century* (Basingstoke, Macmillan, 1996), 37–9.
34 *The People*, 16 March 1919–25 May 1919, *passim*. The SMP notice first appeared on 23 March 1919 and ran until 11 May 1919.
35 IWM, R. M. T. to Aunt Florence, 22 August 1919; F. G. W. interview, 13 September 1996.
36 F. G. W. interview, 13 September 1996.
37 SMC, *Annual Report, 1919*, 45a.
38 IWM, R. M. T. to Aunt Florence, 22 August 1919.
39 See my 'Death of a Young Shanghailander', 285.
40 *NCH*, 18 August 1928, 287.
41 Information on Tinkler drawn from various letters in the IWM collection.
42 IWM, R. M. T. to Edith, 27 November 1921, then *passim*.
43 SMA, U 102-5-471/1, Extracts from Watch Committee Minutes, 11 February 1927.
44 SMA, U 102-5-406, R. M. J. Martin to T. I. Vaughan, 18 August 1930.
45 IWM, R. M. T. to Edith, 16 December 1925. One married a Russian nurse. Of sixty-five marriages where details are known (the majority from church marriage registers), twenty-six of the women who stated their occupation were employed in secretarial positions, and seventeen were nurses; the others included teachers, hairdressers, shop assistants, etc. Lambeth Palace Library, MSS 1564–73.
46 Widdowson, *Shanghai Municipal Police Guide and Regulations*, 56, 66.
47 SMA, U 102-5-471/1, Extracts from the Watch Committee Minutes, 11 February 1927. In fact Parker stayed in the force until 1942, rising to inspector.
48 IWM, R. M. T. to Edith, 10 October 1923.
49 E. W. Peters, *Shanghai Policeman* (London, Rich & Cowan, 1937). Peters never married Sumiko (personal information). Out of a total of eighteen marriages located, a further eleven married Britons, and two Americans.
50 See, for example, Kenneth Balhatchet, *Race, Sex and Class under the Raj: Imperial Attitudes and Policies and their Critics* (London, Weidenfeld & Nicolson, 1980); Hanneke Ming, 'Barracks-concubinage in the Indies, 1887–1920', *Indonesia*, 35 (1983), 65–93.
51 *NCH*, 16 March 1862, 42, 11 May 1861, 75.
52 A fact officially registered by a Municipal Salaries Commission report in 1921, *Municipal Gazette*, 9 April 1921. 113, in SMA, U 102-5-37/7.
53 PRO, FO 917/2656, James Douglas, probate file.
54 SMA, U 102-5-156, S. G. N. Bailey file.
55 SMA, U 1-3-2659, Deputy Commissioner of Police (I/C) to Secretary, 12 November 1926.
56 F. P., interview, 13 March 1996; F. G. W., interview, 13 September 1996.
57 IWM, R. M. T. to Aunt Florence, 10 April, 9 July 1921.
58 PRO, FO 1092/226, Magistrate's Notebook, 18 December 1919.
59 In total six men died in service of disease, and two from shootings. It is impossible to extrapolate any statistically sound conclusion from these figures, but to lose eight men dead from a draft of seventy-four, just under 11 per cent, seems to suggest that service in the SMP was more unhealthy than the norm.
60 Frederic Wakeman, Jr, *The Shanghai Badlands: Wartime Terrorism and Urban Crime, 1937–41* (New York, Cambridge University Press, 1996).
61 Promotion through the ranks was fairly automatic, although it required men to pass exams, and to have passed language tests. All the men were promoted to sergeant in 1921; most could expect a further promotion after seven or eight years' service (sub-inspector) – and if they did not get it tended to leave or be pushed at that point – and again three or four years later men sought promotion to inspector.
62 Interview with J.E.T., March 1994.
63 Another of the 1919 recruits ended up taking this same job a year later.
64 Full details of the incident are in SMP D 6968.

65 IWM, R. M. T. to Edith, 27 June 1925; F. G. W. interview, 13 September 1996; interview with P. April, 1997.
66 IWM, R. M. T. to Edith 16 December 1925.
67 F. G. W. interview, 13 September 1996.
68 Nine of the forty-four whose place of birth is known were Scottish.

CHAPTER ELEVEN

The Russian diaspora community in Shanghai
Marcia R. Ristaino

Shanghai's Russian connection began as a transhipment point for tea from Russian tea factories in Hankou destined for Russia. The Odessa Volunteer Fleet ferried the preferred red teas through the Shanghai port, greatly enriching those Russians involved in the tea trade. In 1860 the Russian government established a consulate at Shanghai which was managed initially by an American. British and American merchant consuls often ran the official affairs of governments with less than substantial interests in the city. By 1880 Russian official and commercial interests came under the charge of the Russian J. E. Reding, appointed to the post by the Russian government.[1]

Russian involvement in China's north-east and railroad construction stimulated Shanghai's development into a banking centre in support of this Russian commercial expansion. Still, the Russian community was small, numbering only about 400 people by 1915. World War I increased demand for products available through Shanghai and increased the size of Russian commercial and official representation. Taken together, these developments produced a growing official, commercial, trading and banking community which was soon to have its stability shaken by political events.

The prosperity of the Russian community became unsettled by the dispersion of Russians from their homeland following the October revolution and Civil Wars. Refugees began arriving in Shanghai by train, and even on foot, and by ship, most of them in destitute condition. White Russian military forces arrived still armed and on whatever ships they could arrange or commandeer for their escape. The steady influx taxed the resources and threatened the stability of the already established and prosperous Shanghai Russian community. To make matters worse, the Beijing government, as part of the aftermath of negotiations with the new Soviet regime, closed the imperial Russian consulate in Shanghai in 1920, replacing it with a Bureau of Russian

Affairs. The latter operated under the Commissioner of Foreign Affairs for Jiangsu Province, but enjoyed only quasiofficial status.[2] In 1921 the Soviet government deprived all Russians living abroad of their citizenship, giving rise to the sentiment among the Shanghai White Russians that now 'we have no country, no government, no consular officials'.[3] In 1924 even the Bureau of Russian Affairs lost its tenuous status once the Chinese government had signed the first Sino-Soviet treaty, recognising the Soviet government and closing the bureau. White Russians in Shanghai were now clearly refugees, deprived of any nationality status. As such, they carried the stigma of being the first European refugee community in Shanghai. These conditions and developments seriously undermined their personal sense of security and national identity.

Poverty and dislocation in the 1920s

In addition to the White military forces, the refugee community was a diverse group, including professionals of all kinds, many of whom had been associated with the major railroad centre in Harbin. There were engineers, technicians, administrators, architects, physicians, lawyers, teachers, accountants and businessmen. Their arrival worried resident professionals, who feared competition from the refugees. Former imperial consul-general V. F. Grosse, under pressure to handle the refugee onslaught, seized opportunities provided by Chinese labour strikes, especially after 30 May 1925, to supply Shanghai with Russian replacements. He provided electric power stations with stokers and foremen, waterworks and gas companies with labourers, shipping companies with crews, cars with chauffeurs, and so on.[4] By 1 August 1925, 953 Russians had been placed, but another 700 were living under miserable conditions and on the verge of starvation.[5] Therefore, with his limited success in hand, Grosse recommended to the Shanghai Municipal Council that effective means should be found to stop further migration of unemployed Russians into the foreign settlements.[6]

The availability of Russian workers to replace Chinese labourers in strikes against power companies, bus companies tram and companies diminished the leverage Chinese strike leaders could apply and caused some strikes to fail. The hiring and replacement trend continued into the 1930s and 1940s, fuelling Chinese anti-foreign sentiments.[7] Once the strikes ended, however, most of the Chinese were rehired, except for their leaders, thus placing the Russians once again in a precarious position.[8] Some of the most fortunate Russian hires worked in the municipal services of the International Settlement or the French Concession, work which paid well and offered the opportunity to receive a financial subsidy upon separation from service. Younger men served in the paid Russian units of the Shanghai Volunteer Corps, a local multinational militia defence force. There was also an active market in Russian bodyguards for rich Chinese, especially as the need for protection escalated in the 1930s because of a general increase in criminal activity, including kidnappings and assassinations.[9]

As the leading White Russian official in Shanghai, Grosse also became concerned with the issue of destitute Russians and public safety. He emphasised the connection between unemployment and poverty and involvement in criminal activities. In just one nine-month period in 1927, 266 Russians characterised by Grosse as 'vagabonds' faced charges in the settlement and French courts for crimes of theft, assault, and drunk and disorderly conduct. To help remedy the problem, which Grosse believed would only escalate with additional destitute Russian arrivals, he called for strict enforcement of the minimum sentences by the courts and more willingness by the authorities to expel 'recidivists and undesirables' from the limits of the International Settlement and the French Concession.[10]

At a time and under circumstances which seemed to call for unity and the harmonious expression of Russian interests, the White Russian community instead engaged in constant quarrelling and petty in-fighting. Its leaders and organisations were regularly at loggerheads, making this notable characteristic a serious weakness of the White Russian community. Notwithstanding the deep divisions, however, it was obvious to all that the community sorely needed a leader and spokesman. Grosse, facing down expressions of resentment over his claim to represent the local White Russian and Slavic communities, asserted his predominant leadership role. In 1926 he established the Russian Emigrants' Committee, which became the administrative centre of the Shanghai Russian community, responsible for some fifty-two affiliated organisations and co-ordinator of the major social and benevolent activities of the Russian community, both Orthodox and Jewish.[11] This committee also became the representative body the Shanghai municipal government organisations dealt with in matters relating to the refugee communities.

How large was the community operating under the supervision of the Russian Emigrants' Committee? By 1929 the Shanghai refugee community had grown to more than 13,000 persons.[12] The Chinese government was not known to have kept statistics on the arrival of the Russian refugees, but the new Russian Emigrants' Committee did record the arrival of refugees in Shanghai. The committee counted 10,454 over the period from 1922 through 1929 (see Table 11.1). The

Table 11.1 Russian refugee arrivals in Shanghai, 1922–36

Year	Arrivals	Year	Arrivals
1922	1,268	1930	1,599
1923	1,968	1931	2,025
1924	877	1932	1,590
1925	1,535	1933	1,389
1926	1,266	1934	1,635
1927	1,036	1935	1,240
1928	1,122	1936	1,094
1929	1,382		

Source John Hope Simpson, *Refugees: Preliminary Report of a Problem* (London: Royal Institute of International Affairs, 1938), 156–7.

White Russian refugees did not find in Shanghai a large Russian community able or willing to ease their accommodation into the city. Rather, in many cases they were shunned by the established locals as 'poor relatives'. Their sheer number, their dire poverty and myriad social, economic and cultural needs overwhelmed the small resident community. In attempting to make the transition in foreign Shanghai, the newcomers suffered from a loss of connection with their native culture and country. Their painful nostalgia for the motherland, and the prevailing hope of an early return, only intensified their social and political dislocation.

Establishing a Russian community in the 1930s

The decade of the 1930s brought many challenges to the growing Russian community. Just prior to the Japanese formation of the new state of Manchukuo on 1 March 1932 the largest recorded exodus of refugees, mainly from Harbin, left for Shanghai. Their arrival further taxed the private and municipal relief services, which struggled to provide soup kitchens, shelters, medical help and employment leads. The undeclared war between Chinese and Japanese forces in early 1932 caused severe damage to the Hongkou and Zhabei districts of Shanghai, where most of the new arrivals settled. Prospects for low-cost housing and living expenses were brightest in these northern districts. Between 1930 and 1936 the Russian Emigrants' Committee reported the steady arrival of 10,572 refugees in Shanghai (see Table 11.1).

Grosse's death in October 1931 set off keen competition among various Russian groups for the recognised leadership role in the large Russian community. Grosse's successor was C. E. Metzler, who, after serving in the imperial Russian mission in Peking, arrived in Shanghai in 1917 to work under Grosse as vice-consul of the imperial Russian consulate. Grosse's death helped bring to the forefront the intense rivalries which existed between the former imperial Russian career diplomats, such as Metzler, and those recent arrivals who had served in the White Russian military forces. To challenge the predominant role of the Russian Emigrants' Committee, a group of former White Russian military officers formed a large umbrella organisation known as the Council of United Russian Public Organisations at Shanghai (SORO). This organisation published its constitution, regulations and by-laws, and, in a clever manoeuvre, applied to the Chinese authorities for official recognition as the body best able to represent the large Russian refugee community.[13] The Chinese granted approval and thereafter SORO leaders claimed that their body had an officially sanctioned legal status which the Russian Emigrants' Committee did not have.

The Russian Emigrants' Committee responded to the challenge by broadening its own organisation and adding to its leadership body some well known and respected figures, notably the Right Reverend Bishop John (Ioann, Maximovich Mikhail Borisovich), the Bishop of Shanghai.[14] In addition, the committee, hoping to completely displace SORO, applied to the Chinese authorities for official recognition as the key Russian refugee body. The local Guomindang authorities, after receiving instructions on the matter from the Nanjing government, took the astute course of not choosing between the two large competing organisations. Instead, they registered the Russian Emigrants' Committee as another 'official organ' for the affairs of the Russian community in Shanghai.[15] SORO's failure to prevail in the struggle to win and maintain sole recognition marked the beginning of the end of its influence, resulting in dwindling membership and organisational affiliations.

Shanghai Russians found themselves surrounded by an alien Chinese culture and generally excluded from close association with other Western communities, owing to their poverty and the social elitism so effectively evinced particularly by the British. In response, Russians looked inward, nourishing and preserving their own cultural heritage through a rich array of religious organisations, schools, libraries, newspapers, journals, clubs, and theatre and arts groups. During the 1930s Shanghai became a major Russian publishing centre of books, magazines, works of literature and poetry, religious works, educational material and patriotic writings. Russian musicians made up 60 per cent of the Shanghai Municipal Council's Shanghai Municipal Orchestra.[16] Russian shops and the Russian language were a prominent feature of the French Concession. The range of Russian enterprises ran from large speciality stores to small kiosks, from distinguished restaurants and cabarets to small cafes and eateries. Refugees also found economic salvation in conducting small businesses such as hat and dress shops, barber shops, pharmacies, bakeries, vodka distilleries, breweries, fur and leather companies, craft shops, jewellery stores, workshops, and automobile service and supply companies.[17]

Russian Ashkenazi Jews played an important role in many of these enterprises. Fleeing pogroms in Tsarist Russia and the terrors of the October revolution, they established a stable community in Shanghai during the 1920s. As indicated by Joshua Fogel in Chapter Six, Ashkenazi Jews in Harbin became victims of growing anti-semitism in Harbin, which in the late 1920s and early 1930s laboured under escalating Japanese pressures linked with fascist elements in the White Russian community. Most Harbin Jews responded to these threats by fleeing south to Shanghai, taking with them the professional and entrepreneurial skills which had made many of them successful in Harbin. They started small businesses similar to those which had thrived in Harbin, such as cafes, cabarets, jewellery stores, pharmacies, dry goods stores and other shops. By the late 1930s Shanghai Ashkenazi Jews, numbering between 4,000 and 8,000, had established a thriving club, an active communal association, synagogues, schools and many other organisations to serve their community.[18] Their contribution to local music, theatre, publishing, and business enterprises was outstanding.

Even amidst these positive aspects, reflecting the gradual formation of a Russian diaspora community, chronic and widespread unemployment continued to take its toll. Within the Russian community, refugee women held the most precarious position. A shocking number found themselves caught up in prostitution in order to survive. Brothels in the French Concession were licensed, but there were throughout the city many disguised forms of prostitution such as the ubiquitous massage parlours, some of which functioned plainly as houses of prostitution. Taxi-dancers and streetwalkers supported a whole network of boarding houses and dress shops which catered to their business and clothing needs. The situation became so acute that the League of Nations commissioned a study of the problem.[19] Reportedly, 22.5 per cent of Russian girls and women between the ages of sixteen and forty-five years were involved in prostitution.[20] League enquiries revealed that the situation had grown worse with new influxes of refugee females from north China. The report stated that, on a cautious estimate, there were at least 800 Russian women engaged in prostitution in Shanghai, and 900 lived in a deplorable state which might force them into prostitution to survive.[21] While hard luck was obviously common, other Russian women did find employment as governesses or gave music or dance lessons to mostly Western patrons. Some acquired practical skills in hairdressing, dressmaking or nursing.[22]

The Sino-Japanese hostilities that began in 1937 took an especially heavy toll of the Russian community. Military operations destroyed Russian shops, workshops, stores and boarding houses in Hongkou and Zhabei. In addition, the Shanghai market became an isolated island cut off from the interior of China, which precipitated a general business decline and increased unemployment among all nationalities, including the Russians.[23] By 1938 the unemployment rate of the Russian community was running as high as 40 per cent.[24] The growing personal suffering involving poverty, unemployment, statelessness, and frequent ridicule and disdain from other social groups helped sharpen the divisions within the Russian community.

The Russian refugees in Shanghai held a variety of political and ideological positions regarding Russia and its future. One group of monarchists was loyal to the Romanovs but remained passive politically, which was prudent, given the restrictions on active political expression in Shanghai. Another monarchist faction envisioned a war between Japan and the Soviet Union as offering the potential for setting up a Russian national government east of Lake Baikal under Japanese protection. A group of young Russians saw change coming from within the Soviet Union, which might effect a combination of the best of Russian traditions with certain revolutionary innovations, including a social monarchy headed by the Tsar but checked by a union of free soviets.[25] Finally, there was the Russian Fascist Party. This body, an offshoot of its parent in Harbin, was fiercely antisemitic, anti-Bolshevik and committed to a vitriolic brand of Russian nationalism which subordinated all personal and class interests to that of the nation state.[26]

Shanghai was not a Russian city, as was Harbin, and, given the fact that the Shanghai Russians were stateless refugees, placing them in a vulnerable political position in the foreign-controlled settlements, factional allegiances generally were not easily expressed. The Russian Fascists did not win broad support in Shanghai, where local Russians were less obsessed with counter-revolution than their compatriots in

Harbin, and were sophisticated enough to recognise the strong hand of the Japanese military authorities behind this organisation.[27] Nevertheless, the Russian Fascists were part of the political landscape in Shanghai, requiring the close attention of the Russian Emigrants' Committee and its leaders.

C. Metzler and the Russian Emigrants' Committee continued to maintain their leading role within the Russian community, but not without challenges. In December 1938 two recent arrivals from Harbin, A. Pourin and General I. E. Tsumanenko, reopened a Russian Club in the Wayside district of Hongkou, calling it a new centre of Russian culture, education, sport and recreation.[28] Both men had backing from Japanese civilian and military leaders in Japanese-controlled Hongkou and therefore were free to express openly their political views, which, of course, matched closely those of the Japanese. But even with these competitors, Metzler still headed by far the largest segment of the Russian community through his leadership of the Russian Emigrants' Committee, a fact which continued to make him of interest and potentially useful to the Japanese authorities.

It is important to appreciate the multiple loyalties which Metzler struggled with in his leadership role. First, there was his allegiance to the motherland, even if it was being governed by the despised Bolshevik regime; next was his necessary recognition of the position of the French authorities in the French Concessions where most Russians lived, and of the Shanghai Municipal Council of the International Settlement, in whose territory many Russians worked. Finally, Metzler had to recognise and cultivate the Japanese authorities, whose power in Shanghai after the outbreak of Sino-Japanese hostilities in 1937 was almost complete. Metzler's response to these realities was to show constantly his patriotism and to encourage the same in others through the strengthening of Russian cultural and educational institutions in Shanghai. He advocated a very temperate political climate within the Russian community, one which would not seriously offend any of the presiding powers. And he tried as necessary to co-opt any serious rivals to his authority, including even those individuals backed by the Japanese, by claiming co-operation with them but at the same time placing them under the direct authority of the Russian Emigrants' Committee. On 24 June 1939 Metzler informed *Shanghai Zaria* that seventy Russian emigrant organisations had registered with the committee, representing a community of some 25,000 refugees.[29]

Metzler's strategy worked remarkably well until mid-1940, when the Japanese announced plans to reorganise the Shanghai Russian

Emigrants' Committee to resemble those already functioning in the north, particularly in Harbin. In addition to forcing all Russian organisations to register with the Russian Emigrants' Committee, a policy which already had been agreed to by Metzler, under the new arrangement the committee would receive its direction and be controlled by the representatives and organs of the Japanese military.[30] Metzler was unable, on principle, to accept this level of Japanese control and, when approached, refused the Japanese offer to let him continue to lead the body during the planned reorganisation period. His demise followed shortly thereafter. On 20 August 1940 Metzler was gunned down by a Chinese hit man just outside his residence on Nanyang Road.[31]

Japanese authorities, still maintaining some caution in dealing with the large Russian community spread out over the city, began immediately to search for another respected Russian leader to replace the slain Metzler. They approached N. A. Ivanov, an attorney and former imperial Russian judge who came from the 'established', or pre-refugee, Shanghai Russian community. Ivanov was quite concerned about the Japanese interest in his replacing Metzler. He approached the Shanghai Municipal Police secretly to learn if they had any information as to whether right-wing Russian elements had assassinated Metzler.[32]

Ivanov gave much thought to the prospect of heading the Russian Emigrants' Committee and consulted with various Russian, as well as Japanese leaders, about his suitability. Russian leaders were somewhat less than approving of Ivanov's just assuming the position, including even Bishop John, who had agreed to fill in as chairman pending a community election of a new chairman. Whatever plans the Russian community had developed for its committee leadership were overridden by the Japanese authorities. On 21 January 1941 the right-wing and Japanese-controlled *Dalnevostochnoye Vremia* (Far Eastern Times) announced Ivanov's appointment as the new chairman of the reorganised Russian Emigrants' Committee. Captain K. Kuroki, the 'Director of the Council for the Affairs of Russian Emigrant Residents in Districts Protected by Japanese Troops', who had ordered and supervised the registration of all Russian organisations with the Russian Emigrants' Committee in June 1939, accompanied Ivanov to Nanking in July 1941, where he was presented to Wang Jingwei, head of the Chinese puppet Reformed Government.[33] Still more evidence of Japanese manipulation of the Russian Emigrants' Committee became apparent in August 1941 when Shanghai mayor Chen Gongbo, operating under Japanese direction, issued a statute explaining that the posts of chairman and vice-chairman of the committee were to be his appointments. The statute went on to define the structure of the newly reorganised committee.[34]

Ivanov's tenure of office was brief. He was assassinated on 9 September 1941 by two Chinese gunmen as he stepped from the car in which he had been riding with his wife.[35] This second murder of the committee's top leader stunned the Russian community, which appealed for co-operation in confronting 'the powers who have twice "beheaded" the Russian community and who aim to disrupt its unity, co-operation and struggle for honour ...'.[36] In the meantime, Mayor Chen appointed a new committee chairman, Colonel N. K. Serejnikov, and on 8 November the city government issued a comprehensive statute renaming the committee the All-Russian Emigrants' Committee of Shanghai and subordinating all Russian immigrants, to include Ukrainians and Russian Jews as well, to its authority. This forced subordination was very distasteful to Shanghai's Russian Jews, who clearly preferred to be left alone like their earlier counterparts in Harbin. Even the heads of the committee's five departments required approval by the mayor, and the committee chairman's term of office was to be limited to one year.[37] The Russian refugee community finally had one unified and legally constituted body, but its leadership and affairs were carefully controlled from outside.

On 8 December 1941, when Japanese military forces entered the International Settlement, Russian refugees, by then reportedly numbering 30,000, were told to co-operate.[38] On 16 December *Shanghai Zaria* instructed all Russian refugees to acquire immediately special certificates of identity which they should carry at all times and show upon demand. The appointment of the new chairman of the Russian Emigrants' Committee was celebrated at a large dinner party held on 31 January 1942 and attended by members of the Japanese military mission, the Japanese embassy and consulate, the Manchukuo consulate, and by officers of the Chinese Peace Preservation Corps. Clearly the Russian community from this point on would have to co-operate with and support the New Order.[39]

The Second World War strains Russian loyalties

The Second World War caused the break-up of the large Russian *émigré* communities in Europe, such as those in Paris, Warsaw and the Baltic countries, which were absorbed either by Hitler or Stalin. Their assimilation left the Russian community in China as the most important group of Russians residing outside the borders of Stalin's domain. The German attack on the Soviet Union on 22 June 1941 aroused Russian patriotism and gradually polarised the Shanghai Russian community between those who saw some merit in the Soviet regime presiding over the motherland and those who continued to call for its overthrow. The emotional undercurrents stirred by the attack began to favour those who wanted to defend the motherland, even as it remained under Soviet domination. Local press reports called for replacing the slogan 'Down with Bolshevism' with the new cry 'Down with the Nazis'.[40]

Responding to the advantageous turn of events, the Soviet authorities began to flood Shanghai with propaganda in the form of books, pamphlets, records and films brought in by ship from Vladivostok.[41] The Soviet Club encouraged visits to its premises and refugee participation in its film showings of both old movie favourites and new ones, including documentaries.[42] An open bar followed the film showings where visitors might drink, discuss and receive additional 'information' about the fate of the motherland.[43] Even more important was the Soviet offer to the stateless White Russians of the opportunity to register for citizenship. In considering their future prospects, many young Russians wondered whether their best interests might not lie with the Soviet Union, especially if they were to pursue a meaningful professional life.

Under the changing circumstances, the All-Russian Emigrants' Committee began to see its power and influence erode as evidence of aroused Russian nationalism and patriotism continued to emerge. This new atmosphere also came at a time of leadership change for the committee. The former leaders, Metzler and Ivanov, had come from the civilian professional ranks associated with the established Russian consular/diplomatic community. Their successors came from the refugee ranks, especially from the military commanders who had risen to prominence during the Russian Civil War. The new chairman, Lieutenant General F. L. Glebov, had received his rank from the fiercely anti-Bolshevik Cossack Ataman G. M. Semenov. Glebov and the committee decided on a firm and uncompromising approach to the slippage in support for the committee. Meeting in October, the committee decided to cut off protection and all services in the form of official documentation to those who sympathised with the Soviet government and in the same month proclaimed an outright ban on member support for the Soviet cause.[44]

The committee's decisions set off a furious round of debate, further inflaming passions on this sensitive subject. Some opposed to the decisions claimed that continued support for the committee should not require members to neglect the danger to the motherland.[45] Others took a more definite stand and urged Russians to stop being refugees and support the Soviet government. They reasoned that assuming this position would enable the refugees to gain the respect of the foreign powers and, at the same time, lead Russians towards reclaiming their lost citizenship.[46] Gaining respect within the established Shanghai community and overcoming their stateless condition were two principal and deeply emotional issues within the Russian refugee community.

The next challenge to the refugee leadership came with Pearl Harbor. Once the United States entered the Pacific War and the American and British consulates, together with their major business interests, closed, the committee leadership had to formulate a response to these key events. The outcome was to caution the local White Russians to lie low, unite around their committee, stay away from political issues, and register with the committee before 15 December 1941. As it was the officially endorsed Russian body it was imperative for members to refrain from any anti-Japanese activity. Committee directives called for newspaper censorship of any rumours, unfounded reporting and anti-Japanese commentary.[47] Seeking to follow their own predilections, but at the same time to satisfy the Japanese, Glebov and the newly appointed committee leaders admonished the White Russian community 'to maintain an irreconcilable attitude towards communism', and warned the refugees against having any relations with the local Soviet community.[48]

But the war news filtering in from the front worked against Glebov and the committee. The Stalingrad campaign showcased the sheer heroism of the poorly supplied Russian soldier, and also suggested that the Nazis were not invincible. Still, the costs were high, as news reports of casualties on the eastern front made plain to readers.[49] The outpouring of local sympathy and support coincided with another push to register for Soviet citizenship which in turn prompted an immediate response from Glebov, who warned that the continued protection of the committee was at stake for those who changed sides.

The Japanese liaison officer, Captain Kuroki, was not satisfied with the degree of control exercised by Glebov and the committee, even after Glebov's unanimous re-election in 1944 by 160 representatives of various Russian organisations, which had also received the approval of the mayor. Kuroki, backed by articles in the Japanese-sponsored press, called for a general re-organisation of the committee and the application of firm administrative measures to carry it out. The result was a general meeting of representatives of various Russian organisations, attended by 143 members out of a total of 166, called to implement the proposed administrative changes.[50]

The newly established bodies tightened control over the economic, administrative and judicial aspects of the Russian community, as supervised by the authorised All-Russian Emigrants' Committee. Russian public bodies were to be examined to determine 'their necessity' and any on-going internal disputes were to be settled by a new Court of Public Arbitration.[51] Even discussion by members of the qualifications or suitability of candidates nominated for office in these key bodies was disallowed. Community resentment against the increasingly repressive character of the committee became apparent in the next committee election, held in December 1944. It was the first general election of the leadership of the Russian Emigrants' Committee to be conducted by secret ballot. Of the 3,000 refugees qualified to vote by being fully registered with the committee and having paid all current and back taxes due, a serious financial hardship which many could not surmount, only 851 cast a vote. General Glebov received 616 votes. The least number cast for a candidate, fifty votes, went to General Tsumanenko, the Japanese favourite.[52] The low voter turn-out further demonstrated the fact that many Russians remained hesitant to express clear political preferences, even by secret ballot, especially with a Japanese-backed candidate on the ballot.

The Soviet–German war brought with it a revival of fascist activity in Shanghai. The new Fascist leader, M. Spasovsky, had close ties with K. Rodzaevsky, the leader of the All-Russian Fascist Union in Harbin.[53] In early 1941 Spasovsky established a secretariat for the organisation in Shanghai and began the weekly publication of *Nash Put*, taking an editorial line closely in tune with its parent publication in Harbin. Spasovsky succeeded in getting the anti-Bolshevik portion of his party's platform heard among his White Russian audience in Shanghai. What was more difficult to convey was the blatant antisemitism and underlying pro-Japanese sentiments which pervaded his speeches and writings. An article published in *Nash Put* entitled 'Can't we dispense with the Jews?' sparked dissent from several quarters. The article attacked the services of two Jewish physicians practising medicine at the Russian Emigrants' Hospital, warning that the health of local Russians had been placed in the hands of Jews. The All-Russian Emigrants' Committee, which had Jewish members on its Advisory Board, responded with an excoriating attack on the article and its authors, noting that even the revered Russian vocalist F. I. Chaliapin, while performing in Shanghai, had entrusted the treatment of his voice to the same Jewish doctors. Clearly, this offensively coarse statement of antisemitic sentiments did not suit the more subtle, guarded and cautious Russian community of Shanghai. This is not to say that antisemitism did not exist among the White Russian community. Rather the expression of any even quasi-political views had, over the years, become muted and subdued in multinational Shanghai, where Russian refugees were acutely aware of their vulnerable, stateless condition, especially after the Japanese occupation.

The Japanese response to this strident brand of fascism presented a different perspective, but one in character with their position in the city. Japanese representative K. Kuroki made it clear that in regard to the 'Jewish problem' it was not for fascists, 'nor for the Germans', nor for 'mere refugees' to determine such a key question as the fate or status of the Jew in East Asia. Rather, these were questions to be handled only by the New Order 'in accordance with the programme approved by the Nipponese Empire'.[54] Kuroki was careful to focus his complaint directly on Spasovsky, whose positions he found presumptuous and destabilising. As for the All-Russian Fascist Union, Kuroki and the Japanese press in Shanghai continued to express respect for its general position and work.[55] In return, Spasovsky began to moderate his public statements and the Union continued to attract followers although not in great numbers.[56]

Daily life during the Pacific War

Life for the 'free' Russians in wartime Shanghai was fraught with struggle to make ends meet under conditions of food and fuel shortages. On the positive side, culture and the arts continued to flourish, with ballet performances at the Lyceum Theatre, concerts, light opera and theatre events. During the months just preceding the Pacific War, the Russian and Polish communities organised evening variety shows, known as the Moonlight Follies, meant to raise monies for the British War Fund. These events demonstrated the peculiar unifying effect which World War II had on the disparate communities in Shanghai, owing in part to the scope and magnitude of the war. The Follies events were held in the garden of the prominent local Jew Ellis Hayim, and besides being attended by local White Russians, Russian Jews and Polish guests, on some of these occasions local Soviet guests also joined in the festivities.[57] At the same time, a similar event reportedly was apt to be taking place at the German compound, raising funds for the Third Reich from a variety of guests in attendance.[58]

Russian refugees retained their freedom after the Pacific War began, unlike the Americans, British, Belgians and Dutch residents, who were eventually interned in 'civic assembly centres', mostly during February–March 1943. The thousands of central European Jews who had fled to Shanghai ended up in a so-called Designated Area, commonly referred to as the Hongkou ghetto. The Neutrality Pact signed between Japan and the Soviet Union in April 1941 offered some protection to the Russians, including the Russian Jews. Some in both of these Russian groups were pro-Soviet or, out of convenience, had accepted Soviet citizenship. At least as important was the fact that the Russians had been in the city for at least two decades and were employed by the Japanese in considerable numbers, especially in the police forces. Thus their services were useful to the Japanese for maintaining a measure of civil order and stability, at least in the initial stages of assuming full control over the foreign settlements. There is evidence, however, that the Japanese had plans to address the issue of the Russian Jews, who had not been placed in the Shanghai ghetto, once they had completed the processing work involved in the establishment of the Hongkou Designated Area.[59] Had the war gone better for the Japanese, allowing them more time to carry out their plans, it is possible that the Russian Jews might have come under even more supervision and control, as well as the large White Russian community.

Black market activity, inflation and speculation increasingly impoverished the White Russian population in Shanghai. From 1942 until August 1945 Shanghai prices increased at an average rate of 26 per cent per month.[60] Utilities such as electricity or natural gas functioned for only one hour a day. Severe shortages in housing, food and fuel, especially coal, compelled General Glebov to convene a Special Economic Council to solicit recommendations for improving economic assistance to the growing numbers of needy Russians. The council sponsored a community kitchen and took other measures to strengthen charitable services to the poor.

When the war finally ended, amid great celebrations throughout the city, the response of General Glebov, leader of the Russian community, remained guarded and cautious. Reflecting the unprotected status of the stateless refugee, still beholden to others and unable to assert an independent identity, Glebov advised the local Russians to remember that they played no role in local political affairs. Rather, he counselled them to focus squarely on their own refugee affairs and exhorted them 'to remain loyal to the government of the country where they have found refuge'.[61] In his last public address, given perhaps to console his compatriots facing new anxieties, Glebov stressed that honest Russians need not fear political repression in the aftermath of the war. This hopeful vision of the post-war Russian future was never realised by Glebov; he died on 10 October 1945.[62]

Post-war conditions and emigration

With the war's end, units of the US Army, Navy, Marines and Army Air Force entered Shanghai in order to help oversee the surrender, disarming and evacuation of the Japanese military and civilian populations. Their arrival brought with it the need for a variety of support services to which the Russian refugees were most willing to respond. Positions became available for drivers, warehouse guards, clerks, PX (post exchange) workers, watchmen, mechanics, and for many other occupations. But the Russians faced stiff competition from the European Jewish refugees who had the efficient services of local and international support bodies to handle and match employment opportunities. At least for the Russians who had spent hours or months in English language instruction, their studies paid off. An additional and very appealing aspect was that those hired would be paid in American currency. Under the inflationary conditions in Shanghai in which prices, between August 1945 and July 1948, increased an average of 33.7 per cent per month and where one American dollar in August 1947 equalled 39,000 Chinese yuan, this was a major attraction.[63] The United Nations Relief and Rehabilitation Administration (UNRRA), in China to provide food, clothing, medical supplies and other services to this war-torn country, became another employer of the Russian refugees, also paying in US currency. With living conditions somewhat improved, the major concern for the refugees became where they would build their future.

Just after the war ended, when the Supreme Soviet issued an appropriate decree, the Soviet authorities offered a period of amnesty during which stateless Russians could receive Soviet passports and return to the motherland. The effectiveness of the local Russian press in evoking patriotic sentiments, especially during the war years, together with the nostalgia and misery of being stateless, caused an estimated 4,000 local Russians to accept the Soviet offer and return.[64] When those who returned began to correspond with Shanghai refugees, their reports portrayed conditions in the Soviet Union at odds with the promises of a good life. Thereafter the tide turned, so that increasingly Shanghai Russians chose the no man's land of statelessness over the growing uncertainty about life back in the motherland. At the same time, the Chinese Civil War, which looked increasingly unfavourable towards Chiang Kai-shek and the Nationalist forces, created a common concern among the Russian community for its safety under a Chinese communist regime.

Until further research is done, a thorough understanding of Russian emigration from Shanghai will remain incomplete. Russians did accept offers of employment in Australia, which recruited the young and able-bodied to participate in the post-war development of its large and underpopulated country. Argentina also offered assistance. Other Russians went to Paraguay and Ecuador, and some to Canada and

France. Before the communist forces took over the city of Shanghai in May 1949, more than 5,000 of the remaining Russian refugees accepted the proposal of the International Refugee Organisation to settle temporarily in Tubabao, off the island of Samar in the Philippines. What was intended to be a four-month stay while the refugees were processed for other destinations turned into two long years, living in jungle-like conditions on an abandoned US naval base, with US surplus tents for housing, a quonset hut and a few barracks for essential institutions like schools and an infirmary, and a good supply of military K-rations and powdered food to make up their diet.[65] Finally, as a result of lobbying in the US Congress by Bishop John, and the attention given to the plight of the Samar Russians by Senator William Knowland of California, legislation was amended to allow the Samar refugees to receive visas and emigrate to the United States. The Russian diaspora in China of more than thirty years had finally reached a conclusion. Unfortunately, the Russian diaspora which had arrived in Shanghai broken and confused left the city with little promise of regaining a sense of cultural pride and national identity, as it dispersed to several countries and locations. These circumstances, together with the pulls and tensions of the wartime experience, caused the Russian diaspora community to end at least as fractured as when it first arrived in Shanghai.

Notes

1 Wang Zhicheng, *Shanghai E qiao shi* (A History of the Russian Emigré Community in Shanghai) (Shanghai, Sanlian shudian, 1993), 4–5.
2 'Origins and Future of the Local Russian Community' (five-part series), *Shanghai Sunday Times*, 26 July 1936.
3 Police report, 15 April 1935, in National Archives and Records Administration, Washington DC, RG 263, Shanghai Municipal Police (SMP) D 5002A.
4 Vladimir Danilovich Zhiganov, *Russkie v Shankhaie* (Russians in Shanghai) (Shanghai, n.p., 1936), 35.
5 V. F. Grosse, 'Report of the Office of the Comptroller of Voluntary Services', 10 August 1925, and Grosse report dated 1 January 1926, Shanghai Municipal Archives (SMA), Shanghai Municipal Council (SMC) Secretariat File, U 1-3-3002.
6 Grosse, 'Report of the Office of the Controller of Voluntary Services', 10 August 1925, 3.
7 Wang, *Shanghai E qiao shi*, 55–6, 238–47.
8 *Shanghai Sunday Times*, 12 July 1936.
9 Lidin, 'Russkaya Emigratsiya v Shankhaie' (The Russian Emigré Group in Shanghai), in *Russkiye Zapiski* (Russian Annals), II, 1937, 315.
10 Report from V. F. Grosse to the Secretary, Shanghai Municipal Council, 21 October 1927, in SMC Secretariat File, SMA, U 1-3-3002.
11 Memorandum from the SMP, 13 June 1933, in SMP D 2882; *Shanghai Sunday Times*, 26 July 1936.
12 Zhiganov, *Russkie v Shankhaie*, 35.
13 A copy of SORO's organisational regulations, in both English and Chinese, and

samples of its official seals, are found in SMP D 2882. SMP D 5002 contains a brief outline of its constitution and a membership list.
14 Police report, 5 August 1936, in SMP D 5002.
15 *North China Daily News (NCDN)*, 3 July 1936.
16 Zhiganov, *Russkie v Shankhaie*, 149.
17 *Shanghai Sunday Times*, 2 August 1936; 'In the Russian Colony', *NCDN*, 10 November 1937; Lidin, 'Russkaya Emigratsiya v Shankhaie', 317.
18 The figure 4,000 is used in *Israel's Messenger*, 32:11 (12 March 1937), 17. Another figure of 5,000 was given by David H. Zysman, Yeshiva University, in his address to the 1994 reunion in Shanghai. *China Press*, 3 July 1940, reports 8,000 Ashkenazi Jews in Shanghai, probably counting in the total number the about 1,000 Sephardi Jews.
19 'Protection of Russian Women', in Shanghai Municipal Council, *Annual Report*, 1935, 33; John Hope Simpson, *Refugees: Preliminary Report of a Problem* (London, Royal Institute of International Affairs, 1938), 158.
20 'Situation des femmes d'origine russe en Extrême-Orient', 15 August 1935, in R4692, Archives de la Société des Nations, Geneva.
21 League of Nations document, *Position of Women of Russian Origin in the Far East*, 15 August 1935 (A.12.1935.IV), and League of Nations report, *Conference of Central Authorities in Eastern Countries* (C.228.M.164.1937.IV).
22 Lidin, 'Russkaya Emigratsiya v Shankhaie', 320.
23 John Hope Simpson, *The Refugee Problem: Report of a Survey* (London, Oxford University Press, 1939), 503. A survey done in December 1937 of unemployment among 6,564 males revealed that, of 553 clerks, only 339 were employed; of 186 bookkeepers, 51 were employed; of 218 electricians, 85 were employed; of 271 engineers, 120 were employed. Noted employment increases were for watchmen. A survey of 3,360 female refugees revealed that, of 165 clerks, 88 were employed; of 346 dressmakers, 124; of 90 manicurists, 46; of 136 nurses, 91; of 89 saleswomen, 42; of 205 stenographers and typists, 110; of 140 teachers, 41. Simpson, *The Refugee Problem*, 504.
24 Simpson, *The Refugee Problem*, 503.
25 Police report dated 30 January 1935 in SMP D 6457.
26 For discussion of the Russian fascist movement in Shanghai see police reports dated 17 March 1936 in SMP D 5835 and 17 March 1937 in SMP D 7478.
27 John J. Stephan, *The Russian Fascists: Tragedy and Farce in Exile, 1925–1945* (New York, Harper & Row, 1978), 74, 155.
28 Police report dated 2 December 1938 in SMP D 8902.
29 Sources citing the figure 25,000 are: *Shanghai Times*, 4 June 1939; *China Press*, 21 June and 3 July 1940; and *Shanghai Evening Post and Mercury*, 28 October 1940.
30 *China Press*, 15 June 1939. Police report SMP D 5002A provides a list of the bodies, dates of formation, leaders and membership of sixty Russian public organisations.
31 *NCDN*, 3 August 1940; *North China Herald (NCH)*, 7 August 1940.
32 'Interview with Mr N. A. Ivanoff', police report dated 5 August 1940 in SMP D 5002A.
33 Shanghai Municipal Council, *Annual Report*, 1938, 17. Wang Jingwei's inauguration took place on 30 March 1940.
34 Russian Emigrants' Committee, SMP MIS 17, 1.
35 *NCDN*, 16 September 1941; *China Weekly Review (CWR)*, 20 September 1941, 84; 27 September 1941, 98–100.
36 *NCDN*, 29 September 1941.
37 Russian Emigrants' Committee, SMP MIS 17, 4.
38 The figure 30,000 is given in *CWR*, 1 March 1941, 441.
39 *Shanghai Times*, 10 March 1942.
40 'Exiled Russians in Shanghai Rally to aid Fatherland', *NCDN*, 12 October 1941.
41 Interview with former Shanghai resident Nikita Moravsky, Ph.D., Washington DC, 16 June 1995.
42 According to the July 1942 *baojia* census, there were 1,666 registered Soviet citizens in the three areas of Shanghai: SMP MIS 17, 9. See also 'List of Soviet Organisations in Shanghai', in French police report, 27 February 1942 in SMP D 13.

43　Interview with former Shanghai resident Joseph Froomkin, Ph.D., Washington DC, September 1995.
44　Wang, *Shanghai E qiao shi*, 222.
45　*NCDN*, 22 October 1941.
46　*NCDN*, 24 October 1941.
47　Wang, *Shanghai E qiao shi*, 308–9.
48　Russian Emigrants' Committee, SMP MIS 17, 3.
49　From 23 February until late March 61,460 Soviets were killed in one sector alone. See *Shanghai Times*, 31 March 1943.
50　Russian Emigrants' Committee, SMP MIS 17, 4.
51　Police report dated 2 April 1944 in SMP D 5002A.
52　Russian Emigrants' Committee, SMP MIS 17, 5–6.
53　Spasovsky's pen name was M. Grott. Other members of the Union included G. A. Hofen, 'Head of the Shanghai Group'; V. V. Ivanchenko, Secretary; and E. N. Chetverikov, Head of the Women's Section. Police report dated 30 April 1942 in SMP D 7478.
54　Translation of article 'Regarding Karganoff-Spasovsky's Letter', in *Novoye Vremia* (New Times), 19 August 1942.
55　Translation of article 'Explanation Regarding the Incident Involving M. M. Spasovsky' in *Novoye Vremia*, 26 August 1942, in SMP D 7478.
56　A meeting for renaming the organisation the Union of National Workers of Russia drew 110 followers. Police report dated 14 October 1943 in SMP D 7478.
57　*NCDN*, 27 July and 28 August 1941.
58　Reported to the author at the Shanghai reunion of former Jewish refugees, September 1994.
59　'Yudaya-jin taisaku ni kansuru-ken' (Concerning Measures *vis-à-vis* Jews), declassified top secret memo No. 69, 18 November 1942, from the Japanese Consul General, Shanghai, to the Ministry of Greater East Asian Affairs: Japanese Ministry of Foreign Affairs microfilm collection, S-9460-3-2556.
60　Shun-hsin Chou, *The Chinese Inflation, 1937–1949* (New York, Columbia University Press, 1963), 23.
61　Russian Emigrants' Committee, SMP MIS 17, 6.
62　Russian Emigrants' Committee, SMP MIS 17, 6.
63　Chou, *Chinese Inflation, 1937–1949*, 24–6, 138.
64　Wang, *Shanghai E qiao shi*, 121. Wang bases this figure on several Chinese newspaper accounts from 1947–49.
65　Interview with Nikita Moravsky, Washington DC, 21 August 1996.

CHAPTER TWELVE

In search of identity: the German community in Shanghai, 1933–1945
Françoise Kreissler

The German presence in China developed relatively late in comparison with other Western powers. This fact made a permanent mark on Germany's relations with those foreign countries which were regarded as competitors seeking to limit the influence of this latecomer to the Chinese scene. Likewise Germans in China, who were very few in number, had insignificant political influence compared with their economic role. Apart from that, until 1871 the Germans regarded themselves as representatives of such German states as Prussia, Bavaria, Saxony, and so on, rather than as German citizens. In 1861 Prussia, the most powerful of the German states and their leader, signed the Treaty of Tianjin with China, which gave it the political privileges which the other Western countries had exacted from China in 1842–44. On the part of the Chinese empire, this was a first step towards the political recognition of the German states. Only after the Prussian victories over Austria in 1866 and France in 1870–71 did China move from *de jure* to *de facto* recognition of Germany as a political, economic and, above all, a military power, one that was resolved to conquer and to affirm its position among the Great Powers.

After the creation of the Reich in 1871, German merchants, missionaries, engineers, physicians, teachers and diplomats became more numerous in China. After its official recognition by China the German Reich made considerable and successful efforts to make up for its late arrival in both the diplomatic and the commercial areas. Its purpose was not to be left behind in the sharing of political and economic power which was to be unleashed in the final years of the nineteenth century. At the end of the Sino-Japanese War (1894–95) Germany gained Concessions in Hankou and Tianjin in exchange for its intervention on the side of France and Russia, when, under their combined pressure, Japan was forced to retrocede Liaodong to China. Up to then Germany had had no Concessions or leased territories in China. Two years later, in 1897, the German Reich annexed Qingdao and the surrounding region by a direct act of aggression, taking as a pretext for the intervention the murder of German missionaries in Shandong. From that time on, Germany had a foothold in China alongside the other Western powers.[1]

Like all other Westerners, the Germans divided their daily life between business, family, the club and various sports and cultural activities. About half the German community lived in Shanghai, where Germans had built up an intense and thoroughly organised community life, with their school (the Kaiser-Wilhelm-Schule), their newspapers (*Der Ostasiatische Lloyd, Deutsche Zeitung für China, Der Ferne Osten*), their associations for engineers (Chinesischer Verband deutscher Ingenieure) and physicians (Deutsche Ärztefirma or Deutsche Ärztevereinigung).[2] Until the eve of World War I the German community lived in relative harmony with the other foreign communities and preserved German national customs and traditions. In 1914 the situation changed completely, when war was declared in Europe and when Germany became the enemy of the majority of the foreign communities in China. Germans were outlawed from non-Chinese society: they were expelled not only from all Shanghai foreign clubs but also from the Shanghai Municipal Council (SMC) and other municipal administrations; in many cases they even lost their jobs in non-German enterprises. This 'cold war' between Germans and other Westerners in Shanghai has been described as follows by the American journalist J. B. Powell:

> It was interesting, at noontime, to see the British and German businessmen passing each other on the Bund without a nod of recognition, each headed for his club for luncheon, where the chief subject of discussion was the war. Each club had a large mounted map of the Western front, but the thumb tacks were on opposite sides of the line.[3]

On 15 March 1917 China broke off diplomatic relations with the German Reich, one of the main consequences for the Germans in Shanghai being the occupation and confiscation by the French of the famous German Medical School (Tongji dewen yixuexiao), which was located in the French Concession.[4] The next turning point in the life of the Germans occurred in April 1917, when the United States joined the *Entente* and declared war on Germany. From then on, German citizens in China were politically and economically isolated. A few months later, on 14 August, China declared war on Germany; it was the Chinese government's turn to take measures against German nationals, who lost all the advantages and rights associated with extraterritoriality.[5] Community activities were restricted: the German press stopped publication, and German clubs were shut down. Nevertheless, the Chinese government asked the German teachers, whose abilities were deeply appreciated, to remain at Chinese schools.[6] Finally, the decisive upheaval occurred on 11 November 1918, the day of the Armistice, on which Germans felt the full effects of the lost war: the victorious British and French took the decision to demand the expulsion of all German nationals from China. Some escaped this drastic measure – missionaries, for example; others got Chinese friends to help them escape repatriation. But the Chinese authorities, who wanted German physicians and teachers to stay, finally gave in to the demands of Germany's enemies.[7]

In May 1921 a peace treaty was signed between the Republic of China and the Weimar Republic. The German community in China got back into their pre-war habits: the clubs and the German schools were reopened, and new cultural associations were organised. But while contacts with Chinese friends and acquaintances were resumed, British and French nationals no longer treated Germans as their equals. Shunned by the other Western communities, the Germans often reacted with an exacerbated nationalism, especially those who had had to leave their homeland in the 1920s because of the post-war political and economical crisis. This justifiable resentment against enemies World War I may partly explain the political affinities of the German community in the 1930s and 1940s.

Table 12.1 clearly shows the decline of the German presence in China beginning with 1917 and proves as well that German business was much more affected than the community as a whole, the main reason probably being that missionaries often could avoid repatriation. During the Weimar era (1919–33) German residents' presence in Shanghai was mainly cultural and economic and, as Table 12.1 shows, German entrepreneurs were back on the China market by the mid-1920s.[8] Since the Germans did not take part in municipal administration (the only German member of the SMC had been replaced by a Japanese member in 1917), many of them gave up social intercourse with other foreigners and chose to withdraw into community life. In the same time this kind of 'self-isolation' from other foreign communities led to closer contacts with China who highly appreciated the new relationship based on equality which ensued from German loss of extraterritoriality.[9]

There is no doubt that the years 1917 and 1918 determined the fate of the Germans in China: they were a turning point which influenced and determined the actions and reactions of the German community, faced with the political and social upheavals in Germany from 1933 on. Without really concerning themselves with the under-

Table 12.1 German firms and nationals in China, 1875–1928

Year	German firms	German nationals	Year	German firms	German nationals
1875	52	367	1917	132	2,899
1880	65	341	1918	75	2,651
1885	57	638	1919	2	1,335
1890	80	648	1920	9	1,013
1897	104	950	1921	92	1,255
1900	120	1,343	1922	184	1,986
1905	197	1,850	1923	244	2,233
1910	238	4,106	1924	253	2,733
1913	296	2,949	1925	318	3,050
1914	273	3,013	1926	314	2,963
1915	244	3,740	1927	307	2,719
1916	281	3,792	1928	319	3,026

Source Chen Chi, *Die Beziehungen zwischen Deutschland und China bis 1933* (Hamburg: Institut für Asienkunde, 1973), 321–3.

lying ideology, the Germans in Shanghai were at first highly sympathetic to Chancellor Hitler's government, which stood up against the democratic powers and announced that the main object of its foreign policy was to wipe away the indignity of the Treaty of Versailles. Such a policy immediately found support within the communities of German expatriates. Germany's strong man had promised to return to the German people the honour which they had lost in 1918, but, as the months and years went by, Germans in Shanghai, like others elsewhere, had to face the facts: it could not be done without making certain concessions, and even if they had reservations, the Germans in Shanghai were prepared to go a long way in making concessions.

The years 1933–45 represent a relatively short period in the history of the community, but one which had a profound impact upon it. However, until now historians have barely touched upon this episode, a fact which can be explained not by its lack of importance but, on the contrary, by the decisive role which those years played and continue to play, and which can also explain the reluctance to confront this period in history. It is common today for those historically involved in the National Socialist era to refuse to draw any parallel with the dominant ideology of the period, and some dispute or flatly refuse any affinity with that ideology. Logically, the political and economic leaders who were responsible after the war for maintaining German political continuity could hardly do other than minimise the role and weight of ideology and politics during the twelve years they represented their country in China. At the same time, they have played down the importance of their own role and function. After 1945 they all had a common reaction: to remain silent about that period. The few pieces written about life in Shanghai were penned by diplomats and journalists who were deeply involved. Keeping silent on the subject of this period and its implications made it possible for people to forget and even, in some cases, to deny the realities of the time.[10]

Let us take a recent example. Erwin Wickert, who was in charge of the German radio station in Shanghai between 1940 and 1941 and the station in Tokyo from 1941 to 1945, served as the West German ambassador to Peking from 1976 to 1980, wrote several books, including novels, and was a member of the German PEN Club until 1995. In November 1996 he made some revealing and characteristic comments, claiming to know less about the twelve years of Hitler's dictatorship than about some ancient Chinese empires.[11] The observation would not be surprising in itself had it not been made during a lawsuit which the retired diplomat had brought against a journalist who dared to cast doubt on the innocence of his wartime career. The journalist was born in 1942 in Shanghai of refugee parents, who had had to escape from National Socialist Germany. Without entering into any sort of polemic, such an example makes clear the perils of tackling the history of the German community in China during this period. For a start, memoirs and recollections written by the principal actors in events, and published at a later date, are unreliable and even tend to lead the uninformed reader down the wrong path. As for interviews with the last remaining witnesses of the period, they are hardly any more reliable than the written testimonies.

This introduction has explained why this analysis is essentially political and less directed towards economic and social considerations. This chapter aims to set up the political framework, essential for the years 1933–45, for a future social and economic analysis.

The implantation of the Nazi party

While the years 1917–19 deeply affected the relations between Germans and other foreign communities, the year 1933 marks a definite break in the community life of the Germans. The political changes taking place in Germany are reflected in the German communities by a more or less rapid process of 'co-ordination' (Gleichschaltung). Well before Hitler's rise to power (30 January 1933), the

Nazi party included a department in charge of Germans abroad (the Auslandsabteilung), which had to control all groups and members of the party living beyond the borders of the Reich. As early as the end of 1933 the Nazi party was beginning to look towards citizens who had settled outside the Reich.

In Shanghai, where most of the Germans in China lived (a population of about 2,000 people), a small group of the NSDAP, with a membership of seven people in all, was set up as early as the winter of 1931–32. In April 1932 this group created the local NSDAP group; Franz Xaver Hasenöhrl (1891–1943), a former officer in the Austro-Hungarian army working as a trader in China, was appointed its chief.[12] His ranking superior in Germany, Ernst Wilhelm Bohle (1903–60), strongly emphasised the quality of the work carried out by Hasenöhrl in China and noted with great satisfaction that the regional NSDAP in China was, along with the one in Chile, certainly the most efficient group abroad.

Nevertheless, until January 1933 the activities of the National Socialists in Shanghai continued to be marginal. In spite of everything, the beginnings of the Nazi party were difficult, as the result of, among other things, the internal conflicts which hindered the rapid implantation of the party and which were due more to personal rivalries than to political or ideological antagonism. For obvious reasons, the German press hardly even recognised these conflicting situations, but some German consular reports, as well as those of the Shanghai Municipal Police (SMP), record the disagreements between the members of the Nazi party in plain language, and even, at times, with undisguised satisfaction.

At the beginning of 1934 the members of the party violently confronted the 'old-established' group with the intention of assuming control not only of the community's political activities but also of social and economic matters which concerned Germany or Germans. This struggle for power began to accelerate when Theodor Hannig took over the direction of the local NSDAP group. His ultra-nationalist attitudes provoked numerous conflicts among members of the Shanghai community, so much so that in May 1934 Hasenöhrl was again sent to Shanghai to reconcile the two parties.[13] This was the situation which Lieutenant-colonel Kriebel (1876–1941), a personal friend of Hitler who had just been appointed consul general to Shanghai, found upon his arrival in the city on 21 June 1934. Perfectly familiar with the political problems there, Kriebel immediately passed appropriate measures and took advantage of the events which had meanwhile taken place in Germany at the end of June 1934. Kriebel summoned all the members of the

German community in Shanghai and tried above all to calm everyone down. The main decision Kriebel took was to limit the powers of the party in the future to political action only, and to proscribe any interference in other questions concerning the German community as a whole, particularly economic questions. All these matters, Kriebel declared, were the sole concern of the consul general. According to one SMP report, Kriebel excluded certain of the party's less accommodating members from its organisation.[14]

An SMP report of 28 November 1934 describes the political atmosphere which reigned within the local German community and noted that, from January 1933, the community had split into two groups: 'a group consisting of persons who accepted the new regime, but were still impregnated with the ideas of the past, and a group composed of 100 per cent partisans of the new regime'.[15] In the former case, they were Germans who were politically relatively moderate, mostly businessmen, long-term residents who wielded a degree of influence on the business world in Shanghai. They were not yet disposed to let politics govern their private and business life. As for the unconditional supporters of the Nazi party, still a minority in 1933–34, they were, for the most part, young members of the Sportabteilung (SA). It is clear that Consul General Kriebel, Hitler's old companion, was one of the people best placed to get a grip on the situation without the slightest fear of criticism or opposition. From this point on the role of the Nazi party in Shanghai was clearly established, and around 1935–36 the organisation of the party was secure. The National Socialists could concentrate on forcing the German community into 'co-ordination'.

'Co-ordination' (Gleichschaltung)

In order to rally the German community to their cause, the National Socialist Party first sought to 'imbue the overseas Germans with the spirit of National Socialism', that is, to persuade them of the fully justified grounds of the new regime and, if possible, make them active defenders of National Socialism.[16] The best way to manage this was felt to be the use of effective oral and written propaganda circulated during conferences and evening discussions organised by the party, which also assumed responsibility for providing clubs, schools and various associations of the German community in China with catalogues of Nazi publications.[17] Nazi publications were distributed free of charge to all the German clubs, even if they had not requested them. For the NSDAP it was a question of turning the Germans away from a certain kind of 'materialism' which they all too easily accepted during the years when they had adopted a rather cosmopolitan way of life.

The unification of the German communities in China posed some problems which were not so much ideological as practical.[18] Although they were not always accepted right from the beginning, in 1933, the local groups of the NSDAP, in Shanghai, Tianjin, Qingdao, Hankou and elsewhere, maintained enough authority, and, especially, enough power of persuasion, to impose their political ideas on those communities. At the same time, there is no doubt that active support for the politics of the Reich on the part of the diplomats, with whom the Germans in China had often had links for a long time and in whom they had confidence, convinced the people that they were making the right decision.[19]

One of the main objectives of the Nazi organisation in charge of the Germans abroad was to put an end, as quickly as possible, to the long-standing German habit of creating a multiplicity of associations, and to impose upon them the 'principle of totality'. The overseas Germans had to be aware of the fact that they belonged to Germany. The 'universal German' who had always tended to be assimilated into his new country had now to give way to the 'total German' who, as a citizen of the Reich, was German 'and nothing but German and therefore a National Socialist'.[20] After having managed to overcome any remaining hesitation within the German communities, local Nazi party groups took charge of the destiny of German people in China. The Nazi party tried to make the Germans understand that it was 'an honour to work for Germany in a foreign country'.[21] German export companies accordingly had to be careful to send only reliable men to China, men who were willing to let the Nazi party exercise control over their private and professional lives.

The unification of the community still presented several problems. Even if the Germans did not show any political resistance to National Socialism, they nevertheless wanted to avoid upheaval in their daily lives. In any case, they refused to follow orders from men who, too often, were totally ignorant of living conditions in the Far East. One of the outstanding cases occurred in 1933 in Tianjin, when Otto Ohlwein, who had been appointed head of the local Nazi group, tried to control the German community. The systematic opposition of the long-term residents compelled him to return to Germany, as none of his compatriots assisted him when he lost his job in Tianjin.[22]

Neither the archives nor the press of the period can give us an account of the reactions of the Germans to the omnipresent Nazi party. For this reason, it is practically impossible to describe individual behaviour in the face of NSDAP control. However, it is obvious that the control imposed by the party on the German population in China did not meet with any opposition, nor even any systematic refusal, and that, without any difficulty at all, that control was exercised on all aspects of community life. It has to be mentioned that there were some attempts at circulating anti-Nazi propaganda, but they cannot be considered really successful, merely attracting the attention of the consulate-general and the SMP. Neither the three issues of the *Shanghai Anzeiger*, a newspaper published in April 1934, nor the leaflet denouncing the political situation in the Third Reich entitled 'Deutsche Shanghai Volksfront/1936-G' which had been distributed to some members of the German community in 1936, or the voluminous document ('A Nightmare comes true') that some Germans found in their letter box in autumn 1939, had any impact.[23]

In the 1930s and 1940s Germans, unlike other national communities in China, accepted strong metropolitan political control over their daily life. Even if they did not join the Nazi party, many of them were members of one of the Nazi organisations in Shanghai, the most important being the Deutsche Arbeitsfront, the NS-Frauenschaft, the SA and the Hitler-Jugend (HJ).[24] In connection with the HJ, for example, the report of the German school for the year 1939–40 proudly indicates that more than 85 per cent of the pupils of German origin were members.[25] In Shanghai the German community finally recognised the leading role which the Nazi party held and which everyone, even the other foreign communities, seemed to accept. In short, between 1933 and 1945 the German community in China showed no active opposition to Berlin's campaign of political consolidation, even if, at times, for personal reasons, it did not much appreciate the German policies in the Far East. It is a fact that Berlin's increasingly pro-Japanese stance, which would lead to the 1936 Anti-Comintern pact, presented risks for German economic interests. The American Olga Lang pointed out, in a 1937 article published in *Amerasia*, that indecision reigned in the Shanghai community at that time:

> The Germans in Shanghai have been suffering from the inconvenient situation of having 'two souls in their breasts' much more than the English Shanghailanders. One German soul, being a good Hitlerite, wanted to help the Japanese ally. The other one, the soul of a businessman, did not want to lose a very profitable and developing Chinese market. The Germans in Shanghai were very dissatisfied with the outspoken pro-Japanese attitude of the German press, and the German Chamber of Commerce urgently coaxed Berlin to change its attitude if 'it does not

want the German business and Germanism [Deutschtum] in China to be done with'.[26]

Politics threaten economic interests

It is clear that the years 1937–38 witnessed a fundamental change in Germany's China policy. By that time Germany had become one of China's main economic partners, since German imports had already exceeded Britain's in 1936.[27] Whereas, up to that point, Germany had concentrated on the conquest of the Chinese market, the new pro-Japanese policy, as demonstrated by the recognition of Manzhouguo (February 1938) and the removal of German military advisers from Nanjing (June 1938), to mention but two examples, largely cancelled out previous efforts which had gone into economic policy. The appointment of a new Minister of Foreign Affairs (Ribbentrop) in February 1938 had brought about a change in the foreign policy of the Reich, as well as in its economic and commercial policies: Germany tried to find a market in occupied northern China and in Manzhouguo.[28]

During the years 1933–37 the German business world, like the rest of the community, adjusted to the political changes – and their consequences – which had taken place in Germany. However, when the Sino-Japanese War began in 1937, Berlin's foreign policy, which was more and more pro-Japanese, began to irritate most of the merchants and businessmen in China, who would have liked their leaders to implement a much more moderate policy of co-operation with Japan. The position the German press took, by expressing enthusiasm over the Japanese military victories during the year 1937, elicited violent protests from the German Chamber of Commerce in Shanghai, which felt that such a position was detrimental to German business in China and unnecessarily undermined Chinese confidence in it.[29]

The chamber of commerce wanted to see an end to all this 'glorification of Japan', otherwise German trade in China ran the risk of being 'definitively wiped out'.[30] Those German merchants in Shanghai whose goods and property were the victim of the Japanese bombings that began in August 1937 did not greatly appreciate the fact that, in Germany, people were claiming that Japan was waging a war in China against Moscow and the communists.[31] Tension mounted during chamber of commerce meetings, for the diplomats, who attended the working sessions, were not prepared to openly support the positions of the German merchants, at least not until they had consulted their ranking superiors in Berlin and received their instructions.

THE GERMAN COMMUNITY IN SHANGHAI

The diplomats found themselves in a situation which was all the more uncomfortable because, unlike representatives of the other foreign communities, they could not allow themselves to protest to their Japanese political allies about the bombing and destruction of German property. What was more, Berlin was asking them to seek friendly relations with the Japanese at all costs. To the leaders of the chamber of commerce it was perfectly obvious that the Japanese occupation of part of China would mean a negative balance sheet for German trade, and they wished their government would be less conciliatory towards its Japanese ally. In 1938 the chamber of commerce's annual report underlined the fact that everyone was familiar not only with the political but also with the economic objectives of the Japanese invasion. The report predicted that a Japanese victory would, without question, be the beginning of the end for foreign trade in China, as the example of Manchuria had demonstrated several years before.[32] German businessmen could feel nothing but regret about the Japanese take-over of business in Manchuria. Every one of them now knew just what co-operation with their so-called 'ally' meant, and they had the impression they were paying dearly for Germany's policy towards the Japanese.[33] The report predicted that, in the event of a Japanese victory, German trade would, at best, be able to serve as a 'stop-gap' and that the primary losers in the war would be 'the Europeans and the Americans, for they have not got the same powers of resistance as the Chinese'.[34]

The business community in Shanghai judged this policy unrealistic, ill-timed and doomed to failure. The pro-Chinese position of the chamber of commerce made a very bad impression in Berlin and the Germans in Shanghai were sharply called to order. The head of the Auslandsorganisation, Ernst Wilhelm Bohle, was given the task of writing a confidential letter to Lahrmann, head of the Nazi party in China, to remind him of the duties of German expatriates: it was their obligation to provide unconditional support for the Führer's pro-Japanese policy and to bear the ensuing economic loss. The personal interests of compatriots in Shanghai should under no circumstances come before the 'great politics of the Führer'. Consequently, it was advisable to avoid, at all cost, giving the Japanese and the Chinese the impression that the Germans in Shanghai were defending a different point of view from that of the Reich.[35]

Following these strong reactions from Berlin, German merchants in Shanghai avoided expressing openly their discontent over Reich foreign policy. The business community quickly understood that Berlin cared little for its commercial interests and that the only thing that really mattered was good political relations with Japan. Taking full measure of this uncomfortable situation, they decided to act accordingly and do their best to protect their economic interests while at the same time keeping politics at a distance. German businessmen in Shanghai were well aware that their government aimed at political and economic co-operation with Japan and ignored at the same time the fact that German nationals were considered by the Japanese only as 'friendly enemies'.[36]

Politics and diplomacy

German diplomats in Shanghai did not show themselves in a good light. Until the end of the 1970s historiography had defined the diplomacy of the Third Reich as an 'apolitical' authority which, for a long time, resisted the Nazi powers, 'without, however, being able to avoid the worst'.[37] Obviously, Hitler's rise to power had immediate repercussions on the structure of the Ministry of Foreign Affairs, but only a few career diplomats were ousted for political or racial reasons. Relations between high civil servants in the diplomatic service and the National Socialist leaders fluctuated between mutual comprehension, arrogant superiority and embarrassed antipathy.[38] One should remember that when Hitler came to power some high civil servants in the Ministry of Foreign Affairs were already members of the NSDAP and even the SS. One of the main reasons why the new government was in no hurry to reshuffle the Ministry was that, traditionally, it included very few members of the democratic parties and its 'non-Aryan' civil servants were rare indeed.

All the diplomats posted in China conformed to the new political rules, while at the same time making an effort to keep their diplomatic sphere intact, and trying to stay clear of direct control by the NSDAP. The racial policy enforced in Germany from 1933 on would, of course, have consequences for the diplomatic community as well. Jewish diplomats in the Ministry of Foreign Affairs were very rare, but Berlin also removed from the diplomatic service all diplomats whose spouses were Jewish and who refused to agree to a separation. Two diplomats in China were victims of such antisemitic governmental measures.[39]

During the early years of the Third Reich, the diplomats managed to keep local Nazi party leaders at a distance fairly easily, making it clear to them that National Socialist methods might be appropriate for dealing with domestic matters concerning the German community, but that they definitely carried risks for German foreign policy. Any direct interference by the Nazi party in diplomatic affairs could only elicit the distrust of the Chinese political class and, what was more, of the international community. The Nazi party authorities could hardly do other than leave the main role in foreign policy to the diplomats. But if a diplomat took one false step the NSDAP would reserve its sharpest criticism for him. As it turned out, the diplomats found themselves drawn much more quickly than they wished, no doubt, into the service of National Socialist ideology, for their job was to represent and defend the new regime which had been set up in Berlin.

Starting in May 1933, German diplomats had to face a wave of protest from Chinese personalities, who approached the consulate-general in Shanghai to express their indignation at the reign of terror for which the National Socialists were responsible, having arrested and persecuted a number of German democrats. On 13 May a delegation from the China League for Civil Rights, led by Sun Yat-sen's widow Song Qingling, was received at the consulate. The delegation included eminent personalities from the Chinese political and intellectual community: Cai Yuanpei, Lu Xun and Lin Yutang, as well as Harold Isaacs, chief editor of *China Forum*. The interim consul general, Behrend, received the delegation and agreed to forward its letter of protest to the German legation in Peking, which, for its part, refused to accept it and sent it back to Song Qingling. According to the plenipotentiary Minister, Trautmann, there was no justification for following up such highly exaggerated protests.[40] The German diplomats declared the allegations of the local press completely lacking in foundation when it denounced the atrocities and discrimination to which, it claimed, opponents of the new regime in Germany were subjected. The allegations were simply intended to discredit the government.[41] This blunt refusal on the part of the German diplomats was greeted with great satisfaction by the local German press. The *Deutsche Shanghai Zeitung* – which had published an article on 16 May entitled 'Mrs Sun Yat-sen at the German General Consulate! Do not meddle with domestic German policy!' – published a letter of protest against the League on 19 May, after the German rebuff. The letter was signed jointly by the 'German community' and the Shanghai Chamber of Commerce.[42]

If the business community at Shanghai did not always approve German foreign and economic policy, in particular with regard to China and Japan, German businessmen still considered that nobody was entitled to criticise the Third Reich's domestic policy. And from the moment Germany's honour was attacked the whole community felt targeted and became involved in defending that honour. When community interests required it, doubts and differences disappeared and the Germans became unconditional defenders of their fatherland

and of their government's position. Moreover, the entire community felt irritated by the violent attacks by a non-official Chinese association on the German government and by the interference in a matter in which no Chinese citizens were involved, an eventuality that had never occurred to any other foreign government.

In addition to their role as representatives of the Third Reich, the diplomats also had to maintain the political unity of the German community. They devoted themselves wholeheartedly to the task in order to avoid being overwhelmed by the men from the Nazi party, who were always eager to take over the leadership of any political activity. In Shanghai, although Germans could not get actively involved in the domestic politics of the Reich, they were regularly called upon to express their opinion about German politics through various referendums. Obviously, the results of these ballots could not be counted, and their value was purely symbolic, but they were an indication of the political tendencies of the German community. Participation in such 'elections' did not commit those who took part in them, but it was unwise for anyone to abstain from the vote and thus demonstrate opposition to the regime, or simply lack of interest in politics. The documents which are available to us show that, on the whole, the results of the ballots were similar to those obtained in the Reich.[43]

More than either the 1934 referendum, organised after the death of *Reichspräsident* Hindenburg, or the 1936 referendum, which dealt with the question of the Führer's foreign policy, the referendum of April 1938, which followed the annexation of Austria, is a good indicator of the growing political commitment to Nazism within the overseas German communities. The *Anschluß* was without doubt the political event which produced the loudest echo among Shanghai Germans. Five years of National Socialism, with its political and economic successes, were enough to bind the German expatriate community to its new metropolitan leaders. Every victory in foreign policy reinforced the position of German expatriates, who for many a long year had been treated as losers. In the days following the annexation of Austria (13 March) the Shanghai Nazis expressed their joy in a telegram to Berlin, in which they thanked the Führer 'for the reunification and the liberation of the *Ostmark*'.[44]

Once the *Anschluß* had been carried out at the political and diplomatic levels, all that remained was to get the German and Austrian communities to accept it. In Shanghai, as elsewhere, this was accomplished through the referendum of 10 April. Of course, Jewish Austrians, like Jewish Germans, were not allowed to vote.[45] In Shanghai, where the ballot took place without any major problems, German and ex-Austrian citizens approved the annexation of Austria, with a majority of more than 98 per cent for the former and more than 90 per cent for the latter.[46] The consul general, Martin Fischer, stressed the importance of this ballot in his report to Berlin, even though the 'Shanghai' votes could not be counted with those of the Germans living within the Reich. He asserted that, once again, the Germans in Shanghai had provided proof that, one and all, they supported their Führer and his policies, which, in his opinion, was all the more important in view of the fact that the cosmopolitan population of Shanghai included many Jews.[47] The annexation of Austria was the last event connected with foreign policy which the German community in Shanghai would celebrate with great pomp and circumstance.

From September 1939 on, the foreign policy of the Reich provoked nothing but hostility on the part of the other foreign communities, who, like many of the Chinese, noticed more and more parallels between the Reich's policy of aggression and that of Japan. From 1938–39 on, Germany's military victories in Europe more directly concerned the foreign communities, and German nationals in Shanghai abstained from celebrating the victories of the Third Reich in public and did their best to avoid any collision with other Shanghailanders.

Antisemitism

Up to this point, we have seen how far the diplomats restricted their activities to carrying out their duties to the best of their ability, with the aim, on the one hand, of defending the interests of the Reich and, on the other, of rallying the whole of the German community behind the new government. These two objectives were, after all, part and parcel of a diplomat's legitimate responsibilities at that time. However, the diplomats also got voluntarily and actively involved in Germany's antisemitic policy. In this connection, it should be pointed out that between 1933 and 1938 German diplomats in Shanghai were not fully acquainted with the 'Jewish problem'. When in 1934 Berlin requested from the consulate-general a report on Jewish activities in Shanghai, the report could indeed mention eight Jewish associations, but their leaders were all Russian or Baghdadi Jews, and it could not mention any activity of the very few Jewish refugees from Germany.[48]

But, starting in 1939, with the arrival of large numbers of Jewish refugees from central Europe, the German consulate-general took charge, not only of writing up general reports on the Jewish community's economic and financial situation, as well as its cultural activities, but also of drafting numerous individual reports, particularly about refugee journalists in Shanghai, who, because of their profession, attracted the attention of the local German community. An examination of the German Foreign Office archives, which remain our only reference source on the subject, shows that in many cases the diplomats provided information on Jewish refugees even before receiving any requests for it from the Gestapo in Berlin or Vienna. In their reports, drafted in the antisemitic terminology commonly used in Germany at the time, the diplomats requested that the journalists in question should be deprived of their German nationality, claiming that they were waging an anti-German propaganda campaign. It is fruitless to ask whether this was done out of political and ideological conviction or not. The fact remains that their behaviour, which could at the very least be described as opportunistic, was greatly appreciated both by the local Nazis and by their superiors in Berlin, even though, in Shanghai, it cost them very little to play the Nazi game to the full. In the final analysis, these diplomats pursued careers as bureaucrats of the Third Reich, with all the ideological and political consequences that this implies. However, the situation was somewhat different in Shanghai as a result of the important role which the city played in the Jewish immigration from central Europe.[49]

Besides the meticulous diplomats, National Socialist propagandists of the German Information Bureau were also active in antisemitic actions in Shanghai. At the end of 1938 an antisemitic pamphlet entitled 'A Warning to all Chinese, Japanese and Gentiles alike – the 'Chosen People' have invaded Shanghai!' appeared in Shanghai. Signed by an 'Anti-Jewish KKK', it was directed at the Jewish refugees from Europe. The Shanghai press – the *China Weekly Review* as well as *Dongfang zazhi* – made mention of it and nobody could ignore the analogy with the antisemitic terminology being then used in the Third Reich.[50] In autumn 1941, a few weeks before Pearl Harbor, a new antisemitic campaign started in Shanghai when on 26 October a leaflet signed by the 'Aryans' Union' was flung from the Park Hotel on to the race course in Bubbling Well Road during a soccer match between the Jewish Recreation Club and the Portuguese Club Lusitano. The leaflet, formulated in English, called upon local 'Aryans' to boycott Jewish businessmen, and there was no doubt that the author was the German propaganda office.[51]

The German community must have been aware of this antisemitic propaganda but apparently did not participate in it. Germans confined themselves to following the instructions of local National Socialist leaders to boycott Jewish shops, cafes and restaurants, but there were also exceptions and some Germans ignored the instructions.

While diplomats, journalists and propagandists were deeply involved in antisemitic actions, the German community in the main did not become active in anti-Jewish activities, even if it did not oppose antisemitism.

Conclusion

After World War I most German nationals abroad did not really identify with the republican regime set up at home and were especially suspicious about the foreign policy of the Weimar government, now mainly focused on Europe, since the Treaty of Versailles had deprived Germany of its colonial empire. Under these circumstances, Germans considered themselves in a way the victim of Western imperialism. In China, where they had been deprived of political – that is, imperialist – influence, they succeeded in exerting economic and cultural influence but no longer had territorial or political interests to protect. Like all German expatriates, they could only with difficulty understand and accept the process of political and social democratisation which took place in Germany. Having lost their political and institutional landmarks, German citizens abroad felt rather isolated and did not consider themselves representatives of the German Republic.

Beginning in 1933, the German community rediscovered a coherent community life. Never before had the Germans been able to assert their national identity with such assurance, in the knowledge that they had the unconditional support of their government. Even if, in the early years of National Socialism, a few internal disagreements persisted, they were aimed at the pragmatic politics in Berlin, but never questioned the official ideology.

More than any other foreign community, perhaps with the exception of the Italians, Germans in Shanghai had to conform in community life with the political process going on in their homeland. At the same time they felt rather proud to be considered citizens of the Reich who were given the opportunity of participating in political life, even if the ballots which took place in China had a largely symbolic function. Without doubt, the National Socialist regime bound together the members of the community who had not felt themselves to be German patriots during the Weimar era. The year 1933 represented a break, a sort of way back to the pre-Weimar situation, even if the Germans in China could not foresee the consequences of the new policy and ideology they welcomed. Paradoxically, it was the diplomats, who were not meant to embody this ideology in their relations with the international community of Shanghai, who became more involved in it than the other Germans. But perhaps we should end this study by going back to our starting point and quoting – once more – Erwin Wickert, who, in his autobiography, justifies his political involvement at the time by observing that no one could know then that 'Hitler's regime would last only twelve years'.[52]

Notes

1 John E. Schrecker, *Imperialism and Chinese Nationalism: Germany in Shantung* (Cambridge MA, Harvard University Press, 1971).
2 Françoise Kreissler, *L'Action culturelle allemande en Chine, de la fin du XIXe siècle à la Seconde Guerre mondiale* (Paris, Éditions de la Maison des Sciences de l'Homme, 1989), 11–20, 65–74.
3 John B. Powell, *My Twenty-five Years in China* (New York, Macmillan, 1945), 55.
4 Kreissler, *L'Action culturelle*, 144–5.
5 Kreissler, *L'Action culturelle*, 23.
6 *Beijing gongbao*, 15 August 1917, quoted in Kreissler, *L'Action culturelle*, 24.
7 Kreissler, *L'Action culturelle*, 25–6.
8 For Germany's influence in China during the period 1918–33 see William C. Kirby, *Germany and Republican China* (Stanford CA, Stanford University Press, 1984), 17–101.
9 Kirby, *Germany and Republican China*, 17–18, 23–4.
10 Françoise Kreissler, 'Nationalsozialisten in China. Ein verdrängtes Kapitel der Geschichte der deutsch-chinesischen Beziehungen?' (National Socialists in China: An Overlooked Chapter in the History of German–Chinese Relations?), in Bettina Gransow and Mechthild Leutner, eds, *China. Nähe und Ferne. Deutsch-chinesische Beziehungen in Geschichte und Gegenwart. Zum 60. Geburtstag von Kuo Heng-yü* (China, near and far: Sino-German Relations in History and Today) (Frankfurt, Bern, New York and Paris, Peter Lang, 1989), 272–4.
11 *Die Woche*, 8 November 1996. Despite his admitted lack of knowledge about the National Socialist period, Erwin Wickert is the editor of the diary of John Rabe, member of the National Socialist Party and Siemens representative in Nanjing until 1938, where he witnessed the sack of the city by the Japanese army: E. Wickert, ed., *John Rabe. Der gute Deutsche von Nanking* (Stuttgart, Deutsche Verlags-Anstalt, 1997) (trans. as *The Good German of Nanking*, New York and London, Little Brown, 1998).
12 *Deutsche Shanghai Zeitung* (*DSZ*), 25 and 27 July 1933; *Mitteilungs- und Verordnungsblatt der Landesgruppe Ostasien der NSDAP* (*MVLO*), 15 October 1933.
13 SMP report, 28 November 1934. National Archives and Records Administration, RG 263, Washington DC (SMP) D 4724.
14 Ibid. See also Memorandum of the SMP, 8 April 1936. SMP D 4724.
15 SMP D 4724.
16 *MVLO*, 15 October 1933.
17 Kreissler, *L'Action culturelle*, 36.
18 Politisches Archiv des Auswärtigen Amts, Bonn (PAAA), Pol. Abt. IV, Po 25 China.
19 PAAA, Pol. Abt. IV, Po 25 China, and Bundesarchiv, Deutsche Botschaft China (BArch/DBCh), No. 3858.
20 Hans-Adolf Jacobsen, *Nationalsozialistische Außenpolitik 1933–1938* (National Socialist Foreign Policy 1933–1938) (Frankfurt and Berlin, Metzner, 1968), 147.
21 K. Kolb, 'Der Deutsche in Ostasien und der Nationalsozialismus' (Germans in East Asia and National Socialism) *Ostasiatischer Beobachter* (Shanghai), 1 March 1934.
22 Report of the Tianjin Consulate, 1 December 1933, PAAA, Pol. Abt., Po 25 China.
23 Kreissler, *L'Action culturelle*, 105–6; SMP reports, 5 February 1937 and 1 October 1939, SMP D 6580.

24 Kreissler, 'Nationalsozialisten in China', 268–74.
25 Kreissler, 'Nationalsozialisten in China', 274.
26 Olga Lang, 'Foreign and Chinese Shanghai faces War', *Amerasia*, 1:9 (1937), 415–22.
27 Kirby, *Germany and Republican China*, 190–232.
28 Kirby, *Germany and Republican China*, 239–44.
29 *Jahresbericht und Übersicht über die Tätigkeit des Vorstandes der Deutschen Handelskammer Shanghai für das Geschäftsjahr 1937–1938* (Annual Report and Survey of the Activities of the Committee of the German Chamber of Commerce in Shanghai for the Commercial Year 1937–1938) (Shanghai, n.p., 1938); Karl Drechsler, *Deutschland, China, Japan, 1933–1939. Das Dilemma der deutschen Fernostpolitik* (Germany, China and Japan, 1933–1939: The Dilemma of German Far East Policy) (Berlin, Akademie Verlag, 1964), 93–7.
30 *Jahresbericht und Übersicht* (1938); 'Shanghais Deutsche gegen deutsche Fernost-Politik', *Die Neue Weltbühne*, 25 November 1937.
31 Ibid.
32 *Jahresbericht und Übersicht* (1938).
33 PAAA, Pol. Abt. VIII, Po 2 China.
34 *Jahresbericht und Übersicht* (1938).
35 Letter from Bohle to Lahrmann, 18 June 1938, PAAA, R.27198.
36 J. O. de Meira Penna, *Shanghai. Aspectos historicos da China moderna* (Rio de Janeiro, Ameri. Edit., 1944), 268; Kirby, *Germany and Republican China*, 236 and 240–1.
37 *Auswärtige Politik heute*, Bonn 1979, quoted in Hans-Jürgen Döscher, *SS und Auswärtiges Amt im Dritten Reich. Diplomatie im Schatten der 'Endlösung'* (The SS and the Foreign Ministry in the Third Reich: Diplomacy in the Shadow of the Final Solution) (Frankfurt, Ullstein, 1991), 13.
38 Döscher, *SS und Auswärtiges Amt*, 67.
39 Wilhelm Haas, 'Lebenserinnerungen' (unpublished manuscript, 1974), 92, 120, 146; *Israel's Messenger*, 3 November 1933.
40 Letter from Trautmann to Mme Sun Yat-sen, 18 May 1933. BArch/DBCh, No. 2325; *China Weekly Review* (*CWR*), 20 and 27 May 1933, and 'A Denunciation of the Persecution of German Progressives and the Jewish People', in Soong Ching Ling, *The Struggle for New China* (Peking, Foreign Language Press, 1952), 57–60.
41 NA RG 84, 1933/800.
42 *DSZ*, 16 and 19 May 1933.
43 Reports of the German Consulates, BArch/DBCh, No. 2217.
44 PAAA, R.27198.
45 BArch/DBCh, No. 2217; *North China Herald* (*NCH*), 13 April 1938.
46 *NCH*, 13 April 1938.
47 BArch/DBCh, No. 2217.
48 Report of 17 May 1934, BArch/DBCh, No. 2323.
49 For the history of the Jewish refugees in Shanghai during the 1930s and 1940s see David Kranzler, *Japanese, Nazis and Jews: The Jewish Refugee Community of Shanghai, 1938–1945* (New York, Yeshiva University Press, 1976); Alfred Dreifuß, 'Schanghai. Eine Emigration am Rande' (Shanghai: Exile on the Periphery) in Eike Middell et al., eds, *Exil in den USA* (Exile in the USA) (Leipzig, Reclam, 1979), 447–517; Françoise Kreissler, 'Die Emigration nach Shanghai. Ein Ghettoisierungsprozeß?' (Emigration to Shanghai: A Process of Ghettoisation?) in Friedrich Stadler, ed., *Vertriebene Vernunft*, II, *Emigration und Exil österreichischer Wissenschaft* (Banished Reason, II, Emigration and Exile of Austrian Academics) (Vienna, Jugend und Volk, 1988), 1028–34; Françoise Kreissler, 'Exil in Shanghai: Problematik und Schwerpunktthemen' (Exile in Shanghai: Problems and Fundamental Issues), in Kuo Heng-yü and Mechthild Leutner, eds, *Deutsch-chinesische Beziehungen vom 19. Jahrhundert bis zur Gegenwart* (Sino-German Relations from the Nineteenth Century to the Present) (Munich, Minerva, 1991), 293–314; see also testimonies and memories written by former refugees from Germany and Austria in Shanghai: Alfred W. Kneucker, *Zuflucht in Shanghai. Aus den Erlebnissen eines österrei-*

chischen Arztes in der Emigration 1938–1945 (Refuge in Shanghai: The Experiences of an Austrian Doctor in Exile, 1938–1945) (Vienna, Böhlau, 1984); Franziska Tausig, *Shanghai-Passage. Flucht und Exil einer Wienerin* (Shanghai Passage: A Viennese Woman's Flight and Exile) (Vienna, Verlag für Gesellschaftskritik, 1987); Hellmut Stern, *'Saitensprünge'. Lebensbericht* (Extramusical Escapades: A Musician's Memoirs) (Berlin, Transit, 1990); Ernest G. Heppner, *Shanghai Refuge: A Memoir of the World War II Jewish Ghetto* (Lincoln NE and London, University of Nebraska Press, 1993); Evelyn Pike Rubin, *Ghetto Shanghai* (New York, Shengold, 1993); Pan Guang and Li Peidong, eds, *Youtairen yi Shanghai* (*Memoirs of Shanghai Jews*) (Shanghai, Shanghai wenshi ziliao xuanji, 1995).

50 *CWR*, 7 January 1939; *Dongfang zazhi*, 16 June 1939. For the complete text of the pamphlet see Kreissler, *L'Action culturelle*, 269–78.
51 *CWR*, 1, 8 and 22 November 1941.
52 *Die Woche*, 8 November 1996.

CHAPTER THIRTEEN

The Shanghai American community, 1937–1949
Mark F. Wilkinson

In 1930 Edgar Snow published an essay entitled 'The Americans in Shanghai'. It is an ugly caricature of carousing hucksters, cross-eyed Bible peddlers and rampant venereal disease. Snow's Americans proudly considered themselves the most wicked, and also the most cosmopolitan, of Shanghai's foreigners – contemptuous of both the colonial British who ran the city and the Chinese who populated it.[1] Like many caricatures, this one contains some elements of truth, but the reality was less lurid and more complex. The purpose of this chapter is to sketch a portrait of the Shanghai Americans in three parts, examining community building in the 1930s, the wartime collapse, and the post-war efforts to revive the American presence. This brief survey suggests that the Americans established a distinctive place for themselves in pre-war Shanghai, while also fitting comfortably within the larger foreign-dominated enclave. But the triple blows of an eight-year war, the demise of the treaty port system and the emergence of the communist revolution conspired to destroy the Shanghai American community by 1949.

In the 1930s the Americans cultivated their businesses, their schools and their community organisations. How did they compare with other settlers? While these were hard, contentious times for the White Russians, the Americans were generally successful and optimistic about their future in Shanghai. They were far better integrated into Settlement affairs than the Japanese, even though the population was tiny by comparison. Americans reaped the benefits of Shanghai's semi-imperial development without having to work as hard as the policemen described in Chapter Ten to maintain that system. In short, they were building a moderately successful, loosely knit but self-consciously American community. They were undone, however, by the political upheaval that commenced in 1927. The Fourth Marines arrived that year because of the tumultuous last stages of the

Northern Expedition. They remained through the 1930s because of the Japanese. Leathernecks on parade were a proud patriotic symbol of American power. But they could not hold back the tides of war or revolution that commenced with the Japanese assault in 1937. After the Pacific War the Japanese were evicted, and the Americans returned, expecting to replace the British as leaders of a new, cosmopolitan Shanghai. But their efforts to rebuild the Shanghai American community were confounded by the destructiveness of the war, the emergence of independent Chinese power in the city and the turmoil of the communist revolution.

Many good recent studies concentrate on the internal dynamics of settler communities, with little consideration of the overarching political frameworks which made those enclaves possible. The results have been important and useful. But the mid-twentieth century was a time of warfare, revolution and anti-colonialism. This chapter advances the modest proposition that those phenomena, too, were tremendously important in the life of colonial communities. How did settlers cope with the loss of imperial protection? How did settlers react to rising nationalist movements or deal with new indigenous power structures? How did the emergence of nationalism or civil war affect private relations between Westerners and Asians in business, in classrooms and on street corners? These issues are worth pursuing for a variety of settler communities in China, India, South East Asia and elsewhere. But the remainder of this chapter will focus on the Shanghai Americans.

Inside the glass bubble: the pre-war Shanghai American community

In 1936 over 3,700 Americans – over one-third of all those in China – lived in Shanghai. Major interests included the Shanghai Power Company, Standard Oil and the Shanghai Telephone Company. There were numerous American trading houses, along with a few manufacturers and a service sector of banks, insurance agents, lawyers and restaurants. The oil, utilities, cotton and tobacco concerns were most important economically, but the leaders of the American business community came just as commonly from smaller, more uniquely Shanghai enterprises, including Henningsen's Produce Company or Bruce Smith's automobile dealership. Missionaries generally comprised about one-third of the population. The Southern Baptists' Shanghai University and the Episcopalians' St John's were the largest and best known missionary colleges in the city.[2] There were also

THE SHANGHAI AMERICAN COMMUNITY

Table 13.1 Americans registered in Shanghai, 1936–49

	January 1936	January 1938	January 1940	January 1941	April 1948	January 1949	May 1949
Men	1,502	1,326	1,171	1,172	n.a.	956	523
Women	1,260	1,057	855	691	n.a.	523	313
Children	1,006	846	829	638	n.a.	267	194
Total	3,768	3,229	2,855	2,501	3,966	1,746	1,030

Source Census reports in State Department decimal files 137 [Census] and 393.11 Citizens. (Gender and age figures unavailable for 1948.)

numerous middle schools, clinics, publishing and administrative offices.

The Shanghai Americans came from disparate backgrounds. Paul Hopkins of the Power Company and Robert Bryan, the municipal advocate, had long, strong China connections because of their missionary parents. After service as a consular officer, Norwood Allman opened one of the most prominent law offices in Shanghai in the 1920s.[3] Jimmy James retired to Shanghai after infantry service in north China. He opened several restaurants and an amusement park. In the late 1930s newcomers joined these American settlers. Episcopal missionary Helen Van Voast arrived in 1936 to teach at St John's. In October 1940 an adventurous Eric Schmidt jumped ship, planning merely to 'bang around' for a year or two in the city. Helen Lyons came to visit a relative but took a clerical job at the US consulate-general in the summer of 1941.[4] And, as Eileen Scully has reminded us, con men, prostitutes and crooked bankers all made up a part of the Shanghai American scene. The US Court for China attempted to curb these 'low roaders' to uphold the law and preserve American prestige.[5]

James Huskey has described the evolution of the Shanghai American community in the 1920s.[6] We need only recap some of the important institutions, practices and shared sentiments that connected them. The chamber of commerce represented business interests while the American Association focused on civic affairs, patriotic festivities and charitable relief. Merchants and missionaries alike sent their children to the Shanghai American School, where they mingled with students from other nations, but in a distinctively American environment. The interdenominational Community Church was a place of worship, but also an important social centre for American Protestants. Catholics attended Sacred Heart, near Broadway Mansions, or Christ the King, in the French Concession. The American Club and Columbia Country Club were the principal social institutions, but retired servicemen might also belong to the local Veterans of Foreign Wars or the Frederick Townshend Ward Post of the American Legion. Randall Gould's *Shanghai Evening Post* and John Powell's *China Weekly Review* kept the Americans in touch with each other and their home country.[7] Thus the Americans had numerous opportunities for maintaining personal, social, religious and functional ties with each other.

Consider the case of young consular officer John Stewart Service. His weekends included barbecue dinners at Columbia Country Club and bridge at the American Club. His partners included a Chinese doctor, several businessmen, other consular officers and a chaplain from the Fourth Marines. Service was on three committees at the junior chamber of commerce, a discussion group at Community Church and a committee to judge student essays at the American school. After work, he frequently ran at the YMCA track with friends. And through it all, he assured his family, he never missed a meeting at the local Masonic lodge.[8]

Americans could move about in this comfortable world only because of the structures of power in Shanghai. Extraterritoriality and the nineteenth-century Land Regulations allowed foreigners to rule the International Settlement through the Shanghai Municipal Council (SMC). The French governed in their adjoining Concession. The SMC jealously guarded its local prerogative, even though the Chinese had won limited representation after the May Thirtieth Incident of 1925.[9] The British clearly dominated, with five of the nine foreign council seats, but the Americans did hold two. Stirling Fessenden from Maine chaired the body for much of the 1920s and then became the secretary-general. (Admittedly, some considered him more British than American.)[10] Americans also served in the Shanghai Volunteer Corps. Norwood Allman organised a mounted American troop as a 'counterpart' to the British Shanghai Light Horse.[11] Participation in SMC or SVC affairs gave the Americans a role, albeit it a small one, in the bodies that dominated the settlement. They were a part of the international club, but retained their national identity. Allman cantered at the head of an *American* troop. Membership undoubtedly helped to bond young men from Boise and Boston together. The American Association hailed SMC elections as the local equivalent of a New England town meeting, promoting a 'slate' of candidates and urging the Americans to go out and vote. Behind the scenes, long-time resident Arthur Basset of the British–American Tobacco Company played the overbearing 'boss' of the American political machine. Elections in the 1930s reflected some jockeying for power within the community, but by the end of the decade that was overshadowed by new calls for Anglo-American solidarity to block Japanese efforts to gain more power on the council.[12] Thus the SMC and SVC helped integrate the Americans in two ways: as a national community and as a part of the settlement community.

Economic, political and social indicators mark the 1930s as a time of growth, with the Americans assuming a higher profile in the city. Their population increased from 3,000 in 1930 to 3,700 in 1936. The chamber of commerce grew from 101 companies in 1928 to 128 in 1941.[13] The United States replaced Britain as China's most important Western trading partner, with Shanghai in the forefront.[14] Eligible American ratepayers for Settlement elections increased from 312 in 1933 to 400 in 1936. That pales beside the 1,200 Britons and 900 Japanese, but it does demonstrate growth.[15] Shanghai movie houses carried the latest Hollywood films while increasing numbers of Chinese went to American schools and clinics. The admittedly biased American Association boasted that Shanghai was embracing 'the American way' along with American goods.[16]

But let us not overemphasise the stature, exclusivity or homogeneity of the Americans. In the 1930s the British lion still dominated the Shanghai Bund. Even though the American population was growing, it was dispersed among the more numerous Europeans and Asians. The Americans flourished, but only because they were comfortable doing so within a larger international body. Studies of 'community' suggest that people may have, in effect, multiple identities, derived from familial, occupational, ethnic or other bases. Thus it seems reasonable that people may belong to more than one community *and* that different communities may intersect while remaining distinct.[17] For the Shanghai Americans, this certainly seems to have been the case. Their nationality gave them one comforting and important basis for identity and community, but it was not the only one. Nor did that commonality assure closeness. Even though missionaries made up a large part of the population, they did not mingle much with the business community. Admiral Kemp Tolley, a veteran of the Yantze Patrol, claimed the missionaries only came out on national holidays 'to mix a little awkwardly with fellow Westerners at the consulate receptions'.[18] Indeed, the two communities were commonly suspicious of each other. Helen Van Voast did occasionally go out dancing or for dinner with non-missionary men, but that was rare. Even church work comes across as rather compartmentalised by denomination. Whether in the Baptist compound, or the law offices of Alllman Davis & Kopps, shared functional ties, spiritual interests or economic opportunities undoubtedly loomed larger than nationality on a day-to-day basis.

The Americans moved easily among the British and the French. What of the Chinese? Did the Americans reach out to form the 'cosmopolitan connection' suggested by James Huskey? Institutions such as the YMCA and the American University Club provided venues where Chinese and American elites mingled. The American Club opened its doors to Chinese members in 1929.[19] Certainly there was interaction. But, just as certainly, it was limited. Even though the Chinese and Americans were in the same place, the lives they lived, the issues they confronted, the social networks they formed were more different than similar. By and large, the Chinese remained 'the other' – amusing, exotic or inscrutable in American eyes. In some cases, cosmopolitanism was actively discouraged. Vice-Consul John Service recalls that his immediate superior opposed working too hard on the Chinese language, lest the foreign service officer succumb to the dreaded fate of 'going native' in his interests or sensibilities. Caroline Service recalled that she really had no Chinese friends at all, but that she had really taken no notice of that fact in the 1930s.[20]

In sum, the Americans constituted a loosely woven national community in the midst of an international enclave. They were fairly cosmopolitan toward the Europeans of Shanghai; less so toward the Chinese, but with a well developed sense of their own identity. Their schools, churches, clubs and associations provided vehicles for interaction, opportunities for shared effort and symbols of distinctness. The fact that the Americans contributed time and money to create these institutions attests to their desire to maintain that identity. To be sure, it was an artificial world, constructed largely by the aggressive efforts of the British Shanghailanders whom Robert Bickers has described so well. In that world, it was as though the Americans were floating along in a 'glass bubble' suspended inside a larger vessel, but insulated from China and the Chinese.[21] By the late 1930s the Americans were generally rather pleased with themselves and looked forward to playing an even larger role in the city. But the turmoil inaugurated in August 1937 would smash those dreams.

The war years – Shanghai endured, Shanghai remembered

Like other foreigners in Shanghai, Americans used an annual series of patriotic rituals to remind themselves of who they were and where they came from. They celebrated Thanksgiving, Washington's Birthday, Memorial Day and, of course, the Fourth of July. In 1937 Judge Milton Helmick opened the Independence Day celebration with a speech on the blessings of democracy, followed by the usual round of baseball games, polo matches, military parades and receptions. The next day a flag-raising ceremony at the race course capped the festivities.[22] One cannot help but feel that they were celebrating not only a patriotic heritage but also their local successes. But five weeks later the crash of artillery and the terror of aerial bombing tore into the heart of that international city. At first, some made light of the fighting among the local 'Orientals'. The mood changed dramatically, however, on 'Black Saturday' – 14 August – when Chinese bombers mistakenly dropped their deadly cargo in the centre of the International Settlement. Among the hundreds killed was Robert Reischauer, a promising young Japan scholar from Princeton University. By some measures, he was the first American casualty of the Pacific War.[23] That fateful August afternoon ushered in more than a decade of uninterrupted turmoil in Shanghai and also marked the beginning of the end of foreign domination in the city.

In 1937 Americans helped to defend the settlement, but ultimately were left with little besides memories and myths of old Shanghai. Clerks and lawyers shouldered arms in the Shanghai Volunteer Corps. The Fourth Marines stood alongside British forces on the south bank of Soochow Creek. Americans volunteered in the numerous refugee camps for Chinese and on the consul-general's evacuation planning committee.[24]

In such times of crisis the Americans expected their home government to protect them. But the Franklin D. Roosevelt administration was more interested in avoiding conflict than vigorously defending Shanghai. The government urged Americans to leave Shanghai unless their presence was necessary. Randall Gould angrily rebuked Washington for shirking its obligations and using the consular service to block Americans from the city.[25] Nevertheless, 1,400 Americans departed in the month following 'Black Saturday'. Although many returned after the immediate crisis, some left for good. Helen Van Voast departed in 1940, thinking her China mission days were finished. The population declined over the following year, leaving about 2,000 Americans to witness the end of an era.[26]

Space permits only the briefest discussion of the war years. The Japanese took over the settlement in December 1941. During 1942 the orphaned taipans shifted for themselves, relying on their own meagre resources and hand-outs from the American Association, the British Residents' Association or the Red Cross. Lucky ones, like Helen Lyons, the sightseer who joined the consular clerical staff in 1941, were repatriated. Some of the less fortunate, including J. B. Powell, were imprisoned and tortured. Most of the remainder, including over 1,300 Americans, were interned. A second repatriation left about 700 Americans languishing in camps at Zhabei, Pudong, Haiphong Road and elsewhere.

The foreigners were challenged as never before. For the first time, they had to endure the penetrating cold of a Shanghai winter without steam heat or brandy. They had to survive the sweltering summers without their country club pools or holidays at their cool mountain retreat at Guling. For the first time, they had to do all of the work previously left to Chinese servants: cooking, washing clothes by hand, hauling garbage and cleaning toilets. For the first time, they were slapped, bullied and terrorised by Asians.[27] They may have been humbled by imprisonment. They may have gained some greater appreciation of the hardships Chinese serving classes endured, but we can only speculate on this point.

As their two-and-a-half-year incarceration dragged on, the foreigners wilted under the strain. By the spring of 1945 internees in Zhabei commonly received only one meal a day, and even that was frequently inedible. Privation, uncertainty and overcrowding contributed to fear, greed and conflict among the inmates. In Zhabei, where British and American families were mixed together, the sense of 'community' was stretched to its limits by the harsh conditions. Some Americans tried, unsuccessfully, to control the distribution of relief goods provided by the American Red Cross. Resentful of British domination of the camp council, some Americans agitated for their own committee, to no avail. Internment did call forth the best in some. Restaurateur Jimmy James worked honestly and tirelessly in the Zhabei kitchen until illness wore him down. Eric Schmidt and others ran schools for children and adults. They put on variety shows and secret Fourth of July celebrations to boost their spirits.[28] Reading the accounts of camp life, one finds much hardship and exhaustion, but also evidence of team work and selflessness. Still, on balance, the Zhabei experience suggests that internment eroded communal spirit more than it bolstered it.

Among the Americans who escaped from Shanghai, a handful wrote memoirs, trying to capture in print a world they had lost in fact. Advertising man Carl Crow, lawyer Norwood Allman and writers Edna Booker, John Powell and Randall Gould published accounts during the Pacific War era, drawing on decades of residence in Shanghai. What did they choose to remember? What sort of Shanghai did they construct with pen and ink?

Crow, Booker and Allman recreate a Shanghai of privilege, private clubs and devoted servants. Crow claimed his houseboys were 'as worried and solicitous as a lot of affectionate children', wondering who would tie his shoes and prepare his meals if he left Shanghai. Except for Crow, these writers portray themselves as open-minded cosmopolitans, alluding to Chinese and European friends, clients and dinner partners. In contrast, Crow writes as an unabashed Old China Hand, confidently assuring his readers that the 'natives' really don't want to go to foreign clubs or parks. Crow's 'compradore' Chinese consider dinner with 'foreign devils' just as trying as Westerners do their encounters with chopsticks. Booker seems to have really known only the household staff. She recalls many misadventures about shopping, preparing for dinners, and the death of a well loved amah. This may reflect in part the more circumscribed world of the American business wife in Shanghai. But it also suggests they were more cosmopolitan in theory than practice.[29]

The war tore old Shanghai apart but, in a way, set the stage for a new era. All the writers describe bestial murders and other atrocities. But, in the midst of tragedy, all praised the Nationalist government for its valiant resistance. Over the years Crow had watched Chinese battles as he would a golf match: with mild interest, occasional amusement and considerable detachment. But the harrowing fighting in 1937 convinced him that 'John Chinaman is . . . a very brave man.' Allman dedicates his book to Generalissimo and Madame Chiang Kai-shek.[30]

Once the Americans and the Chinese became allies, they seemed joined in perpetuity for these writers. Crow predicted that wartime aid would lead the Chinese to 'forgive and forget' the insults of the treaty port era. Booker was 'convinced that the Sino-American friendship which has matured in this war will crystallise in the years which follow . . .'[31] Allman puts this most fervently and personally in his last chapter: 'I'm Going Back.' He was 'prepared to make the adjustment' to post-treaty port Shanghai. Returning 'will be just like going home'. Conjuring up an image of twenty years of cosmopolitanism, Allman predicts a future of mutual respect, collaborative reconstruction and mutually beneficial trade with the Americans at the heart of things. 'Shanghai will rise again.'[32] But Allman was wrong.

The post-war Shanghai American community

In August 1945 American internees were thrilled by victory and the end of their confinement. Even before they left the camps, leaders of the American Association were planning their future in Shanghai.[33] On the other side of the world, stateside China hands were 'straining at the leash' to return. 'Things ought to be darned good for us Americans,' one said. 'No German competition. No Japanese competition. No British competition – I hope.'[34] But these dreams were crushed in a post-war Shanghai mired in political and economic chaos. Not only was it impossible for the Americans to lead in the beleaguered city, they were not even capable of successfully reconstituting themselves as a viable community in its midst.

Four thousand Americans returned to the city, re-establishing their pre-war institutions, including the clubs, the schools and the community organisations. But virtually all of them were hollowed out – weakened by war and inflation; consumed with new kinds of problems. As in the pre-war era, about two-thirds of the community were engaged in business and one-third connected with the missions. The American Chamber of Commerce grew to 152 members by 1947. While there was considerable 'fresh blood' from the States, many of the post-war leaders were former internees like Paul Hopkins of the Power Company. They made up a majority of the 1946 officers of the American Association and one-third of the officers of the 1947 chamber of commerce.[35] But instead of forging a new era of Chinese–American cooperation they spent much of their time trying to recover property occupied by Chinese military forces, raise money to carry out rehabilitation projects and wade through reams of new business regulations imposed by the Nationalist regime. There was little opportunity to build a new sense of community.

The Americans returned to a dramatically changed Shanghai. The Japanese had plundered the city, even tearing out some of the radiators, plumbing and electrical wiring to feed their wartime need for raw materials. American air raids had damaged the Shanghai Power Company's plant.[36] Columbia Country Club had been used as an internment facility. The American School and the mission colleges had been ravaged by occupying Japanese. Rehabilitation was the first priority. Shanghai was also different because, in 1943, the United States and Great Britain renounced the century-old unequal treaties. The Municipal Council was gone, as was the Shanghai Volunteer Corps and extraterritorial legal rights. When old-timers waxed nostalgic about treaty port days, they encountered a new, assertive nationalism. Indignant Chinese invited 'diehards' to leave if they did not like the new Shanghai.[37] They also insisted that the sign at Huangpu Park really had said 'No dogs or Chinese allowed' but vowed that they would never again accept such an insult.[38]

For the first time in a century the Chinese were sovereign in the city and the foreigners were subject. Tragically, the Nationalist regime was corrupt, ineffective and abusive. It never learned how to cope with the combined problems of civil war and economic decay, and the Chinese and foreign populations of Shanghai both suffered as a result.[39] Guomindang economic policies inhibited trade, created semi-official competitors and retarded recovery. With the demise of extraterritoriality and the Municipal Council, the Shanghai Americans lost the protective structure which had shielded them from the Chinese. They were more likely to be accosted on the streets, to have their businesses interfered with or to be hauled into local courts on trumped-up charges.[40] By 1947 the American Chamber of Commerce was warning new American businesses not to come to Shanghai.[41]

Although they condemned the Guomindang regime as greedy and self-serving, Americans had little choice but to work with it. If a plant manager needed to subdue striking workers, he called on the authorities – quite possibly the same men he ridiculed at tiffin for their corruption and incompetence. It was a tricky situation. When workers at the Power Company struck in 1945, Paul Hopkins suspected a Guomindang plot aimed at prising the company away from him. He warned that labour unrest might lead to disruption of the power supply, idle factories and thousands of angry, hungry workers in the streets. When the Nationalists recognised the danger, they reversed course, cracked down on labour and formed an uneasy, imperfect alliance with Hopkins until 1949.[42]

But there was no guarantee of such aid. When workers struck against the American Far Eastern Match Company, and A. H. Henningsen's egg-packing plant, mediators from the Bureau of Social Affairs stood by, seeking a pay-off from the Americans.[43] Thus labour relations illustrate both the enforced collaboration between the Americans and the Guomindang and the tentativeness of that relationship.

The decay of the city confounded the missionaries as well. Inflation, exorbitant real estate costs and unfavourable exchange rates eroded salaries and undermined desperately needed rehabilitation projects. The missions wanted experienced personnel back in the field, but conditions in Shanghai were so difficult that they hesitated to put worn-out former internees back to work prematurely, or to throw novices into the breach.[44] Helen Van Voast returned in late 1946. Compared with others, she was young, healthy and well acquainted with the city. She was stunned by the inflation, the shortages and the decay.[45]

St John's and the University of Shanghai were both in disrepair, swollen by heavy enrolments and eventually caught up in student unrest. In April 1947 demonstrations compelled the Baptists to call in Guomindang police to evacuate the campus, allowing students to return only after they signed guarantees to behave.[46] Van Voast had students and Chinese co-workers who frankly sympathised with the communists. In 1948 commencement exercises at St John's were cancelled because of student demonstrations and the Americans forced the resignation of a Chinese president deemed too easy on the malcontents.[47]

The mention of student demonstrations brings us to an issue that must be considered in the post-war life of the American community: the interplay of national politics, international affairs and local relations between Chinese and Americans. These elements were interwoven in Shanghai in an uncommonly important fashion. Prior to 1937 Americans were generally freer to pursue their economic and social interests. But after the war they could not escape the effects of political unrest. The glass bubble had been shattered.

Part of the problem arose from the twin irritants of American China policy and the misconduct of American soldiers and sailors. The Truman administration gave qualified support to the Nationalist regime of Chiang Kai-shek. Vocal elements in Shanghai condemned this as unwarranted intervention that prolonged civil war. Locally, soldiers and sailors brawled in cafes, beat up Chinese labourers, crashed into rickshaws, assaulted Chinese women and fought with local police. Consequently, demonstrations against American China policy and the personal abuses of the American military were a common occurrence in post-war Shanghai. On 23 June 1946, 50,000 marched in protest.[48] The leftist press complained bitterly about American policy.[49] Liberals and conservatives alike complained about the personal misconduct. As early as December 1945 the liberal *Dagongbao* declared that the Americans were no longer welcome. The conservative *ZhongMei ribao*, associated with the government's own Ministry of Information, cried out for someone to 'Put a Stop to the Unruly Behaviour of US Soldiers'.[50] Anti-Guomindang agitators certainly amplified the problem. But they did not create it. For our purposes here, the inescapable point is that the Americans lived in a more openly hostile, less protected, environment. Certainly, many Chinese and Americans would remain friends and colleagues through the decade. But just as certainly, there was more tension.

To a large extent, Chinese and Americans still lived in different worlds, walking past each other, absorbed with their own burdens. Their mutual images may well have been shaped by the stereotypes and diatribes available in either the Chinese or the American press rather than by personal contact. But where their paths did cross, in the workplace, the faculty lounge or the bus stand, conflict was more likely than in the past. Some teachers at the mission colleges denounced Chinese colleagues for dishonesty, incompetence or communist sympathies.[51] L. K. Little, the American head of the Customs service, bitterly accused some Chinese subordinates of jealousy and disloyalty, while Randall Gould felt 'surrounded by wolves and saboteurs in our own plant'.[52] Students at the Shanghai American School were sometimes embarrassed when Chinese acquaintances pointedly asked to go along to facilities, such as the YMCA swimming pool, which they knew were still reserved to foreigners only. Young vice-consul John Stutesman was shocked when several Chinese accosted him and his date as they rode through town one evening in a rickshaw.[53] Kay Peaslee, the wife of another young foreign service officer, hired a Chinese student as a language tutor. In contrast to the solicitous servants Carl Crow described, this young woman vehemently attacked American foreign policy, said the American soldiers should all go home and admitted participating in anti-American demonstrations.[54]

If the Americans had been able to respond to this hostility with a single voice, it might have actually helped to cement them together in a defensive posture. But they were divided and perplexed. We get a good sense of the range of American opinions from the *Shanghai Evening Post* and the *China Weekly Review*. Randall Gould returned to the *Post*, but John Powell never recovered from his wartime injuries. He died in early 1947. His son, Bill, took over the *Review* in 1945. Powell and Gould both attacked the Guomindang for mismanagement and corruption, but differed on American China policy and the Shanghai scene. Powell criticised the Truman policies as 'dishonest... resounding with democratic phrases' while 'handing out arms for a civil war'. Gould argued that supporting a non-communist regime was the right American policy. He simply wished that the Nationalists were more effective, less anti-foreign and more willing to open China to the Americans.[55]

Gould was quickly discouraged in post-war Shanghai, his editorial style snide and sarcastic. He lashed out at the human failings of any and all Chinese, from the 'cocky and belligerent' rickshaw pullers to the 'cowardly' and 'ungrateful' student demonstrators, to the self-absorbed elite he accused of displaying a 'coolie mentality'.[56] Powell pitied the poor Chinese in the city, even when they tried to extort 'a few pennies' from foreigners in pedicabs. Gould demanded that the police crack down on such lawbreakers. While Gould fumed at anti-Americanism, Powell was restrained. He agreed the demonstrations were excessive, but chided the 'alarmist... taipans' who feared a return of the 'days of '27'. He blamed much of the unrest on legitimate grievances against American policy and the abuses of servicemen.[57]

Bill Powell continued his father's practice of opening the journal to the Chinese community, giving them a forum to speak to the Americans. Here Chinese complained about Guomindang abductions, abusive American military police and Washington's misguided China policy.[58] Powell sympathised with the students and common people, while Gould inherited Carl Crow's position as self-righteous 'Old China Hand'. His barbed editorials struck one Chinese reader as 'the squawk of an injured imperialist' who appeared 'anti-communist, anti-Kuomintang and anti-Chinese all on the same day'. On the other hand, one American advised Powell that the *China Weekly Review* sounded too radical, causing some American businessmen to 'turn purple at the mention of your magazine'. Randall Gould might fly off the handle about trivial things, the letter writer continued, but at least he supported American foreign policy.[59] One may suspect that Powell's editorial stance and openness to Chinese contributors reflected an economic motive: the desire to increase Chinese subscriptions. But Powell relied heavily on American corporate advertising and, more important, relied on the good offices of the American military and consulate to obtain that very scarce and very basic commodity: newsprint.[60] His policies apparently reflected his beliefs. His differences with Gould illustrate the diverse American reactions to the turmoil of the 1940s.

Many of the Americans in post-war Shanghai had been there in the 1930s. But the new Shanghai bore little resemblance to the old days of the International Settlement, as romanticised by Carl Crow and Edna Booker. Nor did the reality conform to the wartime vision of Chinese–American co-operation. They were stymied. As one observer summed it up, the old China hands were 'dazed' by post-war conditions and lamented the loss of their old world. *Everything* had deteriorated. 'A current story had a newcomer to Shanghai remarking one evening on the beauty of a sunset, to which the Old China Hand replied, "Yes, but you should have seen the sunsets here *before* the war."'[61]

By the last weeks of 1948 the People's Liberation Army (PLA) was pushing southward. On 5 November the consulate advised Americans to leave Shanghai unless they had a 'compelling reason' to stay.[62] Many feared a dangerous interregnum between governments and the breakdown of public order, particularly after a post-war era streaked with labour unrest and student demonstrations. One businessman predicted, 'These people can almost certainly be counted upon to riot.' He feared swirling, looting mobs – not of Communists, but of the common people of the city who had effectively been kept at bay by the Municipal Police, the Shanghai Volunteer Corps or the Marines in the 'old days'.[63]

Some businesses elected to remain in Shanghai, believing they could work with the communists. Others simply recognised that post-war inflation and decay had so depreciated their immovable assets, there was no sense in trying to sell out. Among the missionaries, some feared that their work would be compromised under a 'red' regime; some thought that would be the time they were most needed.[64] Helen Van Voast believed that her job was in the classroom.[65] She stayed, but that was the minority decision.

For many Americans the record of the preceding four years was simply too bleak. Within eight weeks of the first warning from the consulate, over 1,400 had left out of a community of 4,000. After PLA gunners shelled the British frigate *Amethyst*, on 20 April, more Americans left. When the communists arrived on 25 May, Consul-general John Moors Cabot estimated there were fewer than 1,200 Americans in the city 'now effectively stranded'.[66]

Conclusion

This chapter has attempted to describe the Americans a little more accurately than Edgar Snow did in 1930 and to set their lives in the broader context of the wars that enveloped them. There has been much good work in recent years on the internal dynamics of settler communities, examining (among other topics) gender and class relations and issues of social control.[67] Some of that good work is reflected in this volume. It is clearly relevant to the Shanghai Americans and has, I hope, informed my thinking about them. But for the years 1937–49 the more potent forces were the Pacific War and the communist revolution. (This hardly strikes me as a bold assertion.) The above-mentioned studies of foreign communities presume a certain framework of international control. This chapter explores what happened to a particular community when that framework collapsed.

In the 1930s the Shanghai Americans were a part of a functioning international community. They played a distinct, albeit minor, role. As the memoirs by Booker, Crow and others suggest, the Americans had a romanticised sense of their position in the city and in the eyes of the Chinese. The wartime alliance added new myths of Sino-American solidarity and Guomindang vitality, causing old Shanghailanders like Norwood Allman to look forward to a heady future. But post-war Shanghai was uncharted territory in many ways. The instruments of Western power, such as the SMC and the SVC, had been stripped away. The communal institutions such as the chamber of commerce and the American Association were badly weakened by war and the emergence of Guomindang authority. Chinese nationalism was more potent and worrisome. Having lost their autonomy, the Americans could neither protect their own interests nor chart a middle course between the Chinese actors, as they might have done at an earlier time. Instead, the fear of unrest and simple political realities compelled collaboration with the Nationalist government they despised. Some were more successful than others. Because the Shanghai Power Company was so important, Paul Hopkins could work directly with the Nationalists and get what he wanted, at least part of the time. (The same is probably true of the large oil companies.) But for the smaller businesses, the kind who figured most prominently in the activities of the chamber of commerce, accommodation was more difficult; satisfaction less likely.

There were attempts to promote cosmopolitanism in the post-war era, but they were feeble and sometimes contaminated by the politics of civil war. By and large, the Americans and the Chinese were still quite distant from each other in the late 1940s. As the differing appraisals of Randall Gould and Bill Powell suggest, there was considerable range in how Americans responded to post-war Shanghai. The differences emerge as one of the more significant dividing factors within the American community after the war. Helen Van Voast and Bill Powell were open to Chinese perspectives. They downplayed the sense of Armageddon in 1949, and both were somewhat suspect among their peers. (The bishop wondered if Van Voast's decision to stay reflected communist sympathies. Powell was subjected to McCarthyite attacks in the the 1950s.) Most of the Americans had lived apart from the Chinese who surrounded them. Thus in late 1948, as the walls were collapsing, it was not so much communist policy they feared as the 'mob' of unruly, unknown Shanghainese. For these varied reasons, the majority of the Shanghai Americans departed from the city.

In general, foreigners, including Americans, had painted a portrait of a Shanghai that was exciting, decadent, exotic and amusing. But it was always a Shanghai in which they had the upper hand. Communal institutions such as their churches, clubs and chambers of commerce had worked well enough in the 1930s, but could not shield them from the problems of the 1940s. The very limited cosmopolitanism of the 1930s did not change much after the war. Thus the Americans were less viable as an autonomous community and not well integrated into the new Shanghai. Most found it an untenable situation, leading to the collapse of the Shanghai American community by 1949.

Notes

1. Edgar Snow, 'The Americans in Shanghai', *American Mercury*, 20:80 (1930), 437–45.
2. B. Hipps, *History of the University of Shanghai* (Richmond VA, Board of Founders of the University of Shanghai, 1964); M. Lamberton, *St John's University* (New York, United Board for Christian Colleges in China, 1955).
3. N. F. Allman, *Shanghai Lawyer* (New York, McGraw-Hill, 1943), 99–144; Paul Hopkins affidavit, n.d. file 266–34, Records of the Shanghai Power Company (SPC), Boise ID; Noel Barber, *The Fall of Shanghai* (New York, Coward McCann & Geohgegan, 1979), 38–9.
4. Helen Van Voast to Friends, 20 October 1936, Record Group (RG) 64, Correspondence; Helen Van Voast Pipe, Oral History, 24 May 1983, Archives, Episcopal Church (EC), Austin TX; Interviews, Helen Lyons, 17 July 1994, San Carlos CA; Eric Schmidt, 25 October 1989, 6 July 1997, Tiburon CA; Jimmy James, December 1987, Dallas TX.
5. Eileen P. Scully, 'Taking the Low Road to Sino-American Relations', *Journal of American History*, 82:1 (1995), 62–83.
6. James L. Huskey, 'Americans in Shanghai' (University of North Carolina, Chapel Hill, Ph.D. thesis, 1985) and 'The Cosmopolitan Connection', *Diplomatic History*, 11:3 (1987), 227–42.
7. J. B. Powell, *My Twenty-five Years in China* (New York, Macmillan, 1945), 13.
8. J. S. Service, 'State Department Duty in China', Regional Oral History Project, Bancroft Library (Berkeley CA, University of California, 1981), 68–70, 158a.
9. Nicholas R. Clifford, *Spoilt Children of Empire: Westerners in Shanghai and the Chinese Revolution of the 1920s* (Hanover NH and London, Middlebury College Press, 1991), 16–37, 150–2; Powell, *My Twenty-five Years*, 326–7.
10. Clifford, *Spoilt Children*, 22.
11. Allman, *Shanghai Lawyer*, 199.
12. J. S. Thomson, 'The Government of the International Settlement at Shanghai' (Columbia University Ph.D. dissertation, 1953), 183–200, 233–50, 290–300.
13. M. Wilkins, 'American Multinational Enterprises', in E. May and J. K. Fairbank, eds, *America's China Trade* (Cambridge MA, Harvard University Press, 1986), 289–92; Roster, American Chamber of Commerce Files (CC), 15 January 1947, in Department of State (DS), RG 84: Shanghai Consulate General (Con Gen) Commercial Section, National Archives, College Park, Maryland (NA).
14. Hsiao Liang-lin, *China's Foreign Trade Statistics, 1864–1949* (Cambridge MA, Harvard University Press, 1974), tables 1, 7a.
15. Thomson, 'Government', 223, 250.
16. American Association pamphlet, 'America's Stake in Shanghai', 12 December 1939, Stanley K. Hornbeck Papers, box 381, folder 'Shanghai: International Status', Hoover Institution on War, Revolution and Peace (HI).
17. T. Bender, *Community and Social Change in America* (Baltimore MD, Johns Hopkins University Press, 1982), 3–13, 59–66; C. Bouton, *The Flour War* (University Park PA, Pennsylvania State University Press, 1993), 22–5, 164–75.
18. K. Tolley, *Yangtze Patrol* (Annapolis MD, Naval Institute Press, 1971), 148.
19. Huskey, 'The Cosmopolitan Connection'.
20. J. Service, 'State Department Duty in China', 141; C. Service, 'State Department Duty in China', 66.
21. Robert Bickers, 'Shanghailanders: the Formation and Identity of the British Settler Community in Shanghai, 1843–1937', *Past and Present* 159 (1998), 161–211; C. Service, 'State Department Duty in China', 66.
22. *China Weekly Review* (*CWR*), 10 July 1937, 214.
23. E. O. Reischauer, *My Life between Japan and America* (New York, Harper & Row, 1986), 62, 66.
24. H. M. Fulcher, *Mission to Shanghai* (New London NH, Tiffin Press, 1995), 162–4; W. F. Nolan, 'America's Participation in the Defense of Shanghai' (St Louis University, Ph.D. thesis, 1978), 125–44.

25 *Shanghai Evening Post and Mercury (SEPM)*, 5 October 1937, 10.
26 F. R. Enghdahl, 'Summary of Activities during Emergency in 1937', n.d., Con Gen file 300: Evacuation; Census Report, 1 January 1941, DS RG 59, Central Decimal File (DF) 137-Shanghai.
27 Reports by camp name in DS RG 59 Special Problems Division; Eric Schmidt papers, privately held; Hugh Collar, *Captive in Shanghai* (New York, Oxford University Press, 1990); E. Booker, *Flight from China* (New York, Macmillan, 1945).
28 Booker, *Flight*, 195; Charles Boynton papers, box 5, folder 'Chapei', HI.
29 Carl Crow, *Foreign Devils* (New York, Harper & Bros, 1940), viii, 196–9, 325–40; Booker, *Flight*, 1–20, 113–19; Allman, *Shanghai Lawyer*, 146–7, 171–213.
30 R. Gould, *China in the Sun* (New York, Doubleday, 1946), 179–82; Powell, *My Twenty-five Years*, 310–15; Crow, *Foreign Devils*, 246, 251.
31 Booker, *Flight*, 233; Crow, *Foreign Devils*, 251.
32 Allman, *Shanghai Lawyer*, 275, 283.
33 Meeting Notice, 24 August 1945, Boynton papers, box 4, folder, 'American Association'.
34 *Shanghai Evening Post and Mercury* (American edition) (*SEPM-A*), 17 August 1945, 5; John Hersey, 'A Reporter in Shanghai', *New Yorker*, 23 March, 1946, 32–6.
35 'Post Report: Shanghai', DF 125.857, December 1946; CC Officers List, 15 January 1947; Boynton papers, Committee List, 1 January 1946, box 4, folder 'American Association'.
36 R. W. Edwards to 'Henry'. 20 November 1963, SPC, box 266-34; Interview, Bill Powell, 24 October 1989, San Francisco CA.
37 *China Critic*, 20 September 1945.
38 *NCDN*, 6, 11, 12, 14 November 1946, 5 (each day); Robert Bickers and Jeffrey N. Wasserstrom, 'Shanghai's "Dogs and Chinese not admitted" Sign: History, Legend and Contemporary Symbol', *China Quarterly*, 142 (June 1995), 444–66.
39 Suzanne Pepper, *Civil War in China* (Berkeley CA, University of California Press, 1978).
40 Memo to Ambassador J. Leighton Stuart, 3 October1946, Con Gen, Commercial file 'Am. Ch. of Commerce Report'; Bruce Smith to K. C. Wu, 24 July 1947, Bruce Smith Papers, box 1, HI.
41 CC Minutes, 18 April 1947, in DF 693.11171/6-2447; Smith to Kinney, 28 August 1947, Con Gen, CC Board Meeting, 5 September 1947.
42 Hopkins to American and Foreign Power Company, 1 October 1945, SPC box 268-14; Hopkin to Henry Bradbury, 15 January 1964, SPC box 266-34, Research and Analysis Report 4208: 'Résumé of Postwar Labor Developments in Nationalist China', 1 November 1946, DS RG 59.
43 'American Far Eastern Match Company', April 1946; 'A. H. Henningsen Company,' May 1947, both in Con Gen file 850.4.
44 Cauthen to Rankin, 28 February 1947, Foreign Mission Board, Southern Baptist Church (BC), box 574, Richmond VA; Roberts to Swift, 29 July, 4 November 1947, EC RG 64, box 154.
45 Van Voast to Friends, 25 October 1946, EC RG 79 box 12.
46 Lorene Tilford Oral History, reel 5, BC.
47 Lamberton, *St John's University*, chapter 15; (Episcopal Church), *Shanghai Newsletter*, July 1948.
48 Mark F. Wilkinson, 'A Shanghai Perspective on the Marshall Mission', in L. I. Bland, ed., *George C. Marshall's Mediation Mission to China* (Lexington VA, George C. Marshall Foundation, 1998), 343–8; Jeffrey N. Wasserstrom, *Student Protest in Twentieth Century China: the View from Shanghai* (Stanford CA, Stanford University Press, 1991), 253–61.
49 For example *Wenhuibao*, 4 July 1946; *Lianhe ribao*, 10 July 1946 in Con Gen, *Chinese Press Review (CPR)* (microfilm).
50 *Dagongbao*, 11 December 1945; 3 January 1946 *ZhongMei ribao*, 16 March 1946 (*CPR*).
51 Frances Roberts (St John's faculty) to Earl Fowler, 7 June 1948, EC RG 79, box 12.

52 L. K. Little to K. T. Ting, 10 June 1946, L. K. Little papers, Personal Correspondence, Vol. 3, Houghton Library, Harvard University; Gould to Wedemeyer, 17 November 1948, Albert C. Wedemeyer papers, Correspondence File, HI.
53 Interview, John Stutesman, Palo Alto CA, 18 July 1994.
54 Alexander Peaslee, unpublished memoir in author's possession, 28.
55 *CWR*, 21 December 1946, 68; *SEPM-A*, 10 November 1945, 5; *SEPM*, 25 September 1948, 1.
56 *SEPM*, 1, 18 February 1947, 31 May, 1 September 1948, page 1 each day.
57 *CWR*, 6 July 1946, 115; 5 June 1948, 5; 25 September 1948, 81; *SEPM*, 25 September 1948, p. 1.
58 See, for example, C. Y. W. Meng, 'Whither Sino-US Relations?' *CWR*, 29 November 1947, 411, or angry letters about mistreatment from American MPs (24 July 1948, 222) or 'I Accuse', by a Chinese recounting her own abduction by secret police, 19 April 1947, 210.
59 *CWR*, 26 June, 3 July 1948.
60 Interviews: Bill Powell, 24 October 1989; Eric Schmidt, 10 August 1998.
61 Earl Wilson (former US Information Service officer), 'Assignment to Shanghai', unpublished memoir in author's possession, 72.
62 Mark F. Wilkinson, 'The Shanghai American Community and the Communist Revolution, 1948–1949', *Southeast Review of Asian Studies*, 17 (1995), 30–47.
63 *CWR*, 11 December 1948, 33.
64 Cauthen to Rankin, 12 and 22 November 1948, BC box 574; Roberts to Fowler, 30 November 1948, EC RG 64, box 155.
65 Van Voast to Fowler, 29 January 1949, EC RG 64, box 162; Van Voast Oral History, 35–9.
66 Cabot to Secretary of State, DF125.0093/5-2449.
67 Ann Laura Stoler, 'Rethinking Colonial Categories: European Communities and the Boundaries of Rule', in Nicholas B. Dirks, ed., *Colonialism and Culture* (Ann Arbor MI, University of Michigan Press, 1992), 319–52.

CHAPTER FOURTEEN

Afterword: a colonial world
John Darwin

The studies in this book portray what is unmistakably a colonial world. They demonstrate, if proof is needed, that imperialism in East Asia was not a marginal case, nor a pale shadow of what is sometimes thought of as an African or Indian 'norm'. Empire building was as central a feature of the region's modern history as it was in tropical Africa or South Asia. Since the 1840s the stakes of empire had been higher, the risks greater, the rewards more enticing and the local resistance more tenacious than in almost any other part of the colonial or 'semi-colonial' world. East Asia, in fact, proved the ultimate test of Europe's capacity to construct a stable and co-operative colonial order. As several chapters graphically describe, it was the intervention of Japan, the dynamic new, but curiously ambivalent, member of the imperial club, which was the decisive factor in the fate of the imperial project and of the imperial communities which had grown up around it.

Imperialism and empire are abstractions. To study them only through the correspondence of officials or the declamations of critics is to grasp little of their historical reality. For many years, historians of imperialism have recognised that empire in any place or time was the sum of the relations – both collaborative and coercive – between imperial agents and the societies into which they had penetrated. Empire was not a majestic edifice of domination but more often a jerry-built shack whose shape changed constantly with the shifting balance of collaboration and control. This is a powerful insight. But, to make full use of it, we need to know more about the local 'agents of empire', the physical embodiment of the imperial project. These were the 'imperial communities' which form the subject of this book. By and large, they have been an unfashionable topic for serious historical research, except where settlers' descendants have formed the majority population (as for example in North America or Australasia). Less

AFTERWORD

earnest writers have been fascinated by the colourful antics of gilded expatriates – as in the numerous accounts of the 'Happy Valley' set in colonial Kenya. But more often the vanished expatriate communities who serviced, exploited and sometimes embarrassed the imperial presence survive only as sketches or caricatures. As a result, empire is still widely imagined as the intrusion of a more or less homogeneous group of (European) settlers, businessmen or officials into zones inhabited by stable indigenous societies enjoying varying degrees of political and cultural unity.

The more we learn about pre-colonial and colonial societies, the more unsatisfactory this conventional picture appears. The supposedly 'traditional' societies into which imperialists stumbled have often turned out to be much more dynamic, mobile and recent than was once assumed. In the modern historiography of India and pre-colonial Africa, the stresses produced by indigenous state formation and social change form the crucial context of the early stages of imperial intervention. Judith Wyman's chapter on foreign Christians in Chongqing shows how East Asian history can be illuminated by a similar approach. She suggests that the changing treatment of Christians in nineteenth-century Sichuan was a side effect of the demographic and political upheavals brought about by Qing colonisation of the province in the previous century and of the way that foreign influence was drawn into local conflicts. But the really striking corrective that emerges from these studies concerns the identity of the imperial communities themselves.

A superficial knowledge of China's encounter with the West might lead us to expect that the imperial communities which were established on the East Asian mainland after 1840 were composed mainly of expatriates moving from Europe, the United States and, much later, Japan, to exploit the opportunities of a new imperial frontier. But the home-grown merchants and missionaries of the treaty ports and the Japanese settlers who went to Korea before and after its annexation in 1910 form only part of the story. The Europeans who made their way to China did not always come directly from their metropolitan homes, and their journey was not always strictly voluntary. Some at least, perhaps more than we know about at present, were serial migrants who had already tried their fortune in other foreign fields. Some may have been Europeans in name only, or, if ethnically European, Asian by birth or residence. Thus the villainous Colonel Caine, in Christopher Munn's account of mid-century scandals in Hong Kong, had reached the colony after an earlier career in India, while the egregious Daniel Caldwell, born in St Helena, had 'probably never set foot in Europe'. The Shanghai police recruits analysed by Robert Bickers were typically displaced men whose social roots had been torn up by world war and who had already developed a taste for overseas life. It would not be surprising if serial migration *was* a widespread phenomenon among China Coasters. The broader canvas of British and European migration suggests that chronic restlessness was common among expatriates. New opportunities in the extra-European world were often first exploited by those on or near the spot with some transferable expertise, like the diggers who 'rushed' from one gold find to the next around the Pacific basin between 1849 and 1896. Secondary migration from one colonial location to another was a universal feature of settler frontiers in the Americas, Australasia and Southern Africa. Even in Asia, where the scope for settlement was limited, wavelets of European migration were set in motion by the building of infrastructure, but ebbed away or flowed elsewhere when the demand for expatriate skills declined.

Involuntary migration, like serial migration, was a key element in European colonialism. The slave trade, indentured labour and the transportation of convicts numbered among the classic techniques of empire-building. In general, there was little demand for European labour in the treaty ports of the China coast. But in the empty plains of Manchuria it was a different story. Russian imperialism was short of manpower. The Russian Jews of Harbin, described by Joshua Fogel, seem to have been unique among the European communities in East Asia in being (officially sanctioned) refugees from religious oppression in the West. But they were not unique in being conceded, as an imperial community, wider freedoms than they could expect at home. Victorian Britain exiled certain categories of its criminal population to the antipodes but granted them wider political rights after the expiry of their sentence than their (non-criminal) social peers received at home. Religious privileges – like those of the Church of England – were upheld longer and more rigorously in the imperial centre than was usually possible in a colonial setting. For some colonists at least, colonial air made them free: in politics as well as economics, the scarcity of manpower could tip the balance against authority. Nor was the Harbin community the only case where Jews were enlisted as imperial pioneers in regions where they were unlikely to compete with other European migrants. There was an abortive project to found a Jewish homeland in the British protectorate of Uganda, and in Mandatory Palestine immigrant Jews were at first expected to play the useful developmental role filled elsewhere by British settlers.

Perhaps the most radical challenge to the conventional image of expatriate communities as the accomplices of imperial expansion is to discover the extent to which in East Asia those communities were both non-European and non-Japanese. Chiara Betta draws attention to the major impact of Baghdadi Jews on the commercial life of treaty port Shanghai and their prominence within the British community where the Sassoon family enjoyed exceptional influence and status. The Sassoons had reached China via Bombay, the chief centre of their commercial operations until the main branch of the family migrated to Britain in the 1870s. Sikhs, Sindhis and Parsis were also represented in treaty port society and Hong Kong as merchants (Sindhis and Parsis) and policemen (Sikhs). In numbers, if not commercial importance, all these groups were dwarfed by the Japanese who had settled in Korea, Manchuria and mainland China; by the Koreans who had left their homeland (partly in consequence of Japanese colonisation) to settle in Manchuria and Mongolia; and by the Taiwanese who moved into mainland China with the status and privileges of Japanese subjects. For Baghdadis, Indians, Koreans and Taiwanese, imperialism had opened up new frontiers of opportunity, or had helped them to escape its oppressions elsewhere. Their migrations remind us that right across Africa and Asia imperialism gained much of its impetus not from the energies of its nominal overlords, but from the vigour with which other subordinate groups took advantage of new political and economic conditions. Bengalis moving up the Ganges valley in the train of British conquest; Tamils colonising the Burma delta in the wake of the Anglo-Burmese wars; Christian Ibos in northern Nigeria; Indian duka traders in British East Africa (once described by Winston Churchill as the 'America of the Hindu'): in all these cases, imperial expansion was supercharged by the labour, expertise and sometimes the capital of colonial or semi-colonial populations more mobile and adaptable than the emigrants and expatriates drawn from the imperial metropoles. Nor can we fail to be struck by the correlation between the rapid growth of Japanese influence after 1895 and the scale of the subaltern communities which colonised under Japan's aegis.

Another way of looking at this phenomenon is to see it at least in part as the co-option of imperial auxiliaries. In East Asia, as in many other parts of the colonial world, there were places and occupations disdained by 'master race' migrants, and others for which they were poorly equipped. Yet without the human capital to create its social infrastructure in less favoured terrain imperialism's costs would have been unacceptably high, and its profits small. The grandest example of this was the recruitment of Indians as soldiers, sailors, clerks, drivers, foremen and labourers for imperial purposes across a vast arc of Afro-Asia from Uganda to Fiji. Without their services, both territorial conquest and the task of building colonial economies able to bear the financial burden of imperial rule would have been impossibly slow and expensive. Barbara Brooks's chapter suggests that the availability of Korean and Taiwanese manpower was of comparable importance to Japanese expansion in East Asia. It would be valuable to know more about the social and economic roles it performed. Claude Markovits explains how Sikhs performed a range of services – especially as policemen and watchmen – which could not be entrusted wholly to Chinese, and in which the number of Europeans could not be increased above an optimum determined partly by cost and partly by the reluctance to maintain too large a European underclass. However, auxiliaries, to serve their turn, could not be left unsupervised. Barbara Brooks emphasises how strictly Japanese surveillance was maintained over Koreans and Taiwanese. The British were equally vigilant against nationalist feeling among Indians in Hong Kong and the treaty ports after 1916. This was a familiar imperial reflex. Ever since 1857 the British had organised their Indian army – the greatest auxiliary of all – in ways designed more to preserve its loyalty than to promote its efficiency in war. In general, the expatriate communities in East Asia, whether drawn from 'master races' or 'auxiliaries', seem to have been permitted very little independence by their imperial sponsors. The one striking exception was the British community in the Shanghai International Settlement, which enjoyed a wide measure of local self-government, in which Americans also shared. But here was an exception which proved the general rule. The settlement had to be defended by imperial troops in the later 1920s – a circumstance usually fatal to settler self-government – and London made little secret of its desire to throttle Shanghailander autonomy as the price of co-operation with Chinese nationalism after 1926. That the Shanghai Municipal Council lasted as long as it did was, perhaps, a paradoxical consequence of Japan's increasingly overt intervention in China after the Manchurian Incident.

Histories of European settlement in the Americas, Australasia and Southern and Eastern Africa were once celebrations of great pioneering enterprises, filling up 'empty lands' and reshaping savage landscapes in Europe's biological and cultural image. More recently the emphasis has fallen upon the destructive impact of predatory and bacterially lethal European intruders upon indigenous human populations, fauna and flora. In East Asia, neither the old pioneer myth nor its modern revision has played so large a part in the historiography (except perhaps in relation to Korea and Manchuria). But the location of imperial communities in China reminds us that there, as in much of Asia and tropical Africa, European settlers were not be found wresting a living directly from the land. Even in the classic areas of large-scale European migration, it was in the processing industries and service functions of the towns that many immigrants found their labour and skills best rewarded. In Asia and much of Africa this urban bias was even more marked. Europeans in India, except when 'on tour' or consciously revelling in open-air pursuits, were concentrated in cities, towns, cantonments or sub-urban hill stations. In South East Asia, most Europeans lived in port cities or the administrative capitals.

It is not surprising, therefore, to find a similar pattern among Europeans in East Asia. But it is striking that even the large Japanese settler population of over 700,000 in Korea was predominantly urban, and that, as Alain Delissen remarks, Korea's cities could be thought of as Japanese implants. The same held true in Manchuria, where the quarter-million Japanese were artisans, merchants, engineers and railway and government officials – a small urban minority in an overwhelmingly Chinese countryside.[1] Japan's Taiwanese auxiliaries in China were similarly urban in occupation and residence. The only exception to this general pattern were the Korean settlers in Manchuria and Mongolia. In a curious echo of the European pioneer myth, Barbara Brooks reports that the wet rice cultivation they introduced was celebrated as symbolic of the superior agrarian civilisation shared by Koreans and Japanese.

Thus both European and Japanese expatriates in East Asia were engaged in building, or imagining, urban communities. The best-known of these are the Shanghai International Settlement and Hong Kong and the straggling tail of treaty ports, each with its Bund. (It would be intriguing to know more about the architecture favoured by Europeans and Japanese in lesser centres.) But it is salutary to be reminded of two other East Asian colonial cities: Harbin and Seoul. Harbin, as Joshua Fogel tells us, was founded in 1898 as the centre of Russian railway imperialism: a kind of Manchurian Winnipeg or Nairobi. It remained a Russian city even after the fall of Tsarism, ruled over by the general manager of the Chinese Eastern Railway. Though by the 1920s its Russian population was being rapidly outnumbered by Chinese immigrants, at over 120,000 in 1921, it was one of the largest European cities anywhere in colonial Asia or Africa. Seoul's population was predominantly Korean, but the eagerness of its Japanese residents to reinvent the city as reassuringly Japanese, displacing Koreans to its real and imagined periphery, offers a fascinating parallel with *ancien régime* South Africa, whose towns and cities were 'white', entered by the black majority during daylight and on sufferance from distant 'townships'.

The absence of agricultural colonists among Europeans and (very largely) Japanese may have influenced their social ethos in other respects. In the Americas, Australasia and Southern Africa, rural settler politics tended to be aggressively egalitarian – though equality was racially bounded – and the myth of the 'open frontier', followed by resentment at its closure, exerted a radicalising effect on settler communities. In East Asia the pattern was different. Among both the British and the Japanese communities, report Robert Bickers and Christian Henriot, there was marked tension between the transient elite of 'company people' or career expatriates on the one hand and 'natives' (the Japanese term) and Shanghailanders on the other. It was the latter who filled the more lowly settler occupations as shopkeepers, small businessmen, clerks, railway, dock or shipping employees and policemen. For some of them, an end-of-service gratuity offered an escape route 'home' – although, as Robert Bickers points out, quite often 'home' was no longer where the heart was. As actual or would-be permanent residents, this group was far more sensitive about Chinese 'encroachment', far less ready to conciliate Chinese nationalism than (in the British case at least) the business elite, whose influence was resented almost as much as that of the diplomats. They bore a family resemblance to other vulnerable settler minorities for whom the loss of racial privilege and return 'home' were equally unpalatable: European railway workers in Northern Rhodesia (Zambia); *pieds-noirs* in Algeria; the white working class in Southern Rhodesia (Zimbabwe). For the Shanghailanders, however, the path of rebellion against imperial 'betrayal', to secure their own *Algérie française* or 'White Rhodesia', was the idlest of dreams.

The dominant fact was the physical insecurity felt by all the imperial communities perched on the flank of China. (The evidence seems less clear in the case of the Japanese in Korea.) This may have been the driving force behind the intense associational life emphasised in many of the chapters of this volume. Treaty port Japanese were marshalled into residents' associations. There was a British Residents' Association, and the British community, like others, maintained internal cohesion in part by a profusion of local publications. A Jewish Association was founded in Shanghai in 1909. Russian Jews in Harbin supported several newspapers, including one in Yiddish. White Russian refugees, argues Marcia Ristaino, turned Shanghai into a major publishing centre for Russian literature. Taiwanese *sekimin* were organised into civic associations. Germans and Americans in Shanghai, according to Françoise Kreissler and Mark Wilkinson, displayed the same passion for community organisations as their British counterparts. So much so, that in the German case, its local Nazi cadre felt the need for a *Gleichschaltung* of their own. Interestingly, it was among Indians that the associational tendency seemed least developed (in contrast to their notorious clubbishness in India and elsewhere). This may have reflected the local strength of the family firm as a social unit (Chiara Betta sees a similar clannishness among the Baghdadi Jews of Shanghai) and the importance of the *gurdwara* as the focus of Sikh communal life.

It is tempting to speculate that the fervour of club and association making was positively correlated with two variables: the depth of cultural alienation from the omnipresent Chinese; and the weakness of family ties among disproportionately male expatriates (at least in the Europeans' case). But until we know more about how far associational life among Japanese, Taiwanese and Europeans was officially inspired and regulated, any conclusion would be premature. Less arguable, perhaps, is the extent to which community consciousness was accentuated by the emphasis upon security and defence. In Korea, as Alain Delissen shows, and notoriously in Manchuria, Japan's military apparatus loomed over its imperial community. In Shanghai, Japanese residents were organised into a militia in 1925. For British expatriates in Shanghai, Hong Kong and the lesser treaty ports, civic life was underwritten by the Royal Navy's gunboats and a garrison easily reinforced from India. The Shanghai Volunteer Corps, a paramilitary defence force, was a key institution for the British in the International Settlement, the focus of Shanghailander loyalty. Mark Wilkinson's chapter shows that in January 1939 marines and navy personnel made up more than a third of the American community in Shanghai, and were twice as numerous as any other occupational group. There was a strong sense in which, however peaceful their avocations, all the imperial communities were extensions of the military systems on which they ultimately depended.

This brings us at last to the intriguing topic of identity. How far were the imperial communities examined here able or willing to construct distinct local loyalties or fashion plausible notions of belonging? On the face of it, the task was far from easy. As Christopher Munn's chapter suggests, the British arrived on the China coast confident of their moral and cultural superiority over a declining and even degraded civilisation. 'Anglo-China', like other reformist projects in India and Africa, would liberate its subjects from the bondage of superstition, corruption and misrule. The conviction that a wide civilisational chasm separated Europeans from Chinese remained the leitmotif of British attitudes, especially, perhaps, among Shanghailanders. It was the great bond which united what would otherwise have been a socially disparate community, riven by divisions of class origins, wealth and occupation. But the price of asserting so vehemently how different Britons were from Chinese was to highlight how anomalous it was to try to establish a *permanent* British society in China. How could settlers feel at home in a world they insisted was hostile, alien and inferior? What made the experiment even more stressful was the uncomfortable discovery that neither government nor business could be carried on without recourse to 'Chinese' methods. In Hong Kong this meant collaboration with the infamous Wong, loyal ally today, pirate chief tomorrow, perhaps both simultaneously. How could the vital sense of intra-communal loyalty be maintained among the British if they were drawn into partnership (with all its necessary compromises) with the Chinese whose manners and morals they affected to despise?

This dilemma was not unique to British communities in China, although it may have been more acute there. In India a tiny British minority, heavily reliant on Indian co-operation and engulfed by Indian cultures, struggled with the same forms of unease. In some ways their position was easier: the British had conquered India; their status was less equivocal; their control much greater. Even so, fear of being 'corrupted' by the machinations of subordinate collaborators (the same fear that Christopher Munn documents so convincingly in Hong Kong) was never far from the surface.[2] And the 'solutions' adopted in British India were strikingly similar to those applied in Shanghai or Hong Kong. Communal loyalty was enforced through residential and social segregation as far as possible, and by taboos against intermarriage. Hyperactive sociability became an affirmation of Britishness, especially manly forms of social life using lethal weapons. The dilemma of collaboration was 'solved' by a careful separation of levels and functions between the British and their indigenous subordinates, so that the two worlds could coexist, partitioned by (dare one say) a 'Chinese wall' over which the British pretended not to look.

This whole rickety structure of fictions was crowned by a set of foundation myths made tangible by statues and memorials. No Briton arriving in India after 1857 was allowed to forget the massacre during the Mutiny of European women and children at Cawnpore, the site of which was carefully preserved as an evocative ruin. Here was the inescapable proof of Indian barbarity and of the ever-present need for racial solidarity. In India, too, the 'Eastern British' made some headway in colonising the landscape – a vital stage in creating a sense of belonging. The hill station; the planned public space like the Calcutta Maidan; the monumental architecture of railway stations like Bombay's; the cantonment and the bungalow; the confident engagement with the natural world through *shikar* and the regulation of forests; the recording of archaeological sites and the writing of India's

AFTERWORD

pre-British history: these were all ways in which the British made themselves imaginatively at home in India and fostered the illusion of permanence. In China, just as segregation was more claustrophobic, the scope for such an empire of the imagination was more restricted. But its beginnings may be glimpsed in the rituals of Shanghailander society.

The experience of other imperial communities in East Asia shows interesting variation on this theme of making identity. Japanese attitudes towards China were more overtly coercive and militarist than those of the British between 1915 and 1922 and after 1930. But towards Chinese culture they were much more ambivalent. Japanese thinking about an imperial role was torn between enthusiastic membership of the imperial club and the resentment and fear of the Western presence reflected in the 'Pan-Asianist' programme for Sino-Japanese solidarity. It is possible that the defensive, separatist mentality which Christian Henriot identifies in Japanese Shanghai was accompanied by feelings of cultural uncertainty, or even, sometimes, by deep attraction to Chinese history and scholarship, breeding a sense not so much of cultural inferiority as of association and kinship. Awareness of a shared East Asian identity similarly complicated the outlook of Japanese settlers in Korea, since Koreans were officially regarded as a branch of the 'common family', practitioners of the same distinctive agrarian culture. After 1910 (the year of Korea's annexation), as Alain Delissen points out, Japanese were treated to all intents on a par with Koreans, and by 1942 both Korea and Taiwan were on the brink of being designated *naichi* territories, parts of the Japanese metropole rather than the empire. Thus the political framework of Japanese settlement ought to have exerted a very different influence on their notions of a 'settler' identity from the British case. But how far, nevertheless, there was a vigorous unofficial sub-culture of racial difference and superiority, fertilised by the large military presence and its aggressive posture towards a fragmenting China, is a topic worth further exploration.

The third case is the most tragic. The fate of the White Russian population which flooded into China after the Russian Civil War graphically illustrates the difficulty of sustaining a strong sense of group identity in a refugee population that was impoverished, consciously transient and lacking in a powerful patron to protect its distinct niche in an alien culture. Language and perhaps religion offered elements of cohesion. But the 'demoralisation' of White Russian society and its failure to develop a stable political leadership were a stark reminder to other imperial communities of what their fate might be without a local administrative structure legitimated by treaty, supported by the apparatus of diplomacy and guaranteed by force. The tragedy of the White Russians (and of the Harbin Jews) is a measure of how dependent all the imperial communities were for their safety and solidarity upon a political and diplomatic regime (rather than their own economic or technical prowess) over which they had, ultimately, almost no control.

So the final impression left by the tale of these communities is melancholic. Each of them embodied (except, perhaps, the White Russians) the hope that East Asia would prove an open cosmopolitan frontier, susceptible to their influence and sympathetic to their styles of economic and social life. In some cases this amounted to arrogant belief in the ability of their culture to transform a backward, decadent world. The response of many treaty port Chinese fostered this expectation, perhaps as late as the 1940s. But the cataclysm of China's terrible wars between 1937 and 1949 obliterated this extraordinary experiment in Eurasian semi-colonialism and restored a seclusion as rigorous as before 1842. But, as China re-engages with the world, the story of the imperial communities in the strange 'open century' after 1842 begins to look less like a dead end. Like the history of migrations and diasporas elsewhere, it is likely to be seen as an essential component of China's part in modern world history.

Notes

1 Isiah Bowman, *The Pioneer Fringe* (New York, American Geographical Society, 1931), 295.
2 For a classic study of this see R. E. Frykenberg, *Guntur District, 1788–1848: a History of Local Influence and Central Authority in South India* (Oxford, Clarendon Press, 1965).

BIBLIOGRAPHY

Primary sources

Archives diplomatiques, Nantes
  Bulletins mensuels de la police, Service politique, 1937–41
  Protectorate religeuse, Sichuan
Archives diplomatiques, Paris
  Nouvelle Serie
Austin, Texas
  Archives of the Episcopal Church
Boise, Idaho
  Records of the Shanghai Power Company
Bundesarchiv, Berlin
  Deutsche Botschaft China
Hoover Institution Library and Archives, Stanford, California
  Stanley K. Hornbeck papers
Japanese Foreign Ministry Archives, Tokyo
Imperial War Museum, London
  R. M. Tinkler papers
Lambeth Palace Library, London
  Mss 1564–73 Baptism and marriage registers, Holy Trinity Cathedral, and Union Church, Shanghai
League of Nations, Archives, Geneva
  R4692 Situation of Russian women in the Far East, 1934–37
National Archives and Records Administration, Washington DC
  RG 59 Department of State, central decimal files
  RG 84 Shanghai Consulate General
  RG 263 Shanghai Municipal Police, Special Branch records
Politisches Archiv des Auswärtigen Amtes, Bonn
  Pol. Abt. IV, Po 25, China
Public Record Office, Hong Kong
  Wright, John Fortescue Evelyn, Diary, 1849–53 (typescript and photocopy deposited by Wright's descendant, Mrs Jocelyn Scrymgeour), 28 April 1851
Public Record Office, Kew
  CO 129 Colonial Office, Original Correspondence: Hong Kong, 1841–1951
  CO 131 Colonial Office, Executive and Legislative Council Minutes: Hong Kong (from 1844)
  FO 228 Embassy and Consular Archives China, Correspondence Series 1, Archives of the Peking Legation
  FO 371 Foreign Office General Correspondence, Political
  FO 372 Foreign Office General Correspondence, Treaty
  FO 678 Foreign Office Records, Embassy and Consular Archives: China Consulates, personal estates correspondence, etc.

BIBLIOGRAPHY

FO 917 Embassy and Consular Archives China, Shanghai Supreme Court, probate records
FO 1092 Supreme Court notebooks, and Magistrates' notebooks
Richmond, Virginia
  Foreign Mission Board, Southern Baptist Church
Shanghai Housing and Property Administration Bureau Archives
  Archives of the Hardoon Company
Shanghai Municipal Archives
  U 1–3 series, Shanghai Municipal Council, Secretariat files
  U 1–9₃ [sic] series, SMP personnel files
  U 102 series, SMP administrative files
Sichuan Provincial Archives, Chengdu
  Baxian collection
Sociéte des Missions Étrangères archives, Paris
  Sichuan Oriental

Published works

Akatsuka Shôsuke, 'ZaiMan Senjin mondai' (Problems of Koreans in Manchuria), 1921 report reprinted in Kankoku shiryô kenkyûjo, *Chôsen tôchi shiryô*, 10, 225–61.
Allman, N. F., *Shanghai Lawyer*, New York, McGraw-Hill, 1943.
Anderson, David, and David Killingray, eds, *Policing the Empire: Government, Authority and Control, 1830–1940*, Manchester, Manchester University Press, 1991.
Anderson, David, and David Killingray, eds, *Policing and Decolonisation: Politics, Nationalism and the Police, 1917–65*, Manchester, Manchester University Press, 1992.
Anglo-Chinese Calendar for the Year 1848, Canton, Chinese Repository, 1848.
Annales de la Société des Missions Étrangères et de l'Oeuvre des Partants (1898–1911), Paris.
Anstey, Thomas Chisholm, *Crime and Government at Hongkong: A Letter to the Editor of the 'Times' Newspaper; Offering reasons for an Enquiry, into the Disgraces, brought on the British Name in China, by the Present Hong Kong Government*, London, Effingham Wilson, 1859.
Arnold, David, 'White Colonisation and Labour in Nineteenth-Century India', *Journal of Imperial and Commonwealth History*, 9:2 (1983), 133–58.
Balhatchet, Kenneth, *Race, Sex and Class under the Raj: Imperial Attitudes and Policies and their Critics*, London, Weidenfeld and Nicolson, 1980.
Barber, Noel, *The Fall of Shanghai*, New York, Coward McCann & Geohgegan, 1979.
Barrier, G. N., 'Sikh Emigrants and their Homeland', in G. N. Barrier and V. A. Dusenbery, eds, *The Sikh Diaspora: Migration and Experience beyond Punjab*, Delhi, Chanakya Publications, 1989, 49–89.
'Bay Area Jews from Harbin, Manchuria', transcripts and tapes from unpub-

BIBLIOGRAPHY

lished interviews held in the Judah Magnes Museum, Berkeley CA, in Russian and English.

Bender, T., *Community and Social Change in America*, Baltimore MD, Johns Hopkins University Press, 1982.

Betta, Chiara, 'Silas Aaron Hardoon (1851–1931): Marginality and Adaptation in Shanghai', University of London, School of Oriental and African Studies Ph.D. thesis, 1997.

Betta, Chiara, 'Myth and Memory: Chinese Portrayal of Silas Aaron Hardoon, Luo Jialing and the Aili Garden between 1924 and 1995', in *Jews in China: From Kaifeng to Shanghai*, Sankt Augustin: Monumenta Serica, forthcoming.

Bickers, Robert, 'Changing British Attitudes to China and the Chinese, 1928–1931', University of London, School of Oriental and African Studies, Ph.D. thesis, 1992.

Bickers, Robert, 'Death of a Young Shanghailander: The Thorburn Case and the Defence of the British Treaty Ports in China in 1931', *Modern Asian Studies*, 30:2 (1996), 271–300.

Bickers, Robert, 'Shanghailanders: The Formation and Identity of the British Settler Community in Shanghai, 1843–1947', *Past and Present*, 159 (1998), 161–211.

Bickers, Robert, and Wasserstrom, Jeffrey N., 'Shanghai's "Dogs and Chinese not admitted" Sign: Legend, History and Contemporary symbol', *China Quarterly*, 142 (1995), 444–66.

Blakiston, Thomas W., *Five Months on the Yangtze*, London, John Murray, 1862.

Booker, E., *Flight from China*, New York, Macmillan, 1945.

Bourne, K. M., 'The Shanghai Municipal Police: Chinese Uniform Branch', *Police Journal*, 2:1 (1929), 26–36.

Bouton, C., *The Flour War: Gender, Class and Community in Late Ancien Régime French Society*, University Park PA: Pennsylvania State University Press, 1993.

Bowman, Isaiah, *The Pioneer Fringe*, New York, American Geographical Society, 1931.

Bresler, Boris, and Gregory Grossman, 'Evsey Domar: In Memoriam', *Bulleten', Igud yotzei Sin* (English Supplement), 350 (1997), 30–1.

British Parliamentary Papers: China 24: Correspondence, Dispatches, Reports, Ordinances and other Papers relating to the Affairs of Hong Kong, 1846–60, Shannon, Irish University Press, 1971.

Brocheux, Pierre, and Daniel Hémery, *Indochine: la colonisation ambiguë, 1858–1954*, Paris, La Découverte, 1994.

Brooks, Barbara, 'The Japanese Foreign Ministry and China Affairs: Loss of the Control, 1895–1938', Princeton University Ph.D. thesis, 1991.

Brooks, Barbara, 'Peopling the Japanese Empire: Koreans in Manchuria and the Rhetoric of Inclusion', in Sharon Minichiello, ed., *Japan's Competing Modernities: Issues in Culture and Democracy, 1900–1930*, Honolulu, University of Hawaii Press, 1998, 25–44.

Brooks, Barbara, *Japan's Imperial Diplomacy: Treaty Ports, Consuls and War in China, 1895–1938*, Honolulu, University of Hawaii Press, 2000.

BIBLIOGRAPHY

Brown, Mendel, 'The Jews of Modern China', *Jewish Monthly*. 3:3 (1949), 158–63.
Cai Shaoqing, 'On the Origin of the Gelaohui', *Modern China*. 10:4 (1984), 481–508.
Cao Linhua, 'Shanghai Riben juliu mintuan gaishu' (A general presentation of the Shanghai Japanese Residents' Association), *Dang'an yu lishi* (Archives and History), 3 (1990), 51–5.
Carroll, John M., 'Colonialism and Collaboration: Chinese Subjects and the Making of British Hong Kong', *China Information*, 12:1/2 (1997), 12–35.
Celestial Empire, Shanghai.
Ch'en, Jerome, *China and the West: Society and Culture, 1815–1937*, London, Hutchinson, 1979.
Chen Dasheng and D. Lombard, 'Le rôle des étrangers dans le commerce maritime de Quanzhou ('Zaitun') aux XIIIe et XIVe siècles', in D. Lombard and J. Aubin, eds, *Marchands et hommes d'affaires asiatiques dans l'Océan indien et la Mer de Chine XIIIe–XXe siècles*, Paris, Editions de l'EHESS, 1988, 21–9.
China Directory for 1863, Hong Kong, Andrew Shortrede, 1863.
China Mail, Hong Kong.
China Press, Shanghai.
China Weekly Review, Shanghai.
Chôkô no nagare to tomo ni (In the Stream of the River Yangzi: Reminiscences of the Shanghai Mantetsu [Bureau]), Tokyo, n.p., 1980.
Chôsen no toyû (Cities and Townships of Korea), Keijô (Seoul), General Government of Korea, 1930.
Chôsen sôtokufu keimukyoku (Bureau of Prison Affairs, Korea Government General), *ZaiMan Senjin to Shina kansen* (The Chinese Authorities and Koreans in Manchuria), Seoul, Gyôsei gakkai insatsujo, 1930. Reprinted Seoul, Seishin bunka sha, 1974.
Chou, Shun-hsin, *The Chinese Inflation, 1937–49*, New York, Columbia University Press, 1963.
Christy, Alan, 'The Making of Imperial Subjects in Okinawa', *positions*, 1:3 (1993), 607–39.
Clausen, Søren, and Stig Thøgerson, trans. and eds, *The Making of a Chinese City: History and Historiography in Harbin*, Armonk NY, M. E. Sharpe, 1995.
Clifford, Nicholas R., *Spoilt Children of Empire: Westerners in Shanghai and the Chinese Revolution of the 1920s*, Hanover NH, University Press of New England, 1991.
Coates, Austin, *China Races*, Hong Kong, Oxford University Press, 1983.
Coates, P. D., *The China Consuls*, New York, Oxford University Press, 1988.
Cohen, Israel, *The Journey of a Jewish Traveller*, London, Bodley Head, 1925.
Cohen, Paul A., *China and Christianity: the Missionary Movement and the Growth of Chinese Antiforeignism, 1860–1870*, Cambridge MA, Harvard University Press, 1963.
Cohen, Paul A., *Discovering History in China: American Historical Writing on the recent Chinese Past*, New York, Columbia University Press, 1984.

BIBLIOGRAPHY

Collar, Hugh, *Captive in Shanghai*, New York, Oxford University Press, 1990.
Condliffe, J. B., ed., *Problems of the Pacific, 1929: Proceedings of the Third Conference of the Institute of Pacific Relations*, Chicago, University of Chicago Press, 1930.
Correspondence, Dispatches, Reports, Returns, Memorials and other Papers relating to the Affairs of Hong Kong, 1862–81, Shannon, Irish University Press, 1971.
Crossley, Pamela Kyle, 'Thinking about Ethnicity in Early Modern China', *Late Imperial China*, 11:1 (1990), 1–34.
Crossley, Pamela Kyle, *Orphan Warriors: Three Manchu Generations and the End of the Qing World*, Princeton NJ, Princeton University Press, 1990.
Crow, Carl, *Foreign Devils in the Flowery Kingdom*, New York, Harper, 1940.
Cumings, Bruce, *The Origins of the Korean War*, Princeton NJ, Princeton University Press, 1981.
Curtin, Philip, *Cross-cultural Trade in World History*, Cambridge: Cambridge University Press, 1984.
Dai Guohui, 'Nihon no shokuminchi shihai to Taiwan sekimin' (Japan's Colonial Rule and Taiwan *Sekimin*), *Taiwan kindaishi kenkyû*, 3 1980, 114.
Darwent, Revd C. E., *Shanghai: A Handbook for Travellers and Residents to the Chief Objects of Interest in and around the Foreign Settlements and Native City*, Shanghai, Kelly & Walsh, second edition, 1920.
Delissen, Alain, 'Kim et Tanaka, techniciens dans la Corée des années 1930: modernisation et division coloniale du travail', *Mouvement Social*, 173 (1995), 97–111.
Der vayter-mizrekh, Harbin.
Deutsche Shanghai Zeitung, Shanghai.
Dicker, Herman. *Wanderers and Settlers in the Far East: A Century of Jewish Life in China and Japan*, New York, Twayne Publishers, 1962.
Die Neue Weltbühne, Berlin, Prague, Paris.
Dikötter, Frank, *The Discourse of Race in Modern China*, Stanford CA, Stanford University Press, 1992.
Dirlik, Arif, 'Reversals, Ironies, Hegemonies: Notes on the Contemporary Historiography of Modern China', *Modern China*, 22:3 (1996), 243–84.
Dobbin, C., *Asian Entrepreneurial Minorities: Conjoint Communities in the Making of the World Economy, 1570–1940*, London, Curzon Press, 1996.
Dongfang zazhi (The Eastern Miscellany), Shanghai.
Döscher, Hans-Jürgen, *SS und Auswärtiges Amt im Dritten Reich. Diplomatie im Schatten der 'Endlösung'* (The SS and the Foreign Ministry in the Third Reich: Diplomacy in the Shadow of the Final Solution), Frankfurt, Ullstein, 1991.
Douglas R., 'Training young China Hands: Tôa Dôbun shoin and its Predecessors, 1886–1945', in Peter Duus, Ramon H. Myers and Mark R. Peattie, eds, *The Japanese Informal Empire in China, 1895–1937*, 210–71.
Drechsler, Karl, *Deutschland, China, Japan, 1933–1939. Das Dilemma der deutschen Fernostpolitik* (Germany, China and Japan, 1933–1939: The Dilemma of German Far East Policy), Berlin, Akademie Verlag, 1964.
Dreifuß, Alfred, 'Schanghai. Eine Emigration am Rande' (Shanghai: Exile on

the Periphery), in Eike Middell *et al.*, eds, *Exil in den USA* (Exile in the USA), Leipzig, Reclam, 1979.
Duara, Prasenjit, *Rescuing History from the Nation: Questioning Narratives of modern China*, Chicago, University of Chicago Press, 1995.
Dusenbery, V. A., 'Introduction: A Century of Sikhs beyond Punjab', in G.N. Barrier and V.A. Dusenbery eds, *The Sikh Diaspora: Migration and Experience beyond Punjab*, Delhi, Chanakya Publications, 1989, 1–28.
Duus, Peter, 'Zaikabô: Japanese Cotton Mills in China, 1895–1937', in Peter Duus, Ramon H. Myers and Mark R. Peattie, eds, *The Japanese Informal Empire in China, 1895–1937*, 65–100.
Duus, Peter, Ramon H. Myers and Mark R. Peattie, eds, *The Japanese Informal Empire in China, 1895–1937*, Princeton NJ, Princeton University Press, 1989.
Duus, Peter, Ramon H. Myers and Mark R. Peattie, eds, *The Japanese Wartime Empire*, Princeton NJ, Princeton University Press, 1996.
Duus, Peter, *The Abacus and the Sword: The Japanese Penetration of Korea, 1895–1910*, Berkeley CA, University of California Press, 1995.
Eckert, Carter J., 'Total War, Industrialisation and Social Change in Late Colonial Korea', in Peter Duus, Ramon Myers and Mark Peattie, eds, *The Japanese Wartime Empire, 1931–1945*, 3–39.
Elliston, E. S., *Shantung Road Cemetery, 1846–1868*, Shanghai, Millington, 1946.
Entenmann, Robert Eric, 'Migration and Settlement in Sichuan, 1644–1769', Harvard University Ph.D. thesis, 1982.
Esherick, Joseph W., *The Origins of the Boxer Uprising*, Berkeley CA, University of California Press, 1987.
Fairbank, J. K., *Trade and Diplomacy on the China Coast: The Opening of the Treaty Ports, 1842–1854*, Cambridge MA, Harvard University Press, 1964.
Felsing, Robert H., 'The Heritage of the Han: The Gelaohui and the 1911 Revolution in Sichuan', University of Iowa Ph.D. thesis, 1979.
Feuerwerker, Albert, 'The foreign presence in China', in *The Cambridge History of China*, XII, *Republican China, 1912–49*, Part 1, New York, Cambridge University Press, 1983, 128–208.
Fleury, le Père François, 'La persecution à Su-tchuen et ma captivité' (My Captivity and the Persecution in Sichuan), *Annales de la Société des Missions Étrangères*, 13 (1900–1901), 2–15.
Fredet, Jean, and Charles Maybon, *Histoire de la Concession française de Shanghai*, Paris, Plon, 1929.
Freitag, Sandria B., 'Crime in the Social Order of Colonial North India', *Modern Asian Studies*, 25:2 (1991), 227–61.
Friend of China, Hong Kong/Canton.
Frykenberg, R. E., *Guntur District, 1788–1848: a History of Local Influence and Central Authority in South India*, Oxford, Clarendon Press, 1965.
Fulcher, H. M., *Mission to Shanghai: The Life of Medical Service of Dr. Josiah McCracken*, New London, NH, Tiffin Press, 1995.
Fumio Kaneko, 'Japanese Colonialism in Taiwan, Korea and Mandchuria', *His-

torical Studies in Japan, VIII, 1988–1992, Tokyo, Yamakawa Shuppansha, 1995, 131–40.
Goodman, Bryna, Native Place, City, and Nation: Regional Networks and Identities in Shanghai, 1853–1937, Berkeley CA, University of California Press, 1995.
Gotô Shinkichi, 'Harubin Nihon shôgakkô' (The Japanese Elementary School of Harbin) in Gotô Shunkichi, ed., Harubin no omoide (Memories of Harbin), Kyoto, Kyôto Harubin kai, 1973, 68–86.
Gould, Randall, China in the Sun, New York, Doubleday, 1946.
Greenberg, Michael, British Trade and the Opening of China, Cambridge: Cambridge University Press, 1951.
Guangyi congbao, Chengdu, Sichuan.
Haas, Wilhelm, 'Lebenserinnerungen' (Life Souvenirs), unpublished manuscript, 1974.
Hane, Mikiso, Peasants, Rebels, and Outcastes: The Underside of Modern Japan, New York, Pantheon Books, 1982.
Hao, Yen-p'ing, The Commercial Revolution in Nineteenth-Century China: The Rise of Sino-Western Capitalism, Berkeley CA, University of California Press, 1986.
Harubin no gainen (The Concept of Harbin), Harbin, Harubin Nihon shôgyô kaigijo, 1924.
Harubin shôhin chinretsukan shûhô (Harbin Commercial Hall Weekly), 2:17 (23 July 1924).
Harubin tsûshin, 6 March 1923.
Hayashi Kyûjirô, Manshû jihen to Hôten Sôryôji (The Manchurian Incident and the Mukden Consul-General), Tokyo, Hara shobô, 1978.
Hayim, George, Thou shalt not Uncover thy Mother's Nakedness, London, Quartet Books, 1988.
Henderson, Gregory, 'Japan's Chôsen: Immigrants, Ruthlessness and Development Shock, in A. Nahm, ed., Korea under Japanese Colonial Rule, Kalamazoo, Center for Korean Studies, Western Michigan University, 1973, 261–9.
Henriot, Christian, Shanghai, 1927–1937: Municipal Power, Locality, and Modernization, Berkeley, CA, University of California Press, 1993.
Heppner, Ernest G., Shanghai Refuge: A Memoir of the World War II Jewish Ghetto, Lincoln NE and London, University of Nebraska Press, 1993.
Hevia, James L., Cherishing Men from Afar: Qing Guest Ritual and the Macartney Embassy of 1793, Durham NC, Duke University Press, 1995.
Higashi Kochiku, 'Urajio yori Harubin e' (From Vladivostok to Harbin) Taiyô, 24:9 (1918), 183–90.
Hinnells, J. R., 'South Asian Diaspora Communities and their Religion: A Comparative Study of Parsi Experiences', South Asia Research, 14:1 (1994), 62–104.
Hipps, J. B., History of the University of Shanghai, Richmond VA, Board of Founders of the University of Shanghai, 1964.
Hsiao Liang-lin, China's Foreign Trade Statistics, 1864–1949, Cambridge MA, Harvard University Press, 1974.

BIBLIOGRAPHY

Hu Hansheng, 'Sichuan Gelaohui Kao' (An Examination of the Gelaohui in Sichuan), in *Sichuan jindai shishi sankao* (An Examination of Three Aspects of Modern Sichuanese History), Chongqing, Chongqing chubanshe, 1988.

Hu Qiwei, *Dazu renmin fanyangjiao douzheng* (The Dazu People's Struggle against Foreign Religion), Dazu, Dazu wenshi ziliao, No. 2, n.d.

Huskey, James L., 'Americans in Shanghai: Community Formation and Response to Revolution, 1919–1928', University of North Carolina, Chapel Hill, Ph.D. thesis, 1985.

Huskey, James L., 'The Cosmopolitan Connection: Americans and Chinese in Shanghai in the interwar Years', *Diplomatic History*, 11:3 (1987), 227–42.

Hyam, Ronald. *Empire and Sexuality: The British Experience*, Manchester, Manchester University Press, 1990.

Inoue Torajirô, 'Kamon ni okeru Taiwan sekimin mondai' (The Taiwan *sekimin* Problem in Amoy),' a 1926 consular report reprinted in *Taiwan kindaishi kenkyu* (Modern Taiwan Studies), 1980, no. 3, 129–46.

Israel's Messenger, Shanghai.

Jacob. b. Abraham d. Sudea, letter (1895), in P.G. von Möllendorf, 'Die Juden in China' (The Jews in China) *Monatsschrift für die Geschichte und Wissenschaft des Judenthums*, 39 (1895), 330–1.

Jacobsen, Hans-Adolf, *Nationalsozialistische Außenpolitik, 1933–1938* (National Socialist Foreign Policy, 1933–38), Frankfurt and Berlin, Metzner, 1968.

Jahresbericht und Übersicht über die Tätigkeit des Vorstandes der Deutschen Handelskammer Shanghai für das Geschäftsjahr 1937–1938 (Annual Report and Survey of the Activities of the Committee of the German Chamber of Commerce in Shanghai for the Commercial Year 1937–1938), Shanghai, n.p., 1938.

Japanese Trade Directory of Shanghai, Shanghai, Japanese Chamber of Commerce, 1940.

Jiaowu jiaoan dang'an (Archives of Missionary Affairs and Missionary Cases) (Taibei: Zhongyang yanjiuyuan jindaishi yanjiusuo, 1974–1981), series 1–6.

Kaetsu Mikio, *Nanasen mei no Harupin dasshutsu* (Seven thousand who escaped from Harbin), Tokyo, published by the author, 1971.

Kai-in meibo (List of members [of the Japanese Club]), Shanghai, Shanhai Nippon kurabu, 1944.

Kanazawa Shozaburô, *Nis-Sen dôsoron* (Studies on the Common Ancestors of Japanese and Koreans), Tokyo, Tôko shoin, 1929.

Kang Man'gil, *Ilche sidae pinmin saenghwal sa yôn'gu* (Poor People's Lives under Japanese Colonialism), Seoul, Ch'angjaksa, 1987.

Kankoku shiryô kenkyûjo (Institute for Korean documents), *Chôsen tôchi shiryô* (Documents on Japanese Rule over Korea), X, Tokyo, Sansei bijutsu insatsu, 1972.

Karaka, Dosabhai Framji, *History of the Parsis; Including their Manners, Customs, Religion and Present Condition*, London, Macmillan, 1884.

Kazama Seitarô 'Kokkyô no machi Harubin tayori' (News from Harbin, the city at the frontier). *Bungei shunjû*, 16:9 (1938), 252–5.

BIBLIOGRAPHY

Kim, Ki-hoon, 'Japanese Policy for Korean Rural Immigration to Manchukuo, 1932–1945', University of Hawaii Ph.D. thesis, 1992.

Kim Chang Rok, 'The Characteristics of the System of Japanese Imperialist Rule in Korea from 1905 to 1945', *Korea Journal*, 36:1 (1996), 20–49.

Kim Il-myon *Nihon josei aishi* (The Sad History of Japanese Women), Tokyo, San'ichi shobô, 1981.

Kimura Kenji, *Zai Chô Nihonjin no shakai shi* (A Social History of the Japanese of Korea), Tokyo, Miraisha, 1989.

Kimura Kenji, 'Zai gaichi kyoryû no shakai katsudô' (Social Activities and Operations of Japanese Residents in the Empire's Periphery), in Ôe Shinobu *et al.*, eds, *Iwanami kôza kindai Nihon to shokuminchi* (Iwanami Series in Colonialism and Modern Japan), 5, Tokyo, Iwanami shoten, 1993, 166–209.

Kindai Nihon to shokuminchi (Modern Japan and its Colonies), 8 vols, Tokyo, Iwanami Kôza, 1992–1993.

Kirby, William C., *Germany and Republican China*, Stanford CA, Stanford University Press, 1984.

Kita Sadakichi, *Kankoku no heigô to kokushi* (Japanese History and the Annexation of Korea), Tokyo, Tôko shoin, 1929.

Kiyozawa Retsu, 'Sekai no jiyû shi, yoru no Harupin' (Free City of the World: Harbin by Night), *Taiyô* 32:7 (1926), 57–65.

Kneucker, Alfred W., *Zuflucht in Shanghai. Aus den Erlebnissen eines österreichischen Arztes in der Emigration 1938–1945* (Refuge in Shanghai: The Experiences of an Austrian Doctor in Exile 1938–1945), Vienna, Böhlau, 1984.

Kobayashi Masayuki, *Yudayajin: sono rekishizô o motomete* (The Jews: in Search of their Historical Image), Tokyo, Seikô shobô, 1977.

Kolb, K., 'Der Deutsche in Ostasien und der Nationalsozialismus' (Germans in East Asia and National Socialism) *Ostasiatischer Beobachter* (Shanghai), 1 March 1934.

Kôno Fumie, *Harubin no sora: Nit-Chû no sokoku o motsu shô Nihonjin no kunan* (The Harbin Sky: Sufferings of a Little Japanese who had both China and Japan as Homelands), Tokyo, On Times, 1996.

Koshizawa Akira, *Harupin no toshi keikaku* (The City Planning of Harbin), Tokyo, Sôwasha, 1989.

Kranzler, David, *Japanese, Nazis and Jews: The Jewish Refugee Community of Shanghai, 1938–1945*, New York, Yeshiva University Press, 1976.

Kreissler, Françoise, 'Die Emigration nach Shanghai. Ein Ghettoisierungsprozeß?' (Emigration to Shanghai – a Process of Ghettoisation?) in Friedrich Stadler, ed., *Vertriebene Vernunft, II. Emigration und Exil österreichischer Wissenschaft* (Banished Reason, II, Emigration and Exile of Austrian Academics), Vienna, Jugend und Volk, 1988, 1028–34.

Kreissler, Françoise, 'Nationalsozialisten in China. Ein verdrängtes Kapitel der Geschichte der deutsch-chinesischen Beziehungen?' (National Socialists in China: An Ignored Chapter in the History of German–Chinese Relations?), in Bettina Gransow and Mechthild Leutner, eds, *China. Nähe und Ferne. Deutsch-chinesische Beziehungen in Geschichte und Gegenwart. Zum 60. Geburtstag von Kuo Heng-yü* (China: near and far. Sino-German Relations in History and Today), Frankfurt, Bern, New York and Paris, Peter Lang, 1989.

Kreissler, Françoise, *L'Action culturelle allemande en Chine, de la fin du XIXe siècle à la Seconde Guerre mondiale*, Paris, Éditions de la Maison des Sciences de l'Homme, 1989.

Kreissler, Françoise, 'Exil in Shanghai. Problematik und Schwerpunktthemen' (Exile in Shanghai: Problems and Fundamental Issues), in Kuo Heng-yü and Mechthild Leutner, eds, *Deutsch-chinesische Beziehungen vom 19. Jahrhundert bis zur Gegenwart* (Sino-German Relations from the Nineteenth Century to the Present), Munich, Minerva, 1991, 293–314.

Kuhn, Philip, *Soulstealers: The Chinese Sorcery Scare of 1768*, Cambridge MA, Harvard University Press, 1990.

Kwôn T'aehwan, 'Ilche sidae- ûi tosihwa' (The Colonial Urbanisation of Korea), in *Ilche singmin t'ongch'i-wa sahoe kujo-ûi pyônhwa* (Colonial Policies and Change of Social Structures in Korea), Sôngnam, Han'guk chôngsin munhwa yôn'gywôn, 1990, 251–98.

Lai Tse-han, Ramon H. Myers and Wei Wou, *A Tragic Beginning: the Taiwan Uprising of February 28, 1947*, Stanford CA, Stanford University Press, 1991.

Lamberton, M., *St John's University, Shanghai, 1879–1951*, New York, United Board for Christian Colleges in China, 1955.

Lang, Olga, 'Foreign and Chinese Shanghai faces War', *Amerasia*, 1:9 (1937), 415–22.

Lanning, G., and S. Couling, *The History of Shanghai*, 1, Shanghai, Kelly & Walsh, 1921.

Lautensach H., *Korea: a Geography based on the Author's Travels and Literature*, Berlin, Springer [Leipzig, 1945], 1988.

League of Nations, *Position of Women of Russian Origin in the Far East*, 15 August 1935, A.12.1935.IV.

League of Nations, *Conference of Central Authorities in Eastern Countries*, C.228.M.164.1937.IV.

Lee Ki-Suk, *A Social Geography of Greater Seoul*, Seoul, Po Chin Chai, 1977.

Lee, Tahirih V., 'Introduction' and 'Coping with Shanghai: Means to Survival and Success in the Early Twentieth Century – a Symposium', *Journal of Asian Studies*, 54:1 (1995), 3–18.

Li Shuxia *Haerbin lishi biannian (1896–1926)* (Historical Chronicle of Harbin, 1896–1926), Harbin, Difang shi yanjiusuo, 1980.

Liang Huahuang, 'Taiwan sôtokufu no taian seisaku to "Taiwan sekimin,"' (The Taiwan Government General's policies for China and "Taiwan sekimin") in Ôe Shinobu *et al.*, eds, *Iwanami kôza kindai Nihon to shokuminchi*, 5, Tokyo, Iwanami shoten, 1993, 77–102.

Lidin, N., 'Russkaya Emigratsiya v Shankhaie' (The Russian Emigré Group in Shanghai), in *Russkiye Zapiski* (Russian Annals), 2 (1937), 308–19.

List of Members of the Shanghai Club, Shanghai, Kelly & Walsh, 1921.

Litten, Frederick S., 'The Noulens Affair', *China Quarterly*, 138 (1994), 492–512.

Liu, Cheng-yun, 'The Ko-lao Hui in Late Imperial China', University of Pittsburgh Ph.D. thesis, 1983.

BIBLIOGRAPHY

Lowenthal, Rudolph, *The Religious Periodical Press in China*, Beijing, Synodal Commission in China, 1940.
Manshû nippô, Fengtian (Shenyang).
'Manshû no suiden keiei ni tsuite' (On the Development of Manchuria's Rice Paddies), *Chôsen oyobi Manshû* (Korea and Manchuria) (May 1922).
Manshû tokuhon (Manchurian Reader), Tokyo, Tô-A keizai chôsakyoku, 1935.
Marshall, P. J., 'The Whites of British India, 1780–1830: A Failed Colonial Society?', *International History Review*, 12:1 (1990), 26–44.
Martin, Brian G., 'The "Pact with the Devil": the Relationship between the Green Gang and the French Concession Authorities, 1925–1935', in Frederic Wakeman Jr and Wen-hsin Yeh, eds, *Shanghai Sojourners*, Berkeley CA, Institute of East Asian Studies, University of California, 1992, 266–304.
Martin, Brian G., *The Shanghai Green Gang: Politics and Organised Crime, 1919–1937*, Berkeley CA, University of California Press, 1996.
Matani Haruji, *Harubin no machi* (The City of Harbin), Tokyo, published by the author, 1981.
McNamara, D., *Trade and Transformation in Korea, 1876–1945*, Boulder CO, Westview, 1996, 119–40.
Meira Penna, J. O. de, *Shanghai: aspectos historicos da China moderna*, Rio de Janeiro, Ameri. Edit., 1944.
Meyer, Maisie J, 'The Sephardi Jewish Community of Shanghai, 1845–1939, and the Question of Identity', London School of Economics Ph.D. thesis, 1994.
Minami Manshû tetsudo kabushiki kaisha, chihôbu nômuka (Regional Agricultural Affairs Section, South Manchurian Railway (SMR) Corporation), 'ZaiMan Chôsenjin nôgyô mondai' (Agricultural Problems of Koreans in Manchuria), 1936 report reproduced in Minami Manshû tetsudô kabushiki kaisha keizai chôsakai (Economic Survey Group, SMR), eds, *Manshû nôgyô imin hôsaku* (Policies for Agricultural Immigrants to Manchuria), 2:1:8, *Ritsuan chôsa shorui* (Survey Materials for Policy Design), 1937.
Ming, Hanneke, 'Barracks Concubinage in the Indies, 1887–1920', *Indonesia*, 35 (1983), 65–93.
Miyazawa Masanori, *Zôho Yudayajin ronkô: Nihon ni okeru rongi no tsuiseki* (Studies of the Jews, Expanded: In Pursuit of Japanese Debates), Tokyo, Shinsensha, 1982.
Morisaki Kazue, *Karayukisan*, Tokyo, Asahi shinbunsha, 1976.
Morris, M. D., 'The Growth of Large-scale Industry to 1947', in D. Kumar, ed., *The Cambridge Economic History of India*, II, *Circa 1757-c. 1970*, Cambridge: Cambridge University Press, 1983, 553–676.
Morse, H. B., *The Trade and Administration of the Chinese Empire*, London, Longman, 1908.
Mou Anshi, 'Zhongguo renmin fandui waiguo jiaohui qinluede douzheng he Zhongguo jindaishi de zhuyao xiansuo' (The Chinese People's Struggle against the Invasion of Foreign Missionaries and Important Strands in Chinese Modern History), in *Jindai Zhongguo jiaoan yanjiu* (Studies of Anti-missionary Incidents in Modern China), Chengdu, Sichuansheng shehui kexueyuan chubanshe, 1987.

Murphey, Rhoads, *The Outsiders: The Western Experience in India and China*, Ann Arbor MI: University of Michigan Press, 1977.
Myers, Ramon, 'Japanese Imperialism in Manchuria: The South Manchuria Railway Company, 1906–1933' in Peter Duus, Ramon H. Myers and Mark R. Peattie, eds, *The Japanese Informal Empire in China, 1895–1937*, 101–32.
Myers, Ramon, and Mark R. Peattie, eds, *The Japanese Colonial Empire, 1895–1945*, Princeton NJ, Princeton University Press, 1984.
Nagano Sueki, *Keijô no omokage* (Scenes of Seoul), Keijô (Seoul): Jijôsha, 1932.
North China Herald, weekly edition of the *North China Daily News*, Shanghai.
Norton-Kyshe, James William, *The History of the Laws and Courts of Hong Kong, tracing Consular Jurisdiction in China and Japan and including Parliamoutary Debates, and the Rise, Progress, and Successive Changes in the various Public Institutions of the Colony from the earliest Period to the present Time* (2 vols., London, Union, 1898).
Ong, Aiwha, 'On the Edge of Empires: Flexible Citizenship among Chinese in Diaspora', *positions*, 1:3 (1993), 745–78.
Owen, David Edward, *British Opium Policy in China and India*, New Haven CT: Yale University Press, 1934. Reprint, Archon Books, 1968.
Pan Guang and Li Peidong, eds, *Youtairen yi Shanghai* (Memoirs of Shanghai Jews), Shanghai, Shanghai wenshi ziliao xuanji, 1995.
Peattie, Mark, 'Japanese Treaty Port Settlements in China, 1895–1937,' in Peter Duus, Ramon Myers and Mark R. Peattie, eds, *The Japanese Informal Empire in China, 1895–1937*, 166–209.
Pelletier, Philippe, *La Japonésie: géopolitique et géographie historique de la surinsularité au Japon*, Paris, CNRS Editions, 1997.
Pepper, Suzanne, *Civil War in China: The Political Struggle, 1945–49*, Berkeley CA, University of California Press, 1978.
Peters, E. W., *Shanghai Policeman*, London, 1937.
Popplewell, Richard J., *Intelligence and Imperial Defence: British Intelligence and the Defence of the Indian Empire, 1904–1924*, London, Frank Cass, 1995.
Pott, F. L. Hawks, *A Short History of Shanghai: Being an Account of the Growth and Development of the International Settlement*, Shanghai, Kelly & Walsh, 1928.
Powell, John B., *My Twenty-five Years in China*, New York, Macmillan, 1945.
Qiao Shuming, 'Kaibu qian daoguo Shanghai de Ribenren' (Japanese who came to Shanghai before its Opening), *Shanghai yanjiu luncong*, 10 (1996), 267–77.
Quested, R. K. I., *'Matey' Imperialists! The Tsarist Russians in Manchuria, 1895–1917*, Hong Kong, University of Hong Kong Press, 1982.
Rabinovits, Shmuel, 'Hayishuv hayihudi be-Sin, sigsugo vekhurbano' (The Jewish Community in China, its Growth and its Demise) *Gesher*, 2:11 (1957), 108–21.
Realty Market, Shanghai.
Reischauer, E. O., *My Life between Japan and America*, New York, Harper & Row, 1986.

BIBLIOGRAPHY

Reynolds, Douglas R., 'Training young China Hands: Tôa Dôbun Shoin and its Predecessors, 1886–1945' in Peter Duus, Ramon H. Myers and Mark R. Peattie, eds, *The Japanese Informal Empire in China, 1895–1937*, 210–71.
Rigby, R. W., *The May 30 Movement: Events and Themes*, Canberra, 1980.
Robinson, Ronald, 'Non-European Foundations of European Imperialism: Sketch for a Theory of Collaboration', in Roger Owen and Bob Sutcliffe, eds, *Studies in the Theory of Imperialism*, London, Longman, 1972, 117–42.
Roland, Joan, *Jews in British India: Identity in a Colonial Era*, Hanover NH, University Press of New England, 1989.
Rubin, Evelyn Pike, *Ghetto Shanghai*, New York, Shengold, 1993.
Samra, Myer, 'The Immigration of Iraqi Jews into "White Australia", 1901–1973', paper presented at the Second International Congress of Babylonian Jewry, Babylonian Jewry Heritage Centre, Or Yehuda, Israel, 15–18 June 1998.
Schrecker, John E., *Imperialism and Chinese Nationalism: Germany in Shantung*, Cambridge MA, Harvard University Press, 1971.
Scully, Eileen P., 'Taking the Low Road to Sino-American Relations: Open door Expansionists and the two China Markets', *Journal of American History*, 82:1 (1995), 62–83.
'Senjin o chûshin to seru Haerbin no kôsatsu' (Reflections on Harbin, mainly on its Koreans), *Chôsen oyobi Manshû* (December 1923), 33–6.
Service, J., *State Department Duty in China: The McCarthy Era, and After, 1933–1977*, with an introduction by J. K. Fairbank, an interview conducted by Rosemary Levenson, Regional Oral History Office, Bancroft Library, Berkeley CA, University of California, 1977–78.
Shanghai duiwai maoyi (The Foreign Trade of Shanghai, 1840–1949), I, Shanghai shehui kexueyuan Jingji yanjiusuo (Shanghai Academy of Social Sciences, Economic Research Institute), Shanghai, Shanghai shehui kexueyuan chubanshe, 1989.
Shanghai Evening Post and Mercury, Shanghai.
Shanghai Mercury, Shanghai.
Shanghai Municipal Council, *Annual Reports*, Shanghai, Kelly & Walsh, 1900–42.
Shanghai Municipal Council, *Municipal Gazette* (1908–43).
Shanghai Municipal Council, *Police Guide and Regulations*, Shanghai, Kelly & Walsh, 1926.
Shanghai Sunday Times, Shanghai.
Shanhai kyoryûmindan sanjûgo shunen kinenshi (Commemorative Volume for the Thirty-fifth Anniversary of the Shanghai Residents' Association), Shanghai, Shanhai kyoryû mindan hen, 1942.
Shanhai Nihon shôkô kaigisho nenpô (Yearbook of the Shanghai Japanese Chamber of Trade and Industry), Shanghai, Shanhai Nihon shôkô kaigisho, 1938, 1939, 1941, 1943, 1944.
Shanhai Nihonjin kakuro rengôkai no enkaku to jishi (Events and Evolution of the Japanese Street Unions in Shanghai), Shanghai, Shanhai Nihonjin kakuro rengokai, 1939.

BIBLIOGRAPHY

Shanhai shôkô roku (Yearbook of Japanese Commercial and Industrial Companies in Shanghai), Shanghai, Shanhai shôkô kaigisho, 1941.

Shanhai shôkô roku (Yearbook of Japanese Commercial and Industrial Companies in Shanghai), Shanghai, Shanhai shôkô kaigisho, 1944.

Shenbao (Shanghai).

Shickman-Bowman, Tsvia, 'The History of Harbin Jewish Community, 1898–1931', unpublished manuscript.

Shinobu Seizaburô, *Taishô seiji shi* (A Political History of the Taishô Period), II, Tokyo, Kawade shobô, 1951.

Shôwa jûyon nendo jimu hôkoku (Annual Report [of the Chamber of Trade and Industry] for 1939), [Shanghai]: Shanhai Nihon shoko kaigisho, 1942.

Siddiqi, A., 'The Business World of Jamsetjee Jejeebhoy', *Indian Economic and Social History Review*, 19:3-4 (1982), 301–24.

Siddle, Richard, *Race, Resistance and the Ainu of Japan*, London, Routledge, 1996.

Simpson, John Hope, *Refugees: Preliminary Report of a Problem*, London, Royal Institute of International Affairs, 1938.

Simpson, John Hope, *The Refugee Problem: Report of a Survey*, London, Oxford University Press, 1939.

'Singminji Chosôn sahoe-rul ottôkhe pol kôsinka' (Reconsidering the Chosôn Colonial Society), *Yôksa-wa hyônsil* (History and Reality), 12 (1994), 11–113.

Sinn, Elizabeth, *Power and Charity: The Early History of the Tung Wah Hospital, Hong Kong*, Hong Kong, Oxford University Press, 1989.

Sissons, D. C. D., '*Karayuki-san*: Japanese Prostitutes in Australia 1887–1916', *Historical Studies*, 17.68 (1977), 323–41; 17:69 (1977), 474–88.

Skinner, G. William, 'Sichuan's Population in the Nineteenth Century: Lessons from Disaggregated Data', *Late Imperial China*, 8 (1987), 1–79.

Smith, Carl T., *Chinese Christians: Élites, Middlemen, and the Church in Hong Kong*, Hong Kong, Oxford University Press, 1985.

Snow, Edgar, 'The Americans in Shanghai', *American Mercury*, 20:80 (1930), 437–45.

Snow, Edgar, 'Japan Builds a New Colony', *Saturday Evening Post*, 206 (24 February 1934), 12–13, 80–1, 84–7.

Société des Missions Étrangères *Bulletin de l'oeuvre des partants* (1870–1898), Paris.

Soejima Enshô, 'Senzenki Chûgoku zairyû Nihonjin jinkô tôkei (kô)' (Statistics on the Japanese Populations resident in China before the War: Preliminary Study), *Wakayama daigaku kyôiku gakubu kiyô, jinbun kagaku*, 33 (1984), 1–35.

Son Chôngmok, *Han'guk kaehanggi tosi pyônhwa kwajông yôn'gu: kaehangjang, kaesijang, chogye, kôryuji* (The Process of Urban Change in Korea, 1876–1905: Open Ports, Open Cities, Concessions, Settlements), Seoul, Ilchisa, 1982.

Son Chôngmok, *Han'guk chibang chedo, chach'i sa yôn'gu* (A History of Local Administration and Autonomy in Korea), I, Seoul, Ilchisa, 1992.

BIBLIOGRAPHY

Son Chôngmok, *Ilche kangjômgi tosihwa kwajông yôn'gu* (Colonial Urbanisation in Korea), Seoul, Ilchisa, 1996.
Sonoda, Hiyoshi, *Sensô, jihen, Shanhai* (War, Incident, Shanghai), Shanghai, Chûgoku tsûshinsha, 1944.
Soong Ching Ling, *The Struggle for New China*, Peking: Foreign Language Press, 1952.
Stephan, John J., *The Russian Fascists: Tragedy and Farce in Exile, 1925–1945*, New York, Harper & Row, 1978.
Stern, Adler Simon, *Jottings of Travel in China and Japan*, Philadelphia: Porter & Coates, 1888.
Stern, Hellmut, *'Saitensprünge'. Lebensbericht* (Extramusical Escapades: A Musician's Memoirs), Berlin, Transit, 1990.
Stoler, Ann Laura, 'Rethinking Colonial Categories: European Communities and the Boundaries of Rule', in Nicholas B. Dirks, ed., *Colonialism and Culture*, Ann Arbor MI: University of Michigan Press, 1992, 319–52.
Stoler, Ann Laura, 'Sexual Affronts and Racial Frontiers: European Identities and the Cultural Politics of Exclusion in Southeast Asia', in Ann Laura Stoler and Frederick Cooper, eds, *Tensions of Empire: Colonial Cultures in a Bourgeois World*, Berkeley CA, University of California, 1997, 198–237.
Sugita Rokuichi, *Isuraeru shi zakkô* (Studies in the History of Israel), Tokyo, Kyôbunkan, 1964.
Sugiyama Kimiko, 'Harubin no ki: watakushi ga doko de mita koto, kangaeta koto' (Notes on Harbin, where I saw Things and thought Things), *Manshû to Nihonjin*, 7 (November 1979), 3–20.
Sugiyama Kimiko, *Harubin monogatari* (Harbin Story), Tokyo, Hara shobô, 1985.
Suh Sang-Chul, *Growth and Structural Changes in the Korean Economy, 1910–1945*, Cambridge MA, Harvard University Press, 1978.
Sweeten, Alan, 'Community and Bureaucracy in Rural China: Evidence from "Sectarian Cases" (*jiaoan*) in Kiangsi, 1860–1895', University of California. Davis, Ph.D. thesis, 1980.
Takahashi, Kôsuke, and Furumaya Tadao, eds, *Shanhai shi, kyodai toshi no keisei to hitobito no itonami* (History of Shanghai: the Formation of a Great City and the Occupations of its People), Tokyo, Tôhô shoten, 1995.
Takatsuna, Hakubun, 'Seiyôjin no Shanhai, Nihonjin no Shanhai' (Westerners' Shanghai, Japanese Shanghai) in Takahashi Kôsuke and Furumaya Tadao, eds, *Shanhai shi, kyodai toshi no keisei to hitobito no itonami*, 97–132.
Takatsuna, Hirohumi, and Chen Zu'en, 'Shanghai Ribenren juliumin guanxi nianbiao' (A Chronology of the Japanese Residents in Shanghai), *Shilin* (The Forest of History), 1 (1995), 93–9.
Takumu tôkei 1939 (Colonial Statistics from 1939), Tokyo, Takumushô, 1941.
Tang Zhijun *et al.*, eds, *Jindai Shanghai dashiji* (Chronology of Major Events in Shanghai from 1840 to 1918), Shanghai, Shanghai cishu chubanshe, 1989.

BIBLIOGRAPHY

Tarrant, William, *Hongkong, I, 1839 to 1844*, Canton, Friend of China, 1861.
Tarrant, William, *Hongkong – Supplement to the Minutes of Inquiry into Civil Service Abuses before the Executive Council, 1860–61*, Canton, n.p., 1862.
Tausig, Franziska, *Shanghai-Passage. Flucht und Exil einer Wienerin* (Shanghai Passage: A Viennese Woman's Flight and Exile), Vienna, Verlag für Gesellschaftskritik, 1987.
ter Haar, Barend J., 'Images of Outsiders: the Fear of Death by Mutilation', work in progress, October 1991.
ter Haar, Barend J., *The White Lotus Teachings in Chinese Religious History*, Leiden, E. J. Brill, 1992.
Tessan, Hiroshi, 'Shinmatsu Shisen ni okeru hanshokuminchika to kyûkyô undô' (The Semi-colonisation of Sichuan in the Late Qing and the Anti-Catholic Movement), *Rekishigaku kenkyû*, 6, No. 529 (1984), 17–33.
The Hongkong Almanack and Directory for 1846, Hong Kong, China Mail, 1846.
Thirkell, George, *Some Queer Stories of Benjamin David Benjamin and Messrs E. D. Sassoon & Co.: Wealth, Fraud and Poverty. Les Juifs entre eux*, Shanghai, Celestial Empire, 1888.
Thomas, Nicholas, *Colonialism's Culture: Anthropology, Travel and Government*, London, Polity Press, 1994.
Thomson, J. S., 'The Government of the International Settlement of Shanghai: a Study in the Politics of an International Area', Columbia University, Ph.D. thesis, 1953.
Timberg, Thomas A., 'Baghdadi Jews in Indian Port Cities', in Thomas A. Timberg, ed., *Jews in India*, New Dehli: Vikas Publishing House, 1986, 273–81.
Tôa Dôbun Shoin Daigaku shi: sôritsu hachijû shûnen kinenshi (History of Tôa Dôbun Shoin University: Eightieth Anniversary Commemorative Volume), Tokyo, Koyûkai, 1982.
Tolley, K., *Yangtze Patrol: The U. S. Navy in China*, Annapolis MD: Naval Institute Press, 1971.
Tranter, N. L., *British Population in the Twentieth Century*, Basingstoke: Macmillan, 1996.
Trotignon, Pierre-Yves, *La France au XXe siècle*, Paris, Bordas, 1976.
Tsai, Jung-fang, *Hong Kong in Chinese History: Community and Social Unrest in the British Colony, 1842–1913*, New York, Columbia University Press, 1986.
Usui Katsumi, 'Kindai Nihon to Chôsen, Chûgoku' (Modern Japan and Korea, China) in *'Chôsen mondai' konwakai* (Discussions of the 'Korean Problem'), 26, Tokyo, Gakushû kenkyû shiriisu, 1984.
Vaid, K. N., *The Overseas Indian Community in Hong Kong*, Hong Kong, Centre of Asian Studies, University of Hong Kong, 1972.
Variam Singh, *Variam Sunehae* (Listen to Variam), Hong Kong, n.p., 1922.
Vespa, Amleta, *Secret Agent of Japan*, Garden City: Garden City Publishing Company 1941.
Wakabayashi Masahiro, *Kaikyô: Taiwan seiji e no shiza* (The Straits: The View towards Taiwan Politics), Tokyo, Shimizu Insatsujo, 1985.

BIBLIOGRAPHY

Wakeman Jr, Frederic, *Policing Shanghai, 1927–1937*, Berkeley CA, University of California Press, 1995.
Wakeman Jr, Frederic, *The Shanghai Badlands: Wartime Terrorism and Urban Crime, 1937–41*, New York, Cambridge University Press, 1996.
Wang Di, 'Qingdai Chongqing chengshi renkou yu shehui zuzhi' (Population and Social Organisation in Chongqing City during the Qing), in Wei Yingtao, ed., *Chongqing chengshi yanjiu* (A Study of Chongqing City), Chengdu, Sichuan daxue chubanshe, 1989, 310–78.
Wang Di, *Kuachu fengbi de shijie: changjiang shangyou quyu shehui yanjiu* (Extending beyond the Closed World: A Social History of the Upper Yangzi Region: 1644–1911), Beijing, Zhonghua shuju, 1993.
Wang Minglun, *Fan yangjiao shuwen tiezhan xuan* (A Collection of Letters and Placards against Foreign Religion), Ji'nan: Qilu shushe, 1981.
Wang Zhicheng, *Shanghai E qiao shi* (A History of the Russian Emigré Community in Shanghai), Shanghai, Sanlian shudian, 1993.
Wasserstrom, Jeffrey N., *Student Protest in Twentieth Century China: The View from Shanghai*, Stanford CA, Stanford University Press, 1991.
Watanabe Ichie, *Harubin kaikikô* (Return Voyage to Harbin), Tokyo, Asahi shinbunsha, 1996.
Wei Yingtao, ed., *Chongqing chengshi yanjiu* (A Study of Chongqing City), Chengdu, Sichuan daxue chubanshe, 1989.
Wei Yingtao, *Sichuan jindai shigao* (A History of Modern Sichuan), Chengdu, Sichuan renmin chubanshe, 1990.
Wei Yingtao, ed., *Jindai Chongqing chengshi shi* (A Modern Urban History of Chongqing), Chengdu, Sichuan daxue chubanshe, 1991.
Wei Yingtao, and Zhou Yong, *Chongqing kaibushi* (The History of the Opening of Chongqing as a Treaty Port), Chongqing, Chongqing difang shicongshu, 1984.
Werhle, Edmund, *Britain, China and the Anti-missionary Riots, 1891–1900*, Minneapolis MN, University of Minnesota Press, 1966.
Wickert, Erwin, ed., *John Rabe. Der gute Deutsche von Nanking*, Stuttgart, Deutsche Verlags-Anstalt, 1997 (translated as *The Good German of Nanking*, New York and London, Little Brown, 1998.
Widdowson, W. H., comp., *Shanghai Municipal Police Guide and Regulations*, Shanghai, 1938.
Wilkins, M., 'The Impact of American Multinational Enterprises on American-Chinese Economic Relations, 1786–1949', in E. May and J. K. Fairbank, eds, *America's China Trade in Historical Perspective*, Cambridge MA, Harvard University Press, 1986, 259–92.
Wilkinson, Mark F., 'The Shanghai American Community and the Communist Revolution, 1948–1949', *Southeast Review of Asian Studies*, 17 (1995), 30–47.
Wilkinson, Mark F., 'A Shanghai Perspective on the Marshall Mission', in L. I. Bland, ed., *George C. Marshall's Mediation Mission to China*, Lexington VA, George C. Marshall Foundation, 1998, 327–55.
Wolff, David, 'To the Harbin Station: The Liberal Alternative in Russian Manchuria, 1898–1914', unpublished manuscript.

BIBLIOGRAPHY

Wong, J. Y., 'British Annexation of Sind in 1843: An Economic Perspective', *Modern Asian Studies*, 31:2 (1997), 225–44.

Wright, Arnold, ed., *Twentieth Century Impressions of Hong Kong, Shanghai and other Treaty Ports in China: Their History, People, Commerce, Industries, and Resources*, London, Lloyd's Greater Britain Publishing Company, 1908.

Wright, Tim, ' "The Spiritual Heritage of Chinese Capitalism": Recent Trends in the Historiography of Chinese Enterprise Management', in Jonathan Unger, ed., *Using the Past to Serve the Present: Historiography and Politics in Contemporary China*, Armonk NY, M. E. Sharpe, 1993.

Wu Jianxi, 'Riben juliu mintuan he Shanghai Riqiao zidi xuexiao' (The Japanese Residents' Association and the Schools of the Shanghai Japanese Residents), *Shilin* (The Forest of History), 4 (1994), 51–9.

Wyman, Judith, 'Social Change, Antiforeignism and Revolution in China: Chongqing Prefecture, 1870s to 1911', University of Michigan Ph.D. thesis, 1993.

Wyman, Judith, 'The Ambiguities of Chinese Antiforeignism: Chongqing, 1870–1900', *Late Imperial China*, 18:2 (1997), 86–122.

Xu Jie, 'Hongkou Ribenren juzhuqu shulun' (A Presentation of the Japanese Quarter in Hongkou), *Shanghai yanjiu luncong* (Collected Essays of Research into Shanghai), 10 (1996), 279–329.

Yamamoto Sanehiko, 'Harupin' (Harbin), *Kaizô* (Construction), 14 (1932), 336–71.

Yamamoto Sanehiko, *Shina* (China), Tokyo, Kaizôsha, 1936.

Yamaura Kan'ichi, 'Kokusai ero toshi Harupin: Manshû ero no fukeizai' (International City of Eros, Harbin: The Wastefulness of Manchurian eros), *Keizai ôrai* (Economic Changes), 6 (1931), 174–9.

Yanagida Momotarô, *Harubin no zanshô* (Harbin's Afterglow), Tokyo, Hara shobô, 1986.

Yokomitsu Riichi, 'Rekishi (Harupin no ki)' (History, Account of Harbin), *Kaizô*, 14 (1932), 2–17.

Yongsan-gu chi (Records of Yongsan-gu), Seoul, Seoul t'ûkpyôlsi, 1992.

Young, Walter C., 'Korean Problems in Manchuria as Factors in the Sino-Japanese Dispute,' *Supplementary Documents to the Report of the Commission of Inquiry*, Study No. 9, Geneva, 1932.

Zai Chûshi hôjin jittai chôsa hokokusho: Shanhai no bu: showa 19-nen 2-gatsu 22-nichi (Report on a Survey of the Situation of Japanese Residents in Central China: Shanghai), [Shanghai]: Zai Shanhai Nihon soryojikan, 1944.

Zenner, Walter P., 'Comparison of the Jews of China and the Jews of India' paper presented at the conference 'Jewish Diasporas in China: Comparative and Historical Perspectives', Harvard University, August 1992.

Zhang Zhongli and Chen Zengnian, *Shaxun jituan zai jiu Zhongguo* (The Sassoon Group in Old China), Beijing, Renmin chubanshe, 1985.

Zhiganov Vladimir Danilovich, *Russkie v Shankhaie* (Russians in Shanghai), Shanghai, n.p., 1936.

Zhu Yong, 'Shanhai kyoryû Nihonjin shakai to Yokohama kakyô shakai no hikaku kenkyû' (The Resident Japanese Population of Shanghai and the

BIBLIOGRAPHY

Chinese Resident Population of Yokohama: a Comparative Study) in *Yokohama to Shanhai, kindai toshi keisei shi hikaku kenkyû* (Yokohama and Shanghai: a Comparative Study of Modern Urban Formation), Yokohama, Yokohama kaikô shiryô fukyû kyôkai, 1995, 399–430.

Zou Yiren, *Jiu Shanghai renkou bianqian de yanjiu* (A Study of Changes in the Evolution of the Population of Old Shanghai), Shanghai, Renmin chubanshe, 1980.

INDEX

Page numbers in *italic* indicate maps.

Abe Kôbô 102
Aberdeen (Hong Kong) 19
Abraham, A. E. J. 41, 49
Adi Granth 64
agency 2, 4
agents of empire 1, 250
Allman, Norwood 233, 238, 239, 245
All-Russian Emigrants' Committee of Shanghai 201, 204
 see also Russians in China, Shanghai, Russian Emigrants' Committee
Amano Motonosuke 114
Americans in Shanghai 205, 231–46, 256
 American Chamber of Commerce 240
 American settlement 41
 business community 232–3, 235
 Columbia Country Club 234
 in Japanese occupation 237–9
 Shanghai American Association 234, 237, 239, 246
 Shanghai American Club 233, 236
 Shanghai American School 233, 235
 Shanghai American University 236, 241
Amoy *see* Xiamen
Anhui 76
Anschluss 224–5
Anstey, Thomas 12, 14–16, 21–6, 28–9, 31–2
anti-colonialism 120, 232
Anti-Comintern pact 219
anti-imperialism 75, 76, 83
anti-semitism 49, 88, 91–3, 96, 100, 101–2

German 204, 225–7
Japanese 204
Russian 204–5
assimilation 88, 109, 144
Australia 207
Austro-Hungarian army 216
Awoon 20, 22

Baghdad 38
Baghdadi Jews in China 2, 38–51, 79, 225
 and French Concession 45–6
 identity 46–9
 anglicisation 38, 47, 48, 51
 in India 38–9, 48
 language 48
 marginal community 38, 49–50
 protection
  British 44
  French 44
 and SMC 45–6
 trading companies
  David Sassoon Sons & Co. 39–43
  E. D. Sassoon & Co. 41–3
  E. I. Ezra & Co. 44
  S. J. David & Co. 44
 women 42–3
Balfour Declaration 99
Beijing 62, 67
Benjamin, Benjamin David 41, 49
Benjamin, Maurice 45
Beth El Synagogue (Shanghai) 42
Boggs, Eli 12, 20
Bohle, Ernst Wihelm 216, 221
Bombay 38, 39, 40, 42, 43, 44, 57, 60, 64, 65, 258
Booker, Edna 238–9, 244
Bowring, Sir John 15–17, 22, 26, 28, 31–2

[280]

INDEX

boycotts 15, 16, 146, 158, 160
Bridges, W. T. 16, 21–2, 29
Britain
  armed forces 237
  British imperialism 71
    China 61
  British Indian Army 254
  British-protected subjects 44, 38–72
    see also Baghdadi Jews in China; Indians in China
  Colonial Office 25, 28, 30
  Dominions 172
  empire 14, 170, 178, 182
    Africa 257
  firms 154, 173
  Foreign Office 43
  intelligence 71, 175
  Royal Navy 12, 14, 17, 20, 27, 30, 257
  see also Hong Kong; Shanghai; Shanghai Municipal Council
British in China 257, 258
  East Asia 256
  Hong Kong 12–33, 258
  merchants 41, 56, 57, 58, 174, 178
  Shanghai 40, 49–51, 147, 170–88, 205, 213, 232, 238, 254, 257–9
  Shanghai British Residents' Association 237, 256
  Shanghai Club 49
  see also Hong Kong; Indians in China; Shanghailanders; Shanghai Municipal Police
British in India 259
British–American Tobacco Co. 234
brotherhoods 78, 82
Buddhism 83, 97
Bund (Shanghai) 175, 235, 255
Burma 63
Bushire (Persia) 38

Cai Yuanpei 223
Caine, William (Colonel, Lt. Governor) 16, 18, 29, 33, 251
Calcutta 39, 43, 258
Caldwell, Daniel Richard 12–33

Caldwell, Mary Ayow 18, 22–5
Campbellpur 64
Canada 207
Canton 2, 14, 39, 40, 57, 61, 62, 65
Cantonese migrants 10
Catholic Church 82
  Catholics (Chinese) 81–2
  French protection 8
Celestial Empire 49, 50
Ch'ongjin (Korea) 98
Chaozhou 110
Chen Gongbo 200–1
Chengdu 80
Chiang Kai-shek 207, 239, 242
China
  anti-British militia 17
  anti-foreignism 75–6, 193
  Chinese Maritime Customs 163
  civil war 14, 207, 241
  foreign threat 79–81
  nationalism 71, 152, 157, 160, 164, 171, 232, 241, 243, 246, 256
  Nationalist government (1927–49) 114, 192, 194, 240, 246
  People's Republic 50
  Qing Dynasty 3, 4, 6, 76, 78, 84, 159, 251
  Reformed Government (Nanjing) 200
  trade with India 38–41, 56–9, 61, 72
China League for Civil Rights 223
China Mail 26
China Weekly Review 226, 243
Chinese
  emigration 75
    Manchuria 90
    United States 19
  merchants 6, 14, 16, 22, 45, 84
  Japan 10
  see also sekimin; Taiwanese
Chinese Eastern Railway 89, 92, 94, 255
Chônaikai 153, 157, 160
Chongqing 76–82, 84, 251
Chônju 139

INDEX

Chôsen *see* Korea
Chôsen Sôtokufu 119
Christianity 79, 83
Christians 75, 76
  Chinese 6, 10, 75–6, 81–4
  Westerners 79–84
Chûgoku (Japanese region) 129
Circuit Intendant 40
citizenship
  Chinese 9, 114, 117
  colonial 2, 5, 109–10, 121
  French 1, 7
  Koreans 117, 132
  Japanese 9, 109, 110, 111, 112, 118
  Soviet 206
clubs
  American 233, 234, 236
  British 49
  German 213, 217
  Japanese 149, 158
  Portuguese 226
  Russian 199
Cohen, Israel 48, 99
collaboration 4, 13
collaborators
  Chinese 2, 13
colonial subjects
  Japanese 7, 59, 61, 70, 79, 90, 94, 98
    in Korea 132, 133, 134, 136
  French 7
colonialism 1, 10, 13
comfort women 94
communism
  China 207, 208, 245
  East Asia 10
compradore 6, 19
coolie trade 29–30
corruption 13, 23–5, 32–3, 184
cotton trade and industry 41, 42, 56–8, 60, 77, 154
Creagh, C. V. 62–3
criminality
  China 13, 14, 112
  Shanghai 5, 174, 176
Crow, Carl 238–9, 243–4

cultural hybridisation 18

Dairen (Dalian) 103
Damao 57
Daotai *see* Circuit Intendant
Dazu 80–2
Denghuahui (Lantern Society) 78
Der vayter mizrekh 101, 102
diaspora 103
Ding Baozhen 78
Domar, Evsey 102, 103
Dongyoumiao pagoda 83
Dutch colonisation 143
Dutch in Shanghai 205

east Africa 171, 178
East India Company 16, 39, 56, 57, 64
emergency legislation 31, 33
Etô Shinkichi 102
eurasians 2, 7, 10, 24, 49, 109, 172
extraterritoriality 2–6 *passim*, 8, 59, 109–22 *passim*, 212–13, 234
Ezra, E. I. 41, 45

Fengtian 116
Fessenden, Stirling 234
Fleury, Père François 79–83 *passim*
France 6, 179, 207
  French Concession, Shanghai 40, 41, 45, 151, 155, 177, 184, 193, 197, 199, 234
  empire 109, 127
French in China
  Shanghai 213
Freemasonry 22, 31, 181, 182, 183, 234
Friend of China 14, 16, 29
frontier colony 13, 33
Fuzhou 111
Fujian 6, 56, 76, 110, 112
Fukuoka 129, 149
Furukin Zôshin i-inkai 162
Fuzhou 2, 39

Gaichi, Gaichijin 121, 134

INDEX

Gaichikoseki 110
Gansu 76
Gedihui 82
Gelaohui (Elder Brother society) 78, 81–3
Germans in China 6, 211, 212, 215, 218, 219, 227
  Shanghai 2, 163, 211–26, 256
  clubs 213, 217
  Deutsche Arbeitsfront 219
  Deutsche Shanghai Volksfront 219
  Hitler-Jugend 219
  Jewish refugees 225–7
  NSDAP Shanghai 214, 216–19, 226, 256
  press 212, 223
  Shanghai German Chamber of Commerce 220
Germany
  associations in China 218
  clubs 212
  concessions in China 211
  diplomats 215, 222, 223, 227
  Gestapo 226
  Gleichschaltung (co-ordination) 215–20
  merchants 221, 222
  military advisers 220
  Ministry of Foreign Affairs 220, 222, 226
  relations with China 211–13, 220–2
Ghadr (Revolution) Party 71
Glebov, F. L. 201, 203–4, 206
Gould, Randall 237, 238, 243–6 *passim*
Grosse, V. F. 193–6
Guandong Army 102, 103, 104, 114
Guangdong 76, 77
Guangzhouwan 6
Guizhou 76, 82
Gujarat 64
Gujarati Muslims 66, 67
Guomindang 9, 120, 196, 241, 244, 245, 246
Gurdwaras 64, 69

Gutzlaff, Karl (missionary) 13

Hakka 76
Hankou 41, 62, 63, 64, 67, 78, 198, 218
Harbin 7, 88–119, 255
  Chinese in 94, 96, 97, 101, 102, 103
  European Jews in 102
  fascism in 103
  Harbin Russian All-Fascist Union 204
  Japanese associations 91, 96, 97, 98
  Japanese community 88, 89–91, 93–8, 101–4
  Japanese enterprises 93
  Jewish press 101
Hardoon, Sila Aaron 10, 45, 46, 51
Hasenöhrl, Franz Xaver 216
Hashomer Hatsair (Harbin) 100
Hawaii 126
Hayashi Yûkichi 162
Hayim, Ellis 205
Hayim, George 43
Henningsen, A. H. 241
Henningsen's Produce Co. 232
Higashi Honganji 162
Hiroshima 129, 149
Hong Kong 3, 12–33, 39, 41, 43, 55, 58, 64, 65, 70, 171, 253
  administration 13
  Baghdadi Jews 39–40, 48
  Bonham Stand 19, 21
  British community 58
  emergency powers (1856–57) 20
  government 18, 29
  justice 12, 14, 15, 25
  Legislative Council 21, 30
  police 13, 15, 63
  Xin'an faction 19
Hongdengjiao (Red Lantern Society) 82
Hongkong & Shanghai Bank 66
Hongkou *see* Shanghai
Hori Isamu 116
Hûngnam 139

INDEX

Hyderabad 67
Hyôgo 149

identities 1, 2, 5, 6, 9, 10, 109
imperialism 1, 2, 6, 84, 109, 126, 128, 250
  historiography 1, 4–7, 10, 109–10, 146, 250–4
Inch'ôn 130, 132, 139
India 42, 43, 48, 56, 64, 71, 81, 149
  British rule 251, 257, 258
  Government (British) 175
  nationalism 55, 62, 70, 71, 232
  trade with China 38–41, 56–9, 61, 72
Indians in China 55, 57, 61, 69, 172
  in British colonial world 253, 254
  Hindus 55, 56, 61, 67
  Hong Kong 39–40, 58, 59, 69, 71
  Ismaili merchants 38, 40, 41, 44, 50
  merchants 38–46, 49–50, 57–8, 65–8, 70, 253
  firms 65–6
  non-economic activities 68
  Parsi community 2, 4, 55, 61, 64, 70, 72
  Pathans 61, 64
  religion 64, 69
  Shanghai 61, 171, 174, 175
  Sikhs 55, 59, 61, 62, 63, 64, 72
    Ghadr (Revolution) Party 71
    policemen 55, 59–60, 62–4, 63, 70, 71, 61, 171, 174, 175, 176, 184, 253
  Sindhi merchants 2, 61, 67, 68, 253
  women 55, 59
Indochina 81, 109, 127, 186
Iraq 44
Irkutsk 92
Isaacs, Harold 223
Italian community in China 227
Iugovich, A. I. 89–90
Ivanov, N. A. 200, 201

James, Jimmy 233, 238

Japan
  China policy 159, 220
  colonial ideology 134, 135, 136
  as a colonial power 110, 146, 250
  colonial power in Korea 115, 116, 119, 129, 132, 134, 135, 139
  consular police 118
  consular service 158, 159, 160, 164
  empire 110, 118, 126, 134, 204, 259
  Foreign Ministry 111, 115, 117, 146, 158, 159
  Imperial Diet 134
  imperialism 110, 114, 119, 120
  Japanese Imperial Army 89, 94, 98, 114, 117, 121, 146, 148, 155, 160
  Japanese protected subjects
    see also Koreans, China; sekimin
  Korea policy 128, 129
  Meiji Constitution 134
  relations with China 115, 117, 147, 259
    Twenty One Demands (1915) 115, 158
  secret police see Kempeitai
  settlements in China 137
  Siberian expedition (1918–22) 94, 95, 96
  wartime 121
Japanese
  colonial citizens (gaichi, gaichijin) 121, 134
  colonial communities 97, 110, 126
  communities in China 97, 121, 127, 132
    Harbin 88–91, 93–4, 96, 97, 102–4; Sôakai (associations in Harbin) 91, 96, 97, 98
    Shanghai 93, 146, 147, 149–54, 156–9, 161, 163–4; Federation of Street Unions (Shanhai Nihonjin kakuro rengôkai) 154, 158–60, 162; Furukin

[284]

INDEX

Zôshin i-inkai (Shanghai Welfare Promotion Committee) 162; Japanese Chamber of commerce (Shanhai Jitsugyô Kyôkai) 159, 164; Japanese Chamber of Trade & Industry 155, 159; Japanese Club 149, 158; Japanese firms 154–7; militia 159, 160, 257; neighbourhood associations 153, 157, 160; Shanghai Japanese Residents' Association 154, 158–62 (Shiminbu (Civil Affairs Department) 162); Shanhai jikyoku fujinkai (Shanghai Women's Emergency Association) 160; Shanhai Seinen Kurabu (Shanghai Youth Club) 160; Shanghai Japanese Entrepreneurs' Association (Shanhai Jitsugyô Kyôkai) 159; Shanghai Japanese Imperial Military Reservist Association (Teikoku Zaigyôgunjinkai) 160; Shanghai Japanese Industrial Club 158; Shanghai Japanese Volunteer Corps 160

communities in Korea 125, 126, 127, 128, 129, 131–2, 134–7, 141, 143, 144
  residents' associations (koryûchi mindan) 96, 132

emigration 7, 89, 94, 116, 125, 128–30, 134, 149, 255
  imin (migrant) 130
  shokumin (colonist) 130, 134
  to China 149
  to Korea 125, 130, 149

naichi (homeland citizens) 111, 113, 118, 120, 121, 143, 259

press
  Harbin 97

settlers 251
  Korea 126, 131, 143, 255, 259
  in Vladivostok 89

see also sekimin

Jejeebhoy, Jametsji 57, 65
Jews 49, 96, 91
  central European 205
  in China
    Canton 39–40
    Harbin 88, 89, 91, 92, 95, 96, 98, 99, 103, 104, 197;
      merchants 95; press 101; religious life 99; schools 99
    Hong Kong 39–40
    Shanghai 38, 42, 43, 49, 172, 197, 201, 204, 206, 207, 224, 225, 254, 257; Jewish associations 226, 256; refugees 225
  India 2, 70
  Siberia 92
  Polish 95, 100
  Russian 7, 43, 47, 98, 194, 201, 204, 206, 252, 256
  Ukrainian 95, 201
  see also Baghdadi Jews

Jiandao 115, 118
Jiangsu 76, 181
Jiaozhouwan 6
Jilin 115
John (Ioann, Maximovich Mikhail Borisovich) 196, 200, 208

Kabalkin, Roman Moiseevich 91, 92
Kaesông 135, 137
Kantô Army (*see* Guandong army)
Karafuto 127
karayukisan 94
Kaufman, Abraham 99, 100, 103
Kempeitai 103
Keswick, W. J. 162
Khabarovsk 89, 90
Khojas 66
Khorvat, Dmitri L. 93–4
King Kojong 131
Kobe 67
kokuseki 111
Korea 4, 7, 109, 128, 253
  Chôsen 2, 125–7, 135, 137
  international concessions 131

[285]

Korean chijông myôn 135
kôryuji/kyoryûchi 130
and Manchuria 114, 254
nationalism 2, 115, 125, 139, 143, 144
relations with Japan 116, 126, 135, 136, 137
sovereignty 128, 130
under Japanese rule 114, 118, 125–44, 254
Koreans 1, 94, 101, 125–44
China 109–10, 114–19, 121–2
Japanese empire 109, 117, 120, 259
Manchuria 115–21, 254–5
Kowloon 17
Kriebel, Consul General 216, 217
Kumamoto 90
Kunsan 130
Kuroki, K. 200, 203, 204
Kyûshû 89, 129, 149

Lang, Olga 219
Lautensach, Hermann 126, 139
Liaodong peninsula 211
Lin Yutang 223
Lu Xun 223
Luo Jialing 46–7
Lyons, Helen 233, 237

Macao 17, 61
Malaya 63
Manchukuo *see* Manchuria
Manchuria 88, 90, 94, 102, 114, 115–16, 118–21 *passim*, 221, 252, 253, 255
Manchukuo 67, 68, 104, 195, 201, 220
Manchurian Incident 68, 88, 103, 111, 115, 119, 120
marriage 9, 14, 18, 32, 88, 182
Hong Kong 24
Indians 67
Jews 43, 46
May, Charles 23–5, 31
May Thirtieth Incident and Movement 158, 171, 176, 187, 234
Meshed (Persia) 39
Metzler, Charles E. 196–200 *passim*
migrants
European 95, 252, 255
migration 1, 95, 129
Sikhs 63
see also Indians in China; Japanese
missionaries 6
American 79, 232, 233, 245
British 79
Buddhist 56
Catholic 84
European 13
French 82
German 212
Protestant 79, 84, 233
Mitsubishi 93
Mitsuya Agreement (1925) 115
Miyamoto Chiyo 90
Mokp'o 130, 135, 139, *140*, 141
Mongolia 115, 253
Mori Gyoin 98, 99
Multan 64
Munson, Bert 178, 180, 184
Murrow, Yorrick Jones 16, 29, 32
Muslims 55, 61
China 76
Shanghai 61

Naftaly (Greenwald), Eve 92, 100
Nagano Sueki 143
Nagasaki 89, 129, 149, 255
naichi see Japanese
Najin 139
Nanam *141*
Nanjing (Nanking) 62
Nazi party *see* NSDAP
Nihon jitsugyô kurabu 158
Nihon kurabu 158
Nihonjin kyôkai 158
Ningbo 2, 39, 41
North America 64, 95, 100, 250
North China Daily News 102
Northern Expedition (China) 232

INDEX

Noulens spy ring 175
NSDAP 2, 216–17, 222–3
  China 218
  Shanghai 214, 216–19, 226, 256

Ohlwein, Otto 218
Okayama 149
Open-Door policy 128
opium trade 14, 16, 20, 39, 41, 42, 44–5, 56–8, 60, 65–7, 104, 112, 118–19, 176, 184
  Koreans in 112, 118–19
organised crime
  Harbin 104
  Hong Kong 14, 17, 33
  Shanghai 176–7
Oriental Development Company (Tôyô Takushoku Kaisha) 114, 130
orientalism 18
Osaka 149
Ossin, Sara 92
Ottoman Empire 43, 50
Ozawa Seiji 102

P'yôngyang 137, 142
Pakistan 64, 67, 68, 71
Palestine 103, 177, 252
Panama 67
Paris 201
Parsis *see* Indians in China
Pearl Harbor 155, 203, 226
Penang 16
People's Liberation Army 244
Philippines 63
Pichon (French minister) 80
pieds-noirs 127, 256
piracy 13–20 *passim*, 23, 30, 32
Po Leung Kuk 33
Polish in Shanghai 205
Portuguese 7, 10, 17, 57
  Portuguese Club 226
Posyolok Sungari *see* Harbin
Powell, Bill 238, 243, 244, 246
Powell, J. B. 212
press in China
  American 219, 226, 243
  British 49, 50, 178, 179
  Chinese 226, 242
  German 212, 216, 219, 223
  Hong Kong 16, 29
  Japanese 97
  Jewish 101, 102
  Korean 127
  Russian 199, 200, 201, 202
prostitution 17, 21, 24, 69, 89, 93, 94, 95, 104, 112, 182, 197, 233
  Japanese 93–4
  Russian 197–8
Pusan (Tongnae) 114, 127, 130, 132, 137, 139

Qingdao 67, 212, 218
Quanzhou 56

Rangoon 43
refugees 163, 193
  Russian 196, 198, 201, 207
Reischauer, Robert 237
religion 6, 42, 252
Robinson, Sir Hercules 28–9
Russia 5, 93, 94
  Bolshevik regime 199
  civil war 192, 202, 259
  military forces 89, 90
  October Revolution 197
  relations with Japan 98, 117
Russians in China 7–8, 59, 70, 192, 201, 259
  and Japanese
    Harbin 103–4
    Shanghai 199–201, 203–4, 205–6
  Harbin 94, 95, 104, 252, 256
  Shanghai 4, 172, 192–208, 231, 260
    All-Russian Emigrants' Committee of Shanghai 201, 204
    Russian Emigrants' Committee 195, 199, 200
    Shanghai Bureau of Russian Affairs 192
    Shanghai Council of United

INDEX

Russian Public Organisations (SORO) 196
Shanghai Russian All-Fascist Union 204, 205
Shanghai Russian Club 199
Shanghai Russian Fascist Party 198–9
White Russian Military forces 193, 196
women 182, 197, 198
Rustomjee D. & M. 65, 66

Sakhalin 114
San Francisco 71, 112
Sassoon family 38–42, 44, 253
  Sassoon, Albert (Abdullah) 42
  Sassoon, Elias David 38, 39, 40, 47
  Sassoon, Jacob 42
  Sassoon, Solomon R. J. 41
Schmidt, Eric 233, 238
Scotland 171, 187
sekimin 5, 72, 110–14, 119–21, 256
  Xiamen (Amoy) 4, 111–14, 121
  Chinese attitudes toward 111, 121
Semenov, G. M. 95, 202
semi-colonialism 88, 250, 253, 260
Seoul (Hanyang) 117, 132, 139, 142, 143, 255
Sephardic Jews *see* Baghdadi Jews
Serejnikov N. K. 201
Service, Caroline 236
settler communities 5, 256
settlers
  Europeans 251
  Africa 254
  Americas 254
  Australasia 254
  see also Japanese, communities in Korea; Shanghailanders
sexuality 9, 17, 24, 32, 32, 69, 70, 175, 182, 188
Shaanxi 76
Shandong 176
Shanghai 2, 4, 5, 6, 7, 8, 39, 40–51, 55, 59–67, 71–2, 146–65, 170–88, 192–208, 211–28, 231–46, 253, 254–7
British settlement 40, 41
Chinese 156, 165, 171, 172, 174, 177–8, 187, 241
International Settlement 7, 40, 41, 45, 46, 51, 55, 151, 152, 155, 156, 158, 162, 172, 174, 177, 178, 187, 193, 201, 237, 257
  see also Shanghai Municipal Council; Shanghai Municipal Police
Hongkou 151, 155, 160, 161, 195, 198, 199, 205–6
Japanese occupation 200, 203–6, 220, 221, 237
Land Regulations 40–1, 234
Mixed court 176, 194
Yangshupu 151, 155–6
Zhabei 151, 155, 160–1, 195, 198
Shanghai Municipal Council (SMC) 5, 7, 41, 45–6, 146–7, 152, 158, 162–3, 173, 178, 180, 182, 193, 199, 212, 213, 254
  and Americans 234–5, 245
  and Baghdadi Jews 45–6
  and British 173
  and Germans 213
  and Japanese 162–3
  and Russians 193
  Public Works Department 183, 186
  see also Shanghai, International Settlement
Shanghai Municipal Police (SMP) 59–60, 63, 158, 163, 170–87, 200, 216, 217, 219, 245, 251
  Chinese 176–7, 184
  Indians 59–60, 62–4, 71, 174, 184
  Special Branch 170, 175
Shanghai Opium Merchants' Combine 45
Shanghai Power Company 232, 240, 241, 246
Shanghai Red Cross 237, 238
Shanghai Volunteer Corps (SVC)

INDEX

174, 194, 234, 235, 237, 240, 244, 257
Shanghailanders 2, 4, 154, 171–3, 175, 178, 180–3, 186, 188, 219, 236, 245, 254, 256, 257, 259
  see also British in China
Shantou (Swatow) 111
Shigemitsu Mamoru 117
Shintô 126, 143
shokumin see Japanese, emigration
Siberia 92, 93, 114
Sichuan 75–84
silk trade 41, 57, 65, 67, 77
Singapore 16, 25, 43, 63, 67
Sinûju 141
Skidel'skii, Lev Shmulevich 92
Snow, Edgar 104, 245
social taboos 9, 47
South Manchuria Railway Company 97, 119, 121
  Shanghai 164–5
Spasovsky, M. 204–5
St Helena 16, 251
St Johns University 241–2
Stalin 100, 201
Sugihara Chiune 102
Sugiyama Kimiko 101
Sungari 90
Surat 39, 64
Surinam 30
Suzuki Nichi-Man Shôkai 93
Swatow *see* Shantou

Taegu 142
Taejôn 132
Taiping rebellion 40, 78
Taiseki status *see sekimin*
Taiwan 4, 6, 109–14, 120
  colonial government (Taiwan Sôtokufu) 109, 111, 114, 120
  Taiwan kôkai (Taiwan civic associations) 111–13 *passim*
Taiwanese 1, 9, 110–14, 121, 127
  see also sekimin; Xiamen
Talati F. M. & Co. 65, 66
Tanaka Giichi 118

Tarrant, William 16, 28–9, 32
  see also Friend of China
tea trade 41, 192
Teikoku Zaigyôgunjinkai 160
Terajima, Consul 113
Third Reich 205, 219, 224, 226
Tianjin 6, 41, 62, 64, 67, 218
  Consular court 67
  German concession 211, 218
  municipal police 63
Tibet 55, 76, 77, 80
Tinkler, Richard Maurice 174, 175–6, 177–83 *passim*, 186–7
Toeg, R. E. 41, 48
Tokumu kikan 104
Tôkyô 129, 149
Tonga Ilbo 127
Tonghak rebellion (1894–95) 131
Toyko Metropolitan Police 163
Traig, Abe 92
Trans-Siberian railway 89, 95
treaties
  Kanghwa (1876) 128, 130
  Nanjing (1842) 2, 39, 40, 58
  Shimonoseki (1895) 110, 120
  Tianjin (Prussian, 1861) 211
  Versailles (1919) 214, 227
treaty ports 3–10, 39, 47, 55, 59, 65, 79, 109, 110, 111, 118, 120, 121, 170, 177, 179, 182, 186, 188, 251, 254, 255, 256
Tsumanenko, I. E. (General) 199, 204
Tsushima, Straights of 135
Tumen river 115
Tung Wah Hospital 33

unequal treaties 128, 240
United Kingdom *see* Britain
United Sates 6, 41, 93, 95, 149
  U.S. Court for China 233
  see also Americans in Shanghai

Van Voast, Helen 233, 235, 237, 241, 245
Veterans of Foreign Wars 234

INDEX

Vladivostok 89, 93, 96, 97, 98, 202

Wakabayashi Masahiro 111
Wanbaoshan Incident (1931) 117
wars
  First Opium War (1839–42) 2, 39, 65, 84
  Second Opium War (1856–60) 15, 17, 41
  Pacific War (1941–45) 9, 137, 160, 161, 172, 203, 205, 232, 237, 245
  Russo-Japanese War (1904–1905) 91, 93
  Sino-Japanese War (1894–95) 71, 128, 211
  Sino-Japanese War (1937–45) 148, 155, 198, 199, 220
    and Germany 220–21
  World War I 42, 70, 93, 94, 97, 99, 154, 179, 192, 212, 213, 227
  World War II 67, 103, 201, 203, 204
White Russians *see* Russians in China
Wickert, Erwin 215, 228
Wong, Ma-Chow 6, 12, 13, 14, 17–23, 25–6, 28, 30–1, 32, 33

Wônsan 130, 132, 139, 141, *142*

xenophobia 75–6, 83
Xiamen (Amoy) 3, 39, 62, 110–14, 121
Xin'an 19, 26
Xinjiang 55

Yamazaki Masao 119
Yanbian 115
Yangshupu *see* Shanghai
Yevreyskaya zhizn' 101
Yi dynasty (Korea) 117, 132, 139
Yiddish 98, 99, 256
Yokohama 41
Yokomitsu Riichi 90
Yongsan 131

Zaibatsu 93, 137
Zeng Guofan 78
Zhenjiang 187
Zhabei *see* Shanghai
Zhang Huanxiang 98
Zhang Xueliang 120
Zhang Zuolin 98
Zhifu 41, 114
Zionism 48, 100
Zoroastrians 64, 70

EU authorised representative for GPSR:
Easy Access System Europe, Mustamäe tee 50,
10621 Tallinn, Estonia
gpsr.requests@easproject.com